1,000 Character Writing Prompts:

Villains, Heroes and Hams for Scripts, Stories and More

Bryan Cohen

DEDICATION

I dedicate this book to the wonderful characters I've met, watched, read and all the characters to come.

CONTENTS

INTRODUCTION

What is it that makes a story most memorable? Do we remember a beautiful setting that is lushly painted in excruciating detail? Do we think back on an intricate plot filled with twists and turns that make our head spin? From time to time, the details of setting and plot do cause us to pause momentarily, but the real trick of telling stories is to create a set of memorable characters. We remember characters from literature like Holden Caulfield, characters from film like Han Solo and from verse like Achilles because they are so completely rendered that they remind us of reality. While these immortal writers have created indelible characters, the writers that are most easily forgotten create cliché-ridden characters that are so typical we look past them like a shredded tire on the side of the highway; in our vision for a split second, but so commonplace as to hardly be noticeable. Why do some authors spend so little time developing their characters?

In some cases it's simply a matter of spending so much time on the other aspects of a book like plot, setting, theme, etc., that they miss out on what may be the most important aspect of the story. Other authors simply don't know how to create dynamic characters and automatically pull from the archetypes they've seen in movies or read in books that were written by similarly unimaginative writers (thus continuing the cycle). In additional cases, writers that may be low in their abilities to understand people other than themselves may just cause them to be completely wrong when attempting to write a particular character type. Their assumptions can make characters ring false or clichéd.

One of the most effective ways to come up with a character is basing it on someone that you know. Obviously, this is a piece of cake if you are writing a story about a family or a profession that you are familiar with and have many people to draw from. If you are writing a story about an alien race and a space captain attempting to work his diplomatic charms on their queen, you may be lacking as far as examples are concerned. If you apply the acting concept of substitution, introduced by Constantin Stanislavski, however, you will quickly find yourself less in want of a space captain type.

Substitution

With many different potential dramas set across various time periods, actors in television and the movies have a variety of parts to play. In many cases, actors wish to draw from their own experiences to make sure that the parts they portray are as realistic as possible. For an actor who is a father of two girls to play a father of two girls, this isn't exactly a stretch. For someone like Bryan Cranston, who is an actor, baseball fan and a father to play a stage-four cancer diagnosed, failed chemistry genius turned methamphetamine drug lord in the show "Breaking Bad" there might be less to draw from. By applying the concept of substitution, however, the actor is able to make equivalent acting choices to situations in the part. For example, while Cranston may never have had cancer, he might have had a situation in his life in which he felt hopeless and he could work on bringing that memory to the surface to portray his character's condition. It is by using substitution that actors are able to bring a personal touch to seemingly foreign roles. In this way, they are able to play themselves in a different set of circumstances that they've never experienced.

Substitution can work the same way for writers when compiling a cast of characters for a story. A writer may want to create a tough cop from the wrong side of the tracks who has a razor sharp wit and a compassionate heart (I realize that example is a little cliché itself, but just go with me here). While the writer doesn't know such a person from his real life, he may know someone who doesn't take crap from anyone, another person who is extremely witty and another who has a tough exterior with a heart of gold. Using the process of substitution, the writer can pick and choose aspects from those real-life individuals to create a character with realistic motivations and actions. Substitution can also be used to lift a few ideas from characters in other stories into your story.

For example, I'm a huge fan of the Joss Whedon created show "Buffy the Vampire Slayer." As an homage to this television classic, I wrote the first book in what will be a series of stories called *Ted Saves the World*, which is about a young teenager who inherits super powers. In "Buffy" there is a character who watches and protects the protagonist, a somewhat stuffy librarian named Giles. Giles is there as the sort of adult voice of reason among a group of teenagers. In my story, I decided to take the idea of Giles, the watcher, and graft it onto a hot cheerleader type who has been possessed by a sort of guardian spirit. I created this cheerleader character to act as both a protector and a love interest of Ted. While you may not be a fan of science fiction and fantasy, there is no question that you may be a fan of a particular character in your favorite story that could fit into your own story in a different set of circumstances.

Writing from Prompts

One of the most difficult parts of writing the beginning of your career. When a writer is inexperienced, it can feel as difficult as lifting a Chevy just to write the first sentence of a story, whether it be for a full-length novel or a short story. The feeling fades over time, but for a writer hoping to become prolific, the starts and stops that come when you have a tough time getting an idea out of your head can feel like an interminable amount of time wasted. One of the solutions to this problem is writing from a prompt. A writing prompt is a short idea, usually consisting of a sentence or two that focuses on a particular subject. On my website, Build Creative Writing Ideas (located at http://www.build-creative-writing-ideas.com) I began writing pages of writing prompts for authors to be able to jumpstart their brains as quickly as possible. After several years and over 70 pages of prompts, I put the prompts into a book called *1,000 Creative Writing Prompts: Ideas for Blogs, Scripts, Stories and More*. I had hoped that writers like me, who were always looking for an idea for a blog post or a story concept would be happy to have a collection of such writing generators. The book sold more copies than I ever thought possible and I knew that someday I would have to follow it up if I could come up with another 1,000 ideas.

While I did write another book of prompts for students called *500 Writing Prompts for Kids: First Grade through Fifth Grade*, this book is the logical sequel to the first, which has sold over 10,000 copies as of this edition. Many of the prompts in the first book deal with plot ideas; scenarios that will help to bring an entire story into being. I realized, looking back on the book, that very few of the prompts dealt with characters. Sure, you can put together an interesting story from a situation alone, but it won't stand the test of time without some characters to help it stand out. Characters literally give a story its character.

And so this book was born and the prompt writing continued. The prompts in this book are divided into 100 different sections, each consisting of 10 different characters of that certain type. You will find sections of major characters like villains and anti-heroes, but you will also find characters that tend to fade into the background like henchmen and children. By making sure that all of your characters, down to the barista at the local coffee shop, are three-dimensionally developed, you will ensure that your story is extremely readable from cover to cover.

Writing from a prompt is a simple process. You flip through the book until you find a section with a character that you wish to create. Look through the prompts and pick one that seems to be in line with your writing sensibilities. Read the prompt to yourself and begin writing a scene featuring that character. I've tried to give each prompt a large amount of detail so that you can pick and choose which details you want to keep and which ones you want to drop. In addition, each prompt ends with a question which acts like a little "choose your own adventure" for the character, letting you take it in its own direction. It is my hope that by including these open-ended questions with each character prompt, that many different readers would be able to turn the same prompt and the same essential character into hundreds of distinct characters.

Ways to Use the Book

While you can simply take any prompts in the book and begin creating a new story and character right then and there, there are many different ways that you can use this book for your writing purposes. Say you have a character who doesn't seem to be adding much to your story. You can flip through this book and find one that has a bit more panache and alter that character into your story. Another idea is to take one of the characters and to change the gender, the profession, the age or the background until you find one that fits into a story you're writing. You can also take a character from this book who would normally be a protagonist and shift him or her into the background to add pop to your secondary or tertiary characters. With 1,000 ideas to choose from and many ways to manipulate each prompt, you may be able to find endless uses for its contents.

In order to create these 1,000 distinct characters, I have used a bit of imagination, some of my favorite characters from television, books and movies and people I know from world history and my history. You may recognize some traits from stories you've read and you may even know a person or two like the people you read about here. In all the characters I've generated here, I've made an effort to make each persona new and unique so that none of them feel directly ripped from the headlines, pages or memories.

In addition, I've made an even balance of male and female characters with 500 of each. In many movies, books and other stories, female characters tend to be given short shrift. Of course, this is ridiculous in this day and age and stories like those told in movies like *Bridesmaids* will hopefully enable the shift to more female-driven tales to counteract the male heavy ones.

I hope that you find this book extremely helpful to any character-related writer's block that you're experiencing. I think that we live in a world where there are many tools such as this guide that can make writer's block a thing of the past and if we can avoid the distractions that come with a digital world long enough to sit down for some writing time, we can all create something extraordinary. Happy writing!

Sincerely,

Bryan Cohen

Author of *1,000 Character Writing Prompts*

CHAPTER 1: CHARACTERS BY ARCHETYPE

Heroes

It's a bird, it's a plane, it's...a blue guy in red tights? While Superman may be losing his red tights in the newest movie adaptation, you can't take the hero out of this classic character. There have been a lot fewer heroes in movie and books as of late because they've been moved to the side for the much more popular anti-hero. Heroes are as much mocked as they are revered for being steadfastly opposed to evil and cynicism in a world where many have negativity as their only defense mechanism. Let's not forget the heroes by including one in our stories: even as a side character.

1. Upon hearing screams, you look up into the air and see a man falling to his death from a rooftop tour. All of a sudden, a bulky man in a camouflage jumpsuit swoops in, grabs the man and parachutes them both to safety. You catch up with the man afterward and it turns out he's part of a secret project to protect citizens. This hero joined the Army shortly after a terrorist attack, hoping he could make a difference. He spends time away from his family while on assignment but he has a deep love for his wife, treating her with respect and appreciation. Why does he feel so compelled to help people he barely knows?

2. With his country in ruins, a second-tier baron in a monarchy assumes control of his nation with peaceful rhetoric. He prevents a near civil war by granting rights to the commoners of both sides and within a decade of his rule, the kingdom is flourishing economically after a long period of darkness. It was his father's steady hand and great sense of compromise that taught him the secrets to governing and he is extremely thankful daily. He does not look like a king, clean-shaven, a large nose and bright green eyes make him appear more like an elf, but as soon as he opens his mouth you realize the power he wields. What goals does a man like this seek for his name in posterity?

3. She quickly rose through the ranks of the large city's police department to become the youngest superintendant and the first woman of the position. In a place and career hounded by corruption, she was able to weed out those who were exploiting their power within a few months. By removing the bad seeds, she was able to reduce crime and the department's budget during her tenure. She works hard and has had a difficult time keeping in touch with family. Her demeanor warms some and intimidates others. What is a typical day like for this high-ranking cop?

4. An accident with medication quickly left this mid-ranking civil servant blind at the age of 30. She wallowed in misery for nearly a year before coming to terms with her ailment. Since she loved seeing the world around her, she determined that if she would never be able to look at herself again, she would make her life as wonderful as possible instead. That would be the beauty she could see. She founded an organization to help those in her situation to cope with their condition and rehabilitate their lives. Just twenty years after her accident she was a loving mother to three and a beacon of hope to thousands. What's the next step in the life of a woman who has done so much?

5. You attend a workshop led by a man who seems too good to be true. At the age of 25, he wrote a book that changed the world and has since been giving seminars to change people's lives. He looks more like an NFL linebacker than a transformational coach, but when you finally get a chance to meet him face to face he warms your heart and invigorates your soul. It's something about the way he connects with you. You are fortunate enough to sit down with him at a coffee shop after the workshop. What is the first question you ask him?

6. A war has broken out between a large country and its colony. One man steps forward to lead the colony in a battle that nearly seems impossible. This leader came from humble beginnings and despite this sense of humility he is able to command the attention of everyone he comes into contact with. His personal life may be the only aspect of his life that is not commendable as his luck with the ladies is far below his battle acumen. What is the outcome of this war and does it help his social life?

7. She had been on the job for about nine months when she noticed the accounting error. It had been two weeks since her boss told her to ignore the issue and a week since the accounting matter mysteriously disappeared. It turned out her company had been essentially stealing from the Medicare program and even though it might cost her job, she scheduled a meeting with her state attorney general. She was incredibly torn because since she moved to the city, she'd had few friends and all of them were at work. She stuck to her guns, however, and though she lost her job and

her friends, she received a percentage of the state's settlement agreement. What will she do with the money and what is the next step for her?

8. As you wait in the emergency room for a friend to be treated for a minor injury, you notice several gurneys entering into the hospital at lightning speed carrying gunshot victims. One doctor at the hospital takes charge of the situation quickly. She commands respect with a deeper than normal voice and authority that can't be trumped. At the same time, however, she seems to reassure the patients with true compassion. Later on, as your friend is checking out, you see the doctor joking with a co-worker provoking a laugh. You approach her and ask if everyone is OK. Not only are the gunshot victims going to survive, but the doctor asks about your friend by name. What has made this woman as strong-willed and perceptive as she is today?

9. In his stage life, he was a professional wrestler who was loved by the masses. The people upstairs never dared turn him into a villain, especially because he was such a cash cow as a hero. To continue in this lifestyle, he was away from home most of the year and his personal life suffered. Despite how tired he was on a day-to-day basis, he still stopped by local charities and made as many appearances as possible to boost awareness for important causes. Between charity, travel and wrestling, he didn't have much time for friends but kept a positive attitude nonetheless. Why does he work so hard on his career and charitable causes and what will he do when his wrestling career ends?

10. She was bullied throughout high school because of her sexual orientation, but she never stopped joking around with her friends and teachers, making her one of the most revered kids in school. When she went to college, she began a campaign to prevent such bullying in high school and she became a national sensation. Despite her ability to coast on account of her rapport with people and her blond, cheerleader looks, she determined early on that she would follow a higher calling. How does she react upon hearing that her girlfriend from high school has been assaulted and what does she do next?

Villains

Just as there aren't as many full-fledged heroes written about these days, there are also fewer absolute villains. The line between a villain and an anti-hero has certainly been blurred. A couple of years ago, the animated movie *Megamind* turned this concept on its head by turning the villain at the beginning of the story to the hero by the end. Comic books and movies in last two decades have made a point to stress that villains are simply heroes who reacted different to their circumstances. Here we will stick with the absolutely vile, worst of the worst villains of yesteryear.

11. He is a powerful wizard who once fought with the side of good. After decades of appearing to love and help the local townsfolk he has gone into hiding and has started to breed an army of evil. He is tall and wiry under his flowing robes and nobody knows his exact age. He was in love once with a woman who was unwilling to love him back due to his black heart. Upon turning evil he brainwashed her from afar and she now helps him in his schemes. What are the wizard's dastardly plans and why has he changed his ways from the light to the dark?

12. You open up the newspaper one day to find out that one of the largest charity magnates in the world is a complete fraud. The founder of several charities for children has apparently been bilking his own charities for millions of dollars over the past few decades. The man was a frequent guest on television and had an almost Kennedy-like appearance of perfection. He spoke in such a way that everyone would listen to the tune of many charitable donations. Why would a man with so much influence resort to taking money from children and what will he do next?

13. A day after your store refused the protection of the mob, you were thrown into a van and taken to see the kingpin. When your hood is removed, you are surprised to see a housewife, dressed in an apron as if she is about to do some evening baking. She speaks to you just as a mother would and uses this charm in an effort to convince you to pay for said "insurance." When you reach for your pocket, she pulls out a gun and fires it over your shoulder, just to make sure you're playing straight. How did this incognito mobster rise to power and why does she keep up the appearance as a housewife?

14. A woman from a small town with big dreams came to the Midwest in search of a calling. After finding a group of nomads in the countryside, she decided to con them by faking a vision of a message from God. The group became so infatuated with her ideas that they began to recruit more to their ranks. Before long, the woman was

running a cult of over 50 people. She determined to use her power for personal gain by having them commit petty thievery in the nearby area. Her wide eyes and curly, black hair would make her adorable to most, but she could be vicious if pushed. What started her on this path to cult leadership and what will she do to take the cult to the next level?

15. After a great deal of pestering from your spouse, you decide to visit your neighbor. You ring the doorbell and see what appears to be a sitcom dad from the 1950s looking back at you. He welcomes you in with open arms and a hearty handshake. You tell him you just moved in next door and the man seems to really connect with you, getting you to open up in record time. Just as he's telling you he thinks you'll love it here, you hear a scream from downstairs. The man smiles. What makes the noise downstairs and why has the man decided to keep it away from view?

16. Before the age of 16, this candidate for the United States presidency had resolved to listen to whatever his mother told him for the rest of his life. He knew that she had influenced him to do some horrible deeds but in a way he liked them. His athletic build and catalogue model looks let him bed whatever women he wanted and his wife was none the wiser. The adultery aside, he had a darker secret that would completely ruin his political chances. What is the secret and what is his political platform?

17. She was the girl that everyone else adored at Sandy Ridge High School. She was the cheerleading captain, the class president and she had been accepted to Stanford the following year due to her high academic marks. She worried slightly that the web of manipulation she'd created in her school including sleeping with teachers for grades and blackmailing the principal would be difficult to create halfway across the country, but she knew it always just took a little acting and a little planning. When did she start acting deviously and will it continue throughout her life?

18. Her entire life she'd only wanted two things: power and money; and she was willing to do whatever she could for them. Her position as a judge in a corrupt city made her life that much easier. Her salary was already quite high, the hard work at the best law school in the country made that a certainty, but it was the payouts that were the most satisfying to her. It was difficult letting some obvious offenders free, because they made her skin crawl, but most of them were hard workers she completely related to. Does her family know about her illicit legal dealings?

19. As your blindfold is taken off, you realize that you recognize your captor. While you can't place the name at first, you know that he is some kind of brilliant computer scientist who has been featured on television. He asks you what you know about his weapon and you feign ignorance. He pushes a button on a keypad and pain goes shooting down your spine. He says that he doesn't like to lose and that you wouldn't like to see him when he's...less than amused. What is this man's project and how does he hide his evil organization from the public?

20. She looked through the crosshairs of the sniper rifle and everything was set up perfectly. She had a pang of loneliness for a second. It was difficult sometimes, traveling around the world alone. Killing and then disappearing without a trace. Her parents never asked her where she'd gotten the money for their swanky retirement home, then again, she didn't stick around long enough to hear the answer. She could have told them she kills bad people for a living, but of course, that would be a lie. What does the future look like for this master assassin?

Sidekicks

There's nothing like having a friend to help you out of a sticky situation, or one that gets into sticky situations frequently. Whether your story is a cop drama, a family comedy or an action-adventure, there is typically a hero and a sidekick. While the hero is steadfast in his beliefs, the sidekick is frequently the voice of reason, sarcasm and occasionally, the trouble. Sidekicks can be the best part of a story or one of the most grating aspects. I'll try to keep to the most enjoyable ones in this list.

21. As you scan the radio, looking for crime to defeat, your partner in heroism is practicing extreme martial arts on a punching bag to your left. As the bag snaps off a chain link and comes crashing to the ground, you wonder more about your partner's origins. He was practically adopted by your family decades ago and he never speaks of his original home. He is strong, fast but also cold and it's exceedingly difficult to get him to crack a smile. Where did this partner of yours come from and why does he spend his time with you?

22. You have decided it's time to let your sidekick go. He's been tagging around you since elementary school, coming over your house, finishing your sentences and calling you practically every night. While he has a good attitude and he's been there for you in tough times, you may have outgrown his partying ways. He frequently lets you know about his lady conquests and those aren't the kinds of conversations to have around your family. You tried to break things off with him a few years back and he nearly cried. What is the next step with this lifetime friend and how will he react?

23. She is quiet, mousy and she is the key to your business. It has just been you and her for the last three years with you baking the pies and her keeping the books balanced. Words are not her forte, as she seems to tremble when she speaks, but she is extremely devoted. If you talk about your love of the company, you can see tears well up in her eyes. You've only seen her open up once or twice when alcohol was involved and unlike most, she says nothing but nice things when she's drunk. What do you believe caused her to be so reserved and why does she like crunching the numbers?

24. As you land the jet you turn around and marvel at your co-pilot. "She saved my life again," you say to yourself as you give her an embrace. She lets down the guard of her extreme professionalism and utters a nervous laugh. She is all business in the air and the warmest person you've ever met on the ground. To get to where she is, she needed to work harder than anyone in school and throughout her training. She's the best in the business and without her, you'd be toast. What goes through her mind in the air that keeps her so calm?

25. For years, your name has struck fear in the heart of criminals throughout London, but when it comes down to it, you're just the front for your brilliant sidekick. Sure, you've had to fight villains with your bare hands, but if it wasn't for your deductive partner, you would never have gotten to the end of each criminal maze. You are truly the brawn and the pretty face to go with his detective work. He is married with two children and has no need for the flash and excitement that you tend to enjoy. What has helped him to become the man of pure intelligence he is today?

26. As you attempt to save a village, you are forced to partner up with a wanted thief with a heart of silver. He says he's after treasure buried in the center of town, but he slips up and you realize that his love of riches is subservient to his desire to see the boorish warlord pay for his crimes. Behind his moustache and his ability to work his way out of a sticky situation, there is a loyal and honorable man there. He covers it up by boasting about how amazing he is, but you can see right through that. How did this good man end up a thief and your partner?

27. As you wonder to yourself, "Why did I take on such an ambitious play?" your assistant director comes up behind you and puts her hand on your shoulder. "Get it together," she says with a smirk. She's not the lovey-dovey type. If she were a food, she'd be salty and sour. If it weren't for her, you'd have quit multiple times but she peps you up like a football coach and sends onto the field. You are grateful that such a strong-willed woman agreed to partner up with you in the first place. Why has she relegated herself to number two when she could easily lead the group herself?

28. As you walk across the alien planet, you are glad to have your sidekick close at hand. Not only is she extremely perceptive but she can actually see danger before it comes. You're still not sure if you believe in the second sight thing, but you've certainly seen her in action enough to know it can't all be coincidence. She often seems burdened with what she says are the many possible futures that could occur. She is kind and playful when you get to know her and you wonder if she sees a future together with you. When did she inherit such a gift and how has it shaped who she is?

29. When you won the heavyweight championship, you had no idea that one of your biggest supporters would be your brother-in-law. Sure, he's mooched off your success to a certain extent and he's had his share of trouble but he's literally been in your corner for every fight since. He's worked at the same job for decades and getting a little bit of luxury from you has made him happy as a clam. He's always there for a quick verbal jab at you when you're getting cocky and he's just who you need when you don't see the obstacles to a situation. How do you think he feels getting a chance to be taken care of after taking care of himself for so long?

30. You're getting old, but she won't let your fan base see or feel that for a second. She is your personal relations mastermind and without her, your movies might have been relegated to the bargain bin years ago. She is calculating but never cold and her wit is easily able to defuse any situation. Last year, you slipped in the shower and broke your hip and she spun it into a motorcycle accident. Brilliant and strong, she does her job better than anybody, though you know little about her home life. Who is she really and how does she get her kicks?

Rebels

There's nothing we love more than character who is willing to rebel from the norm. Similar to antiheroes, rebels may often take part in heroic actions, except rebels are usually found shaking things up simply to shake them up and to cause trouble for authority. Rebels may be looking to take back what is rightfully theirs or to just show the flaws in a tyrannical world. One of the most well-known rebels in cinematic history is James Dean's iconic *Rebel Without a Cause*, who really spoke to a generation at the time the movie was released. Creating a rebel appropriate for your own place and time can likewise make a character that your readers identify with.

31. Even though they mocked his clothes and his antics, most of the people in your high school wanted him or to be with him. He showed up to every class at least five minutes late, had his food delivered to the school at lunchtime and had several artistically rendered and visible tattoos on his neck and back. He was easily able to deflect anything negative that was said to him or about him due to his quick wit. He rarely fought back verbally, though he was easily able to make the person talking to him sound completely foolish. What was this rebel's cause and how did he come to be who he was?

32. He was a comedian who had gathered a bit of fame through his writing and acting projects. When he finally had the opportunity to head up his own television show, he was astounded by how little creative control he had. He couldn't come close to creating the dark, demented show mirroring his life that he wanted. After two seasons, the show went off the air and he got to thinking. He accepted a tiny contract from a cable network that wouldn't allow any executives to give him notes of any kind. Unsurprisingly, his show was beloved by critics as something that had never been done before. What are some of the other ways in which this funny man rebels against the norm?

33. When other companies were using animal testing on products to save money, she was spending three times as much to avoid harming any of nature's creatures. Despite these efforts to be socially conscious, her company thrived because those who were like-minded flocked to her progressive business. She never thought her company would be anything but the source of a regular salary for her and her family. The fact that it was bringing in enough money to employ thousands of people was enough for her and spending the profit on keeping her soul intact was the best kind of bonus she could pay herself. What are some of the aspects of her upbringing that made turning a profit far below number one on her list of priorities?

34. She refused to participate in convention when she walked into school and saw the designer fashions and high-priced accessories that adorned the other girls in her class. First of all, she wasn't even close to having enough money to buy them, but secondly, she loved designing her own stuff and being her own person. She was mocked by some of those who could afford some of these items, but others thought her to be an amazing example of independence and free will. Twenty years down the line, she would be a fashion designer who was making outfits the popular girls could only dream of wearing, but for the time being, she had to grin and bear the consequences of her individuality. What are some other ways in which she rebels against convention?

35. He had spent the last decade of his life learning to be the best teacher he could be. As kids grew more and more inattentive, he knew that he would have to do something drastic to keep their attention. He started to bring to the classroom more than a few unconventional teaching methods. He would bring in word for word explicit rap lyrics and connect them to Shakespeare. He would photocopy graffiti and other various vandalism from bathroom stalls. He even showed his students intense scenes from movies and television shows involving drugs and sex. He got in trouble plenty of times, but the administration couldn't complain too much. After all, test scores were way up amongst his students. What are some of the wilder things he's done to teach his students?

36. It was true that he'd gotten a legitimate medical degree and was well on his way to becoming respected in the field of medicine. When an illness struck his wife and traditional means couldn't cure it, he reached out to a doctor

who was famous for using homeopathic and biologic medicines to treat athletes. Within a few months his wife was cured and he was a changed man. He ditched his practice and learned more about alternative medicine. He started a new office in which traditional and alternative healing came together, which was a huge success, even though he was shunned by those who used to call him a colleague. What are some of the new methods he uses and how has his opinion changed about being a doctor in general?

37. In a time when women were treated vastly different when it came to wages, she became a symbol of rebellion. When she realized how much more her male friends were being paid for a job in the textiles industry, she staged a strike, forcing the employers to become more aware of the income discrepancy. It took many hard hours of work, but her strike was the straw that changed the nation. Now almost 30 years later, because pay was by no means equal. She continued to spread the word through her writing and activism. While having a family and growing older might cause some women to soften, she never budged an inch with her fiery personality. What in her upbringing gave her the strength to be such a force for positive change?

38. She was one of the hardest working movie stars in Hollywood and yet, it didn't really matter that much to her. She'd already saved up for her retirement and her kids' college funds. Monetarily, she had achieved 10 times what normal people did through their entire lifetimes. Upon a visit to a poor third-world country, she decided that she would donate her total salary for the rest of her lifetime to charity. For an actress making over $10 million a film, this was no small sum. She was reenergized and began working harder on as many movies as she could in a year. The public caught onto her donations and began frequenting her movies with new aplomb. Her salary rose and the studios even got in on the action, donating at least 10 percent these movies' profits to charity. What were some of the ways in which her funds were used and how did she feel when she wired over that money?

39. He was born into an extremely corrupt fascist government. His parents were completely wired in and were willing to do anything for a horrible tyrant so that their son could grow up to the age of adulthood in the same warped system. He began to organize secret meetings of his friends and cousins who would plot over the course of a decade to overthrow the regime. He even got a job for the tyrant himself, to bring down the empire from the inside. Whenever he planned an attack or instigated a protest, he thought of his mother and how hard she had to work for so little. When the full plan went into effect, he was the worldwide voice of the rebellion and became a beacon of hope for many. What were some of the atrocities he witnessed growing up and how did they shape him?

40. She was one of the most outspoken politicians in the world on the rights of homosexuals to marry, despite the fact that she was a heterosexual conservative with a family of five. A few years ago, her granddaughter came out to her and asked this proud and educated woman to put aside her beliefs of "the family" and to think about her own family. Her granddaughter wanted to marry the love of her life, her soul mate and this staunch conservative knew upon seeing them that it was meant to be. She wrote editorials to newspapers, made speeches to gay rights groups and mounted support in the Senate to pass a new rights act extending the ability for gays and lesbians to marry. Her late-in-life cause was thoroughly invigorating. Did her about face on the issue of marriage cause any changes in her other beliefs?

Antiheroes

Antiheroes are some of the most popular characters of the last few decades and have been seen in mediums ranging from comic books to mumblecore independent films. The antihero may have a dark past such as that of Mal in the short-lived television series "Firefly." The character may have multiple unlikeable characteristics but when push comes to shove, the antihero will rise to the occasion to do the right thing. Antiheroes work well as protagonists in many stories, as most people are no longer willing to accept "the perfect hero" anymore like they might have half a century ago.

41. While it's true that he was running from the law, it wasn't exactly a fair assessment of the kind of guy he was. After all, he had been in the Army and was all ready to move up the ranks and become a good citizen for Uncle Sam. The world had other plans, however, as he saw something he wasn't supposed to and was immediately framed as a terrorist. His skill allowed him to escape and he was now doing everything he could to both unearth the conspiracy and clear his name. He'd grown a bit tough and sarcastic through this process, but he persevered with hopes that the

country would reveal the truth. Has he been able to contact his family and if so, what do they think about his situation?

42. He wasn't in it for the chance to discover some great artifact or to bring an ancient scroll back to a museum, he was in it for the money. No matter how hard he tried, however, innocent people tended to be put in danger looking for same treasure he craved and he had to do his best to save them. He may have loved money, but he didn't value it above human life. The skills he'd obtained in becoming a sort of treasure mercenary served him well in both causes. When he had the thought that his mom and dad would be proud of who he'd become, he laughed and took a shot of whisky. In what other ways has this tough guy softened during his attempts at protecting innocent life?

43. She was one of the most hated girls at school due to her ability to spread rumors that would ruin people's place in the popularity spectrum. She had always felt a great power from talking about others, making her feel she was important in the grand scheme of things. When she was the witness to an illegal crime perpetrated by the teachers and principal, nobody believed her due to her previous rumor mongering. She gathered the few real friends she had left and played detective to stop the crime and save her reputation. She was surprised to find that her battle for the forces of good made her feel more important than spreading chatter ever could. If she got out of this sticky situation alive, she considered toning down her gossip mill as much as 50 percent. If successful, will she turn over a new leaf or will old habits prove hard to break?

44. From a young age, her and her parents did not see eye to eye in the slightest. There were constant fights and screaming matches about how they didn't understand her at all. When she was 18, she was out the door with the hopes of never returning to her "screwed up" family. After traveling the world for a few years, she came back to find her family completely in shambles. She hated being there and every step into her parents' house made her cringe. Despite that, it was up to her, as both an insider and an outsider to patch things up before her family fell apart forever. What is the situation she has to diffuse and what are some of the skills she's learned abroad that she can bring to the table?

45. He had the reputation as a conniving politician and his larger than life personality made the label stick. Despite how he appeared from the outside, he was actually one of the most honest men you'd ever meet, a major departure from most on the campaign trail. When he realized that the federal government was attempting to secretly pass a bill that would limit the rights of Americans everywhere, he chose to fight back. At his own expense and against the wishes of his party, he slowly but surely toured the nation to counteract his image and tell the people the truth about the bill. Was his attempt to preserve the rights of his nation successful?

46. He wondered from time to time if his parents would be proud of him as the captain of his very own ship. He often thought of his folks when he recalled the rebellion. He and his family were on opposite sides of the conflict. When his side lost, his parents tried to reach out to him, but he was worried that if they connected with him, they would be labeled as rebels. He also thought about his parents during every job he and his crew did that involved something labeled as illegal. He stole but he wouldn't kill. He refused to rob from anyone who didn't have it coming to them. What are some of the other aspects of his tenuous moral code?

47. She was imprisoned for a crime she didn't commit and while her children and husband loved her, they thought she was as guilty as the court "proved" she was. In her public relations work, she had accidentally crossed a major player in an international drug ring. The syndicate had enough power to ruin her life and take the people she loved away from her. She escaped from prison and a nationwide hunt for her, dead or alive, began. She knew this was her only chance to prove her innocence and to save the lives of thousands who were under the thumb of the man she crossed. With every television station flashing her face, how will she be able to take down the life of the man who took away hers?

48. She loved money. Not enough to kill for it, but enough to work her way to the top of a criminal law firm to defend the accused in high-profile cases. She had successfully proven the innocence of many that the public had already mentally sentenced. This lined her pockets with millions and gave her a life of luxury. When she successfully exonerated a man who she later found out to be guilty; she changed her tune. She could no longer defend the people who were taking advantage of her charisma and the flaws in the legal system. She began her own practice with the

money she'd saved up and she started to protect the innocent for the first time in her life. What are some of the old habits she's had to get rid of in her new line of work?

49. Even though he was on the right side of the law, it didn't mean that he always abided by the rules. He was a complete junkie and he often stole evidence to get himself high. He was also a great cop and he did everything he could to be clear headed and strong when he was on duty. He had a problem and there were few people who knew enough about it to help. When a low-level drug dealer identified him as a client, it was his word against the dealers. Instead of coming clean, he vowed to take down the supplier and to eradicate his drug problem cold turkey at the same time. This wasn't going to be easy. How did he get addicted to drugs in the first place and how able to function is he while detoxing and railing against drug dealers?

50. She felt a little bit like Robin Hood sometimes. After all, she led her own merry band of warriors through the forest and they tended to take what they needed but not from those who were worse off than her. She had a reputation throughout the kingdom that painted her as an evil witch who was more likely to cut your throat than shake your hand. Those who met her saw that she wasn't dastardly, she was just a charismatic leader looking out for those who were mistreated. She had to do things from time to time that made her feel uncomfortable, like ripping the purses from privileged young girls, but sometimes to survive you have to ruffle even your own feathers. How did she become an outlaw in the first place and will she ever have to rebel against the oppressive kingdom?

Rivals

Some of the best stories are formed from rivalries in many different settings of the world. There could be a rivalry in school, in a club, at the workplace and even in the home itself. Rivalries typically pit a protagonist against an equal that tends to be working for the opposite side of either good or evil. Some rivalries have played on this quite literally with characters like Evil Superman, Evil Hercules, etc. Some rivals are a bit stranger, such as Max Fischer's rival Herman Blume in the movie *Rushmore*. Rivalries often perpetuate the action in a story, so it's best to make sure the rival you include is well-developed.

51. No matter how hard you tried, no matter how suave you looked, he would always be the one to get the girl. You'd been "best friends" for nearly your entire life, much to your chagrin. You were too timid to break off a friendship, especially with someone so well-regarded. But every time you had a crush on someone, he would quickly say that he did as well, before snatching up the girl as his very own. You couldn't wait until college when you would go far away and leave his shadow. The only problem, he just told you that he was going to the same school as you. Will this rival of yours follow you around the rest of your life and how does he always come out on top?

52. When you first went to college, you were overjoyed to find out that your dorm had a ping pong table. You'd been the champion out of a group of friends who were all quite skilled at the sport. That was until you met the foreigner who had been the captain of his high school's ping pong team. He was strong and fast at a sport that had never passed the point of a hobby for you. Every time you played, he always countered your slams and his chances of making an error were extremely low. Outside of the games he seemed kind and a pretty cool guy. Inside the games, however, there was nobody you hated more. How will you describe this rival to your friends when relating the story after college?

53. She was intelligent, overwhelmingly popular and funny to boot. You felt that even though there was little to no chance for you, you wanted to go up against her in the race for student body president. She felt like she was a shoe in and assumed she would be running unopposed. One day she came up to you and said that a war was brewing, a war that you would lose. You were just interested in student government. She was interested in winning at all costs and began launching an all-out smear campaign against you. You had no idea what her issue was, after all, she was probably going to win anyway. Making your life a living hell made you want to get even. What are some of the ways in which this queen bee creates a campaign to smear your good name?

54. She had been your best friend through thick and thin. But when the two of you both had the hots for the same guy, this created a conflict that the two of you couldn't get over. You went from speed-dial to mortal enemies within a week. You began to sabotage each others' chances. Your friend even got to the point of slashing your tires when you secured a date with the dreamboat. You couldn't believe that you once hung out with the same girl who

was pulling such dastardly tricks on you. When the guy eventually fell for someone else, you wondered if you'd ever be able to think of your former friend the same way again. Will your former friendship with this rival be salvageable?

55. Despite the fact that you were a hard worker and devoted most of your life to your job, he always seemed to be one step ahead of you. While you were hired at the same time, he got a promotion well before you. He was under-qualified for his added responsibilities and he seemed to show up to every meeting unprepared. While you picked up his slack, he used his charm to weasel his way out of his obvious shortcomings. You had no idea what else you could do to get a leg up on him. You already came off as smart and harder working but he was always in first. What are some of this rival's qualities that make him so revered at the office?

56. You were one of the morning warriors, getting to the gym each day before the sun came up. You were happy to be the strongest person pound-for-pound in the place and others marveled at your small stature and large capacity. That is, until he came along. He was like a superhero. He weighed 20 pounds less than you and he looked like a strong gust of wind would blow him over. Despite his size, he was able to lift more weight than you in almost every exercise. Your title of strongest small guy went out the window and you desperately wanted it back. How will you face the challenge of this small, but powerful rival?

57. You didn't understand how she was completely unknown popularity-wise when you all left school for the summer. When you all came back, she went all "Sabrina" on you and had completely transformed into a popularity hurricane. All of a sudden, you were no longer the queen bee; you were no longer the girl people looked to for the next trend. It was her. She went from nerdy nobody who had once been the subject of embarrassing nicknames to someone everybody wanted to be around. And she was totally nice about it, which really made you fume. How did this girl go from zero to hero over the summer?

58. You loved your students more than anything and their respect and admiration were important to you. That's why you hated the new math teacher. She was barely competent enough to lead study hall, let alone 10th grade geometry. She had a brash method of instruction that used real world examples that only vaguely connected to the subject material. She also gave out insulting nicknames and candy to the kids. Now your students couldn't stop talking about her and you were incredibly jealous. What are some of the other qualities of the new teacher in town?

59. You were content being a house husband because you were the most amazing dad on the block. You participated as a coach or a chairperson for almost every activity. Your kids loved you and you seemed to have it all. When your neighbor left his job, however, he threw himself as wholeheartedly into every activity as you did. Before you knew it, the two of you were competing to be the baseball coach, the head of the PTA and the carpool driver. Then he started playing dirty by saying disparaging remarks about you behind your back. You had no ill will toward him, until his kid punched your kid due to a misunderstood insult. This meant war. What has caused this fellow house dad to challenge your status as "the coolest" dad in town?

60. When your husband got remarried, you mostly hoped that his new wife would be decent to your children so that the post-divorce transition would go smoothly. Deep down though, you really wanted her to be a complete shrew so that your kids would want to come running home to their biological mommy. Fortunately and unfortunately, she was a real class act and as a result, your kids were frequently talking about how great she was. You did your best to up the ante with gifts, better cooking and an attempt to find a new high-paying job. Despite your efforts, she outdid you in every possible facet and lavished them with both toys and attention. What will you have to do to win their affection back from this new mother?

Goons and Thugs

Just as villains are the counterparts to heroes, goons and thugs are the corollary to sidekicks. Not all goons and thugs are involved in some kind of organized crime business. Some may just be creepy folks who are prone to following the evil that exists in any part of society. When you're creating a villain in any profession, such as a shady doctor or an evil drama teacher, you also want to come up with a second-in-command that holds his or her own. Let's get beyond the clichés of a muscle head or a yes man and find something memorable about these goony characters.

61. While it wasn't very well known as a profession, every political campaign needed a guy to take care of the dirty work. He was that guy. Some of his day to day tasks included keeping people with information quiet and letting them know "what's best for them." He never "hurt" anybody, though he did show off his impressive muscles to those looking to do damage to his boss' chances of staying in office. At the end of the day, he collected the benefits of a government employee and kept his family well fed. How did this thug get into the business of politics and does he like his job?

62. There was something he hated about the word, "torture." He liked "coercion" or "compulsion" much better as he felt these words were more professional. He wasn't just some two-bit crook who chopped off thumbs and pulled fingernails apart. There wasn't any style to these methods. He was an expert when it came to making people say what needed to be said. His employers loved his style because it wasn't bloody and it didn't elicit screams, because it was more psychological than physical. He was willing to draw a little blood if needed, but it was a last resort, because pain came in many forms and some were much less messy. How did he get into the "coercion" business and what does he enjoy most about it?

63. She didn't mind that she had to use her sex appeal to get some jobs done for her employer. Sometimes, she would seduce a guy and handcuff him to the bed so that her employer could talk to him alone for a few minutes. She had also used some lock picking and athletic abilities to steal a few important items here and there or to extract a phone number or contact for her boss. She felt like a spy or something most of the time, not like an object. She was treated extremely well and got nearly everything she needed financially for her troubles, though she had been put in danger more than a few times. It was a difficult life sometimes, but she was happy to be able to take care of her family, even though her job wasn't on the up and up. What are some of the most difficult "assignments" she's had to take on?

64. She was one of the most important assets for the mob. Despite that, most in the world of organized crime hated her with a passion. Only a few at the top of the organization knew that this high-ranking policewoman was actually a double agent, truly working to keep those in the top of the mob world out of trouble. She had put a ton of low-ranking mob personnel in jail, but when the police had a major opportunity to deal a blow to the organization, she quickly informed her real employers of what they needed to do to escape. The police couldn't figure out how the force seemed to miss every major opportunity for victory and the double agent was proud at her ability to keep things secret. How and why did she decide to be one of the bad guys when she was revered as one of the best cops in town?

65. His parents were always worried about how he'd fit in. He was much bigger than his classmates throughout school and he had failed three grades along the way, leaving him behind the intelligence level of most of his peers. It wasn't until he got a gig as a goon for a crime syndicate that he found his true calling. They were scared that he'd get arrested and that they'd have to bail him out, but he seemed to really enjoy his job and more than anything else, he loved being valued. What are some of his best skills as an extremely strong goon for a less than reputable employer?

66. By trade, he was a loan shark's money collector, but he fancied himself a bit of a poet. Yes, it's true that he was hired because of his boxing background and that if called upon, he could easily break someone's thumbs or ankles. On the other hand, much of the violence of his job was uninspiring to him. He wrote love poems, sonnets and odes to the nature and music he experienced every day. He didn't have a whole lot of people to share his work with, so he went to open mics and poetry slams as frequently as possible. How did this man who punches for a living learn to have such a love for words?

67. When your line of work is breaking into high security areas, it helps to have someone who can get into and out of tight spaces. This former gymnast and martial artist was so precise in her movements that she could leap between infrared beams of light to avoid tripping alarms. She could use her skills to climb high walls and narrowly avoid pressurized floor sensors. In addition, she was such a cute, young looking woman, that if something went wrong on a mission, she could use her charm and her big blue eyes to diffuse a situation. How did she get into the business of breaking and entering and what are some of the benefits and detriments of such a high risk career?

68. She was the main squeeze of the gang's leader and she was quite a woman. After all, how many women can lift a small vehicle off the ground? She was a former professional wrestler, turned bodyguard, turned object of affection, as there was nothing the boss loved more than strength. While others might have been afraid of getting mixed up in a gang leader's business, she wanted to be as involved as possible, especially when it came to "taking care" of people who had fallen out of line. She knew that she was leading a dangerous life, but she was doing it for love and for her love of bashing heads in. What is her relationship like with her gang boss boyfriend?

69. He wasn't particularly big or strong. He didn't strike fear into the heart of the people he threatened or the cops he laughed at when he was being interrogated. He seemed like a perfectly normal guy on the outside. That is, of course, until he snapped. He had a temper on him that burned as hot as the fires of hell. And when he got mad, it wasn't just about anger, he was absolutely crazy in both his emotions and his actions. For instance, when he got into a sticky situation and was trapped in a room with five attackers, nobody knows exactly what happened, but when he opened the door, he was the only person left alive. The stories, now that's what made people afraid of him. How did his temper come to be and is he ever able to calm it down when necessary?

70. Where she grew up, it was a challenge just to stay alive, and she learned many tricks from her parents to preserve herself in a difficult world. When she moved to the United States, she was recognized for her talents when she poisoned a gang member who was trying to take advantage of her. Soon enough, she was being paid for her aptitude as a sort of jack-of-all-kills, with an array of ways to take certain people down before they took her down first. She loved her new life now that she was no longer on the bottom, but she felt strange about killing people who hadn't directly wronged her or her family. When given an opportunity to get out of the business, will she take it or continue to live in the lap of luxury?

CHAPTER 2: CHARACTERS INSIDE AND OUTSIDE THE LAW

Law Enforcement

Back in the day, many members of the law enforcement community were portrayed as blue-clad, donut-eating, moustache-donning officers who squeezed in cop activities between naps and home life. With the grittier stories of the last couple of decades, there have been entertaining cop stories that feature the "super cop" who runs around town at breakneck pace putting criminals behind bars. The super cop has been parodied in works like *Last Action Hero* and *The Other Guys*, reminding us that some police officers are normal people who want to make a difference. However you decide to portray your cops, it's likely that the doughnut downing diner cops are long gone in more recent cop tales.

71. He was a normal sheriff in a town full of incredible geniuses. He happened to stumble upon the town while driving across the country and he ended up taking a vacant spot as the head sheriff, solving mysteries and crimes perpetrated by government officials working in secret in the middle of nowhere. As the brilliant aren't always known to have common sense, he provided it in droves for scientists who were able to do everything from teleporting to miniaturizing. His mind was blown by some of the things he'd seen, but what kept him most grounded was thinking of his family. What are some of his wild adventures like in the midst of this crazy town?

72. He knew he only had a few more hours until the end of his shift, but he could barely keep himself from shaking. He wondered if his partner knew about his addiction and he wondered how much longer he could continue to lead this double life. He tried to calm himself by thinking it could be worse, after all, he'd never stolen evidence or anything like that. He used his own money to buy drugs and he hadn't used his connections as an officer to fuel his habit. He knew that what he was doing was unsustainable, because a man with a drug problem walking around with a gun is a recipe for disaster. He tried to get anonymous help, but he was worried that his friends and co-workers would find out. He attempted to tough it out cold turkey, but he got so sick he ended up in the emergency room. Will he be able to put his demons behind him to be a model citizen and policeman?

73. The second that the teenager pulled out a gun, she immediately shot him in the side. The gun went flying to the ground and she quickly cuffed him and put pressure on the wound. She knew that the kid wasn't a killer, but she'd seen kids do stupid things too many times to let him do something that would define his life. She remembered back when compassion toward a teen had nearly gotten her partner killed. She knew that in a tough situation, she had to use her incredible aim to neutralize the threat. Her new boyfriend had told her he wanted kids, but to her, all kids were targets or delinquents waiting to happen. She couldn't bear the thought of bringing kids up in such a dangerous world. Will her perilous job continue to reassert her opinion about having a family or will something cause her to change her tune?

74. How else was she supposed to support her family on a cop's salary? That's the question she always asked herself when she got a call from that mysterious cell phone - the one that rang whenever she had to do someone a favor. The favor was always something that only she could do as a police officer and it was what allowed her to continue to pay the bills for her mother and her sister. She always did her best to convince herself that she was in a way doing the right thing, but she'd never felt so dirty in her life. She hoped that by toeing the line between morality and immorality she might have a chance of doing both. How long will she be able to keep up this double life and what are some examples of favors she's had to do for her anonymous benefactor?

75. It was almost as if he were some kind of hero movie cop. Not only did he always get his criminal, but he was in incredible shape and knew the ins and outs of at least 10 different fighting styles. He was an expert at firing multiple kinds of weapons and he had memorized every single law and how to uphold it. His abilities were beginning to lower the morale of the other members of the police force. They knew they would never be able to hold a candle to him and many of them considered other fields, such as becoming organic food grocers. His superior officers told him they still wanted him to be extremely proficient, they just suggested that he be a little less overt about it. He tried

his best, but his attempts to portray imperfection were unconvincing at best. What are some of the ways in which he's tried and failed to show flaws in his law enforcement abilities?

76. As a kid, he was nothing more than a petty crook. He and his friends would go around knocking over mailboxes and putting stink bombs in the girl's locker room. One day, after he got caught setting off a firework inside a gymnasium, one of the policemen took him aside and gave him a speech he never forgot. During this chat about civic duty and wasting your life, the officer gave him a pamphlet for a young police program. The program nurtured youth with no direction and made them feel like a part of the force. It gave him something to do away from his crook friends and he ended up becoming obsessed with being an officer of the law. His friends gave him a hard time, but he realized that this gang of his would give him an enjoyable adolescence and a horrible adulthood. He soon became a real cop and the clash with his old friends began. Who will come out victorious in this battle on the mean streets?

77. When her fellow detectives asked her how she came to be an expert on serial killers, she said that her father taught her everything she knew. They took this to mean that she was a detective just like her dad, when in actuality, he was one of the most notorious murderers in the history of the city. She had witnessed awful things that would scar most children for the rest of their lives. She'd even witnessed her mother's murder. She knew her calling then. She would never let what happened to her family happen to anybody else's again. Through the intense study of psychology and criminology, she became an extremely well known profiler. She made every effort to keep her history with her father a secret, but it was incredibly difficult as he was made into a comparison for every related killing that occurred in the tri-state area. It also didn't help that her father was still alive, serving a life sentence due to a compassionate jury. What are some of her visits with her dad like and what has she learned from his evil deeds?

78. She was the only sister to five brothers, yet she was the tough one. Her scrawny siblings were often picked on in school, but she would quickly intervene and diffuse the situation. She got into fights from time to time, but they were always in an attempt to preserve her brothers' honor. She was proud when three of them came out of the closet and she made it her goal to protect not only her family, but those who were picked on for who they were. Her brothers weren't surprised at all when she became a cop and they knew that her presence alone would improve the safety of the town. Her co-workers tried to label her toughness as the result of abuse or being a butch lesbian. She had no problem standing up to the gossip just as she had for her brothers years earlier. What is her proudest achievement and why?

79. He wondered if he was truly making a difference anymore. After having been a high ranking officer in the force for years, he hadn't seen any action in the field in ages. He knew that he was doing his best to nurture the younger officers and he did a lot of important behind the scenes delegation work. He didn't feel particularly important though. When officers would get gunned down in the street, he would wish that he was killed instead of them. When it came time to take down a large human trafficking organization, he stepped away from the desk and got back into the field for a large bust. Will his itchy trigger finger get him in hot water or will this case be his greatest success?

80. During a criminal investigation, she had tracked a shipment of drugs halfway across the country, where she knew she had absolutely no jurisdiction. She threw caution to the wind by faking a vacation there and she continued to look into the case. Between her sex appeal and her sharp tongue, she could talk her way out of any situation. She got into trouble on multiple occasions with the local police force, but eventually smoothed things over to create a sort of working partnership. When she found out that the operation was even bigger than she'd thought, she worried she'd bitten off more than she could chew. With the help of the local precinct, she led a small task force to take down the heavily armed and angry drug cartel. At this point, her words and charm would have to be superseded by the aim of her gun. How did she come to be the detective she is today and why?

Government Officials

The officials of local, state and federal governments take on many different forms. They might be pencil pushers who have the ability to strengthen or weaken your business or personal life simply by sending you a particular form in the mail. They may be of extreme importance politically, hoping to win voters and to move on up the political ladder. They might also be idealists who have gotten into the government in hopes of changing the world for the better. There is a lot of potential for government officials in stories like superhero yarns, espionage tales and political thrillers along with many other genres.

81. He didn't meet your portrait of a typical Internal Revenue Service employee. After all, he actually had a sense of humor and wasn't just about numbers. He was willing to help you understand more about your taxes free of charge, and on several occasions he saved you from being on a dangerous list of people to be audited. The thing is, he didn't really love his job, but because he was so good with numbers, it was an obvious fit after he was recruited in college. He stayed with the job for 40 years. How well does he fit in at the IRS and how satisfied has he been with his career path?

82. Everybody knew that he was a nice guy who wanted to make a difference. He was on the county's board and he'd been elected due to his trustworthiness and his honesty. When a sleazy lawyer who'd recently moved into the area wanted to take his seat, the lawyer dug up as much dirt as he could about the kind county board member. In an advertisement that ran on all the local channels, the board member was painted as a philanderer who was involved in seedy activities throughout the night. The lawyer twisted the words of friends in interviews, cutting them up and pasting them together to sound angry and hateful. Suddenly, people began treating him differently and he considered not running again for his seat on the board. What will his strategy be to counteract the negativity of his opponent?

83. She was born and raised in a small town in the middle of the country and yet she had some massive dreams. Many girls dream that they will be the next president of the United States, but few of them actually follow through with a government career. She began her efforts in a small department in the town she grew up in and was easily the most dedicated and involved person there. She successfully ran for a spot in the state's House of Representatives and before long she had become a major contender for the state's U.S. Senate seat. One thing that set her apart from most was that she was willing and able to work harder than all of her peers. If she came to a place in which people were working harder than she'd previously experienced, she'd simply kick it up to a higher level. What are some examples of her extreme overachievement and will she be able to realize her dream?

84. She hoped that her forgetfulness wasn't part of a larger issue. She double checked the lockbox under her desk that held secret funds she'd skimmed off the top of the payroll. She made sure that all the bank receipts she'd forged were in proper order in case someone took an attentive look into her files. She just knew she was forgetting something and as a dirty treasurer in the state government, she knew that one wrong move could get her into a lot of trouble. In her efforts to keep on top of her job, she started taking memory supplements and even some brain classes. She knew she would have to pull out all the stops to keep her brain sharp, her family safe and herself out of jail. Will she survive an upcoming internal audit and what made her decide to go dirty in the first place?

85. As an interim mayor who had no chance of being elected, he knew that he had to make an impact in the short time he would be in office. As a major patron of the arts, he understood how hard it was for artistic organizations to function. In his last three months in the position, he would create a massive festival that celebrated the local art scene, including theatre, music and dance and he would make it completely sustainable through sponsorships and ticket sales. He pushed so hard to make the festival a reality that people started to get excited. Neighboring cities began to inquire about the festival and he had to expand the number of vendors exponentially. The event became the largest in state history and brought a huge amount of revenue to the city. Will this big boost in awareness give his potential future candidacy a chance or will he be known more as a "one hit wonder?"

86. As the new head of the Department of Natural Resources, he literally wanted to "clean up this town" from top to bottom. What he found though, was that most companies that were guilty of dumping chemicals or creating pollution refused to admit fault. They would much rather drag out months or years of litigation as opposed to simply dealing with the problem. He realized that all of his time as the leader of the town's environmental initiative was in court as opposed to being in the trenches. He started to campaign for his efforts exclusively with the online generation of 20-somethings and slowly but surely, his causes became nationally known through viral videos and podcasts. In a massive burst, the companies tried to preserve their images by settling their litigation, leading to

millions of dollars to be used for cleaning. What were some of the things he said in his campaign to get the youth fired up about making the state a cleaner place to live?

87. If there was anything important to her, it was the well-being and safety of her children. This was one of the reasons she ran for and won the seat of chairwoman of the school board. Now that she was in power, she would do everything she could to protect her kids from scary, bullying students and teachers. One of the plans focused particularly on the school band, which both of her children were a part of. She highlighted several problem children, all of whom had at one time or another gotten into fights with her kids. The ideas and remedies she came up with were sound, but unless an idea had to do with her family in some way, she was prone to shoot it down. Will she continue to use her seat of power to influence the schooling experience for her "little munchkins?"

88. She knew that there were a lot of people who hated the fact that she was now in power. As the first female president of the United States, she realized she would be held to a higher standard than most. Her emotions and the causes she fought for would be especially scrutinized. She ran on a campaign that she'd rather be a one-term president who did everything she believed in with full force, no matter how it reflected on her approval rating. She made a major push for worldwide woman's rights and pushed for a legal precedent on par with the Universal Declaration of Human Rights. She used her domestic power to veto ordinances that she didn't agree with and she used her speaking skills to take down any candidate from the opposite party who stood in her way. She even dissolved the BCS in college football. Will her strong beliefs and a lack of wavering make her into the one-term president she prophesied?

89. Every day of his life he'd followed his parents' wishes. Since they had gone into politics, he was required to as well and through their help, he was elected to head the county clerk's office. He was in control of a staff that dealt with thousands of forms and filings every day. He was bored out of his ever-loving mind and desired a more exciting life in which there were risks. The only risk in his job, he said, was getting a paper cut. At the close of each work day, he'd head to the coast and surf as long as the daylight held out. When his parents found out about his leisure activities, they threatened to cut him out of their will. Will he once again yield to his parents or decide to follow a more laid back existence?

90. He didn't like the term that he was "in somebody's pocket." It's true that he was not above taking money as a consultant to a pharmaceutical company here and a defense contractor there, but he felt like he was providing a service. When he made more money as a Senator, he felt like he was more able to run an effective campaign and keep himself as one of the leaders of a great state. When a major crackdown on lobbyists occurred, he did his best to weather the storm, though his name was being dropped frequently in documentaries and testimonies. He was glad to have saved up enough money to keep his lifestyle afloat for years, though he didn't enjoy the protests outside of his house. What was it about his upbringing that made him feel as though taking money to influence the law was a legitimate practice?

The Armed Forces

At any given time there are tens of thousands of soldiers from the United States all around the world. They may have extremely risky lives overseas in a war zone or they may be involved in a humanitarian effort. They might have families living on a base with them or they might have a family waiting for them thousands of miles away. There are many different kinds of members of the Armed Forces and to try to portray them all as strong-willed soldier types would be clichéd and inaccurate.

91. His friends had mocked him in college for his bachelor's degree in Peace, War and Defense because they saw no practical application for it. Then again, most of them took on English and Dramatic Art degrees, so he couldn't help but quietly snicker as he prepared to get into law school. He wanted to become part of the Judge Advocate General Corps, or JAG Corps for short. He had to go to boot camp and he had to deploy overseas in certain instances, but his main responsibility was to be a legal advisor for his commanding officers. He loved wearing his uniform, he loved supporting his country and he loved being legally knowledgeable. What is day-to-day life like for this Armed Forces lawyer?

92. He was an elite killing machine, though to you, he'd always be your best friend from high school. You knew that he would be involved in some kind of military career. It was obvious from the way he would absolutely destroy you and your other friends in military-based video games and how extremely seriously he took them. You weren't surprised when he enlisted and you were even less surprised when he told you he'd be involved in a very covert position doing sniper work. When he returned from duty, he was an extremely different person. He explained that he might act strangely when he entered a room, because he was still in a mind frame of killing and avoiding death from his time spent in some of the most hostile territories in the world. You wondered if he'd ever be able to get over such a psychologically altering life-or-death mentality. What are some of the weird things he does that are different from his time before the military?

93. She simply couldn't get enough of the rush. Even though she had a family to tend to, and even though she was no longer required to go on any more tours, she continued to re-enlist in an effort to keep the high going. She was brought in to diffuse bombs because of her steady hand and her fearless attitude. She continued to do it because she was completely addicted to the thrills of being on the front line and saving men and women from terrorism. She knew that she was supposed to be home, watching her daughter grow up and teaching her about life. But every time she spent a month or two back there, she became bored out of her mind, no matter how many extreme activities she did on the weekends. What was it that initially got her to be obsessed with danger?

94. All their lives, her parents had saved up to send her to the college of her choice, but she asked them to save the money, because she could go to school later on the GI Bill. They were completely floored by the news. Their daughter had joined the Navy and it was the last thing they expected to hear. They were so surprised because she seemed like such a normal girl. Then again, they did realize how much she'd enjoyed boats her entire life, and she was the happiest she'd ever been during the cruise they took a few summers back. She quickly calmed them down, which was one of the skills she'd developed over the past couple of years. What are some of the reasons she chose to join the Navy right out of high school?

95. He liked to make the joke that "he was building a bridge to victory," but his parents never laughed. They asked him why he couldn't build bridges and buildings in safer parts of the world. He'd always been particularly patriotic and while he was hardly the kind of guy to go to war, his skills with metal and electronics were direly needed in the war effort. He felt a certain pride that his creations - the bridges that he constructed would be ridden by the best fighting force the world has ever known. He spent his down time playing cards and avoiding the expensive purchasing habits of his peers, so that he could save up to start his own construction company upon his return. He hadn't been in too much direct danger during his time overseas and returned to a relatively normal life, living just a few blocks away from his overjoyed parents. What are some of the most difficult tasks he endured working for the military?

96. Through the use of simulations, he'd been training for this for nearly a decade. But just because he had worked as a nuclear technician and knew exactly how to fire a nuclear weapon, didn't mean that he was prepared for the order to do it. His sub had received word that a full on nuclear attack had been launched on the mainland and that retaliation was both authorized and necessary. As they moved into position, his hands moved as they had dozens of times before during computerized drills. Unlike then, however, he had a huge number of emotions coursing through his brain. He wondered if he'd be able to push the button to condemn potentially millions to death with the push of a button. He waited until the last possible second, making sure that this wasn't some kind of mistake. He fired the weapon. What will the aftermath of this nuclear scenario be for him and his ship and what will his thoughts be when he looks back on it years later?

97. It didn't matter what religious background they had, she was willing to accept them and listen to their crises of faith as they fought the war. She was part of a new breed of chaplains, armed with knowledge of many different faiths and able to provide spiritual comfort to anyone who needed it. She'd only gotten involved with the military in the last few years and had previously bounced back and forth between religious and charitable causes. She saw a documentary on post traumatic stress disorder from the military and realized a new calling: to help bring back men and women from the war, spiritually in tact. She was personally able to help over a thousand soldiers to cope with

stress and to trust in God. She also felt as though she got closer to God in the process. Detail at least two conversations she took part in with servicemen and women.

98. She had joined the military in an effort to reach her full potential. She'd never been adept at school and she wasn't the prettiest girl or the best athlete. She knew she wanted to make a difference in the world and thought that being on the front lines of the war would make her find out who she was. However, after being sexually assaulted by male peers on several different occasions, she figured out that her lot in life was not to be a quiet statistic. She filmed one of the assaults for evidence and took it to both her commanding officer and his boss. She wrote a piece for the New York Times and from within the military, she became a voice of female empowerment. Her friends asked her why she didn't leave the service that had let her and many other women down. She said they would have to drag her out kicking and screaming to prove that she was a quitter. How has her life changed since that fateful day when she decided to fight back?

99. He had spent over two decades in the military and he had become extremely close to fulfilling his lifelong dream, to become a four-star general. He had held his position of lieutenant general for around five years and he proudly served under the most decorated soldier in a generation. It was assumed that when the general retired, he would be moved into the position, but he was surprised to find himself passed over. After being passed over several additional times, he asked what more he could do to make himself general material. Without a clear answer from his few superior officers, he began to search for the answers within himself. During a vacation, he took a three-day course of complete silence to find out if what was holding him back was internal instead of external. The answer came to him on the third day and it completely shocked him. What was the answer that he determined about the future direction of his career?

100. Throughout her childhood, her father had raised her to become an expert in combat of every kind. A heart irregularity kept him from enlisting, dashing his dreams but allowing him to graft them onto his child. She spent at least an hour a day learning about the various weapons of the world and three hours training in martial arts, boxing and general physical fitness. By the time she reached high school, she was miles ahead of her classmates and won several awards as an athlete. But those accolades meant little to her, since she knew that she was destined to be camouflaged. There had never been a father as proud as hers was when she enlisted. He was hardly surprised when she came back one of the most decorated female soldiers of all time. She knew that her dreams had been heavily influenced, but she was happy to achieve them. What was her childhood like, training so hard for a predetermined goal?

Spies and Secret Agents

Some of the most entertaining characters to write about are those who aren't exactly who they say they are. While classic characters like James Bond paved the way for the next several decades of secret agents, newer television shows like "Chuck," "Burn Notice" and "Leverage" have brought the wonders of updated technology into the espionage world. If you plan on creating the next amazing superspy, make sure to play around with unique back stories and strange and unusual talents.

101. He had a way with the ladies like no agent before him, mostly because he was gay. Women in the field tended to open up to him much more than the chauvinistic womanizers who were usually working for the agency. He was extremely proficient at hand-to-hand combat and he possessed an especially mean streak reserved for anyone who called him something derogatory. What are some of this spy's vices and what was his path to the top of the agency like?

102. His parents, Mr. and Mrs. Bond, didn't think much of it when they named him James, but it was attached to him like glue for the rest of his life. This was especially true when he actually decided to become a spy. He was mocked throughout his training which pushed him to become one of the strongest agents available. He even used his name at times to catch bad guys, making them laugh before taking them down easily. Would he ever consider changing his name and what are some of his best spy skills?

103. Her European looks and her ability to match countless dialects and regional accents made her an important asset in the agency. In her real life though, she thought of herself as a true country girl who was raised on the farm.

Having daily chores and multiple brothers made her tough, but it was her mother who fueled her love for accents and other cultures. How did she become a secret agent and how often is she able to get home to the farm?

104. She had grown emotionally cold during her years in the field and she hardly seemed to know the difference between right and wrong anymore. She simply followed orders and carried them out whether it involved burning down a village or safely transporting a diplomat across state lines. Deep down, there was a part of her that hoped she was still fighting the good fight. Unfortunately, that part was growing quieter and quieter with every mission. How has she changed over time and what would have to happen to right her moral center?

105. After witnessing a horrible crime while overseas, he was taken into protection by a spy organization. It was obvious that he wouldn't be going anywhere for a while and after some convincing on his part, he began to train with the spies. It turned out that he was a quick study and he often surpassed the skill levels of many of the other spies. Within six months, he went from protective custody to working on his own case. How successful will this accidental spy be in his new agency?

106. One day, he received a strange phone call that vaguely threatened his wife and children. After the caller proved himself with some drastic shows of power, the man was on a plane the next day with specific instructions to obtain information from his employer's headquarters. There was nothing he cared about more than his family and he was willing to do whatever it took, including getting his assistant to figure out who was after him and how to stop this person. Will he be able to stop this threatening situation and save his family in time?

107. She a powerful agent who was known as ruthless and cunning and she was typically hired to do the dirtiest work that the agency had to offer. Everything changed when she found out that she was pregnant in the middle of an incredibly delicate assassination situation. She was determined that it would be her last job and she fled the agency she'd worked at for over a decade. She didn't want to be a mother but she took it as a sign that she had the ability to be something other than a killing machine. What happens to her in her quest to escape?

108. She had risen up the ranks of the CIA for nearly two decades after being inserted into a high school military academy by a rival country as a sleeper cell. When the time was right, she was to poison the very government that she worked for. When the time came, however, to attack the United States where it would hurt, she had fallen in love with a man she'd never be able to see again if she was locked up for treason. She began to form a plan in which she, the man and the United States would all go unharmed while her origin country would be left in the cold. What did she do and what happens when agents from her birth country catch up to her?

109. He was never meant to be a field operative and he was much more comfortable behind a computer than he'd ever been behind a gun. When everyone in his unit was killed, however, he was forced to access whatever training he had to safely return home. Hacking into ATMs and gaining security clearances were no problem for him, but he knew that at some point he'd be faced with his weak point, hand-to-hand combat. He elected to use his brain rather than his fists to exit the situation. What does he do to avoid fighting as he escapes from a sticky situation?

110. She was known in the agency simply as "The Cat" and there were countless stories of her saving the country, hostages and preventing terrorism all over the world. She was older now, but she became more refined and deadly with age. The only issue with her was that in the last two months she had completely gone off the grid and there were worries that she'd gone rogue. It was up to you and your team to find her before she could tarnish the reputation she'd built up during her storied career. That is, if she was still alive. What happens when you meet "The Cat" and how does she compare to the stories you've heard?

Drug Dealers

Television, especially after-school specials, tend to portray drug dealers as evil peddlers of poison who are more likely to give their products to young children than they are to smile or say something kind. Now, while I'm in no way supporting drug dealers, to portray them as such malevolent souls would lead to very one-dimensional characters. Movies like *Pineapple Express* have shown us that some drug dealers are just idiots while shows like "Breaking Bad" have given us the conflicted, backed into a corner dealer character. Keep away from the clichés and give these characters a bit of panache with their stash.

111. When he got into the business, his friends always told him never to sample too much of his own supply. Before they even finished the warning, he was too high on marijuana to even remember the advice. He may have been a bit of an idiot but he wasn't mean-spirited. He frequently gave money to the homeless and even volunteered at a shelter once. He kept things simple and wasn't in the business for the money. He wanted to make enough money to sustain his habit, pay his bills and allow him to get some decent Christmas presents for his family. How does he feel morally about selling drugs?

112. It didn't start out with kids, he kept telling himself. He never wanted to be that guy who messed with kids' education, but before he knew it, he was providing product to high school students. It all started when his cousin started begging him to be a part of the business. He didn't want to say no to family, since family had always been important to him. He tried to make it clear though, that he shouldn't spread it around to his friends and especially not anybody younger. His cousin didn't listen, but found a way to nearly triple the money being pulled in within a few months. When he made the final payment on his mother's house, he was excited to reach a lifelong goal but hated the way in which it was achieved. Will he stop peddling his product to kids or will the lure of the added money be too great for him?

113. It wasn't hard for her to get her night's work complete within an hour or so. After all, she was a very attractive girl and people usually came up to her in the booming club whether or not they knew she had drugs. Her goal was to unload enough ecstasy and other products to get her through the next month and she had little to no problem doing that on a good night. She had become an expert at doing the exchange of money and pills discretely and she had a reputation as a bit of a ghost, sneaking in and out of the club so quickly, you'd swear she wasn't there. She rarely took part in the drugs herself as it wasn't good for her bottom line. Besides, while others had a good time letting go of their inhibitions, she much more enjoyed being in control while counting her earnings. How did she get into this business in the first place?

114. People had a lot of pain and she wanted to be the one to fix it. She'd grown up in a household of drugs and when her family was having trouble, she naturally gravitated toward selling drugs as a way to get out of it. She made a few deals with some local corrupt doctors to procure a seemingly endless supply of pain pills like OxyContin. She found her appropriate demographic as young adults who felt the world was too much for them. They would take the pills straight up or crush them and snort the powder. The pills were extremely addictive and she tried and failed to avoid addiction herself. She felt like a zombie walking around and selling the drugs at a heck of a profit. Even when she'd more than dealt with her family's financial worries, she kept the routine up because she felt too zoned out to do much of anything else. What will be the end result of her attempts to dull her pain and the pain of others?

115. Crime had been a part of his life since he was a baby, which was why his parents moved the family to the states when he was a teenager. He didn't have much problem adopting the language but he hated being labeled as one of the poor kids. He shoplifted multiple times until he was caught and thrown in juvenile hall. That's when he learned that drug dealing could be a much more lucrative trade. He began dealing whatever drugs he could find, but made sure to do it all from his car, so that the police couldn't track him to one location. His parents were both unemployed, so most of the money he made went to them. They knew what their son was doing, but they were proud that he was willing to risk his life to take care of them. Has he ever had any close calls with the law or with unruly customers?

116. When people asked him if he was a "drug dealer," he laughed. After all, most people viewed drug dealers as those having to deal with crazy addicts and run from the cops every night. He was on the top of the food chain. He was the one who brought product direct from the "factory" and sold it to regional dealers at a 10 to 1 profit. He only dealt with people he knew well and he kept his spending discrete so as not to raise a lot of attention. He didn't really think too much about where the drugs were going, he mostly thought about his own life and his own problems. Anyone who got addicted to the stuff he was pushing in their general direction had to deal with their issues on their own. How did he become so high up in the area's drug trade?

117. She was recruited to be a holder at the age of 11, because nobody would suspect a tiny, little girl to be holding onto drugs and guns. Then again, she was holding these things for kids only a few years older than her. As

she got older and she began to blossom into a devilishly cunning young woman, her friends realized that she could use her skills to get into places most of them couldn't. She began making deals with people running drugs in clubs throughout the city. She enjoyed getting the chance to dress up all nice and pretend to be 21. She even flirted her way out of a cop searching her boss' car on the way to a deal. Why did she decide to continue in this line of work throughout her teens instead of branching out and doing her own thing?

118. When her husband was locked away for a long time, she had no idea what she was going to do to keep her family going. She hadn't had a job for years, because her husband's drug dealing had kept them secure as long as she'd been a mother. She realized though, that she still had all of her husband's contacts and that it wouldn't be hard for her to do what he had done all these years, after all, she'd watched and even accompanied him throughout all his activities. She decided to use her children to move the product, making it look like they were delivering birthday presents to family friends and loved ones. She felt a pang of sorrow, recruiting her kids into such a dirty business, but she knew that if she was going to put them through college, all of them were going to need to work a little harder. What are some of the ways in which she works differently than her husband did?

119. He went to college to learn how to run his own business, though he never expected he'd be running that business while he was still attending. He'd never really been into drugs himself, but he quickly noticed that the people moving the stuff around campus were doing it in an extremely inefficient way. He worked his way into the group and eventually took over as he was obviously one of the smartest of the bunch. He quickly grew their organization and eventually they were selling nearly twice as much to the sororities and fraternities on campus. He even made some connections with campus police to keep them safer from authorities. By the time he left school, he had become an expert in the area. How would his college life have been different if he hadn't gotten into the drug trade?

120. Most people knew her as the kind, little old lady who lived at the end of the block. Her closest friends knew her as their marijuana supplier. The woman, in her 70s, had started growing the drug because it helped her with some of her ailments such as back pain and depression. Now that her husband had passed away, she didn't have much to do aside from tending to her marijuana garden. When friends inquired about it, she shared pot brownies and cookies with them to heal their own pain. Word eventually got out and the woman's crop was taken from her. She decided to fight back in court and try to get special dispensation for those who needed medical marijuana. How successful will she be in her efforts be become a dealer once again?

Criminals

While the people who occupy our nation's prisons may seem almost alien to us in their actions, they frequently aren't so different from you and me. Whether it be in a state of desperation or of extreme emotions, they took part in an action that will dog them for the rest of their lives. Even if the crime is small in proportion to something like second-degree murder, they may have difficulty getting a job after serving a prison sentence. Those who have been caught committing a crime will typically pay for it and revealing that payment is especially interesting when portrayed in a story.

121. After failing to get a job out of high school, on his eighteenth birthday, he decided to take up a life of crime. Three days later, after a robbery attempt gone horribly awry, he ended up in jail for the next 20 years of his life. He'd barely had a chance to figure out who he was and now, due to his poor choice, he was stuck. A few years into his sentence he began taking college courses offered to inmates through the prison system and he learned a lot about right and wrong and the kind of person he could be if he put his mind to it. What will life be like for him once he gets out of prison?

122. This master thief had only been caught a few times doing what he did best: stealing million dollar jewelry. The only issue for the local police force was that the thing he did second best was smuggling himself out of prison. He was notorious for his escapes and there had even been a television movie created about his exploits. As he grew older and considered settling down, he wondered if he would really be able to start his life over or if he'd always be a petty crook. How will this lifelong criminal learn to live with a life beyond thievery?

123. One of the words frequently used on her in her youth was "innocent," because she looked like she was straight out of a 1950s perfect suburban sitcom. As she got into her twenties, her innocent looks nowhere near fit

her actions when she was charged with several brutal murders of her friends. She and an accomplice had done an expert job covering their tracks and two juries had been unable to convict her. Eventually, a third jury came to the correct judgment and forced her behind bars for the rest of her life. How could this childlike veneer be hiding an angry murderer underneath and why did she do what she did?

124. She loved being a woman because it typically predisposed people to think that she was clueless when it came to computers. In reality, she was a world-renowned hacker who would and could steal anything from government secrets to bank account access codes. By dressing and acting like a floozy, she had been able to get out of multiple sticky situations. One or two slip ups though, had her in jail for a very long time. She felt a bit guilty for putting her family through her incarceration and she planned on making it worth their while. What will she do to improve her family's lot and will she consider using her technological expertise to get herself out of prison?

125. This small town young adult had always hated when people acted differently from the norm. In school, he was one of the most popular kids because he had perfect looks and an athletic build, and he was brutally mean to those who were of a different race or sexual orientation. He and a few friends got drunk one night and brutally attacked a gay teen who was walking home from work. The teen survived to tell the tale and the small town boy was put away for the next 25 years. He was reviled in the media for continuing to stick by his bigoted viewpoint and in several Internet polls, he was voted the most hated man in America. What would his reaction be upon seeing those polls and what in his upbringing taught him that such acts were the right thing to do?

126. He was supposed to be nothing but a getaway driver. He would take a small cut of the money and then he would use it to pay off some looming gambling debts that were causing him and his family a lot of grief. When his associates killed two security guards at the bank, however, he was made an accessory to murder and he went to jail for over a decade. When he was there he realized how good he'd had it before and a sense of peace washed over him. He became something of a wise man in the jail and even the prison guards began looking to him for advice. What was it specifically about prison that made him so grateful for life on the outside?

127. She hadn't felt in much control whatsoever throughout her entire life. She wasn't traditionally attractive and her great desire to be in a relationship made her take up with some very domineering men. She was extremely lonely and she just wanted to be held some nights. She became a high school English teacher and one of her students became the person she wanted to be with more than anything. She was the boss of the relationship, which she'd never experienced due to the men she usually saw. After she was caught having sexual relations with a minor, she would never be able to teach again and she was sent to prison. Did she feel her relationship was worth it and how will she cope with being labeled a sexual predator?

128. Early in her career as a cop, she was known through the force as one of the toughest, most righteous individuals, regardless of her gender. As the years went on, she grew greedy with power and began manipulating her position unlawfully to get what she wanted. After years of running several money related schemes, she was caught and was sent to jail in a prison populated by people she'd once put away. Life was harder for her there than it ever had been in her early days on the force. What ultimately caused her to cross over to corruption and what is a typical day like for her in her new surroundings?

129. Outside of prison he was one of the most feared mob bosses in existence. In prison, he was even scarier as he'd been put away for life and he had deep connections on the outside. Nobody dared mess with him, prison guards included, for fear that his "friends" would kill family members, even children, of those who treated him badly. Since he was already in prison, there wasn't much investigators could do and they had no idea how he got his messages to the outside so quickly. Due to his larger than life presence, how is he usually treated during a standard day in the prison?

130. During a routine investigation, she had been found guilty of many counts of animal cruelty. She'd run a dog training and breeding facility that had been a public nuisance for years as she'd essentially locked the dogs in a room in the dark, fed them poorly and had neglected to clean up their feces. She'd even killed several of the dogs she'd bred when they wouldn't sell and it was only speculated what she did with their bodies. During her trial she was lambasted by animal rights organizations and local townspeople. When she entered prison, she was treated like scum

by animal loving inmates. What caused her to treat animals so badly and why did she take up the business in the first place?

CHAPTER 3: CHARACTERS BY OCCUPATION

Bosses

Many stories, especially those that spend time in an office or a police station are prone to showing overbearing and angry bosses. The recent movie *Horrible Bosses* portrayed these division heads as sharks, jerks and even nymphomaniacs. While many bosses are not well-versed in the ways of effectively running a team of employees, not all of them are mean and a few of them are even revered by their employees. In addition, unless a boss has the letters CEO on the front door of the office, he or she has one or multiple bosses to report to. While it may not be easy being an employee, it can be even more stressful to have both employees and bosses to deal with.

131. He was one of the most laid back people you've ever met and as a result, your office never got anything productive done. He'd come around to everybody's desk and chat with his employees for what seemed like hours. Any goals he set he'd change if anybody made even the most minor complaint. You loved not getting yelled at, but in a way, you missed the authority. Why is he so laid back and how will he keep his job if he fails to reach all of his quotas?

132. Everyone at the office knew that he was corrupt, but they were too afraid to do anything about it. People talked about him as if he had connections to the mafia, and with the tough-guy clothes he sported, almost everyone was willing to believe it. He openly talked about stories of his old days on the streets of Brooklyn. You weren't sure if they were true but they were intimidating. Is he actually corrupt or is he simply blowing smoke to appear intimidating?

133. There were those at the office who believed she only earned the position because of who her father was, but when she settled in, it turned out she was effective enough to write a book on the subject of management. While her dad was known as a ball-buster who ordered everybody around, she trusted people and seemed like more of a mentor than an employer. What in her life caused her to be such a respectful boss?

134. You two were hired at the same time, but here you were still languishing at the same position while she had become your boss after several successive promotions. It didn't seem like she was that much more special than you. As far as you were concerned, you were equals. Then again, she did have one of the best attitudes you'd ever seen. Will she continue to move up the business ladder?

135. He's only a year or two away from the Baseball Hall of Fame and now he is going to be your manager. Your previous coaches had always said you weren't living up to your true potential, but your new boss wouldn't say anything of the sort. He watched you swing a few times, motioned you over and had you watch him a few times. He didn't say anything; he just hoped you'd pick it up. You weren't completely surprised to end up with the best year of your career. How well does this new coach do for your team as a whole?

136. It was impossible not to smell your boss coming from a mile away as he reeked of alcohol. He would rarely attend meetings, even the ones he called and he could usually be found sitting in his office wearing a pair of sunglasses. He seemed nice enough when you chatted, but you never knew if you were talking to the real him. When did he become such a drinker and will he ever be able to overcome it?

137. She fancied herself extremely creative and full of new, strong ideas. One of the reasons she rose to the top was because she was always coming up with new plans that management seemed to love. When she finally became your boss, however, she drove you crazy with her flip-flopping and always changing one more detail in a project to make it perfect. She even rearranged your desk once without asking for your permission. How will she do as your boss and is she creative or simply scatterbrained and why?

138. She was an extremely diligent employee and when she was promoted to manager, nobody blinked an eye because she had certainly paid her dues. She always shows up early and stays late. She is perpetually punctual and kind. Her only issue is that she has no idea how to manage and frequently gets frustrated and confused about what to do with her new responsibilities. How will she cope with these changes to her job description?

139. As you moved up the ranks in the White House, you never expected you would move as high up as one of the personal assistants to the President himself. He is extremely intelligent and always busy trying to solve all the

conflicts in the world. He knows everyone on the staff by name and as the man who picks out his wardrobe and takes his food orders, you are privy to a very inside look into who he is. What was one situation in which you saw the true him come to the surface?

140. Motivated, energetic and powerful are words you'd use to describe her personality, but absolutely nobody in the office can figure out exactly what she does. You all know that she has an office and that she never seems to be in it. She rarely responds to e-mails, her assistant tends to do that for her. Some days she doesn't show up at all and her assistant says she was away "on business." What are a few things, if there are any, which she actually does as your boss?

Servers, Baristas and Bartenders

Yes, the people who get you food, coffee and beer are people, too, and they frequently lead interesting lives with their own families and problems. There have been some wonderful tales that focus on the existences of these unique people that help us by laughing or listening. While I haven't personally spent time as a server or a bartender, my theatre life allowed me to see many different service employees during their off-hours and I've heard enough stories to write hundreds of characters. My time as a barista at a major coffee chain taught me a lot about life, but also about the types of people who enter the service industry. Let's push past our stereotypes of service people and try to create well-rounded characters with thoughts, hopes and dreams.

141. Always serving your coffee with a smile, you wonder how somebody could be so incredibly perky at such an early hour. When you comment that he must knock a few back before the shift starts, he says that he doesn't drink coffee and he's naturally this way. He frequently cracks jokes and keeps the mood very lively in the room. Has he always been such a naturally early riser and what does he do outside of work?

142. When you step into church, you are surprised to see your favorite bartender sitting at the pew next to you. He is usually your go-to guy when you need someone to tell a lewd and crude story to and now you feel embarrassed. You start to apologize and he waves you off. He says he is happy to do his job. How did a man of God end up tending bar and why?

143. No matter what time of day you come in, it seems like she is always working at the diner. When you ask her about her story, you are surprised to find out that she is part-owner of the place. She works on the floor nearly all day long because she can barely afford to pay employees. She got into the business because she loves people, and gets to be around many more people than she did with her last job as a pencil pusher. Will her business succeed? Why or why not?

144. She looks like the epitome of the indie coffee shop: covered from head to toe in tattoos, multiple piercings and when she works, the radio is always tuned to the local college's station. You ask her about a Harvard diploma you see on the wall next to a painting and it turns out it is hers. She had previously been on the track of becoming a biology professor but decided to go the opposite direction of the prim and proper world of academia. Is she happier now that she's able to express herself and why?

145. He isn't just a server, he is hell-bent on being the best server in town. Even though awards aren't important to him, he had won the local newspaper's "best server" trophy three years running proving his superiority when it comes to caring about the customers. He had been a strung out drug addict only a decade earlier when someone told him that his life's reward will be equal to his service. He took that advice literally. What are some of the things he does to make his service superior?

146. They love him when he bartends at one of the most popular night clubs in the Boys Town neighborhood in Chicago, but they truly adore him when he does his drag act on Sunday nights. Sure, he remembers all the customers and practically has their drinks ready before they get to the bar, but they go completely mad over his outfits, his songs and his comedy. He's says that if he makes enough money from drag, he would even consider giving up tending the bar. What are some of the satisfactions he gets from serving people at a bar and how do those differ from what he gets out of his performances?

147. While some people have their swimsuit calendars and others have their Internet obsessions, you are in love with your barista. The way she smiles at you and hands your drink over the counter, lingering just long enough to rope you in before moving onto the next customer's concoction. Whenever you have trouble getting out of bed for work, you think of how pure her skin looks and the dimples on her face when she grins. What does she do outside of slinging coffee and does she secretly harbor a crush for you as well?

148. When you put together the schedule for your bartending staff, you always try to give everybody a fair amount of high-money weekend shifts. You often cringe when you have to put down your niece's name. As a favor to your brother, you gave a job to the angriest, most energy-sucking creature you'd ever encountered and despite her extremely good looks, she seems to have only lost you business in the three months she's worked for you. What happens when you confront her over her bad attitude?

149. When he graduated from one of the best universities in the country, his parents expected him to go far in this world. After he defied their expectations by trying his hand at acting, he returned to his birthplace and became a full-time server at a popular restaurant. He continues to do shows every once in a while, but slowly but surely, serving took over his entire life and now he works every weekend, giving him no availability for acting. Will he continue to be a server for the rest of his life and why?

150. On the surface, it seems like she is a simple server of frozen yogurt at the local soft-serve station. In actuality, it is a cover, because she is a spy for a government agency, looking after an important asset in the area. She hates when people look at her like she didn't have high aspirations in life, like she hadn't learned to nail a target from hundreds of yards away with a powerful sniper rifle. She sometimes wishes she could use that skill on unruly customers. How does she cope with the monotony and is her mission successful?

Teachers

When it comes to most stories, teachers tend to fall into one of two categories. In one corner, we have the life-changing educator who truly reaches his or her students on a deep level. In the other, there's the nasty instructor who seems to be constantly out to squash the students' excitement. Of course, from our own experiences in school, we know there are many shades of grey and there are as many different kinds of teachers as there are students. Let's embrace these workhorses of the educational system by portraying teachers realistically and genuinely.

151. At first glance, if you saw this gangly, pale man with glasses, you might be able to figure out his profession in three guesses or less: high school math teacher. He wasn't the kind of teacher who wanted to prepare his students for a standardized test, nor was he a Robin Williams-esque stand on the desk to get the students pumped type. He teaches his students math, plain and simple, and he does it in a way they understand. A former volleyball player in his student days, he is tough, but never intimidating. He once pulled an all-nighter at school working on test papers during a hurricane that prevented him from returning home that night. What got this man into math and how did he become such a strong teacher?

152. Even though he likes to start class with a joke, he usually keeps things serious, because the lives of men, women and children are in his hands. He's been teaching EMT certification courses for over a decade and takes pride in his instruction. If he doesn't teach a subject correctly, how can he face his wife and son when he returns home? Even though he is a strong-willed man, he always cries upon receiving a message from a former student who saved a patient's life. What line of work will he take up if he ever loses his teaching job and why?

153. As she sent her oldest child away to school for the day, she put on her outfit for work. It consisted of a sports bra, a tight-fitting tank top and a pair of yoga pants that hugged her svelte frame. She is the primary instructor of the "workout challenge" class at the local gym and she works hard to put her students through the ringer every week. While her friends marvel at her physique after having had two kids, they don't realize how much work she has to do to maintain an exercise teacher's body. She is always quick with a joke to lighten the mood and she connects to her students, always available for long chats after class. What made her decide to embark on this sweat-soaked teaching journey?

154. As you paw through your old elementary school yearbook, you wonder about what happened to your fourth grade teacher. The one who taught you the value of proper planning. By the virtue of being so painstakingly

organized herself, she made you understand how you could be organized. You remember her being a bucket of laughs as well as her long, wavy red hair. She got married a few years after you had her and you marveled at her ability to keep a classroom organized while planning a wedding. She must have worked extremely hard and as a result she remained impressed on your mind. What ended up happening with her and how has she impacted the lives of other students?

155. You decide to buy the next round of beers as your friend gives you another piece of advice about dating. Since you've always been a bit timid in that area, you have been happy to latch onto this wise soul and his deep understanding of the opposite sex. He's even written a book on the subject and is well-known around the area as a mentor to men in love. You know him as a regular guy who loves playing video games and performing comedy at a local club. He is a wizard when it comes to analyzing relationships, and you hope that some day he will find a love that measures up to his standards. Why has he made romantic relationships such a focus of his life?

156. With five minutes left to go in class, he stared at the second hand moving slowly around the clock. He gave the students 20 minutes of silent reading and told them that if anyone said a word he would dock them a letter grade. He got into teaching because he thought it'd be easy and for the summer vacations, but he'd gotten more than he'd bargained for. After four years on the job, he resolved to spend as little time in the building as possible and was always ready to dash for the door. How does he typically interact with his students and will he continue to be a teacher for the rest of his working life?

157. You've heard of fathers who learned a lot from having a daughter, but this was ridiculous. Despite the fact that she had yet to reach puberty, your daughter was your best kept secret as your life advisor. This was due to a wisdom she possessed that was well beyond her years. How many little girls read self-help books and meditate? Despite a love of pigtails and frilly dresses, she has more to offer than most expensive therapists and personal coaches. You wonder where she got such a propensity for helping people through life's toughest times, because it certainly wasn't from you or her late mother. What are some pieces of advice she's given and what kind of person will she grow up to be?

158. She is built like a truck and has a haircut like someone who might drive one. She's also a health teacher required to show you the "Miracle of Life" video and teach you about sexually transmitted diseases. Anyone teaching fifth graders about this subject might be a bit awkward, but she wanted to do a fantastic job and was over thorough about every aspect. She lives alone and plays on several recreational softball and soccer teams. How would she react if a student asked her an intentionally inappropriate question?

159. In his youth, he was filled with anger and hate, but a trip to Tibet completely changed his life. He saw the peacefulness of the Buddhist monks and embarked on an existence of meditation and love. Upon returning home, he chose to teach this peaceful lifestyle to those who had a difficult upbringing like his own. How is he able to defeat his inner-negativity and what is his current day-to-day life like?

160. Her life goal is to change how other women think about money. She realized in her late twenties that she wanted to understand more about finances and stop depending on male bosses and financial planners. As she learned more and more, she became a voice of reason and advice to women she knew, which turned into a class. The class turned into a book and before long she was appearing on national talk shows promoting her ideas. While she is happy to be helping so many, it is difficult for her social life and she has a tough time keeping up with the friends who helped to catapult her to fame. Why did she choose to focus on teaching about money and what future does it hold for her?

Landlords

Not all of us have been fortunate enough to deal with such colorful characters. Landlords have been much maligned in stories as being greedy, unlawful and angry with few positive qualities. I have not personally had too many landlord troubles, but I have heard many tales from friends about "the landlord from hell" which makes for a vivid character in a story. To keep away from clichés, we will intersperse some landlords who are simply looking to provide tenants with a positive experience, for better or worse.

161. When he came by your apartment on your move in day, you thought it was a kind gesture. When he repeated that gesture for the next 13 days, you started to wonder what you'd gotten yourself into. He is only about a decade older than you, so it isn't completely strange for you to be hanging out, only you weren't friends in the first place. He eats your food, plays your video games and constantly reminds you that he has a key to your house. You wonder if he was violating some apartment ethics code or if he was just friendly and weird. What are some of the stranger things he has done in your apartment?

162. This man is so cheap, you wonder how he ever ended up owning a condo. When you rented from him, he said that he had a repairman available 24 hours a day, but you never expected it to be him. He had absolutely no technical skills to speak of. When he came to fix a noise in the refrigerator, he ended up rendering it completely useless, spoiling all your food. He wears thrift-shop clothes that are clearly too big for him and he asks for the rent a few days early each month if possible. How did this cheapskate come to be a landlord and what other corners has he cut?

163. When you had the cops called on you for a noise violation, she quickly pointed out that she had the right to do so in your lease agreement. The only problem, there was no noise coming from you apartment because you had been sound asleep. She seemed a little off when you first rented from her, but the cops were called five nights in a row and you started to get the hint that she was completely off her rocker. She even once asked for payment in meat instead of a check. How did this woman become so off and will she continue to interfere with your life?

164. While her name isn't Mrs. Robinson, she certainly acts like it is. She frequently calls you over to her apartment to help her with chores and to reach things from low places. It took you a few times to realize that she isn't just looking for help with odd jobs. She even asked if you would stay with her one week when your apartment was being fumigated. Eventually, her requests became more and more forward until you falsely told her you were in a relationship. This didn't stop her in the slightest and she began sending you lewd pictures of herself. Will she ever be successful at coaxing you into her life or will you have to do something drastic to call it quits?

165. A couple of months after you signed your lease, you finally grasped that your landlord speaks exactly no English whatsoever. When you moved in, you must have dealt with the landlord's son or brother from out of town because communication with him was literally impossible. He would knock on your door around midnight on the last day of the month asking for the rent. You've had absolutely no luck getting him to come over and fix things, he just hangs up on you. How did this man become a landlord and will he get in any trouble for being a poor one?

166. After experiencing a natural disaster, you expected at least a little human sympathy from your landlord. Instead, he sent you a letter announcing that he'll be raising your rent over 20 percent. He threatens to kick you and the rest of your housemates out unless you pay the raised rates. You don't know what to do as you certainly can't afford the price hike. You wonder to yourself what kind of jerk would take advantage of people like that as you make your way to your local alderman's office. Why did this landlord decide to take advantage of his tenants and what will be the result of his money grab?

167. Her parents were trying to teach her self-reliance by handing over the deed of the building to her. The only problem was that this made an 18-year-old girl your landlord and she wants absolutely nothing to do with it. When her and her boyfriend come over to assess issues, you feel like you are hiring an irresponsible babysitter, not trying to get your apartment fixed. You even caught them making out on your couch once when they were supposed to be fixing the kitchen tiles. You knew that they said that girls tended to mature faster than boys, but she seemed to be the exception to the rule. Will she learn self-reliance or just take advantage of the freedom she was given?

168. When you open the door to your apartment, you expect it to be empty. It isn't. It is completely full of people and it's all because your landlord is having an every floor of the building party. She acts surprised that she never told you and hands you a drink, made up of materials from your own liquor cabinet. Your landlord seemed pretty laid back and fun when you met her, but you aren't sure if you are laid back enough to let this party stand. Before you can say a word she is already running off in the other direction toward a table of Jell-O shots. Does she do these sorts of things with all her tenants and why would she think your apartment was fair game?

169. He is large and in charge and you are deathly afraid of pointing out any issues in the apartment. The first time you reported a problem, no water pressure in your shower head, he literally cranked the sockets with his hands until the pressure worked. He left his hand imprints there on the metal as a reminder only to call him for emergencies. He looked like a bouncer at a top-tier night club, not the guy you give your rent money to. You even heard a disturbing story about how he treated the last tenant who was late on the rent. How did this hulking creature become a landlord and what does he do for fun?

170. She is a little, old lady who owns the entire block. She is content spending her time inside, offering cookies to those who come by and flipping through photo books of her grandchildren. She has employees to handle all of the technical work in the houses, but appreciates when people come by to chat with her when dropping off their rent checks. They are amazed to see how much she's done in her time on this planet as if it were several lifetimes back to back. She has been all around the world and has stories to tell about various historic events that you can only read about nowadays. What are some of the things she's done, how did she become a landlord and what are some of her regrets in life?

Hosts, Correspondents and Reporters

We see them on television, hosting our favorite reality shows, reporting on the news going on in our areas and analyzing what certain life events mean to our way of being. These television, radio and online personalities are there to facilitate our understanding of what goes on in our favorite entertainment and news programs. These hosts, correspondents and reporters are an interesting breed of celebrity as they become notable from telling us "what is what" as opposed to making some major breakthrough on their own. The stereotypical way to portray them is nice on camera but a jerk behind the scenes. Let's play around with a few more shades of grey than that stereotype.

171. He is the host of one of the first and most popular reality shows set in remote locations throughout the world. Despite the condition of the contestants, he is always impeccably dressed and he seems to get tanner and more handsome each year. Though you can't tell on screen, he only works a grand total of 50 days a year and is left to his own devices otherwise. He feels lucky that the work keeps him well compensated, but he wonders if all he is meant for is hosting a glorified, tropical game show. If and when the show is cancelled, what will this bronzed host do with his life and why?

172. No matter where there is conflict in the world, he wants to be on the front lines to cover it. He marvels when he looks back at a reel of his best-of footage and sees locales such as Iraq, Bosnia, Afghanistan, Somalia and more. He's been closer to gunfire than most police officers and he's feared for his life on multiple occasions. It is exhilarating to him and if you asked if he'd rather die while reporting or safe at home in his bed, he'd laugh at you and say, "Isn't it obvious?" What is his proudest accomplishment and why?

173. She is a correspondent for a completely tongue-in-cheek news organization. She's always been interested in politics and sarcasm and this position completely met those qualifications. Her friends have told her they've learned more about what is going on in the world from her and her program than they ever have from most legitimate cable news channels. If only they knew how much the people in the writer's room knew about the basics and not-so-basics of government. Her and her writers work hard to strike the right tone in their program and she feels blessed to be a part of it. What is one piece of news she particularly enjoyed spinning into comedy and what does she do during her free time?

174. Her talk show is an inspiration to women around the world and she's had the fortune of interviewing heads of state, celebrities and others who were remarkable in their own right. When she returns home at night, she is tired. It's a lot of pressure keeping up a positive image when she doesn't always feel that way. To her, the world is quite damaged and she isn't sure if her little show can do everything she wants to do to fix it. The negativity of the news and political scene can't help but contribute to this world view. What are some of the things she plans to do to continue her cause of a happier and healthier world?

175. He is a powerful reporter who is much beloved by the older generation. They believe that everything he reports on is true because he has what seems like an unshakable sense of integrity. This trait is not inherent, however, and to learn it he went through periods of addiction to gambling and alcohol. It wasn't until he received treatment at

a well-known facility that he determined to be the most reliable person on television. Through his efforts, he became the man he is today. What are some of the things he learned so he could improve upon his integrity and does he ever feel a burden by being so honest in a world rampant with dishonesty?

176. When he heard of the most dangerous animals in science class, he always asked to learn more. His student research led him to a degree in biology but he felt that it wasn't enough just to read about animals. He embarked on a quest to study these animals directly and through a series of coincidences, he would become the charismatic new host of a show about dangerous creatures. He loves having the opportunity to share these wild beasts with his audience and the kids at home who embrace his passion. He has sustained injuries on multiple occasions during filming but he figures it's just part of the job description. What was it that attracted him to animals so much in the first place and what does he like the most about hosting?

177. She felt like she wasn't getting her due. After all, she's attractive, well-read and has amazing ideas, yet here she is stuck as the junior reporter at a local news station only 10 miles away from where she grew up. In order to promote herself, she knows she will have to reach a younger audience. She takes to the Internet and begins to make videos about the stories around the world that don't get much coverage such as the tales of inspiring women from third-world countries. Her videos receive millions of hits and she turns them into offers at major news networks, though they might not give her as much time to continue the videos. What will the next step be in her career and why?

178. Her conservative views and strange accent made her a treasure trove of comedic material for liberal comedy news shows, but she doesn't care because she is doing what she loves. She only wants to make sure that those on the right side of the political equation know what is going on and she wants to accomplish this by stating things as simply as possible. When her friends told her it makes an intelligent woman like herself look like an idiot, she knew from her high television ratings and infamy from the other side that she had to be doing something right. What is the achievement she's the most proud of and from where to her beliefs originate?

179. He had been the host of a major game show for nearly three-quarters of his adult life and he had finally decided to retire. His money-based program had given him more than enough pension to live on wealthily for the rest of his time and he wondered what he was going to do with himself. He'd been a game show host for so long and didn't really know if he could do anything else. Everybody who passed him on the street spouted his hosting catch phrases back at him and his grandkids never tired of stories about the famous people he'd had on the show. The world seemed to see him as a host and nothing more. What will he do in his final decades and will he ever go back to hosting?

180. She knew that being a reporter in places of conflict was dangerous, but she never expected to be captured and ransomed by an evil dictator. Every few days she would tell a camera that she was healthy and treated well, and for the most part she was. She wished she could see her husband and young child just for a second. It had been three weeks and the two countries were at a stalemate for her release. She questioned if she had gone into the right field and if journalism was what she should be doing. Is anything that keeps her away from her son the right career choice? What is her day-to-day life as a prisoner like and how will her situation become resolved?

Emergency Workers

Emergency workers have always been in the background of medical shows like "ER" and "Grey's Anatomy," so it's refreshing when they're brought to the forefront in works like Martin Scorsese's *Bringing Out the Dead*. There are thousands of paramedics, firefighters and other first responders that are on call throughout the world trying to save people from certain death. There is heartache and pain for the people in this position, as well as joyous emotions from bringing someone back from the brink of death. Bring in a character from this category to add some morbid depth to your story.

181. He decided to become a firefighter after he saw the dedicated hard work of those who'd come to the rescue of the 9/11 attacks. He lived in a much smaller area than New York, but he knew he could make a difference if he was even half as brave as they were. The training was hard because he was overweight, but he trimmed down a bit from the work he put in. His ability to take in all knowledge about fires, buildings and health made up for his lack of

athleticism. He saved fire victims and his peers on several occasions with the information he'd absorbed. Is he living his dream of helping people and why or why not?

182. If there was an unknown chemical substance in the field, he was the person who could identify it quickly and simply. He was a first responder as part of a hazmat team and whether it was powder in an envelope or an unmarked barrel in a basement, he was one of the best in the county to deal with it. He could have become a professor, but he was always more interested in helping people directly. He kept so up to date on the news of chemicals and terrorism, his wife joked that he could barely carry a conversation without bringing terrorists into it in some way. What are some situations he's responded to and how have those situations affected his world view?

183. She had been an emergency medical technician for only a few months when she was called to one of the most gut-wrenching car accidents her city had ever faced. It felt like half the emergency workers in the city were there trying to save the lives of the people stuck within the massive pileup. She unintentionally took on a leadership role and stayed calm throughout the ordeal. She always said that growing up in a tough neighborhood taught her that keeping your cool meant keeping your life. How does she save people during the accident and what are some of her EMT experiences afterwards?

184. She worked hard to become the first female firefighter at her station and she knew that to keep her position she'd need to train twice as hard and be twice as good as most. Since she was smaller and stronger than half of her peers, she was able to get into tight spaces which had led to several saved lives over the few years she'd been there. She was single and actively dating and most men were turned on by the firefighter thing. She quickly dispensed of those men. Why was she so determined to be a firefighter and what will she look for in a partner?

185. He just wasn't sure if he could handle all of the lost causes anymore. Most of the time the people his team of paramedics would encounter simply needed a trip to the hospital to be bandaged up. It was those who had already passed away or those who were obviously too far gone that got to him. Maybe it's because he cared that he was so good at what he did. He hated giving up and on several occasions he felt like he had snatched people from the imminent grasp of death. Those who he hadn't saved gave him nightmares. Will he continue on in the job or will his demons get the best of him?

186. He was in charge of coordinating the departments in the case of a city wide emergency like a terrorist attack or a natural disaster. He was a small man with a powerful voice, and people gave him respect for his accomplishments. He'd been awarded several medals for working with the Armed Forces and when he left the service, he moved up the ranks of emergency management and was said to have saved the lives of thousands by acting quickly during the bombing of a large office building. He made sure every department was up to speed with frequent inspections and tests and kept his red notebook at the ready with all his extreme emergency plans. What would he have to do for something like a major earthquake and how did he become such a strong leader in his field?

187. She was one of the first on the scene when the epidemic began, setting up quarantine areas and working around the clock to determine the disease. She was the head epidemiologist for the region and she would have to work quickly as the symptoms were spreading. People were passing out left and right from the airborne disease and the radius of the illness was tough to determine. After losing a childhood friend to a tropical disease when on a college abroad trip, she knew that stopping diseases in their tracks was her calling. This disease was unlike anything she'd ever seen, but this was what she was born to do. Will she be able to stop the disease from spreading and how?

188. She came to people in one of the most difficult times of their lives and she did her best to get them the help they needed. As an employee of the Red Cross, she would assess damages from fires and accidents and determine how much financial support the organization could provide to these families and individuals. She had numbed a bit to the fear and pain of people who had lost everything and a several day per week bar hopping routine helped with that internal deadening. She frequently thought about what she would do if she lost her possessions and grew extremely depressed. How has she reacted to some of the situations she's seen and will she able to be snap out of her emotional funk?

189. He was a park ranger who had received special emergency certification to be the best ranger he could be. Due to the many hunting and boating accidents that occurred under his watch, he figured it was best to be prepared.

He had always been interested in nature from the time he was a young boy and knew that taking care of the forest would be involved in whatever he did. His training has come in handy as he even was able to treat a woman with injuries from a bear attack, which she survived from thanks to his help. What are three of the things he loves about the forest and what would cause him to lose his cool in an emergency situation?

190. As a school nurse, she decided to be as prepared as possible in a violent world by becoming first responder emergency certified. Nursing was her second career and she was happy to be back in the school her children went to, though things had changed. The school now had metal detectors and the police department on speed dial. When she heard about the casualties a few years earlier at the school from gang violence, she knew that she had to do something to help. She went from housewife to nurse and when the chemistry laboratory disaster occurred, she was the first on the scene and was happy to be able to help. How will she handle herself as the accident unfolds and what do her children think of her new career?

Chefs and Cooks

I'm a little bit addicted to the Food Network and I'm not ashamed to admit it. I'm especially intrigued by the show "Chopped" which features four chefs from different backgrounds competing against each other to cook the best food possible. I think that we rarely think of who puts our food together and how much training and love has gone into it. I love when I'm able to catch a glimpse of the food preparation specialists working at the back of a diner, cafeteria or restaurant because I can see how focused these people are on creating me a gastronomical delight. A cook or chef as a protagonist in your story may be just want you need to delight your readers' palette.

191. As an executive chef at one of the highest-rated restaurants in the country, he had a reputation as being brilliant, bold and kind of a dick. If one of his chefs created something below his standards, he was quick to yell and it took the owner to restrain him from firing the victim on the spot. He wanted nothing more than to make every customer obsessed with the food, especially when it came to French and Italian cuisine which was his specialty. His temper hampered his ability to connect well with people, but he didn't need people, he thought to himself, he had food. How did he become so proficient at cooking and what are his life goals?

192. He was a world traveler growing up, like a seed hitched on the pant leg of his parents who seemed to read their passports more often than they read to him as a youth. As a result of his frequent travels, he experienced the foods of many different cultures, giving him an opportunity to pick and choose the aspects he enjoyed the most. He went to culinary school and used the knowledge of rare spices and techniques to rise up the ranks to become a well-known New York chef. What other aspects of these cultures has he picked up to use in his life?

193. She was a pastry chef at a vegan bakery and loved creating the most extravagant displays of sugar and dough she could think up. She came from a rough family life with several different foster families taking care of her. It was with these families that she learned about cooking and realized it was her calling. She loved the look on people's faces when she brought them something they enjoyed. Her work was featured in many different local publications and she's even had several celebrity clients. What would the members of her family think of her accomplishments?

194. When her doctor told her that she would need to be much healthier to live past the next decade, she took up cooking healthy foods. She never expected a change in diet would lead her to being one of the top healthy chefs in the region. She had always been the kind of person to take on a project head on and in its entirety. Her attempts at being healthy started with classes and a part-time job and ended with her writing a book and owning her own health food restaurant. She even took up running and started doing 5Ks with her friends to look the part of a healthy chef. What are some dishes she prepares in her restaurant and how has her life changed since becoming healthier?

195. He was anything but ordinary as a half-Cuban, half-Irish mix and as a result, his cooking was anything but ordinary. He loved pulling multiple cultures into one dish and he even started a restaurant called "The Coin" where every dish had at least two sides to it. His parents had always hammered home the point of never forgetting where you came from and he stuck to it with every aspect of the restaurant. Even the decor smacked of both Ireland and Cuba at the same time. Unsurprisingly, in his relationships, he was drawn to those of multiple races and wondered what it'd be like if he had a child who started his own four-culture cuisine dining facility. What other aspects of his life combine his multiple cultures?

196. He was one of the most well-known pastry chefs in the entire world. His specialty was desserts that didn't hit the normal taste buds, concentrating on savory and bitter flavors and making them absolutely delectable. His fame from his pastries earned him a chain of dessert shops and even a hit television show. Even though he craved and created bitter flavors, he was one of the sweetest people you'd ever meet. He always added energy to every room he entered, in part because he was so grateful for everything that he'd ever experienced. What would filming an episode of his television show be like and where did his sugary demeanor come from?

197. She was large and in charge and everybody at her restaurant knew it. She had catapulted to fame in the last decade on her "butter first, ask questions later" style of cooking and her restaurants were wildly successful as a result. In a world where healthy was becoming a more prevalent choice, fat and food lovers rejoiced at her recipes and her menu in which health consciousness was thrown out the window. She had lived her life by the maxim that "life is too short" and she wanted everybody who tried her food to feel like he or she was getting a real treat. What are some other ways in which she is "old school" in her sensibilities?

198. Her life had been a series of difficult decisions. Her family had wanted her to go into medical school and by becoming a chef, she knew she would disappoint them. When she realized the love of her life was keeping her away from her love of cooking, she had to let him go to follow her dreams. She never had a difficult choice picking what to cook as she had an uncanny sense for what her family and customers would want and it showed. She was willing and able to use whatever ingredients she had in her kitchen to create something unique and delectable. This creativity was something she felt she would never have realized in her medical career or with her practical-minded partner. She felt guilty for these choices she'd made, but she never felt anything but joy when she was cooking. Will her parents ever forgive her for her decision and what will her future hold as a cook?

199. He loved to cook, bake and create, the only problem was that he was no good at it. Sure, he could follow a recipe and make sure that a meal turned out exactly as it was supposed to. That's what he did all day long at the local grocery store. When he returned home, however, his family was frequently disappointed at his attempts to "invent" new recipes. The attempts often turned out disastrously, but it was the creation that brought him true joy. He felt like a sort of maestro for a symphony orchestra when he was making a meal, and despite his family's protestations, he continued to try out wild and crazy concoctions at least three times a week. They began to secretly order pizza while he was at work. What are some of the dishes he's put together for them and will he ever become more successful with his creations?

200. She couldn't believe that her life had come to this. After all, she'd gone to school in the hopes of becoming some amazing sous chef at a fancy steakhouse or something. Her talent wasn't supposed to be used to cook for hundreds of little snot-nosed kids every day. She was tasked with creating appetizing and healthy meals for the elementary school she went to as a child. She'd always wanted to move away and see where her talent would take her, but it just didn't seem to be in the cards. She felt validated when the kids came back for seconds. What held her back from her dreams of moving to a big city and becoming a town-renowned chef?

Actors, Musicians and Artists

In many stories I've read that are steeped in cliché throughout all of their characters, the actors, musicians and the artists are portrayed the least realistically. Having been an actor for many years, I have definitely witnessed the pompous, stuck up, "what is my motivation?" type of creative artist, but they are certainly few and far between. There are many more that are grounded in reality, often with a 9 to 5 job to pay the bills and a desperate effort to blend their creative passions with what the world actually wants. I've been fortunate to meet multiple successful creative types in the acting, music and artistic fields of various personalities, some of which I'll share or create with you here.

201. He looked like he belonged on underwear billboards. He didn't want to settle just for using his body though, he wanted to be an actor on the big screen. The problem being that he was absolutely terrible at acting. After years of always depending on his looks, he didn't have much in the way of an analytical brain or a functioning brain at all. He wasn't able to take direction well and he even had issues with things like hitting his mark. What will this prized specimen of humanity do about his dream of becoming an actor?

202. He'd been a completely internal person all his life and anything spur of the moment was far from being in his wheelhouse. In college, he discovered his untapped powers of improvisation, which transitioned into serious acting. It turned out that his many years of an overactive internal monologue worked quite well for his ability to externally monologue. His parents and friends were completely surprised when he invited them to his first performance, in which he completely killed it and received a standing ovation. Will he continue to act after college and in what ways has his introspection improved his acting abilities?

203. She wasn't the prettiest, she wasn't the most talented, but she was extremely fearless in all of her performances. She had absolutely no shame and she used this ability to take on roles that would have scared any other actors out of their wits. She'd been naked on stage in front of her peers as a freshman, she'd played men, transsexuals and she'd even had her head computer generated where a woman's genitalia was supposed to be in a wild music video. In addition to her lack of stage fright, she was tough as nails and was willing and able to defend herself in a battle of wits or fists. How did she become such a tough cookie and what are some of the ways her lack of fear have helped her career?

204. She had a voice like an angel and by the age of 22, she had already front-lined several successful bands. The only problem was that none of them had ever really taken her anywhere and she wanted her voice to get out to a larger audience. She struck out on her own and moved to New York City. She started by playing night clubs and teaching lessons to make ends meet. Just as she had hoped, she was discovered by a producer and she was even able to produce her own solo album. Now, all she could do was wait to see if it was picked up by the local and nationwide radio stations. Will she achieve her dreams of success and how will her final result make her feel about her career?

205. For most of his life he'd felt like he was in great pain. His circumstances didn't really demonstrate that, he had loving parents, he grew up in a decent area, he wasn't bullied or mocked, but the smallest amount of discomfort would cause him agony. His parents assumed he might be able to channel this pain artistically and they were right. He began taking art classes and he noticed similarities between his personality and the personalities of the other artists. His work was quickly snatched up by local galleries and they were hailing him as a homegrown talent. He was pleased by his success, but the pain was still a part of his life and he used drugs and alcohol to calm it as much as he could. Will his art ever be enough to calm his pain or will his methods of suppression consume him?

206. When he told his family that he wanted to paint and draw, they pushed him toward engineering, as it seemed a practical version of an artistic career path they would never choose for him. He had an uncanny ability to render both blueprints and the human form and when he was away at college he took classes in both subjects. He was a half-decent engineer, but his artistic abilities began to attract attention throughout the university. It wasn't until a family friend visiting the school saw one of the drawings that his parents found out. They rushed to school and told him he would have to quit this "artistic nonsense." Will he listen to his folks or will he continue to pursue art as a potential career path?

207. She was something of a young Martha Stewart, as she was able to take objects like paper plates, popsicle sticks and buttons and turn them into something fantastic. Pictures of her creations had been making it into magazines for nearly a decade before she was persuaded to write a book on the subject. Her tome of crafting ideas was a best-seller and she toured her work around the country for all to see. She didn't feel like making sculptures out of such silly materials was really art, but she did thoroughly enjoy herself while she was doing it. She was happy that her success gave her an opportunity for the finer things in life, even though she used such simple objects to bring her visions to reality. Where did her artistic abilities come from and how high will her success take her?

208. She loved to sing more than anything and at the age of 15, she decided to record herself singing her favorite songs on YouTube. Millions of views later, she had been contacted for a record deal and she would be touring around the country. She loved her sudden rise to fame, though she missed getting to see her friends and her favorite teachers. She had a private tutor to help her educationally while she was away but it wasn't the same. She would often cry to a friend on the phone in the evening when she tried to go to sleep. Will she continue to live the life of a pop recording sensation or will she try to go back to being a regular kid and why?

209. On a whim, his parents took him for a casting call at the age of two and he'd been acting ever since. He became a child star, getting to play opposite major adult actors and holding his own quite nicely. As he grew up, his acting matured as well and he was able to weather the storm of the transition from child star to indie teen actor. He knew he had a great talent and that he'd earned his parents enough money to retire as a result of his hard work, but he wasn't completely sure that he still wanted to do it. Acting wasn't as easy as it looked and as a sort of method actor, he often felt sad when he played sad characters, which was bringing him down. Will he decide to continue in this career or try something new and what will his parents think?

210. She didn't just want to be an actor or a singer or a dancer. She wanted to be all of them: a triple-threat. She had her parents send her to all of the camps and the classes so that she could absorb all those skills into her tiny body. She wasn't bad at any of the three skills, but she wasn't exceptional either, which only forced her to work harder. She was so involved in her love of musical theatre, that the other kids at school poked fun at her. She resolved the only way to beat them was to become the best in the world. She stayed up late and practiced singing every night and each morning she'd get up early to exercise for dancing. She put most of her work into her acting class and she dreamed each night of becoming a star. Will she be able to realize her dream and if so, how will she get there?

Clerks, Cashiers and Receptionists

They deal with your service requests, take your money and receive your phone calls every day. We often make every effort to get around them as quickly as possible but as writers we must take every opportunity to understand the people around us. I've been a receptionist before for a temporary staffing agency and in a clerk position for various other gigs and I've worked among some amazing and driven people working their ways to the top along with people who hate their very existence. These people, of course, all have their stories and can be extremely fleshed out as amazing characters by the writer who puts in the effort.

211. All day long he rang up customers at a health food grocery store and he wanted every customer to enjoy their time at his register. He would use strange accents, funny hats and a strong sense of caring during each encounter. After a while, he knew almost all the regulars' names and this made his job even easier, since those customers knew to expect the best from him. They almost always tried to get into his line because he simply made the shopping experience more fun. What does he enjoy the most about being a cashier and what is his future in the grocery industry?

212. He was a temp on his first day when the company began to take a downturn. He was tasked with answering the phones, but there were so many calls that other employees were helping out. In a climate of fear and panic, he had nothing to worry about, since his job was only going to last a couple of days anyway. This gave him a calm demeanor and made him a sort of go-to guy as the company began to crumble. This further reinforced his belief that working full-time for someone is dangerous, while filling in every now and then had the benefits of low accountability. What are some ways in which he's able to help the company in its final days?

213. She had been a personal assistant for this up and coming male executive for about five years now and she'd come to one conclusion. She could completely run his business for him and it would thrive without all of his stupid mistakes. She was caught in the plight of being the brilliant Watson to a bumbling Sherlock Holmes and she was tired of it. She began taking evening courses for a masters degree in business management and using the contacts she'd gained to find a new job. Her end goal was to have her former boss working for her someday. Will she achieve her goal and how well does she do when actually running a business herself?

214. She was faking it. If she smiled at you while you were purchasing something from her retail store, it was because she was faking it. If she gave you a kind glance and discussed merchandise with a giggle, it was because she was faking it. She absolutely hated everything about her job and when she went home, she immediately fixed herself a vodka tonic. She didn't have any aspirations of a higher position or becoming the store's manager, she just wanted to get her paycheck and not think about what she did for a living on the weekends. What are some jobs she might actually enjoy and what left her so cynical as far as life goals went?

215. He'd tried his hand at many different trades. He'd worked in automobile repair, insurance sales and even a bit of gardening. Through opening his big mouth or doing something uncouth, he'd lost every single one of those jobs. Now, a cousin had given him one last chance of making copies and typing up invoices at his small business. He was in deep credit card debt and knew he couldn't afford to lose this last-ditch job. He was nervous almost every minute of his position and he tried to act like the perfect gentleman who was practically mute. He'd had several close calls of almost saying something that would have gotten him canned, but he relented just in the nick of time. Will he be able to keep this job and what are some of the things he's said to get kicked out of previous positions?

216. When people asked him if he just, "Answered the phones," he responded with a big belly laugh. He was much more than a simple receptionist at his job, though he didn't expect other people to really understand that. From his perspective, he kept the entire business together. If it wasn't for him, meetings would run late, accounts would be unbalanced and the company would crumble. Sure, he answered the phones, but he actually connected with the people on the other end. Every day it was his goal to be the best administrative assistant in the business, with hopes of getting a raise and increasing his pride. What are some things he did to stand out from your average admin?

217. Whenever she put on her uniform as a grocery bagger, she felt proud. After all, she was only 16 and she was already helping her mom pay the bills. She kept a little bit for herself so she could go to the movies every once in a while, but she knew that adults needed more money than teenagers anyway. Her mom always gave her a giant hug every two weeks when she handed that money over. The job wasn't terribly exciting but she enjoyed seeing the multitudes of different people every day. She thought to herself that maybe she'd be like the businesswoman in the pantsuit one day or the mom lugging around two toddlers. She wasn't sure what she wanted to be yet, but it was just amazing to her to have the option of growing up to be like any one of the adults who came into the store. What was it that made her so loyal to her family and what will she decide to do upon graduating from high school?

218. She had been a housewife for her entire life and when her marriage fell apart she knew she'd have to get a job. She landed a position working for an up and coming online publication. She barely knew how to type at first, but one day, she stayed at the office nearly all night long and learned every aspect of the system. She ended up becoming a major asset to the company, giving a middle-aged perspective when it was needed. She even got a promotion and gained her own column on the website at one point. How did she feel as a member of the working world after having been out of it for so long?

219. He loved working the cash register at night, because he was a master at skimming just a little bit off the top. He made sure that the amount he took wasn't noticeable and that aside from his thievery he was a model employee. He was smart enough to cover his tracks so that his bosses thought that an item was damaged here or stolen by a customer there. They were never suspicious over the five years that he worked at the store and they actually praised how observant he was, since none of the other employees ever seemed to report lost or stolen merchandise. He didn't feel bad about stealing from his bosses, after all, they weren't exactly the most moral people he'd ever met. What was it that made him think that stealing was a legitimate choice for him in his job?

220. She was hired for her looks, but nobody expected that she applied to bring the company down to its knees. She was a spy for a rival organization that was looking to get a leg up in the market and she was the perfect candidate. Absolutely gorgeous, smart as a tack, but easily able to feign ignorance when accidentally logging into classified parts of the company. It took just a few months for several important e-mails to be leaked to the general public and for the system's accounting to go haywire. She wasn't a vengeful person, per say, but the company had fired her father several years earlier for what seemed like no reason at all. And nobody messed with her daddy. Will she feel any sort of satisfaction when the company files for bankruptcy a few months later and why?

Writers

There is a tendency for some writers starting out to portray their own kind as shut-ins with little in the way of social graces. There is no question that some writers embody those traits and wouldn't know a conversation if it hit them in the back of the head. Some writers are the exact opposite and use writing, speaking and touring equally in their profession. Other writers are freelancers who work on their craft in an effort to support their family. There are also writers who work primarily online in an effort to build up a community and spend their nights out with their friends. These many different people come together to make an eclectic bunch of characters who just happen to be writers.

221. He'd always been a numbers guy, which was why he got into freelance writing. He crunched the numbers and realized that with little training but a lot of gusto, he could make considerably more money as a writer working per hour and have tons more freedom than he ever would as a math professional. He studied every aspect of copywriting like it was a formula and he then put that formula into practice. After a few years, he was able to command a rate of over $200 per hour, with just as many clients as he wanted. Writing, to him at least, was a science after all. What does he do with the time provided by his career's freedom?

222. He was a well-known author throughout the world for his portrayal of complex, government-espionage scenarios. He inspired video games, movies and dozens of copycat authors. The books often featured the worst-case scenario for spy and terrorism-related missions, which came from his extreme fear of death and his unshakable pessimism. It was his editors that forced him into endings where the good guys won and his press team that shielded the public from his dire beliefs. His family kept a close eye on him to make sure he didn't take his negativity to the next level. What caused such him to have such a dystopic viewpoint?

223. Her books were like comfort food to women who were looking for something more in their lives. The books featured wild romance and women-empowerment and they usually sat at the top of the best seller's list until the following one came out. It turned out, the reason she wrote these books was because her own life lacked the happiness she wished for as a child. She created characters who had crazy adventures and amazingly happy endings that she could never seem to get for herself. Now a millionaire, she was finally able to live out some of her fantasies in reality. What is her typical day of writing like?

224. There are plenty of advertising copywriters in the world, but her ads are the best-selling by far. When she came onto a campaign, there was a hush throughout that particular office, waiting to see what brilliance she would come up with next. Singlehandedly, she had brought many brands in the United States to the top of the heap. The agencies paid her handsomely for her work and she lived on a breathtaking property in the countryside with her family. She had an uncanny ability to know exactly what people wanted. What are some of her specialties and successes in the business?

225. His picture was literally in the dictionary next to the word "prolific." After years of writing 364 days per year, taking only Christmas off, he'd written over 250 novels, several short story compilations, multiple non-fiction tomes and even a book of childish poetry. There was an iconic image of him hunched over his office desk writing that could be found as inspiration in the houses of many writers throughout the world. His family loved and appreciated how he provided for them, but they couldn't help but wonder why his books were so much more important to him than they were. What are his opinions on family and his family's ability to put up with his abundance of work?

226. He was one of the most popular female authors for young adults of our time. Although, he wasn't a woman at all, because he was actually a ghost writer for a popular publication house. When his books became overwhelming popular, the publisher decided to keep his identity secret to preserve the mystery until the hysteria died out. His legend (as "her") only grew over time. After his books had sold over 30 million copies and he'd earned nearly a billion dollars in royalties, his publisher finally conceded in letting him reveal his identity. He'd had a good sense of humor about the whole thing and in his first interview mentioned his consideration of cross dressing or getting a sex change. What was it about his books that made him so popular?

227. When you wanted someone in your life to feel better, you would almost always enlist her help without even knowing it. She was a successful greeting card writer who knew, with the perfect blend of tongue-in-cheek humor and love, how to get anybody out of a funk. Some of her cards had even been medically proven to increase the chances of healing. Her parents had major health problems when she was growing up and it had been almost a part of her nature to try her best to make them feel better. They always encouraged her well wishes. To make a little extra money in college, she applied to a greeting card company. The rest was history. What are some of her most used cards and how does she feel when she makes someone's health improve?

228. In her youth, she wanted to be a teacher, but she never imagined that she'd have a hand in teaching millions of students every single year. For over a decade, she had been one of the most prominent textbook authors for both middle and high school and her books were featured in nearly every classroom. She had an uncanny knack for explaining complicated concepts in ways simple and entertaining enough for kids to learn. At the end of her day, she came home feeling satisfied that she had contributed to the education of so many people. What are some of the things that set her textbooks above the others on the market?

229. He often remembered back to when he had trouble reading as a youth and wanted desperately to create books that would help kids like him to become literate. He not only created children's books but did his best to distribute them throughout the country to disadvantaged families like his own had been. Writing wasn't his initial trade as he'd done quite well for himself in the business world, though it always called to him and when he'd made enough money to retire, he decided to act. It was estimated that his organization cut illiteracy in half over the course of five years. What are some of the feelings he experiences when he helps a kid to read for the first time?

230. If she could name one problem she believed the world had and could solve, it was a lack of self-esteem. She'd led seminars for over 20 years on the subject of self-worth and self-love and had gained quite a following. Her friends and co-workers thought she should make the transition into writing about her passion and when she did, the response was enormous. Her book was featured on every talk show throughout the country and it quickly became a best-seller. Her honesty mixed with her wit struck a perfect tone and the royalties would make her set for life. What is next for this best-selling author and how much has the book changed her life?

Camp Counselors and Instructors

I have many fond memories from my 13 years at Willow Grove Day Camp in Pennsylvania. I went from the tiniest of tots to the step just below counselor during my time there. I came to love the camp as a whole, but it was really the people that made it for me. Some of my counselors were incredibly memorable and now that I'm older I truly appreciate them spending their summers working for little to no money to entertain me and my peers. Counselors may not always love what they do, but hopefully for most, there are moments that make the long hours and little pay completely worth it.

231. When he became a teacher over a decade ago, one of his big dreams was to become a baseball coach on the side. Unfortunately, the school he taught at had a coaching staff in place and he was barely even allowed to work the concession stand. When a friend gave him the idea of being a camp counselor to get some coaching experience, his eyes lit up. He became a counselor for one of the oldest groups of kids in camp, but more importantly to him, he took over the coaching gig for the travelling team. They certainly weren't the best bunch of kids he'd ever seen play the game, but he enjoyed helping them to grow over the summer months, and he came back summer after summer to do what he loved. What are some of his summer coaching highlights?

232. This wasn't supposed to be what he was stuck doing all summer. When his parents told him that he wouldn't get his customary summer allowance unless he got a job, he thought they were kidding. They said he had to learn something about the working world if he was going to live under their roof and at the last second, the only job he could find was as a camp counselor. He didn't even like kids. He did enjoy trying to date some of the female counselors, which is how he spent most of his energy that summer. Would he learn anything from his counselor experience or would he be the same old rich kid?

233. She loved kids and thought she could affect their lives the most by teaching them the intricacies of soccer. She had played for her middle and high school team and she knew she had a lot to offer. Unbeknownst to her, for many of these teens and tweens, her biggest gift was that she looked like a goddess. Unintentionally, she had become the object of affection to a great number of the campers and counselors alike. During school, she didn't care much about dating because she was so busy with soccer. Now that she had some downtime during the summer, she began to notice the attention of a whole bunch of people. She was asked out on a date at least once a day during camp and some of them she said yes to. After all, she was allowed to have a little bit of fun while she provided a service to the community as well, right? What is it like for her to be the quintessential "bombshell" of the camp and what are some of her dates with the other counselors like?

234. She hated seeing her kids cooped up in the house all summer. She knew that one of the easiest solutions was to become an instructor at the local day camp, since it would allow her to send her kids there for free. She became the arts and crafts director and was tasked with coming up with projects that close to 1,000 kids would work on throughout the 8-week camp season. She didn't have much to work with, mostly popsicle sticks and glue, and it was hard work providing creative guidance for so many, but she was happy to go through with it for the benefit of her kids. What is one of her camp days like from beginning to end?

235. He was a real lifer when it came to his camp. Ever since he was a little kid he dreamed of being a counselor there, because he truly looked up to them for the decade he'd been attending. He loved it when he and his peers ran circles around the teenagers and grown men and he figured it'd be just as fun to be on the other side of the equation. He'd been a counselor in training, then a junior counselor and now he was ready for the real deal: a head counselor position. He felt proud to be leading a group of young men through a great camping experience. What are some of the things he likes the most about being a counselor? What does he like the least?

236. He couldn't stand how soft kids were getting these days. With all of their Internet games and their Facebook profiles they were forgetting to become men. He figured he would do something about it by volunteering to teach several important subjects at a summer camp. He would head up the archery, marksmanship and wood working stations to ensure that kids would learn these important manly skills. He worked hard to make the subjects both entertaining and extremely informative. He knew that these kids would go home to their iPads and would continue to be babied by their parents, but at least he had made some small contribution to their adulthood. How do some of the kids react to his attempts to get them to "man up?"

237. She hadn't become a swim instructor for the extra money or to keep herself in shape. She was there to make sure that when kids were in a sticky situation in a pool, they would come out of it alive. She wasn't concerned with fun or water sports, she wanted these kids to learn everything about swimming and how to save each other from drowning. To hear her describe a pool is like hearing most people describe some sort of water-laced death trap. Some of the owners of the camp had asked her to tone down her apocalyptic pool talk, but she still scared the kids half to death with her stories of pool-related fatalities. Sure, they learned to swim, but they rarely ever wanted to go into the pool again. What are some other things she is a tad melodramatic about?

238. Her whole life was surrounded with slimy little creatures...and that was just the kids! She was a much bigger fan of lizards, amphibians and tiny mammals than she was human children, but the best market for her animal loving skills was to show them off to kids. After all, she figured that by teaching them about these awesome organisms, she might create a few animal loving adults. This is why she took the position of Nature Instructor at the camp. It kept her in one place for a couple of months instead of touring about from school to school and it gave her the opportunity to hang out in a pristine wooded area instead of the city. It was a win-win, though working with so many snot-nosed kids all day made her yearn for her apartment which was full of cats, frogs, birds and other non-human friends. What is it that makes her enjoy the company of animals more than humans?

239. When most of the kids went to the computer building, they were expecting to play non-stop games that mostly involved blowing each other up. But their computer instructor, an old-school guy who had been involved with computers when they were still punch cards, had different ideas. He wasn't there just for fun and games but to teach these kids the cool things they could do with the ancient machines located at the camp. He gave them basic web design lessons, had them print out three-dimensional airplanes and toys and gave them history lessons using interactive videos. If he had his way, kids wouldn't rot their brains with high-frame rate explosive games, but they would learn important skills. How successful are his attempts at keeping computer time educational?

240. While most of her friends were sitting poolside and waiting for senior year to begin, she was slaving away trying to take care of 20 bratty kids each day. After a financial hardship or two, her parents could no longer afford to support her spending habits and told her if she wanted to have fun that summer she would need to work for it. After several attempts at getting a job in retail or waitressing, she found the only job that would hire her. She hated the outdoors and she saw her kids as 20 whining versions of her annoying little sister. She cried and whined as soon as

she got home every day but her parents wouldn't and couldn't relent. Did she learn anything from her summer of working and will she ever come back to do it again?

Technical Crew

When we visit a sporting event, movie theater, play, concert or fireworks display, we don't often think of the technical crew behind the spectacle we are beholding. These are often extremely intelligent people who have taken their talents to the long, black cords and the complicated mechanisms of behind-the-scenes work. Some of them have taken umbrage to the lack of appreciation they get. Others are just happy to be a part of such technical wonderment. Don't make the same mistake that most entertainment goers make, include members from this esteemed group in your story.

241. When he was dangling hundreds of feet above the stage, hanging lights in an elaborate setup, he felt like God, even though he didn't believe in him. He was one of the most death-defying members of the crew who would balance at strange angles on the catwalk to get lights into the perfect position. He could tell just from looking at a lighting setup how it would look on the stage and he was a well-regarded member of the team. He'd be in even higher regard if he wasn't so cocky about how good he was. Why did he get into technical lighting and what are some of his hobbies that make him continue to feel superior to others?

242. He was the guru when it came to designing a set that would evoke some sort of major emotional response. He knew exactly how an audience would respond to the way a set looked upon watching a particular play. His work was often cited in reviews as being "genius" or "the stuff of legends" and hundreds of pictures of his sets could be found in dramatic art textbooks. Personally though, he felt as though his best work was still ahead of him and that he had never created "the perfect set." This quest for perfection drove him and the people around him a little bit crazy, but it helped him to create some amazing masterpieces. What do some of his sets look like and why did he get into this business in the first place?

243. As a director, you originally thought that the most important people to have around you were actors who could do anything artistically that you wanted. You were wrong. When you met her, you assumed that she was just some acting dropout who couldn't cut it and chose technical theater instead. That was where you were extremely wrong. She was able to solve every single problem that came up in the production side of your show. You had almost prepared for the production aspects to be faulty, because something always seems to go wrong when you least expect it. It was almost comical how you could start a sentence, "Well, what about the – " and she would always end it, "I took care of it." The technical aspects of your show were flawless and it was all because of her incredible abilities to eat problems for breakfast. What are some of her magical talents and how did they manifest in the show?

244. You thought you knew the definition of tough before you met her. When she carried those large pieces of wood in with her tiny frame and seemed to defy physics with her strength, you changed the definition just a tad. The previous year, she'd even been knocked in the head with a steel beam during a play production and within three months, she had completely rehabbed and was back in action doing the technical production work she loved. She wasn't just tough, but she was cute as well and the two of you joked between moments of her showing some incredible feats of power. What is it that has made her so interested in the technical aspects of theater and how did she become so tough?

245. If he were a superhero, his power would be his amazing sense of hearing. This was the perfect guy to have on board at a concert hall with shows going seven nights a week. One of his most important abilities was to hear when the sound system was even a little bit off and he had the knowhow to get it to sound exactly right. He could also sense when a speaker was about to blow or malfunction in some way. It was like he had a sound sixth sense or something. He was well-known in the area as the guy you wanted working your band's set to make you sound incredible to any producers who were in town. What are some other ways he employs his super hearing ability?

246. He thought building up elaborate fake buildings and coming up with awe-inspiring set imagery was a perfectly fine way to make a living. His favorite part, however, was tearing it all down to rubble. At the end of every show, while some set pieces could be preserved or sold, most of the set needed to be torn down to bits. That's where he came in. He was a master when it came to a quick, efficient and violent end to an award-winning set. In a process

known as strike, he was the strike king. He even secretly hoped that shows would not be particularly successful, so that he could tear them down more quickly. What are some of his favorite memories of set destruction?

247. She was the one who had the supreme power when it came to making sure you looked your best or your worst. She was the costume designer and she had no problem tightening up your clothes a size or two if you had done her wrong. When the two of you dated, she had spent extra time making you appear like the most attractive person who had ever stepped away from the chorus. Now that the two of you had broken things off, she was still making your costumes, but her meticulous stitching ability was used in other ways. During one performance, your pants split right down the middle. During another, a button on your shirt popped off due to tightness. What are some other ways in which this costume mistress has been vindictive?

248. She was at the same time the most feared and the most respected woman on the technical crew. She wouldn't take crap from anybody and it showed in how smoothly and successfully the show could run. She was the quarterback, the captain and the den mother all rolled into one. She was the stage manager and without her, the show would be a complete disaster. One of her main talents was her ability to point out and find mistakes before they happened so they wouldn't disrupt things. It's the same talent that gave her a 4.0 GPA in college and made her frustratingly annoying to hang out with. Why did she decide to get into the stage managing business and why is she so good at what she does?

249. As a dazzling array of brightly colored tapestries rustled through the theater, to the delight of the audience members, he was up on the catwalk controlling it all, while eating a pastrami sandwich. This particular show had been running for several consecutive years and he had the process down to a science. He knew what levers to pull and buttons to push like the back of his hand and as a result, he didn't need all that much concentration. He was happy to be paid for his time up there, but for most of the three plus hours, he did nothing but sit there and wait for his cue. Slowly but surely, he gave himself more freedom about what he could do while he was waiting. Today, that freedom had reached the point of "pastrami sandwich eating." What are some of the other strange things this member of the fly crew was willing to do on the catwalk?

250. She was always just waiting for her opportunity. In high school, she signed up for the crew when she didn't get a part from her audition and while she loved gracing the stage to move set pieces, she yearned to have even a single line. The same thing happened in college, when her audition went awry, she took the stage...but only to move some backdrops from here to there. All in all, she'd been on stage more than most of the actors at her schools, though she'd never realized her dream of saying just one line. A few years later, a community theater audition gave her the first acting part she'd ever had. A maid, who had exactly what she wanted, just one line. What does she love the most about the theatre and what are some things she learned from her time backstage?

Scientists and Researchers

At any given point of time, there are thousands of scientists and researchers throughout the world who are taking part in countless tasks to develop chemicals, create medical countermeasures and learn more about people. Billions of dollars go toward these researchers to fund the next advancements in science that can help us to live longer and safer lives. Many scientists portrayed in stories seem to take on the "mad scientist" archetype, when in actuality, most scientists work hard, have families and do what they can to forward human progress. In stories of disease, weaponry and sociology, try playing around with a scientist or two for credibility's sake.

251. When he was a kid, most of his peers were running around the neighborhood or watching TV. Meanwhile, he had his nose firmly pressed against the pages of a book at the local library. There was something about information that he just couldn't get enough of. During high school, he took an internship researching for a historical fiction author and it was the most fun he'd ever had. Later on, he would take on larger and more professional roles than helping the latest bestseller, but no matter what project it was, he simply loved getting paid for accumulating more knowledge. What are some of his favorite subject matters to learn about and why?

252. He was doing some of the most complex scientific experiments in the world that could protect humanity as we know it from a deadly epidemic. But when he got home, he only cared about two things: being a good husband and a good father. He'd seen some of his colleagues become so consumed by their work that it ruined their home

lives. Even though he had the same number of degrees as they did, he refused to ignore his most precious experiment: his family. From time to time, he'd get a little detail obsessed around the house, like wanting to stop a leaky faucet or a sputtering snow blower with his brilliance. His wife helped him to rein it in, because after all, fixing problems was for work and living the solution was for home. How do the other scientists treat this family man who actually keeps his work and home life separate?

253. She had absolutely no problem being the only woman in a field typically filled with men. After all, she was one of the few female PhD candidates in her program and she was the only one who made it through. Also, by being the only woman in a sea of men, she became something of a prized commodity. She was fawned over and well taken care of with free meals and drinks at most conferences she went to. She wasn't interested in a relationship, since it distracted her from her work. Fortunately, most of the younger scientists she met felt the same way. As a result, she worked extremely hard, putting in 13 to 15 hour days when necessary and she played even harder than that. She wondered what all those boring popular kids from high school would think of her now. What are a few of her main goals in life and how does she work at achieving them?

254. She wasn't the biggest fan of people, after all, they'd always sort of mocked her long face and her glasses. She didn't love reading or writing either, but it gave her something to do while other people were off apparently having fun. She had an aptitude for science and enjoyed it, even if nobody wanted to be her lab partner. She vowed that one day she would create something, perhaps a new polymer or element, and she would cement her place in history. This way, while everyone who mocked her would be forgotten shortly after their death, the memory of her achievements would continue on forever. What are some of the fields in which she is attempting to solidify her legacy?

255. He had been born into a family of scientists. His father had made a pioneering discovery about surgical techniques involving the heart. His mother was the first person to develop a vaccine against several kinds of cancer. Needless to say, the pressure was on him to create something or discover something even grander than his parents. He followed their lead into some of the best scientific programs in existence. He achieved high marks and seemed destined for greatness. There was only one problem: he didn't really want to be a scientist, he wanted to be an actor. Will he be able to tell his parents of his true passions before he's forever locked into a life of science?

256. He wasn't what most people would call stable and he had some radical political beliefs that he kept pretty silent when he was considered for a position with the U.S. government. He fashioned himself somewhat of a sleeper cell, who would infiltrate the Centers for Disease Control and Prevention and use his knowledge to create a bioterrorist act so heinous, the country would scarcely be able to recover from it. He kept his life as normal in appearance as possible, getting married and having two lovely children. After seeing how precious they were, he wondered if he still wanted to go through with a plot he'd been planning for most of his life. What are his reasons for wanting to do something that could kill thousands and what are his reasons against it?

257. People who knew her back in college thought it was funny that she'd gone from busting heads to trying to protect them. She was a star lacrosse player at the same time that she was a budding chemist. She had seen players get injured despite wearing helmets and padding and she became interested in finding new compounds for protective gear that could prevent those injuries. She interned at large athletic wear companies, only to eventually begin her own lab that looked into developing lightweight and extremely strong materials. She continued to play sports on the side, if for nothing else than testing out some of the gear on the field. Some of the technology that her and her team developed was later licensed by the athletic wear companies to be used by millions of young men and women. What does she enjoy more, lacrosse or chemistry and why?

258. When the signal came from another world, she was the one to detect it and decipher it. She wanted to be the one to make contact with another form of life when the two races connected. She'd always held out hope that life existed elsewhere. It was a statistical improbability that they were alone in the universe, like she had been for the last decade or so. It was extremely hard on her when her parents passed away and she took their favorite activity, stargazing, to heart. She devoted her life to the stars and learning the answers to the questions of the cosmos. The signal proved that something was out there and if she was chosen to make first contact, she knew that somewhere

beyond the stars, her parents would be proud of her. Describe the selection process and what will happen if she is picked.

259. It's funny how things work out sometimes. He developed the time machine on the same day that the world was about to end. He had no time to test it, so he had to go back himself in an effort to protect civilization. He survived his trip backwards one day and learned all he could about what happened to cause the Armageddon. He'd spent so much of his life developing the device as a gateway to fame and fortune. If he was unable to save the planet, however, there would be no such thing as fame, fortune or even him. He was no hero and hadn't thought much of others along the way. Now he was their only hope. What are some things he learns about himself in his attempts to save the world?

260. All scientists would like the opportunity to change the world for the better. When she discovered a legitimate, renewable, safe energy source that could replace fossil fuels, she automatically became the most famous researcher on the planet. It was the impact of her work that was important to her, not the fame, and when she was making talk show appearances, she wished she could be perfecting her discovery. She knew that if this energy source could be used in cars and power plants, the planet could begin to recover from some of the ways people have ravaged it over the last several hundred years. For a long time, she'd wondered if all those times she worked through the night and all those normal activities she'd ignored (like starting a family) would be worth it. On this day, she believed it truly had been. Will she be successful at implementing her new power source?

Pilots, Attendants and Crew

It's amazing to think that just a century and a half ago, there was no such thing as air travel. Nowadays, there are thousands of flights zigging and zagging across the globe to get people to their destinations quickly and easily. The people that make it happen are the pilots, flight attendants and flight crew that get us safely from point A to point B. If you go flying frequently, it can be easy to take these hard working people for granted, but we can make up for it by including them and their stories in our work.

261. He became a pilot because of Tom Cruise. Well, not directly, but the movie *Top Gun* had certainly made an impact on him. He figured that he'd be some amazing fighter pilot going all over the world ending the lives of bad guys. Through a series of life events, such as starting a family and having to tend to his aging parents, he ended up becoming a commercial airline pilot instead. He never did achieve the glory of a "Maverick" character, but he was happy with how his life had progressed. He enjoyed interacting with the thousands of passengers he transported each week and his family was proud of him. He didn't need the glory anymore. How close did he become to being a fighter pilot and what caused his change in direction?

262. He'd lived a full life but there was one thing he wanted to do that he never got around to. That's why he decided to take up flying lessons at a local airport. He did this without telling his children because he knew they would worry about him. He just told them he was going to the YMCA to do some water aerobics classes, since they'd never have the time to accompany him. Ever since his wife passed away, he knew that she would have wanted him to cross everything off his "bucket list." Flying a plane was near the top of the list. The funny thing was, he was actually quite a natural at flying and his instructor said he was one of the best beginners he'd ever taught. He felt a pang of regret, wondering if flying was actually what he was supposed to do. What reactions will he receive when he tells his kids the truth of his afternoon excursions?

263. You had been on many flights before, but this was the first time you'd seen a female pilot. She was calm and appreciative of her opportunity. After all, she knew that people were looking at her, simply expecting a male pilot and co-pilot at this point. People who hadn't noticed her before takeoff practically jumped when they heard a woman saying, "This is your pilot speaking." When the flight landed, you spoke to her for a few minutes asking about her experiences. She said that she'd met a lot of resistance from both her peers and her parents, but she always knew she wanted to fly planes. She recalled telling herself upon her first plane ride that she would pilot planes when she grew up and she never looked back. What is some of the resistance that she faced during her attempts to be a pilot?

264. She was amazed every day with the amount of crap people brought with them from city to city. She understood that some vacations required a hefty amount of clothes, but she could tell from the magic of matching

luggage exactly how many clothes some believed they needed. She was on the runway six days a week loading possessions into and out of planes all day long. She had struggled to find a job after college and found this to be a bit mindless and labor intensive but well paying enough to live on. She felt like she was helping people with their peace of mind, making sure that bags made it safely and securely to their final destination. What are some of the most interesting items she's seen been transported on an airplane and what was her reaction to them?

265. He came to be a flight attendant because of his love of traveling. He found it difficult to engage in the fun parts of travel, since most days he was completely confined to the small cabin space in his assigned airplane. He loved his co-workers and he more or less enjoyed the clientele, he just wished he could be in more wide open spaces during the day. From time to time, he'd stay in a destination city to explore the area, but he was usually too tired from his job to go as wild and crazy as he'd like. In addition, while he was allowed to end up in a different city on some weekends, he had to deal with all of the room and board expenses. He wondered if he'd gotten into the wrong line of work and now dreamed of being a traveling food critic. What are some of his best experiences in the cities he has traveled to?

266. He felt like he had one of the most rewarding jobs in the air travel industry. When a plane had a technical issue, it was up to him to quickly identify it and fix it, making sure it was safe, sound and ready to transport people from place to place. If he didn't do his job properly, people could be in danger. Pilots and flight attendants knew that he was one of the best in the business and they trusted him implicitly. He relished the pressure that was put on him every single day and there was nothing he loved more than getting his hands dirty on a faulty airplane. He had a perfect record of repair, as there had never been a problem with his planes after he dealt with them initially. He planned to keep that record perfect the rest of his life. What kind of skills has he had to develop to deal with such high-pressure situations?

267. She had been in the business a long time and she'd seen it all. From her beverage dispensing walks down the aisle to her seat belt demonstrations, her job had changed a great deal over the last 30 years. She remembered back to when she was a pretty young thing, getting ogled by businessmen in first class. Those days were long gone and a lot of flight attendants who started with her had long moved onto other professions or motherhood. She'd practically run away from home to become a flight attendant, defying the wishes of her parents to get something more secure and husband-attracting. They said that all she wanted was a trip to the "mile high club," which she was proudly still not a member of. She was good at her job and was happy to have done it well for many years. What are some of the wildest things she's seen in her line of work?

268. Her position was so secretive on that and other flights, that even the flight attendants didn't know she was there. Her job, as an undercover air marshal, was to travel on flights to major cities like New York and Los Angeles and make sure that there were no terrorist or criminal activities. She went through a special security screening and did her best to look like an average businesswoman. She'd never had to pull her gun or stop any strange activity and frankly she was glad. She never really liked air travel in the first place and it tended to make her queasy. She wondered how well she'd be able to handle a terrorist with a bomb when she was reaching for her sick bag. How was she initially assigned to be an air marshal and what kind of situations is she trained to diffuse?

269. He didn't see how someone could fall asleep while doing his job. He was an air traffic controller and from the beginning to the end of his shift he was completely wired. He saw things more three-dimensionally than most and his spatial reasoning ability was off the charts. He didn't need anything like caffeine or sugar to keep him focused, because his job made him incredibly excited. He felt a duty and a responsibility to be the best he could at his position and he took that pride home to his family every single day. He'd always had the skill to corral multiple variables at once, which showed during his high school ability to plan parties and his college ability to date multiple people at the same time. What are some of the other qualities he must exhibit to be the best he can at maintaining airport safety?

270. She was dry, she was witty and she knew exactly how to make the safety speech stick in your head at the beginning of a flight. This flight attendant had done "the spiel" so many times that she began adding her own little quirks. She mocked the fact that they had floatation devices for a flight over land. She made fun of the people sitting

in the emergency exits. She even insulted herself and her own crew to get a chuckle out of her passengers. She spent the entire flight cracking jokes with the pilots, her peers and her customers, who were frequently in need of a laugh. She remembered back to when she was bright-eyed and bushy-tailed, doing her best to stick to every aspect of protocol imaginable. She had gotten jaded from saying the same things over and over again and adopting this sand-dry attitude was her best way of coping. Has she ever gotten in trouble for her wittiness?

Dentists

If you had to choose one person to be on the good side of, you might choose the trained professional who will be tinkering around inside of your mouth. Even though I've only had a few dentists in my time, their personalities have been all over the board. There was the European woman with the iron fist who wouldn't let any plague escape her grasp, blood or no blood. I've seen the friendly old man who follows up every appointment with a sugar-free treat. I've even seen the one who plugs himself and his business in silly TV commercials. While we only get to see dentists once or twice a year, it's never a bad idea to see them often in your stories.

271. He knew early on that to survive in a town of many dentists, he needed to create a brand for himself. For the front of his store and the top of his car, he ordered a giant plastic dancing tooth wearing a lab coat with his name on the back. He started booking radio and television ads, focusing on him and the dancing tooth. He even got on several local talk shows to discuss dental health and his business. As a result, everybody knew him as "the dancing tooth guy" and began to frequent his business. His wife didn't love all the attention, but they were both glad to have a successful business in a tough market. What are some of the other ways in which he had advertised his dancing tooth brand?

272. Even though his office had been updated to include the latest in dental technology, those who entered his examination room still referred to it as "the dungeon." After all, about 30 years ago when he decorated the place he'd given it a sort of medieval motif because he loved that kind of stuff. Unfortunately, since it hadn't been updated since he'd gone into business, it now resembled more of a torture chamber than the typical bright and cheery, kid-friendly offices that most dentists use. The fact that he'd grown old and a bit scary looking, only added to the medieval mystique. Will this dentist ever realize that his decor might be scaring off potential customers?

273. In Hungary, children knew that a trip to the dentist wasn't about sugar-free treats and bubble gum fluoride, she thought to herself. The children in the United States whined and cried about her making their mouths bleed with her aggressive gum line picking. She responded to them by saying they should floss more, admitting no fault of her own. She was a fantastic dentist as far as keeping her patients' mouths clean, but she was never much of a people person. When she began to lose customers, she wondered what her next step should be to bring in business. What will she decide to do to keep her practice afloat?

274. She made men want to come to the dentist. She was extremely attractive and she prominently displayed some old pictures of herself including some from her high school cheerleading days. She was more or less oblivious to these men scheduling more than four dental appointments each year, as she had the photos displayed so her patients would get to know her. In reality, they wanted to get to know her much better and before she knew it, she was getting requests for her personal phone number. She didn't really feel comfortable dating her patients so she almost always declined. She just wanted to clean teeth and she wasn't interested in breaking hearts. Why did she get into dentistry and did she ever think her appearance would be both a benefit and a detriment to her practice?

275. One of the things he loved the most about being a dentist was having a captive audience. After he'd failed in his efforts of being a stand-up comedian while going to dental school, he realized that he could make whatever jokes he wanted while people had cotton balls shoved in their mouths. As a result, he began trying out new material on his patients, though he found that if he did get a laugh, it really disrupted his work. He wondered if he would have to make a choice between trying to be a funny guy and being a dentist. As he began to tone down his exam room comedy, he started to become a better listener. As his listening skills improved, so did his stand-up comedy open mics he would do on the weekends. It turned out the dentistry was exactly what he needed for his comedy. What other positive traits has he gained from his dental work?

276. He seemed like a bit of a sleazebag, but he had the best prices on dental work in town, which got him a good deal of customers. He was the kind of dentist who gives dentists a bad name. When he put people under for dental surgery, he would take a couple of bucks from their wallets and record them saying funny things when coming out of a drug-induced haze. He loved blurring out their faces and putting the videos up on YouTube, giving him some additional advertising revenue. He had been sued on more than one occasion, but he'd gotten out of most of them due to a brother who works at the state attorney general's office. In his personal life, he was just as much of a jerk, using his high salary from his dental practice to buy flashy cars and to take superficial women out to a constant party at his favorite club. Will this immoral dentist continue to succeed or will one transgression too many spell the end for his practice?

277. One of the defining events of her life was when she was hit by a car while riding her bike during her middle school years. She survived the ordeal but despite wearing a helmet, her jaw was shattered and her teeth were completely destroyed. If it weren't for dental reconstructive surgery, she would have looked like an absolute freak. The way her teeth were taken care of amazed her and she vowed to go into dental work to help kids and adults to heal, like her dental surgeon had done for her. She worked hard in school, especially because science wasn't a subject that came naturally to her. When she failed an important exam along the way, her parents advised her to give up. She thought back to her laying there on the pavement, mortified at the state she was in and began working even harder. She passed the exam and all future exams to become the dentist she knew she could be. What are some other ways in which she remembers the dentist who saved her mouth?

278. Her family hadn't exactly been the pinnacle of dental health when she was growing up. There was nothing resembling floss anywhere to be seen in the house. There was even sort of a contest between the kids to see who could get the most cavities. That is why she was surprised by her own decision to go to dental school about halfway through college. Part of her choice was made after seeing how meticulously her roommate dealt with her hygiene. This dentist-to-be never realized that teeth could be so well cared for. She also knew she wanted to help people health-wise, but she wasn't as interested in the many years of medical school that would be required. When she told her family they nearly popped a filling. Will she be able to reform her family's decades of poor dental health?

279. He tried to come off like the "cool dentist," but he more closely resembled the crazy, nitrous fanatic in *Little Shop of Horrors*. He loved singing to his patients and thought that such a joyful attitude would set his patients at ease. In reality, they were never sure what exactly he would do next, which completely frightened them. His wife made every effort to tell him that he was making people uncomfortable but he refused to change his ways, causing him to lose most of his patients. He needed an image adjustment or he'd literally never work in this town again. He began researching the most successful dentists in history and tried to mimic all of their best business practices. He had a grand reopening of his business and hoped that giving up being the "cool dentist" would get him back on track. Will he be successful at his second effort despite not being "cool?"

280. She knew that her time was almost up, though she didn't want to admit it to herself. She had been one of the few female dentists in the state when she began and now nearly 45 years later, she was happy to see the balance had shifted. In her younger days, she would go around to the schools preaching the benefits of good dental hygiene. She later had several adults come up to her, telling her how her message had really stuck with them. Dentistry was what she was meant to do in this world and if she retired, she figured it was like signing her own death warrant. She knew it was getting tougher and tougher to do her job though and she decided to hang up her metal pick. What was it about dentistry that made her get into the profession in the first place?

Bakers, Butchers and Farmers

In a world that is becoming more and more digital and mechanical, it's refreshing to see a character have a profession that involves doing something with his or her hands. It can be remarkable watching a baker whip up an out-of-this-world cake, seeing a farmer till a massive property and observing a butcher prepare succulent pieces of meat. Writers tend to portray these characters as less able mentally than those in more computer-based, modern-world professions, but there are many different reasons that these food-producing people work in these get-your-hands-dirty food-based careers.

281. He'd grown up idealizing his mother and the way she carried herself in the kitchen. His dad was rarely around due to travel and as a result most of his childhood life lessons were lightly brushed with flour. His mom had a small side business baking pies and hid some of the money from her husband so he wouldn't spend it on liquor. When he asked his mom if this was a form of lying, she said that freedom was more important than anything else. As he grew up and worked as a baker at several different bakeries, he always kept that phrase in mind. He started saving money until he had enough to start his own bakery, employing his mother's secret pie recipes. He dedicated the shop to her and her fantastic food by calling it "Mom's." What are some of the other things he learned from his mother while growing up?

282. When people asked him how long his family had been in the business of farming he laughed and told them he came from city folk. He had actually been a corporate lackey for nearly half a decade before he decided to pick up his family and move them to a vacated farm. Now about 20 years later, he had used a great deal of his corporate earnings to build a fully sustainable organic farm from the ground up. He didn't miss the urban life, as it was affecting his health and stress levels and he worried his kids might grow up in the wrong kind of crowd. It took him a while to get used to the "Green Acres" lifestyle, but once he got the hang of it, he much preferred it to the busy streets, the smog and the general bad attitude. What are some of the things he misses about the city life and what is his biggest farming challenge?

283. She was loud, she was boisterous and she could wield a meat cleaver like nobody's business. After attempting and failing to strike out on her own as an event planner, she came back to the family business of butchery. She realized that there weren't many women in the industry but she figured if her mom could cut a slab of meat, she certainly could too. After she became officially certified she settled into life as a full-time butcher and planned to take over for her parents when they passed away. As a local business, it was tough surviving in the recession, but her youthful energy and intuitive marketing ideas kept the store going when it might have gone under. Will she ever attempt to leave the business again to start her own path and why or why not?

284. Her alarm went off indicating that it was time to make the donuts, as well as the cakes, the pies and the other pastries. She worked for a chain sandwich and pastry shop and because everything was made fresh each day, she had to get up at what she called "the butt crack of dawn" to get over to the shop for baking. She was glad that she had very specific recipes and guidelines to fulfill, because she knew she wasn't the most creative crayon in the box. She hated having to rise so early, but she did enjoy her co-workers and all the wild morning pranks they would pull on each other. Every once in a while, hours after her shift ended, she would come in from lunch to see how well the pastries she made were selling. Though she wouldn't admit it to many, she had a sense of pride from seeing them sell out. How did she become a baker in the first place and what kind of job might she leave it for?

285. He seemed like your typical meat slicer, though a fateful late night trip proved you didn't know him at all. He had run his own butcher shop for what seemed like forever and you remembered how intimidated you were of him the first time you saw his burly muscles and heard his thick accent. He didn't do specials, he didn't do commercials and he didn't do compliments, but he did prepare the best meat in the county. Upon a suggestion from a friend, you attended a poetry slam and you were surprised to find out that he was one of the frequent contributors. Some of his poems were about meat, while others were about his life after immigrating to the U.S. You were amazed to see the sensitive side of a guy who cuts into dead animal flesh for a living. How did this butcher get such a tough exterior with a gooey poetry center?

286. He had grown up as something as an animal activist on his father's farm. His father did his best but was unable to keep up with all the responsibilities that came with the job, especially treating the animals well. He knew that when he took over the family farm he would make sure that all the animals were raised with the finest food, the freshest water and even better living accommodations than he had. He even created a short video to put online, in an effort to demonstrate that his farm was nothing like the frightening conditions that vegetarians often use to show inhumane animal practices. The farm's conditions became a viral hit and his meat sales shot through the roof. Just before his father passed away, he told his son that he was proud of everything he had done to keep the farm alive. Knowing that his father loved him and was proud of him, was something he'd waited his whole life for. What are some of the more modern ways he farms in comparison to his father?

287. Her life growing up on a farm was probably a lot like what you might think. She had to get up early to do her chores and she was probably dressed in too much flannel. But being a farmer for life was not anywhere close to her dream. She worked hard to make sure she didn't pick up an dialect from living in the middle of nowhere. She made sure to go to a college that was far away and when she got there she dumped all her old clothes and barely spoke of her home life. When she returned home one summer to find her father and mother deathly ill, she started to reconsider her desire to put the farming life behind her. On a whim she decided to bring her boyfriend to the farm and to powwow over whether or not she should stay to watch over the farm that they'd otherwise have to sell. What will she decide to do and what is the thing she disliked the most about telling people she had grown up a farmer's daughter?

288. She hated being told what to do, especially when it came to the kitchen. Her mother wanted to teach her everything about baking from day one and all she wanted to do was to create her own concoctions. While her mother stuck to old recipes using what seemed like ancient equipment, her daughter was all about the newest technology, molecular gastronomy and vegan or vegetarian methodologies when she put her pastries together. Every year around the holidays, these two very different bakers would practically square off in an attempt to get the most adoration from the family. Unsurprisingly, the adults sided with her mom but the younger cousins and siblings always loved what the daughter came up with. What are some of the reasons she decided to become a baker like her mother, while using completely different methods?

289. He needed a miracle and he never expected it to come from anything resembling the Internet. His farm was in trouble and despite government assistance it looked like it might go under. Most of his family had moved off to less rural areas long ago and a distant niece helped him to try for a last ditch effort. She was going to help him crowd fund the farm. The two of them came up with a video and the proper campaign and rewards he would offer as part of a small donation to his business. He didn't really understand how it all worked and for most of his life he'd resented such "new-fangled" technology. When the donations began rolling in, allowing him to continue the work he'd done his whole life, his resentment turned into gratitude for such amazing technology. How will this newly funded farmer embrace the worldwide attention his online campaign has given him?

290. She was a farmer, beekeeper and urban sophisticate all rolled up into one. She had always loved seeing fresh jam and honey stands throughout the south where she grew up. Despite the fact that she lived in one of the coldest major cities in the country, she wanted to give her southern traditions a go. While most of her friends were off partying on the weekends, she tended to fresh fruit and raised bees in her backyard. She invested hundreds of dollars in the proper equipment, despite not having much income in the first place and she began to tour the farmer's markets with her city-raised products. It certainly wasn't easy and she realized on many occasions why most farmers dealt with their craft in a more remote location. She knew that despite these difficulties, she had found her calling, creating preserves and sweet spreads just a few blocks from a major freeway. What are some of the aspects of her vocation that made her want to do it in the first place?

Doctors and Nurses

We hope that whenever we are ill or if our loved ones are injured that they will be taken care of by proficient doctors and nurses. Writers tend to use one of two viewpoints of doctors. They are either experts and spend every waking moment thinking about the health of others or they act like high school students trying to have sex with each other at any given moment. It's up to us as the writers of the future to create more well-rounded characters that have flaws but don't act like morally vapid sex-maniacs either. Nurses are frequently portrayed as angry or careless individuals who get in the way of healthcare. It's time to push past the clichés and create some flawed but realistic doctors and nurses in our stories.

291. His entire life he knew he was going to be a doctor. This wasn't necessarily a result of an extreme desire on his part, more so it was his parents' desire. As immigrants to this country, they wanted their son to be extremely well off so that they could easily be flown back and forth between their homeland and here. After his parents drilled the idea of being a doctor into his head for so many years, he couldn't help but examine it from every side. He wanted to please his parents and he enjoyed helping people. Could he have put those desires to other ends? Sure, he thought,

but why not keep his parents happy and save some lives in the process. What did he use as motivation through medical school and will his parents ultimately be happy with his hard work?

292. Despite his best efforts to turn his hospital into something resembling the show *Grey's Anatomy*, all he got was a series of sexual harassment charges. He'd been a full-fledged doctor for a few years before someone turned him onto a show where doctors and nurses have sexual relationships and more drama than you can fit in a trauma ward. He knew that his hospital didn't quite work like that but he wondered if he made a few advances here, a bouquet of flowers there, if he might be able to spice up his work life a bit. His flirting only resulted in allegations of inappropriate behavior and his attempt to send flowers to a married co-worker turned into a stand-off at the local watering hole. He supposed that his life helping people and having polite conversations with co-workers would have to suffice. What are some of the other aspects of medical dramas did he try to infuse into his place of work?

293. To say she grew up in a bit of a backwards family was quite the understatement. When she informed her parents that she wanted to become a doctor, they immediately refused to help her with even one penny toward such an education-intensive profession. They wanted her to find a husband who would take care of her and pay for anything she needed. When she said she wanted to help people who were sick, they said that she could go to a two-year nursing program after she had a child or two with this hypothetical wealthy husband. She worked twice as hard to cobble together the money for the parts of her education that loans wouldn't cover. After becoming a doctor, she made it a point to speak in front of youth organizations, telling them never to give up on their dreams, even if their parents say that they will never happen. What are some traits she needed to develop to put herself through her education?

294. Medicine is a field that requires perfection from day to day and she was just the person to spread that message. This taskmaster dealt with the interns when they arrived at her hospital each year and she had no issue putting the fear of God into them. She didn't yell or single anybody out, she simply had the sternest demeanor you've ever seen and a look from her could get you to quickly back off of whatever point you were trying to make. She was a brilliant doctor as well and her esteemed reputation had been earned in many ways over the past decade at the facility. If she had one shortcoming, it was her difficulty sympathizing with those who were related to a patient. She felt that the best thing for them to do was to let her do her job as opposed to putting extra pressure on her to succeed. What are a few of the reasons she got into medicine in the first place and has anyone ever broken through her gruff exterior?

295. He knew from a young age that he wanted to be a doctor; he simply didn't have the academic chops to back it up. His friends and family advised him to give up on his dream so that he didn't experience the disappointment they knew was coming. He simply smiled and kept working. Throughout his undergraduate education he had multiple tutors pushing his D's up to B's. He studied for the MCAT for nearly a year just to get himself to the point of the bare minimum required to get into a sub-par medical school. He continued to employ former medical students to tutor him. He gave up relationships and countless social events to that he could work and study as long and as hard as he needed to so that he could succeed. He did eventually become a doctor, though it took him two more years than most. Despite his low grades throughout his schooling, he ended up becoming a pioneer of many surgical techniques in the industry. What was it about being a doctor that motivated him so much to succeed?

296. He was a beer guzzling, sports watching kind of guy and his friends teased him endlessly about the fact that he was a male nurse. The only reason he was willing to accept it all was because this was the first time he'd felt like he was meant to do something in life. He'd be a tough kid and was on the outskirts of several gangs in the inner city. When a friend of his was shot, a male nurse helped him to cope with the situation and convinced him to find a new group of friends. From that point on, he knew that he wanted to help people in the same way that nurse helped him. When his friends mocked him, he almost always had the same retort, "When you guys have a beer-induced heart attack, you're gonna be glad I became a nurse." Has he experienced any resistance to his career choice from his family and peers?

297. She laughed when her peers asked if nursing was her first career choice. After all, her 50th birthday coincided with her first day on the job. She had been a part of a series of jobs throughout her life. She had once been

a librarian, a day care worker and a Sunday school teacher. Once her children were all grown up and out of the house, she looked in the mirror one day and asked herself what she truly wanted to do. The answer was to heal the sick. She went back to school for a nursing degree and within three years she had finally found her calling after five decades of life. The experience she was able to bring to the profession was invaluable for her peers and the hospital was very happy to have her there. She'd done many things that provoked pride in her life, but her daily routine in her new job topped all of them. What made her decide she wanted to help the sick?

298. Throughout her education, one thing that her teachers noticed about her was that she was skilled at multitasking. No matter how many different projects, assignments and activities she had on her plate, she could deal with them all. She later applied these skills to a successful nursing career. While many believed that the advanced technology of medicine now did most of the work for doctors and nurses, it was still often up to her and her peers to notice small changes in the health of their patients. She was better able than most to keep in mind the very specific health conditions of multiple people per day, allowing her to notice even the slightest dip in health in a patient. This unique ability had saved the lives of dozens over the years and she was proud to be able to pull off such a balancing act from day to day. What are some of the other ways in which she employs this ability outside of her job?

299. He felt like something of a failure. All of his life he'd wanted to be a doctor but life continued to intervene. When he and his girlfriend became pregnant, there was no way he'd be able to go to medical school and leave his new son with a mostly absent father. He settled instead for nursing school, which was no picnic either, but it gave him more time to start his family off right. When he couldn't get a job at any hospitals nearby, he picked up his family and moved to the middle of nowhere so that he could get a job at a country doctor's office. His girlfriend hated moving away from the city and rarely let him hear the end of it. He kept envisioning a different life for himself in some different dimension in which things had gone differently. He wished he could have been a doctor and felt ashamed every day. What are some of his other life goals that he has been unable to achieve?

300. Her whole life she'd been a follower. Her best friend was charismatic and interesting and she could only dream to have qualities like that. When her friend went to school to become a nurse, of course she signed up in hopes of securing a career in which she could follow her friend for the rest of time. When her friend quit school with a week remaining to run into the arms of a statuesque Cuban immigrant, she wasn't sure what to do with herself. Her friend was moving over a thousand miles away and she was just a week away from a degree she wasn't sure she wanted. She began reading self-help books about self-esteem and being your own person. She found a job in her field and figured out how to find joy in even the little things she did there. She still thought of her friend from time to time but was glad that she was finally able to strike out on her own. What had caused her to be such a follower earlier in her life?

Lawyers

Lawyers get a bad rap as money-hungry, greedy, slimy characters who are as willing to get an obvious perpetrator off the hook for a horrible crime as they are an honest soul; as long as a paycheck is involved. In reality, there are lawyers of many different varieties, many of whom aren't even found in a court room. Sure, there are lawyers that you see on television that are involved in high-profile cases, but there are also government employed attorneys who make an effort to get restitution for citizens who have been ripped off or otherwise taken advantage of. In addition, due to a rough economy, those who attend law school are not always assured a hefty salary, especially if they go into business for themselves. Test out a few off-kilter lawyers in your story to keep the clichés at bay.

301. He'd spent most of his high school and college days assuming he would be a protester for the environment. About halfway through his undergraduate years, he realized he might be able to do more from the inside and readied himself for a path of environmental law. He knew it would be a lot of hard work but he wanted to be able to make a difference while at the same time sustaining himself through a high paying job. Over the course of a decade, he worked his way up into one of the country's top environmental law firms and had a hand in important legislation that could improve the health of the world. What do his protester buddies from college think of his ascent into the corporate aspects of environmentalism?

302. When he decided to go to law school, he was completely in it for the money. After an internship at the state attorney general's office, however, he became infinitely more intrigued by the political side of the legal profession. He knew that by being part of a high-ranking firm, he would make more money than he could ever dream of. But he didn't realize how much lawyers in the government can affect policy and literally change the face of how people conduct themselves and their businesses at the local, state and national level. Sure, he would be able to help the disadvantaged to fight back against wrongs they had been dealt, but he wasn't in it for the charity. He wanted to be an attorney general so that he could have power and influence. What is it about him that have made money and power so important to him in his career?

303. To say she didn't like losing was putting it mildly. This high powered criminal prosecutor had never lost a trial despite being a part of many difficult and controversial cases. She had been competitive her entire life, going back to her youthful dance competition days, up through high school field hockey and eventually with perfect grades in high school and college. During those earlier years, her emotions frequently got the best of her when she wasn't able to succeed. She learned emotional control techniques and went to years of therapy to keep herself calm under pressure. Ultimately though, only one tried and true method prevailed: not losing. She knew that if she could win every case, she would effectively prevent herself from having another emotional breakdown. What is her formula for success to winning consistently in the court room?

304. As she chased down yet another ambulance, she wondered how her life had gotten to this point. She once believed that her quest to become a lawyer was going to be the perfect combination of her vast interpersonal skills and her desire to help people in need. She truly felt pride in her work when she was offered a position at a major firm. A few years later, however, a poor financial market caused them to let all their newest employees go. She tried to start a private practice but found that unless she worked all day long to find clients, she wouldn't be able to afford the car and high-rent apartment she'd purchased during her initial position. She hoped in the end this would all be worth it. How does she feel that her current position has compromised some of her earlier ideals?

305. He was in the middle of law school when it happened, a drunk driver careened into his car as he was pulled over to the side of the road. He lost the use of his legs and he battled the depression that came after it by dedicating himself fully to physical therapy and his studies. He always saw when businesses and regular citizens were breaking the law as he grew up, that's one of the reasons he got into the industry. Seeing the world from a different angle as a disabled person made him realize just how little people cared about the American Disabilities Act. He once again threw himself into his work to find the businesses and individuals who were preventing those with disabilities from leading a normal life. After becoming one of the most well known lawyers on the subject of the ADA, he no longer regretted what had happened to him; it was all meant to be. What are some examples of ways he's improved the lives of the disabled?

306. His peers made fun of the fact that he was so close to his family, even though in part, they were jealous of him. His mother was actually famous for the time she came late into the legal library to bring him a midnight sandwich. He was never embarrassed by their conduct, even when they hooted and hollered the loudest when he received his law degree. There was no question that he would go into family law, attempting to help families to remain civil during some of the most difficult times in their lives. He felt grateful every time he heard a divorcing couple argue or when parents would scold a damaged, runaway child. He knew it could have easily been him with such a complex and painful family situation. He eventually became a father himself and truly knew the gift his parents had given him. What are some of the lessons he learned from his family that he was able to use in his practice of law?

307. She had made it fairly clear early on, she was in law for the money. This was the main reason she got into corporate law. When millions if not billions of dollars changed hands, adding in a paltry six-figure number for legal costs wasn't much of an issue. Ever since she'd read stories of the famously rich families like the Waltons or the Buffetts, she knew she wanted to be rolling in the dough. She'd worked so hard during high school and college, she actually had enough to pay for law school before the first tuition bill arrived, allowing her to save much of her inordinately large salary right away. She didn't love the 70 plus hours of work per week, but she was willing to do nearly anything to be financially well off. When she made the final payment on her beach front property, she kicked

her feet up and knew that all of it had been worth it. What caused her to be so interested in money as to make it her life's focus?

308. While she'd always wanted to be famous, her talent and looks weren't as kind to her as her ability to argue her way around anything. She had to settle for being "the lawyer to the stars," and her clients were frequently on the front covers of magazines and on the top of the Hollywood box office. When she thought back to her childhood desires to be famous, she wondered what the allure was. She was already invited to some of the biggest and fanciest parties, had millions of dollars to spend and spent time on movie sets around the world. What she didn't have to deal with was her name in the papers every other day with paparazzi coming from every direction. She had everything Hollywood had to offer without the drawbacks. Who were some of the most famous people she worked with and what was her favorite part about supporting those in the limelight?

309. Every year, he wondered if what he was doing meant anything. He'd gotten into scholastic law in an effort to help kids to be protected from the system, but more and more he was finding that kids were the aggressors. There were more children bringing weapons to school and participating in horrible acts. The worst thing in his opinion was that they were receiving support from their parents to continue such heinous activities. He had been thoroughly bullied in school and thought that being on kids' side could prevent bullying in the future. Defending a child during an assault trial in which the student obviously perpetrated the crime against his teacher was not this lawyer's idea of making a difference. He considered changing careers, but his own family was already dependent on the amount of money he was making. He felt as though he was completely stuck. Will he be able to figure out a way into a new career or will he somehow improve the condition of his current job?

310. She chose her words carefully, since she was in the business of carefully and not so carefully chosen words. When someone wrote or said something slanderous, she was there to defend that person, using every legal crutch at her disposal. She had grown up in a country where free speech was not possible and by standing true to this fundamental right, she felt like she could make a difference in the world. She often thought back to her youth and how she could tell how much more her mother had to offer by the intelligent glances she would give her every single day. She felt that if someone tried to take away these rights, it would be like the world had adopted the policies that shut her and her peers up as females and children. She still had to choose her words carefully in court, but she was able to speak them with passion and truth and for that she was grateful. What are some of her earliest memories without free speech and how does she exercise this right outside of the courtroom?

Child Care

Due to two-income households and extremely busy parents, child care has grown by leaps and bounds in the last few decades. As the son of a mother who is in the child care industry, I know that there are high highs and low lows in getting to experience these important moments in a child's life. Some people involved in child care have had their hands in the development of many children, while some are simply looking for gainful employment. In addition, there are a few child care professionals who are more involved in the lives of kids in their care than the children's parents. This leads to some very interesting dynamics between children and their caretakers.

311. Every morning he stared for a few minutes at his college degree. He wondered if all the bills he was now paying off were worth it. After all, he hadn't gotten a job in his field of journalism despite his best efforts. Since he couldn't get a job, his mother hooked him up with a family who needed a nanny. He was so proficient at his job that other families in the neighborhood began to snatch him up for evening babysitting jobs. He went from his dream of becoming an editor for some large publication to working 70 hours a week as a child care enthusiast. The thing is, he was actually a better nanny than he ever was an editor and he was raking in a small fortune from these suburban parents. Had he actually found his calling in child care or was this just on stop in the road to his dream?

312. When he told his parents he wanted to take care of children professionally, they pushed him in the direction of being a pediatrician or a child psychologist. He yielded to their demands for a while and even got so far as medical school before he started his own day care center. He loved the idea of helping kids to grow, not to heal them when they were at their lowest, like the professions his parents forced him toward. He didn't want to see children in pain, he wanted to see happy kids and to help them to become happier. He knew that to appease his parents though, his

business would need to make as much money as a doctor and he struggled every day with the business side of things. Will he ever be able to convince his parents that this is what he's meant to be doing?

313. Her kids were all grown up now and they'd moved out of the house to start their own lives. She missed lugging around her boys and thought long and hard about getting back into the parenting business for someone else's kids. She found a job as a nanny for a pair of lawyers who were too busy to deal with the day-to-day kid-related tasks. As a mom, she was perfect for the job and she'd always wanted to have a girl. This job would give her three of them. There were challenges as she wasn't as fast as she used to be, making it difficult to chase the little tykes around. Despite some issues every now and then, she felt completely renewed and she spoke about her "second family" whenever she got the chance. What are some of the things she likes the most about nannying?

314. She had scored one of the cushiest jobs for an actress in the big city: a nanny gig. A great deal of her friends who were slaving away at temp jobs were completely jealous. Her job paid more and had better hours. What they didn't know was that it was tough work! It was true that she had no trouble acting silly with them and keeping them entertained, but there were tears and colds and bathroom issues to deal with. The parents wouldn't always get home on time, making her late to rehearsal and hangouts. Despite these difficulties, she wouldn't trade her job for the world, as it was giving her valuable experience for the far off day (she hoped) when she would become a mom herself. What are some of the ways in which she uses her acting talents to entertain the kids?

315. You and your spouse were hesitant before the interview, after all, how many male nannies had they ever even heard of before? Still, they wanted to be open-minded about the process and when they met him, they were glad they did. He was the most organized, well-trained and kind person they had ever met. He showed them pages and pages of references, certificates and even hand-drawings previous kids he'd watched had made him. They observed him with their infant for a few minutes and they were amazed to find that he was much more level-headed with him than they ever could be. He was the perfect manny. For formality's sake, they waited a day before hiring him for the next five years. How did this individual become so good at his job?

316. He was pretty much your last ditch effort. Your kids were pretty close to being old enough to watch themselves but you knew you needed a semi-adult to keep an eye on them in case they did anything stupid. Bring in your next door neighbor's son, who wasn't exactly the sharpest of saws. He'd asked on more than one occasion if he could watch your kids over the last couple of years, and he was perfectly nice, despite being a complete moron. You'd heard your neighbor talking about the dumb things their son had done when he was younger, such as almost burning down the house on multiple occasions. But you hoped that he'd become more mature over the last few years because you absolutely had to have a night to yourselves for your sanity. When he came over wearing a marijuana propaganda T-shirt, 20 minutes late, you wondered if you made the right decision. Describe this babysitter's evening trying to make sure that he and your kids wouldn't do something stupid.

317. She was elderly, infirm and she didn't get around nearly as well as when she had kids of her own. Oh, and she was absolutely free because she was your mother-in-law. She absolutely loved to be responsible for your kids and gave you a much needed date night every two weeks or so. You weren't sure exactly what she and the kids did together but afterwards it seemed like both parties were completely beaming. Your kids wanted her to come back as often as possible and your mother-in-law felt the same way. You had to know what they were doing that was so fun as to nearly prefer her over you and your spouse. You set up a hidden teddy-cam to find out the answer. What are they doing while you're on your date night and why is it so fun?

318. She could not believe how long it took her parents to leave her alone with her little brother. They finally trusted her to watch over him after years of her begging to do it. She loved her brother, even though he could be a pain sometimes and she really wanted to take care of him for a whole evening. She had it all planned out, she would make him a snack and they'd watch a movie together. It would be amazing. There was only one problem. While she was making the snack, her brother snuck out of the house and she had no idea where he could have gone. Will she be able to resolve the situation before her parents come home and will they ever trust her again?

319. When your father, a retired Army colonel, said he wanted to watch your kids for the night to give you two an evening on the town, you were worried. Your dad wasn't always around due to constant touring and training but

when he was, he was quite the disciplinarian. You felt like he had a tough time discerning between kids and Army recruits. Then again, since you and your spouse were quite pacifistic, perhaps your kids could stand for their butts to be kicked a bit. You gave it a shot and noticed the next day that your children were acting a bit differently. They were actually behaving. What did your dad do with the kids to get them more in line?

320. After receiving the news that she'd never be able to have children of her own, she decided to devote her life to taking care of kids that weren't hers. She started by watching her sister's kids whenever her sister had to go out of town. She followed it up by volunteering at Church every Sunday watching the kids of the congregation. Eventually, she got several certifications and began working in a high-end day-care facility, surrounding herself with kids every day. When she met her husband, a single-father whose wife had passed a few years earlier, she was overjoyed that she finally had the chance to raise a child of her own for the long haul. Will she ever attempt to utilize a fertility clinic to attempt to have a child of her own flesh and blood?

Sailors, Captains and Fishermen

From *Moby Dick* to "The Deadliest Catch" we have always been amazed by the wonders of the sea. While exploration and expedition is no longer a major part of our culture, in the past, journeys by sailors like Sir Ernest Shackleton led to amazing tales to far-away lands that we could only dream about or YouTube today. Devoting your life to the sea at any point in history has always been difficult on a family due to the many days, weeks and years out among the waves. In addition, many jobs and sojourns across the sea can be dangerous and when accidents occur, medical help may be far away. If you plan to take your story to the seas, make sure to include a few of these salty dogs.

321. When the ship became stuck on the ice, hundreds of miles away from the nearest civilization, some of the new men in the crew worried. Those who had been through it all with this mythical captain knew that they had nothing to fear. Despite the dangerous expeditions they had endured in water riddled with icebergs, pirates and gargantuan sea creatures, he had never lost a single man on any of his missions. Immediately, this storied leader began assigning tasks to crew members to keep them from worrying about their predicament. He created games and contests and essentially turned the boat into a sort of working cruise while they all waited to get free from the ice. He never did make it to his final destination, but he knew that it wouldn't have been worth it if he'd lost a single man. How did this leader get such perceptive qualities when it came to dealing in crisis?

322. He staked his reputation on catching his own personal white whale. It wasn't really a whale though, it was more like a large salmon who had evaded his ship earlier in the month by biting the tip of the captain's finger off. The captain had become the laughing stock of the fishing industry and he'd lost the respect of his crew. In order to get back his sea-cred, he took his ship back out to sea to find the salmon who'd taken the tip of a finger that was very near and dear to him. He pushed the crew to the brink of exhaustion and refused to let them sleep in more than four hours shifts. He had never been so angry in all his life and as a result, he pushed his logic far back in his brain. Even if a crew member was able to calm him down for an instant, whenever he looked back at his bandaged finger, the rage sprung up anew. Will he be successful at catching this "evil" salmon and if so, will his personality return to normal?

323. She loved the feeling of the salty air against her cheeks as her crew worked to get her as many fish as they could handle. Many of the grizzled, bearded seamen who had a stranglehold on the industry laughed when she took up the trade. She didn't care what they thought though, because she'd always known she was meant for the sea one way or another. She put together a rag tag crew of fishermen that everyone had given up on. They reminded her of herself and she knew should could light a fire under them. Through appealing to their sense of pride from great achievement, she created a bonus and award system that made them push farther and harder than they ever had on the other boats. She was also kind and compassionate, which catered to their low levels of self-esteem. How did she come to be a part of the industry and what kind of satisfaction does she get from it?

324. It had never occurred to her that she was the leader of her friends until they were dealing with a major crisis situation. A freak storm during a tour caused the captain of the boat to fall overboard, leaving them alone, none of them with enough boating experience to deal with the situation. They needed a leader and as a frequent party planner

and all around fast-talker, she became the person in command quickly. She calmed down those who were freaking out and she started giving orders that forced other people to listen to her. She felt a strange sensation, as if she was finally coming into what she was meant to do. Through her leadership, they retrieved the fallen captain and made it back to shore. She'd never felt so alive and wanted to continue that sensation by becoming a non-accidental captain. What are some of the qualities she was able to exhibit during a tense situation?

325. On every fishing boat, there were certain types of people that you wanted to have on board. One of those people was the good luck charm, the person who always seems to stumble on the best possible catches too often to call it random. The crew called the man who held the position on your boat, "The Fish Whisperer." It was like something out of a movie. He would sit on the side of the boat for a few minutes, simply looking down and whistling. When he was done with his routine, he would direct you where to take the boat and nine times out of 10, you returned with the biggest haul you'd ever seen. A few of the crew members thought that he must have some kind of deal with the devil and you wondered sometimes if he had an occult connection. Then again, perhaps he was just a fish savant that you were lucky to have. How would he describe his own fish whispering ability?

326. When he first said he wanted to come on board as a deckhand, his family laughed uproariously. After all, he'd always been the weakest and youngest kid in the family and they still laughed about an incident in which he'd been blown over by a strong gust of wind as a child. He knew that this would be the opportunity to prove himself, to finally rid himself of the stigma of being a weakling. His father rode him hard while they were out trying to catch fish, mostly because he wanted him to give up and go back to the safety of land. This intense scrutiny only made him work harder and over time, he became one of the strongest members of the crew, though his father wouldn't admit it. He even saved his father's life when the proud captain fell overboard into freezing Arctic waters. He was the "baby brother" no longer; he was a man. How does he feel now that he has a new level of respect from his family?

327. She wasn't there for fish or a desire to breathe in the salty air. She was there for love and to keep her boyfriend alive as he embarked on one of the most dangerous jobs in the world. She took on a position as a nurse, which was direly needed due to the frequent injuries of the men on board. She didn't want her love to go, but since he wouldn't relent, she forced her way on board to keep an eye on him. Don't take her devotion to mean any sort of weakness, though, because her strong will eventually became the glue that held the ship together. She was boisterously funny and it wasn't until he saw her interacting with the rest of the crew that he knew she had to be the woman he spent the rest of his life with. What are some situations in which she had to use her skill and strength to protect the boat's crew?

328. Plenty of kids had used their parents money to become the youngest ever to circumnavigate the world. She had no chance at that title, since she was pushing 75, but she did have another championship belt in sight. She wanted to be the oldest woman to perform the feat alone. Her husband had died a few years ago and with her family paying little attention to her, she began training for her new life challenge. She had always been a fan of the water, but since the love of her life abhorred the ocean, she was relegated to lakes and swimming pools. When her family found out about her impending journey, they tried to stop her and even made an effort to put her in a home. She laughed and did it anyway without their permission. It was an incredibly difficult task and on several occasions she almost didn't make it through alive. In the end though, she was victorious. How will her family treat her now that she has made her way into the record books?

329. As the clock reached five in the afternoon, he took the last papers out of his inbox and began writing a note. The note acted as his immediate resignation. This paper pusher nudged his glasses back up the bridge of his nose as he thought of his exciting impending adventure. He had used all of his 401k and his retirement funds to buy a boat. He would no longer be bound by his boring tasks at work and he promised himself he'd never have an inbox again. He set sail on a foggy morning and he never looked back. He became an expert fisherman and a decent cook. He met others who had embarked upon the same lifestyle and he knew that this was what he was meant to do. On the one year anniversary of his decision, he came back home and threw a giant party that was attended by hundreds he'd met throughout the year. After decades of cubicle captivity, he finally felt free. What are some of the challenges he's faced living on the water?

330. Your boat spotted an archaic ship floating in the waters and moved in its direction. You and two of your crew members boarded the ship after attempting to elicit a response. You were amazed at what you saw. A woman, dressed in clothing from hundreds of years ago was passed out on board. After reviving her, she began speaking in an English that hadn't been used since the time of the British colonies. You could barely understand what she said, but soon you realized that her and her ship had somehow been transported hundreds of years in the future. She was delicate but tough and gave off a prickly vibe to most of the crew except for yourself. As you described the events of the past few hundred years, she laughed, and seemed to take it rather well considering. What will this sea-woman from the past do with herself in the present day?

Salespeople

The most effective salespeople in the world are simply people who have a way with words who have determined to turn their talent into profit. There are many different types of salespeople from the honest car dealer attempting to give your family the best deal possible to the telemarketer who has sold thousands of dollars worth of insurance policies using less than forthcoming coercion. While sales can be a part of many different jobs (for example, a writer must sell himself as an expert in his field or type of fiction), master salesmen have the ability to craft words perfectly and understand exactly what a customer may want.

331. He'd been working in promotional gigs for several consecutive years. He had planned on being an actor or a speaker but this area of work held his interest because he was good at it and his skill enabled him to earn multiple bonuses. Whether it was juice, salad or shoes, he sold nearly double the company average because he knew how to talk to people. He would almost affect a different personality for each person who came by in an effort to mimic their energy and seem like he was on the same wavelength. He had been something of a nerd in high school and college, but he learned how to connect with all people positively to become more popular. He was now using that skill for financial gain. Will he continue to stay in sales or will he use his new skills for another line of work?

332. Ever since he was a little kid, he loved the concept of the telephone. All he seemed to want for his birthday or Christmas each year was either a toy phone, a phone accessory or someone to talk to. He couldn't stop talking and his parents enrolled him in a public speaking class that was mostly for older students and adults. It didn't matter how young he was, he ran circles around the other members of his class. When his dad found that his son was referring customers to his lawn care business at a rapid pace, he got his protégé started with a cold calling job that got him extra allowance. Soon, his father's business became one of the biggest in the state, due to his son's incredible ability to sell. Eventually, he left for college, getting into an Ivy League college almost completely because of the interview. What are some of the techniques this super salesman uses to convince people to act?

333. When her friend started one of the first daily deal companies in existence, she considered leaving her relatively cushy job in insurance sales. After all, she'd built up a nice little nest egg for herself already and the job would probably still be there for her if the deal company crashed and burned. It didn't. Not only did she secure major stock options for herself by being one of the first employed by the company, but she also was the first to broker national deals that would be purchased by millions of people. Within three months of signing on, she had become a millionaire through commissions. Her friend saw her skill and appointed her to nearly every national deal the company tried to lock down, which allowed her to make nearly a million dollars a month for the next seven months. She knew that she was lucky to be in the right place at the right time and she was grateful for the extremely high earning position. What will this lifetime salesperson do with her millions?

334. One day when she was calling her mother to pick her up from school, her mother said, "Honey, will you stop using that sexy voice when you're talking to me?" She didn't understand, because that was her normal post-puberty voice. It turned out that even though she was relatively average in most ways, she had a voice that tended to drive both men and women crazy. She took a summer sales job before college to pay for some incidentals and quickly became the top selling person in the company, despite only being there for three months as a glorified intern. Her commissions alone paid for her first two semesters at college and she could hardly believe it. She found a similar job each summer and by the time she graduated, she was ready to put down a hefty deposit on a house. What is it that causes so many people to succumb to her attractive voice?

335. The rent was due and he felt like his luck had finally run out. After a promising business career, he'd been fired from his last three jobs due to a misunderstanding, a company bankruptcy and a lack of aptitude. He took up a straight commission job because it was the only one he could find. He was terrible at it at first and he dreaded coming into work. While attending a little league baseball game of his nephew's, he realized that the kids who did the best weren't always the strongest, they were the most enthusiastic. He began employing as much enthusiasm as possible while he was at work and he started to become much more excited about his job. Within a month, he had risen in the ranks and was making more than enough money to keep his apartment. He gave his nephew a huge gift for his next birthday. What are some of the ways in which enthusiasm helped him to grow as a salesperson?

336. As he walked down the row of cubicles, he saw so many unhappy faces of his fellow salesmen and women. He wondered how so many people could be glum doing a job that he personally loved every second of. Unlike some of his co-workers, he wasn't in the sales business to earn a wage, make the big bucks or to convince people to get something they didn't need. He was a believer in the sales principle that you need to see what a person actually needs and then help him or her to get it. Not only had this philosophy kept him near the top of the sales rankings each quarter, but it also made him feel like he was doing something worthwhile, which is a much better motivator than money ever could be. He woke up every day with a smile on his face and couldn't wait to clock in. How does this optimistic fellow apply this philosophy in other parts of his life?

337. She was hardly a natural at anything she did, but she was a sponge when it came to information. When she wanted to become a softball player, she read every book possible about swinging, running and catching and she ended up being the captain. When she had trouble with French in high school, she absorbed books and books about the language and the culture and she blew the teacher's socks off during the final oral exam. When she got a sales job after high school, she nearly got fired in the first week for screwing up left and right. Over the next few weeks, she read every book possible on the subject and turned herself into a sales making machine. During a winter sales contest, where the first prize was a major bonus, she had nearly double the sales of the second place runner up. What was it about her that allowed her to take in so much knowledge from her book reading?

338. She was nervous, after all, she'd been out of work for nearly five years while taking care of her kids. She hadn't been completely without income, of course, as she'd been a prolific online re-seller during most of that time. She started buying items at garage sales in her spare time and reselling them on an online auction site, in an attempt to bring in a bit more income. She found that she was a natural at selling these items using her elaborate descriptions and soon she was the primary bread winner in the family. Business had been slow in the past year and now that her kids were growing up, she thought she'd try her hand at a sales job she actually had to put dress pants on to do. She hoped that her skills would translate over or she'd be as sunk as that Troll doll she tried to auction. Will she succeed at the job and if so, what parts of her experience will she be able to use?

339. He loved talking about his days as a door-to-door salesman. He would travel all over the country testing out products like vacuum cleaners and laundry detergents in a world where you could actually knock on doors without being afraid for your life. He still did some sales-related work on the Internet and had actually built up a good income for himself in an industry usually thought to be for the younger kids. He had no trouble adapting, just like he'd adapted when his wife passed away. He knew she wouldn't want him to spend his life crying over her, that he had to continue to be who he was: a salesman. His favorite story was when he sold a woman, who was starting her own cleaning business, on over $250 worth of equipment, back when that was worth a lot. He took pride in knowing that the woman's business was still functioning in a modern world. What are some of his other favorite stories to tell about the good old days?

340. All his life he wanted to follow in his father's footsteps. He saw his dad unloading cars left and right so quickly that on several occasions they ran out of vehicles to sell, so the story goes. His dad explained to him exactly how to judge what kind of vehicle a person wanted and how to keep the potential sale from walking out the door. He looked up to his father so much that as soon as he got out of high school he began trying to sell cars at a dealership across town. Once he had the experience, he figured his dad would hire him to work side-by-side. The only issue was, he was a terrible salesman. Whenever he tried to use large adjectives to describe a vehicle he felt like he was lying. In fact, the entire time he was selling he felt like he was doing something wrong that would damage the

lives of families who could do just as well with a used car. Will he be able to get past his mental blocks to become a car salesman like his dad?

Models and Dancers

While many of us have now been privy to see the lives of models and dancers on shows like "America's Next Top Model" and "So You Think You Can Dance," for me, it is impossible for me to think like characters of this type without referencing the movie *Zoolander*. Ben Stiller and Owen Wilson portrayed such ridiculous, hilarious male models, that you couldn't help but mock such self-centered, self-conscious individuals. Obviously, not all models and dancers fall into that mold, but it's important to remember the comedic potential of characters that must so meticulously maintain their outward appearances.

341. His parents were at the top of their respective fields: psychology and philosophy. They had written books on the subject and they were regarded as far beyond intellectual. When he realized that he was never going to come close to their level of wisdom, he embarked on a quest to find an industry he could be at the top of. He had the height and the build to be photographed and he joined up with a local modeling agency. They told him that if he looked flawless and exercised incessantly, he could be featured in advertisements from New York to California. He worked incredibly hard and he became an icon in modeling. What are his parents' thoughts about his career choice and how does he react to their opinions?

342. He had been one of the chubbiest kids in school, but he was active and doctors told his parents that when he hit puberty he would lengthen out to a healthier weight. But his doctors never expected this. As he grew and his features filled it, he became an absolute dream to look at. His classmates quickly forgot the heavy kid they used to poke fun at and began losing themselves in his looks each and every day. On a summer trip with his parents, he earned a modeling contract in California and the entire family moved out there to support him. With his advertisements in magazines and catalogues, now it was more than his classmates that were staring at him. Despite all this, he couldn't help but still think of himself as a chubby kid. How will his less than attractive beginnings affect him as he continues in this line of work?

343. She was one of the top candidates on a modeling reality show and she felt she had exactly what the judges were looking for. She had sex appeal but it wasn't too overt. She was skinny but she wasn't too thin. Plus, she had a way of getting under the other models' skins without them knowing she was the one planting a seed of doubt. She would pretend to love and compliment the others, when in actuality, they were backhanded compliments causing them to feel awful about themselves. Through the weeks of the competition, she had singlehandedly caused about three of the eliminations. When it finally came down to the last three, all of her vindictiveness finally came out and the judges questioned if she was honest enough to be a part of the industry. Will she be able to rise above her personality to win the competition?

344. She was living out her dream as a successful model, but she barely had any time to enjoy it. Almost every day involved 16 or more hours of runways, casting calls and hair and makeup sessions and she felt like she never had a chance to breathe, let alone eat during it all. Before she found her success, she was at the gym three hours a day to keep herself in shape. Now, the constant working and the mini-food that she found at each event was causing her to lose weight despite the lack of training. She wondered if she had made the right decision, after all, part of having a career she loved, was about sitting back and appreciating what she'd accomplished, she thought. Will she continue on in modeling or will the tough schedule cause her to burn out?

345. When he got into dancing, he knew what he was getting into. After all, he figured out that he wanted to be a dancer after watching the musical, *Billy Elliott*, in which a kid gets bullied for dancing. He never kept things secret and immediately told his friends and his family the kind of life he wanted. He wasn't surprised when his dad tried pushing him back in the direction of more masculine sports. He also wasn't surprised when his friends asked if he was gay. He told them that dancing had nothing to do with his sexual preference and it was just something he loved. Through all of this he persevered and put it all in the back of his mind for his first New York audition. What are some of the other hardships he's faced as a young dancer?

346. When other kids had pictures of buxom babes on their wall, he had pictures of sleek dancers who caught his fancy. While others were saving up their money for comic books and movies, he was trying to pay for dance classes in secret. When he tried to convince his parents to let him go away to dance school, he thought they would be completely unsupportive. It turned out, they loved the idea of him following his passion and they encouraged him 100 percent. After all, all he talked about was dancing and famous dancers, they had a sneaking suspicion he wouldn't be going into politics. With one hurdle down, how will he ultimately break into the industry that he knows and loves?

347. As she primped up her hair for her 10-year high school reunion, she laughed when she thought about herself back then. She wasn't ugly, sure, but she was completely average in every way. It freaked her out at first during her first year at college when she began to sprout up. She was a late bloomer and the extra six inches she gained in a single year turned the "Freshman 15" into the "Freshman Fabulous." Her parents barely recognized her when she came home for Christmas that year. And now here she was, a full-fledged model who spent most of her days posing. It sure beat her efforts waiting to get asked out for senior prom, she thought. She would never have any problem with that sort of thing ever again. How has her personality changed since those days of being "average?"

348. She felt like some of her friends assumed because she was dancing in amazing shows that toured the country that she was set for the rest of her life. They had no idea how little pay she had to live off of and they rarely knew how tenuous her hold was on the roles she had. She spent every day thinking about how hard she had to work to stave off the new additions to the company. If she ever had an injury or illness to contend with, it didn't mean she had the day off, it meant she had to work just that much harder. Being a dancer was her life dream, but keeping it was more like a nightmare. Will she be able to keep hold of her profession and why or why not?

349. For most of his life, he'd been naturally gifted with a chiseled physique and the ability to move at a lightning pace. He worked less hard than most of the other dancers in his company because for the most part he didn't need to. When he hit the age of 30, however, everything began to change. His metabolism dropped through the floor and he needed to start dieting and exercising like crazy. His muscles grew weary with fatigue much more quickly than usual and his conditioning needed to be superb to keep up with the others. He was finally getting a taste of what the others had felt for years and he was not happy about it. How will he cope with his newfound hardships?

350. She knew that her parents would never visit her halfway across the country and so she had no problem telling them she had gotten a part with a dance company. What she didn't tell them was that it was a job dancing exotically for a strip club. All her life she'd wanted to be a ballerina and she worked hard for it. When all of the opportunities dried up, along with her bank account, she decided to use her talents to make enough money to renew the search. When an opportunity came up to dance for money, she took it. She'd been on stage for years and yet, this new job rattled her due to the strange clientele. The money was good and she hoped her parents might understand some day. How has taking this new job affected her psychologically?

Laborers

The summer after I graduated from college, I had a surreal experience as part of what was called "The Ready Crew," that prepared the dorm rooms for the incoming residents. As I was leaving this academic institution, I was putting in hours of hard labor cleaning, moving and lifting. It was tough work and yet it was much less difficult than the jobs I see people doing everyday on construction sites, landscaping properties and loading docks. Some people love that kind of work while others are simply doing it to get by. Whatever their background, they have a story behind every brick they lay and each truckload of mulch they dump.

351. He wasn't your average Mr. Fix It as he was skinny and short with blond hair and blue eyes. Despite this, he was a travelling handyman who went throughout the city fixing and building at a discount. He would do the little things like assembling a bookcase and larger issues like re-wiring an entire house. He was fully certified for all these tasks, he simply didn't look the part. There was something he loved about helping people to complete their homes and that love came through with each customer he helped. What does he do during his spare time to continue his love of helping people and why?

352. If you saw him on the street and he had a mad look on his face, you might want to cross to the other side. He was an older guy, but he was incredibly tall and built. He handled certain jobs building houses and other buildings

that three men would strain to do. And yet, he was extremely kind and soft spoken. He loved his kids and his wife and treated them with an overflowing love. While he'd gotten a tough upbringing and his tough exterior genetically from his parents, he knew that he would have to be the one to turn the corner with compassion. What kind of pride does he take in his work building up houses for other families?

353. People gave her strange looks when she told them she drilled oil for a living. They assumed that was work for reclusive tough guys who wanted to escape from society. For her, it was a way of life and it was how she could provide money for her family, who lived in a cramped house on the mainland. She wasn't just trying to pull in enough for her kids and her husband, but also her sister's family and that was what kept her going every day. She was fortunate enough to have a skill set to do some difficult and thankless work that was well paying enough to keep everyone afloat. What are some of the things she misses the most when she has to work on the oil rig for days at a time?

354. When you saw this cute, little blond with a tool belt, you laughed a little to yourself. When you saw her assisting her peers in hauling large chunks of metal and wood in constructing everything from sheds to theater sets, you were thoroughly impressed. When she was away from the long-sleeved shirts and beat-up jeans of her work, she wore loud, attractive clothes that were a clear departure from her day job. She said that she'd gotten into work with her hands during college and that she'd kept it up because she loved being one of the guys and defying expectations. What is her day-to-day life like on the job and how does it contrast with her nightlife?

355. He always thought he'd be doing more with his life. His best efforts at college weren't enough to earn a degree despite multiple attempts and he found a job pouring cement for housing foundations. While some of his peers saw it as a sort of metaphor, building foundations for growing families, he couldn't help but see it as a disappointment. He hated talking about his job with his friends and he looked at himself as a failure. His parents were surprised that he was so unhappy, because they were proud of him and his long-standing job. All of the pressure in his life seemed to be coming from himself. Will he ever be able to find something to be grateful for in his job?

356. He wasn't the kind of person who built things up. He was a destroyer of walls, furniture, windows and anything else that needed breaking. He took a certain pride in swinging his hammer as if he was Thor or something. His peers warned employers not to get on his bad side, but in reality he was more of a jokester than a hothead. He just happened to be good at turning things into rubble. He loved pretending to be a scary dude to someone he'd never met, before slapping the person on the back and laughing uproariously. How did he get into such a destructive, enjoyable line of work?

357. As she put the finishing touches on the final bush, she stepped back and marveled at what she'd done. She'd been one of the main landscape artists for a transcendent mansion property in town for several years, but this was her finest creation yet. She'd created a close to life-size replica of Noah's Ark in the form of shaped bushes, trees and flowers. Her employers were major figureheads in Christianity and had given her instruction to use a prominent biblical tale. She went above and beyond anything they thought was possible and she felt incredible satisfaction. What are some of the other creations that have come as a result of her hard work?

358. When her father had two daughters, he assumed that the family legacy working on the Ford assembly line would be kaput after two generations. He had no idea that one of them would continue the path by taking his place shortly after his retirement. She loved making her father happy that the trend of car manufacturing could continue. After all, he'd taken so much pride in his handiwork growing up that his daughter couldn't help but fall in love with cars as well. She knew more about vehicles than most mechanics and she even assembled cars with her dad in the garage during her spare time. What are some of the things she likes the most about working on cars?

359. He felt like a real daredevil sometimes, but in actuality, he was just a roof repairman and cleaner. He had seen a perspective of his city that few other than low-flying pilots could obtain. He loved telling people the things he did on a day-to-day basis because they all thought his death-defying roof heroics were impressive. For the most part, he was quite safe up there due to having the proper equipment, though he had experienced a few close calls in his time. He recently got into one of his first long-term relationships and his partner has given him a lot of guilt about

putting himself in such danger. Will he decide to stay with the profession or will he pick to stay safe and keep his partner from worrying?

360. While most of her friends were getting ready for their senior prom, she was working all throughout the night on her trade school final project. She was one of the best welders her school had ever seen and she loved it so much she made it a job and a hobby. During the day, she welded together parts of heavy machinery. By night, she was a semi-successful sculptor who used what she could find in junkyards and trash heaps to turn into art. There was something she really enjoyed about connecting and creating metal objects. The first time she saw the blue flame and the mask during a lesson in trade school, she somehow knew it was what she wanted to do the rest of her life. What are some examples of machines and sculptures she had worked on?

CHAPTER 4: CHARACTERS BY ACTIVITY
OR AFFILIATION

Athletes

We are living in a fitness conscious world, people! It's not always apparent for writers who are not frequently the fittest bunch, but if you are writing about an urban area, it's very likely that there will be tons of runners, bikers and other athletes moving through the city at rapid speed. Not all athletes are hardcore and not all of them are muscle heads, so if you plan to include a character who is an exercising fiend in your story, here is a list to check out.

361. You couldn't have told by looking at him in his suit and tie, but your co-worker is secretly a weekend warrior. You'd known that he worked out every morning, but it wasn't until you got a gym membership that you realized to what extent. Several miles at an Olympic pace, followed by power lifting and a hilarious aerobics routine. It turns out that in addition to being a sales genius, he competes in triathlons all over the country. How did he get into this hobby and what kind of satisfaction does he get from it?

362. You asked him for a spot during your bench press attempt and you were amazed by how easily he picked the bar off your chest. He was massive. You were even more amazed when your friend took you to a drag show and the spotter was the main attraction. After the show, he recognized you and gave you a huge bear hug that nearly suffocated you. It turned out that lifting weights was a diversion for him, while being on stage seemed to keep his spirit alive. What is it that makes him happy about both pursuits?

363. With a baby-face that kept her looking fresh out of high school, the hardcore former-gymnast pushed the hefty bar over her head to the cheers of her fans and teammates. At first she seemed like your average Hollywood youthful blond, but under the sun dresses and beneath the smile, beat the heart of a warrior and the muscles of a boxer. Add in an impeccable sense of timing and you have a woman who could melt your heart, crack you up and beat the pants off you, depending on the situation. How do people's reactions to her tend to shape her opinion of the world?

364. She is large, in charge and she doesn't take crap from anybody. Oh and she's also a marathoner. You nearly choked on your water when she first told you. While the woman may be 50 to 75 pounds overweight, at the end of the day, she could outrun you. Your friends have told you she's a joy to run with, cracking jokes and shouting at passing cars. Since you have wanted to take up running, you go for a jog with her one day where she tells you an amazing story about how she got into running. Write about her story and why she made running a part of her life.

365. As you paw over the walls of your new friend's apartment, you ask him how he earned his varsity letters. It turns out that he is your college's mascot! Not only can he do flips and leap through the air with the greatest of ease, but he can do it all while wearing a giant costume. Quiet and reserved, you wouldn't assume he would be responsible for firing up tens of thousands of fans multiple times a week. When you ask him why he became a mascot he says, "Well, you only live once, right?" What kind of career do you think this athlete will take on after graduation and why?

366. You've made friends with the toweringly tall, blond barista at your favorite coffee joint and you sit down for a cup with him after his shift. It turns out that he is a jack-of-all-trades in a big way. He had a stint in minor-league baseball and he still plays semi-professional ball as a starting pitcher. While he recovered from major elbow surgery a few years back, he finished his PhD and studied in Europe. To pay the bills, he trains local young baseball players and gives motivational speeches to youth groups. You marvel at his goal-setting abilities. Where did he get his sense of hard work from and will he ever make it to the big leagues?

367. Sitting across the bar you can't help but recognize the muscular woman looking back at you. As you approach her, it becomes clear that she is one of the buxom, buff women from the popular television professional wrestling league. You've seen her kick butt on multiple occasions and she's portrayed as one of the toughest women alive. When you get to talking to her, you realize it's not just a persona. She tells you stories of bar fights and brawls she's had off camera. That being said, she also talks quite kindly of her parents and sisters. How did she get into this line of work and what's her drink of choice?

368. She recently celebrated her 80th birthday with a morning swim. This isn't so surprising considering she's swum about 25 laps every weekday for the last two decades. Unsurprisingly, she looks more fit and younger than most of her counterparts at Church, where she is a major official. She loves her grandchildren and hopes one day they can all go for a swim together. How long do you think she'll keep up this healthy and life-extending athletic habit?

369. When you made it a point to interview the man who started your favorite charity, you never expected to be staring up at a seven-footer. It turned out, this former pro-basketball superstar had a heart as big as his massive hands. After growing up in a rough neighborhood and losing his brother to a gunshot wound, he knew that he would be back to change things. A strong listener and a slow-speaker, he is one of the best interviewees you've ever encountered. Are there any other surprises to learn about this caring, hulking man?

370. You had never even heard of the X-Games (short for extreme) until a co-worker invited you out to see her friend. You expected to see an ugly, over-tattooed, pasty girl who clearly batted for the other team. After seeing an amazing skateboard routine, your friend's friend took off her helmet to reveal a face like a movie star. With long, black hair down to her shoulders and a perfect smile, you weren't surprised to hear that she had sponsored lining up for her. When you all sit down for a drink, what is the first thing you ask her and how does she answer?

Nerds, Geeks and Dweebs

One of my favorite developments of the last decade or so is that nerds, geeks and dweebs have gone from social outcasts to cool in one generation. There are several examples you can point to, but one of the best is the success of the show "The Big Bang Theory" which is one of the top-rated shows on television despite its nerdy tone. These types of characters tend to take on some stereotypes such as living in their mom's basement and going to comic conventions, but nerds, geeks and dweebs are positively ruling the digital world, which gives you a lot more room to work with.

371. Online, he was a warrior like no other in one of the world's most highly populated massive multiplayer online role playing games (MMORPG), and the game developers had a difficult time keeping up with his quickly leveling character. What the players in the game didn't realize was that he had devised method to exercise furiously while playing online. His desktop was attached to a contraption of his own making that incorporated cardiovascular exercise and weight training. Nobody on the streets would ever be able to tell by his six-pack and massive biceps that he used the computer nearly 15 hours a day. What was he like before his gaming/exercise combination and how has his physique changed his life?

372. As one of the original Star Wars geeks, he was first in line to see the new trilogy when it was released in the late 1990s. He remembered back to his childhood of how much the first movie had affected him and how he'd seen it more than 20 times in theaters. He even considered naming his first child Luke, until his wife rightly denied him. After watching The Phantom Menace, however, he changed his tune. No matter how he spun it, he felt that George Lucas had ruined the series he loved like a member of the family, and he decided he would never trust the Star Wars creator again. Was he able to keep himself from seeing the next two movies and how does this change his opinions of the original trilogy?

373. She was a blond, tan cheerleader who was extremely popular and could be found dating the quarterback of the football team. She was also an avid Magic The Gathering player, and on her free weekends she would play in a tournament at the local gaming store. She had two older brothers who were both geeks and she grew up playing the card game. As her brothers were both away at college or grad school, playing the game as often as she could brought her a special joy. Her friends made fun of her for it and were never able to quite understand the game, but she continued it because she wasn't about to let other people tell her what to do. Will she continue to play the game when she herself goes away to college and why or why not?

374. She had the calendar marked nearly eight months ago for her favorite week of the year: San Diego Comic Con. She had been preparing her cosplay costumes for months and was just putting the finishing touches on the sais of an Electra outfit for her first day. She had a different dorky uniform for each day of the festival and she already had her tickets to her favorite television shows and the most promising upcoming movies. She and her friends went

a little crazy last year and hooked up with some out-of-town MIT guys. While she considered toning it down this year, she always believed that what happened at the Con stayed at the Con. Why is she such a big fan of the convention scene and what adventures will this year bring?

375. People never interested him as much as numbers did. When he needed to succeed in a required communications class, he actually created a formula that would allow him to devise a successful speech to pass the class as opposed to learning the skills needed to communicate, and it got him an A. He was at the top of his class through his undergraduate work and his PhD in applied mathematics. Whenever he went to parties, he talked about math, made math jokes and frequently changed more interesting conversation topics into math-related discussions. He did hope to find love someday, but he calculated the probability as low. What will the future hold for this lover of numbers and will he ever find the square root of true love?

376. While most gamers look up and marvel at the top players on the multiplayer online versions of games like Halo, he's always looking down the list. Because he's almost always #1. He's been one of the best online players at first-person shooting games ever since Quake in the mid-1990s, and he's actually learned to make a living from his skills. By coming in first place in international gaming tournaments, he's been able to supplement his salary as, you guessed it, a game tester. He'd considered going into development, but he worried it would take away from his considerable amount of practice time. Will he ever meet his match and how well does he interact with people in the real world?

377. The real world never held much interest for her and when she was asked to be a beta tester for the virtual world of Second Life, she jumped on the opportunity. She always had an acute mind for business strategy and it didn't take her long to realize how to make a living buying and selling virtual real estate in the game. She also developed a group of friends and even found a partner to marry in the game (and later in real life). Since she was making a decent income and experiencing an exciting social life in Second Life, she found little time for anything else. Via her doctor's wishes, she would go to the gym three times a week, but that was one of her few trips outside, most weeks. Why was she so interested in a virtual world and what would a day be like for her when the Second Life server went down?

378. You knew that she was well-versed in all things nerdy, but you never expected that she would be able to quote you the movie The Princess Bride from beginning to end. She knew the script perfectly as if she was reading it from your eyes, and she even did different voices for each of the characters. Throughout her recitation as you watched the actual movie out of the corner of your eye, her smile was wide, creating dimples on her freckly cheeks. Her blond hair glistened from the glow of the television screen and you smiled back. You were already smitten, but being able to quote one of your favorite nerdy movies verbatim was the icing on the cake. What other nerdy or normal qualities did she possess and what practice did she take part in to accurately quote the movie?

379. He had watched all 500 plus episodes of "The Simpsons" and though the quality had dipped, he made sure to keep up with the show so that his library of quotes could continue to increase. He and his friends used to get together for each new episode in middle and high school and they would go back and forth quoting the show endlessly. While some of his friends had moved on, they would still have quote-fests from time to time. It was rare that he would go an entire paragraph without inserting at least one Simpsons quote or voice. What do his friends and family members think about their never ending Simpsons dictionary of a loved one?

380. She had a recurring dream that she was a warrior princess who had been pitted against a large group of orcs and a golden dragon. These dreams stemmed from the huge amount of fantasy books she had read during her lifetime and that she would continue to read as long as she lived. She was always one of the first in line at midnight to attend large releases like Game of Thrones, but she also read the books from less well-known series. She loved the fantastical worlds created between the pages and she frequently pictured herself in the place of some of the main female characters. What are some of her main goals in life and when did she get so into reading this genre?

Ninjas and Samurai

Ninjas and Samurai have a special place in my heart as one of the favorite video game character types of my youth. During elementary and middle school, I could be frequently found playing Ninja Gaiden or Teenage Mutant

Ninja Turtles, both 8-bit Nintendo games. Ninjas are elusive creatures with amazing skills and backgrounds that are shrouded in mystery. Samurai are warriors with a code of honor that runs deep, and they are portrayed wonderfully in movies like The Seven Samurai and Yojimbo. While most traditional stories will not employ these character types, it never hurts to bring in the elements of a strong-warrior from an ancient tradition into an action-adventure set in the past.

381. He was a powerful warrior who had learned the art of ninjitsu at a young age from his domineering father. He escaped home as early as he could to go off and study with other masters, and due to his persistence he was able to learn techniques that most would have given up on. He became feared throughout the land as a man who could easily kill with a single touch to just the right areas. He grew tired of his dominance and settled down with a family of his own. He soon realized that unless he worked on his attitude, he would be just like his own father and drive his family away. What will this master ninja do to master himself?

382. As one of the last samurai, he knew that it was up to him to impart the wisdom of his culture to future generations. He opted to become a teacher at a large school, both to pass down the teachings of the samurai and to avoid a war so that he could put those practices into a book. His book ended up becoming one of the most popular volumes of all time in his country and he achieved his goal of spreading the word that fighting was often not the answer and that self-reliance and compromise was the best combination for any situation. What other lessons did this master have to impart to future generations and why?

383. You were the commander of a small fleet of soldiers and you and your men were currently being decimated by a cloaked figure. After the ninja had taken out most of the soldiers, she took off her mask to reveal that she was a woman. Not just any woman, though: she was the daughter of the very war criminal you were trying to apprehend. It turned out that the man had taught his daughter exceptionally well from a young age. She didn't understand the severity of her father's crime and believed that protecting him was good for the country. She loved her father deeply and would kill every man that came for him. Will it be possible to make her understand that her father is actually an evil man?

384. The ways of the samurai were not frequently taught to women, but hundreds of years after the last true samurai was lost, she opted to bring the culture back strictly with women. She formed what started as an exercise club at the local gym and turned it into a way of life. Women who were intrigued by the art of mastering the self and learning aspects of martial arts came back week after week. It wasn't the samurai practice itself, however; it was the founder's enthusiasm with it and her desire to bring it into reality. How did the woman feel about creating such a movement and flipping the gender balance of samurai worldwide?

385. He was able to fly through the air as if gravity couldn't hold him down. Then again, he was in a high school full of boys and girls who could do the same. He was one of the top students and the other ninjas-in-training marveled at his skill. If only they knew the fear he harbored inside. After losing his parents at a young age, he was incredibly afraid of dying at any moment, and it was this fear that pushed him to be better than all of his peers. He knew he needed to be the fastest in the world to prevent unnatural death, and he was close to achieving it. Will he ever be able to overcome his fear and if so, what will do it?

386. He was certainly able to fight and he often won, but he was no true samurai. He had made efforts to be brought into the group of samurai warriors protecting the village, and while they appreciated his help, they did not acknowledge him as one of them. They believed he hadn't had the proper training and his bawdy actions with women and his frequent drunkenness disqualified him from their ranks. He wanted nothing more than to prove himself to them, and he figured he'd do that by showing off his skills defending the village. Is he successful in his quest of proving himself to be a samurai?

387. She had trained her whole life so that her family would be safe from the impending attacks. While she survived, the rest of her family fell to the new tyrannical regime. She could think of only one way to avenge her family and that was to go over to the other side and destroy them from within. She heavily applied makeup, hid her painful past and pretended to be the perfect woman, which gained her the favor of many suitors including the new dictator. She faked falling deeply in love with him and she was eventually married. When a rebellion began to brew,

she took this opportunity to strike. What will she do to avenge her family and what will she feel like upon exacting her revenge?

388. Staying at home and hoping for marriage when there were men out there losing their lives? This was no life for her, she decided, and with the help of her friends, she changed her looks into that of a man's. She quickly picked up on the fighting style of the warrior and rose through the ranks while keeping her secret. She learned much about what men said behind women's backs and felt completely at home. She never wanted to go back to her original life. Will this fighting woman be able to keep her secret from the men she now calls friends?

389. When he started being bullied at school, he determined that despite his fate, he would not be tempted to do something stupid like getting even. He instead opted to learn all that he could about the way of the samurai warrior. He learned from books and from after-school classes and he was able to defend himself. He never used his ability to strike back, however; he simply deflected every attack using the momentum of his attackers. Eventually, the bullies grew tired of their inability to hurt him and turned toward other students. The problem is, he had decided to defend everyone in the school at all times. Now that he was safe, why did he decide to protect the other students?

390. Her warrior ways had always been looked down upon by her parents, who wanted her to become a good bride and nothing more. When her brother was kidnapped, however, they changed their tune, hoping that she could use her skills to return him to the family. She travelled across the land, hoping to save her brother and get back in her parents' good graces. She was successful in her mission, but only a few months later her parents were back to asking her about giving up this "silly ninja business." She decided that the only way for her would be to lead a double life. How did she go about this and what will the rest of her life be like?

Pirates

When creating 100 categories of characters, I was bound to have a few categories that some might find to be extraneous. I don't consider pirates to be of that ilk due to the newsworthiness of the Somali pirates a few years ago and the success of the Pirates of the Caribbean movie franchise. Pirates can be used as a dastardly villain or simply a bit of comic relief in a sea adventure. While not all pirates will be as memorable as Captain Jack Sparrow, you are bound to find some enjoyable traits within these 10 scurvy dogs.

391. He was one of the most cunning pirates of all time, according to the stories, and his legend had grown hugely. This was, of course, far out of proportion with the truth. While people were being truthful when they spoke of him winning large battles with inconceivable odds, it was almost always an accident. He once tripped over a lantern, which allowed him to avoid a direct hit to his body and sent a cannon ball directly into the weapons cache of another ship, blowing it to smithereens. A similar incident allowed him to defeat 10 men when a rope he was nervously gripping ended up tripping the men and sending most of them overboard. Who is this man really and how does he react when he hears his legend?

392. He was a terrible captain and nearly all of his crews had mutinied on him. Almost being the operative world. His great charm knew no bounds. Even though he frequently sent them on the wrong course and put them in bad position, he was able to flatter each man in just the right way. He eventually had his first mate secretly give all the orders as he used his talents to get secrets from the men and women of local towns to score riches for all the men on his ship. His mother had always taught him the best way to speak to person was by first listening. Will his charm be enough to keep him safe and alive during the rest of his tenure as a captain and why?

393. She was bawdy and rude, and in a game of chance she'd won her very own pirate ship. As she'd been looking for a change from her brothel life, she took a few of her girls and opted to become a woman of the sea. By leveraging the services of her women, she was able to gain the respect of her mostly male crew and to stage several successful attacks on local sea merchants. She loved this new life, and within a few years she became one of the most feared pirates on the seas. What was the stickiest situation she ever got into as a female pirate captain and how'd she get out of it?

394. She didn't know the rules of the water and had disdain for pirates, yet when push came to shove, she could fight her way out of any situation. After a bloody battle, she inherited the position of first mate of a crew that could help her to achieve her goal of revenge. At first, a few of her fellow shipmates thought they could take advantage of

her, but after one lost an ear and another an eye, the rest of the crew left her alone. She was even willing to act as bait for other ships as a "defenseless woman" trapped in a lifeboat. Once she boarded, she strategically rigged the ship to explode from a cannonball in the right place and dove off once her ship came near. She knew that eventually the ship she destroyed would include the captain who killed her father. How did she learn to be such a fierce combatant?

395. He'd always had a difficult life on land. He was cross-eyed and was certainly lacking in the dental department. On sea, however, he was able to find camaraderie and power that dry land couldn't offer him. It turned out that pirate ships were often a group of people just like him with one or multiple deformities. Nearly everyone on the ship was willing to look past these if he worked hard and kept out of trouble. He even once spotted a ship in the distance that led them to a major score. He knew that this life was dangerous, but his felt his happiness was worth it. How will his time on the ship change him when he returns home to visit his family?

396. He was a frustrated teen who was tired of the iron rule of his parents. He opted to stow away aboard a pirate vessel for hope of a change. He quickly found that as an errand boy for an entire ship of pirates, it was almost as if he had ten times as many chores. Now that he was hundreds of miles away from home, he began to appreciate what he had with his parents and he lamented his decision. Since the pirates considered him a slave, it was up to him to escape upon reaching the next town. Is he successful in his attempts or will he be a pirate slave forever?

397. She no longer wanted to live a life as herself and decided to elaborately hide her gender and take to the seas as a fisherman. Only a month into her journey, she was captured by pirates and only revealed her gender to prevent certain death. The pirates had recently lost their cook and assumed that finding a woman in the middle of the ocean was a blessing. She soon became one of the boys and she loved telling lewd and crude jokes with the kind of men who would appreciate her. She even found love with one of the pirates. What will the rest of this pirate cook's life be like and why?

398. She was the daughter of the king of the pirates, at least until she killed him to take over. She was ruthless and showed little in the way of mercy, regardless of the situation. If any fellow pirates would ever cross her, she would quickly end their lives, and so many of them were scared of her, there was hardly ever a peep of an uprising. She had determined that her and the pirates must attack and defeat an armada of ships from a nearby nation and she took them to war. There was something she wanted from them. What did she want and why was she willing to kill her father to gain the power to do it?

399. He was of little use to the rest of the crew, aside from unintentional comedic relief. He had one glass eye because of a fishing hook mishap and an unfortunate cannon incident had left him perched on a wooden leg. No matter how tough the seas looked and how gloomy the men were, they could always count on this accident-prone man to cheer them up. At first, he looked at it all as an unfortunate burden but as the time and laughter went on, he almost relished in the cheer he brought to the other pirates. Obviously, he'd never run or blink with his left eye again, but he was able to tell jokes no matter what his deformities. What is a typical joke he would tell and what other accidents might befall him during his lifetime?

400. When her son said he wanted to become a pirate, she agreed with one condition, the condition being that she come along to keep an eye on him. The pirates on the first ship he sailed on laughed at him in the beginning, but they soon learned that his mother was no woman to mess with. She was able to stare down and guilt any man, woman or child, and she would stop at nothing to make her child safe. She even once attacked and defeated a man who made fun of her son behind closed doors. This only added to her legend. It was unsurprising then that she eventually became captain and made her son first mate. How did this woman learn to become so strong-willed?

Knights and Warriors

In my nerdy days of playing medieval-based games full of dragons and princesses, one of my favorite character types was the knight. This dashing hero was able to battle where lesser fighters couldn't and was frequently seen dashing across the page or screen on a white horse. If you are creating a more modern tale that wouldn't work well with these heroes, feel free to adapt them to a modern setting, like the police or the Army. In addition, to keep up my fairly balanced character total, I will be placing female warriors related to knights here among the ten.

401. He seemed like the fairest knight of them all with long, blond hair and muscles that barely fit into a suit of armor. What those in the town did not know is that in his youth he was one of the most mocked children of his small village. Overweight and underappreciated, he knew that he would have to become the most handsome knight in the land to gain respect. He ran away from home and trained himself to live off the land. He missed reading and writing, which were his initial passions, but upon his return to civilization, he was the perfect candidate for knighthood. Was he ultimately happy with his decisions and would his past ever catch up with him?

402. No matter how hard he trained and how many damsels in distress he saved, he was always going to be second best to the most famous knight in the world. He was most certainly an amazing rider and fighter and if he were to battle said knight one on one, there would be a chance that he'd win. The problem was that he simply wasn't charismatic enough to bring in the same kind of support for his exploits. It bit at him sometimes that if he'd been born in a later generation, he might have been thoroughly hailed for his skill and strength. Because he came about when he did, however, he would be second banana for his entire life. Will this somehow second-rate knight do something about his plight or let it play out?

403. She lived a great deal of her life as a lie. When her parents were killed in a village raid, she used her riding skills to escape injury, and she ended up in a much larger town where she could blend in. She knew that the best way for her to get back at those who wronged her was to become a knight, but there were no women knights in her country. She cut her hair short, affected a deep voice and dressed in boy's clothing for the next five years, as she trained to become a protector of the realm. She was able to keep up the ruse long enough to be knighted and to confront the people who killed her parents. Once she has exacted revenge on those who wronged her, will she continue to pretend she is a man so she can best utilize her training?

404. She couldn't help but laugh when she saw these heavily armored men walking through her territory. They appeared ready to take on an entire army, but they would be no match for her. After they fell into a few of her carefully placed trapped, she quickly disarmed them with her speed and asked them to tell her what their business was. They laughed at seeing a woman threaten them until she placed a sword tip right next to one of their necks. As their laughing ceased, they asked for her help to lead them through the woods to find a kidnapped girl. She agreed, and over the course of the next few days, she wowed them with her many abilities to survive in the wilderness. How did she end up being the warrior she is today?

405. His whole life he knew he was born to be a conqueror. One of the first armies he led was successful in conquering a great nation after barbaric tribes had been attempting to do the same for decades. The only issue was that he was a fantastic vanquisher, but not much of a political leader. After his battles were successful, he was so popular that he was a unanimous choice to lead the new nation. This wasn't something that appealed to him in the slightest, though he knew it was his duty to take up the position. He made horrible decisions that angered the populous, though they were very beneficial to his warriors. Soon enough, he had a coup on his hands and led his army into battle. What will the end result be of his ability to fight and his lack of an ability to lead?

406. He was trained to attack and destroy anyone and anything his paying employers told him to. When he was sent to raze a village of innocent men, women and children; however, he decided to change his colors. He felt a sort of kinship with the people there and he quickly turned his team of men into protectors for the area. He knew that his employer would send others to attack, and he did his best to train the members of the village to protect themselves. It took a lot of work and he was by no means the best teacher in the world, but when the second wave of mercenaries came, they were ready because of him. What was it he saw in the village that made him change his mind about proceeding with his orders?

407. In an ancient land where women were worshipped instead of relegated to the house alone, she was the most powerful knight in the realm. Men were not allowed to lead in this place and she was glad of it, since many of the men she knew were weak and easily influenced by their impulses. In her experience, women were strong and focused and could defeat any obstacle. When her realm clashed against a realm of male warriors, she knew that it would be no match for her well trained soldiers. In this literal battle of the sexes, will this powerful female warrior be successful in her war?

408. To the untrained eye, she and her friends seemed like average middle-aged women who were ready to concentrate on creating a family. In reality, she was the leader of an elite fighting team that kept her city safe from the gangs and mobs that were slowly taking over. She had learned multiple fighting styles and movement skills to train her group in tactics that would let them move silently throughout the area. She listened in on an extra police scanner she borrowed from her husband, allowing her and the team to get the drop on any criminal activity. When did she and her secret band of warriors decide to take the city back into their own hands?

409. After his country lost most of its knights in a major battle, they really had to scrape the bottom of the barrel to find a set to replace them. He was one of those candidates. He'd always wanted to be a knight, but he wasn't fast, strong or smart enough to ever make the first string. The thing he had that set him apart from all the candidates though was the fact that he had a huge heart. He loved his country and fought for nothing but the love of the men, women and children who deserved freedom. Through his hard work and his love, he quickly became the leader of this new band of heroes and he was successful where the first group of knights had failed. How did he develop such heart and what are some of the adventures he and his new team of soldiers will go on?

410. When she was kidnapped from her kingdom, most thought that there would be some kind of large ransom for her safe return. No ransom would ever come, because the kidnapping was staged by the princess herself. She wasn't interested in the slightest in becoming a princess. She wanted to escape from her parents who forced her to be girly and avoid what she really loved: saving people who needed saving. She was no damsel in distress, but she was more than willing to save an actual damsel. Slowly but surely she learned from teachers in the wilderness how to take care of herself and become the warrior she was born to be. What were her reasons for wanting the opposite of a royal existence?

Royalty

One of the reasons that I found European History such an interesting subject in high school was because of the wild eccentricities of royalty in countries like England, France and Germany. For hundreds of years, these countries were ruled with an iron fist, not just by kings, but by earls and duchesses as well. The gap between the haves and the have-nots was drastic, and many members of royalty were able to do whatever it was they pleased. A story set far in the past or one in a fantastical world could do with a few royals interspersed throughout.

411. When he was young, he travelled among the commoners as often as he could to learn what would control them. As he ascended toward the throne, he knew that they responded more to religion than they would to anything else. Rule the church, rule the country. He slowly but surely tightened his grasp around religion, bringing church and state together and giving him power and wealth no king had known before him. What he couldn't have expected, however, was for another religion to rise. What will he do when the country devolves into civil war because of this new religion?

412. He had always had everything he wanted handed to him (literally) on a silver platter. When his family fell out of favor, however, and it looked like he would no longer be in line for an esteemed position, he had to learn to live with less. At first he whined nearly every day about eating less food and having nearly no diversions at all. It was only when his parents took him to a nearby village where the residents had almost nothing that he got it. He not only had to live with less stuff but he also wanted to help the people who were around him to receive more. What will he do to achieve this new quest and what are some of the things he misses about royal life?

413. She became queen by appearing to be the perfect candidate: shy and religious and easily controlled by her uncles and cousins. All of the qualities, of course, were a complete and utter lie, and the only thing she truly wanted was the power of ruling a nation. She ruled the country with an iron fist and knew much more about politics and geography than her uncles and cousins ever assumed. Her policies were occasionally in line with theirs, but some of her decisions seemed to make absolutely no sense to them. Within decades, the country began to improve financially and morale-wise. What are some of the things she did and what do her family members think about her hidden competence?

414. She was once a commoner, but there was nothing at all common about her. Her beauty seemed to spring up from the earth itself and it was not long before she was noticed by those from outside the village. She was courted by

a duke and was wed shortly thereafter. It was difficult for her to adjust to such a royal lifestyle. She wanted so much to be able to split her portions with the servants, who were once her closest friends. To achieve these ends, she became a bit of an activist, helping to improve the lot of those not as fortunate as her. Her husband didn't love these qualities of hers but couldn't argue with her growing self-reliance and confidence. How has she changed since marrying into royalty?

415. He was in the process of being groomed for the throne, and his father could only dream that he'd stop hanging out with such lowlifes. There were stories of him gambling, drinking and spending late nights with seedy women. The King wondered how his legacy would live on. It turned out that the prince was learning how the country worked from the ground up, while keeping his reputation low. If he was able to make himself seem lowly, then he believed his rise to power would make him seem even more of a natural king. Also, he particularly enjoyed some of the partying. Will his theory be correct and how would this theory succeed in the modern world of constant media?

416. A distant cousin to the throne who was appointed the earl of a small farming area, he knew that he was fortunate to be given any royal standing at all. Despite this position, however, the men and women the he "ruled" were more likely to make fun of him than listen to him in the slightest. He was portly, he had a stammer and he was accident-prone. One time when he gave a speech to his "subjects," he fell down a stone staircase and was laughed at for weeks. Behind all of this, he was a decent earl, doing his best to secure rights for the people in his town. Why didn't he attempt to get back at the people who mocked him and how will the rest of his "reign" go?

417. After a wave of the plague swept through the country, she was surprised to find out that her son had an outside claim to the throne. She'd previously devoted her life to being a good wife, but now she knew that being a conniving plotter of death would be her best role as a mother. Her favorite form of murder was poison, as she had paid a few of the servants to poison certain cups of tea before going into hiding. Slowly but surely, she forced her son to the top of the ladder of royal candidates. Some people at the top expected her, but she acted to kind and sickly for her to be evil, right? Will she be successful at her plot and how will her life change if she is?

418. While she had always been a high society woman, it wasn't until she caught the eye of a young prince that she considered she might become royalty. When he asked for her hand in marriage, it finally struck her that she would be one of the most public figures in all of the country as a princess. She accepted the proposal and began preparing for her new life as a beloved figure. There was only one problem. Despite her best efforts, she was a reviled princess and she accidentally insulted the commoners on many different occasions. When a revolution came to pass, she was one of the first sent to prison. Why was she so hated and how will she fare behind bars?

419. Before his birth, it was believed that he would be the future king, but after the deformity was revealed, he was placed behind locked doors, rarely allowed to experience the rays of the sun. He spent most of his time reading old texts and figuring out a day that he could reclaim what he believed to be his divine right. By wearing custom clothing, he was able to hide most of his ailment and he started a small rebellion in the midst of his family to get him placed on the throne. Those who wanted nothing to do with his grotesqueness plotted to kill him. Will he survive these attempts on his life and what are some of his positive qualities as a potential king?

420. She was just a normal teenage girl, going to high school and trying to navigate the perils of popularity. Her life changed when she was told that she might be the last descendant in a long line of royalty from a country she'd never even heard of. She travelled to the country and learned everything she could about it and wasn't sure if she could handle such responsibilities. After all, she'd only just learned how to drive. She'd always wondered if she'd find Prince Charming, but she might actually be the royalty in the equation. Does she decide to pursue her potentially royal heritage and why?

Coaches and Athletic Trainers

Not everyone has had the esteemed pleasure and pain of being a high school or college athlete and dealing with a coach. Every single one of my coaches up from township t-ball was a character, and I have many great memories of sports as a result. In addition, personal and team trainers are integral parts of an athletic experience for those working out at a gym or in the higher levels of athletics. It's sometimes tough to look past the mega-personality of professional athletes to see the coaches and trainers who have made their athletic prowess possible. If you have athletics or a gym as any part of your story, don't forget to have some coaching and training involved.

421. While he was an incredibly tough wrestling coach who could pound you into a pulp, after someone pointed out his idiosyncrasies to you, it became difficult to take him 100 percent seriously. At the end of every sentence, he had a sort of nasally whine like you might expect a professor or butler to have. Whenever he had an arm or leg torqued the wrong way, instead of yelping in pain, he would laugh. He literally laughed at pain. In addition, when he took you all out on a jog, his head would wobble back and forth like a turkey's might. You made every effort to learn from him after his quirks were pointed out to you, but even if he had the best advice in the sport to give to you, you'd still be concentrating on that strange nasal whine. What would he do if someone called him out on his own habits?

422. You figured that if you were going to learn soccer from anybody, it might as well be someone who was born and raised on the sport as this Brit had been. Your team had some decent players and you hoped he would have some fantastic pointers to get you to the top of the league. Unfortunately, his hands-off approach mostly consisted of watching you all play and blowing his whistle every once in a while. If something didn't go your way, he'd say, "Unlucky," and continue to watch. During the many losses you endured as a team, the word unlucky was used many, many times. Where do you think he got his coaching habits and would they work well on a different type of team?

423. As a young guidance counselor to-be, she was coerced into volunteering for a coaching position with the girl's volleyball team. She had played a bit in high school and thought it would be easy to put together a respectable squad. Despite her best efforts, however, the team was quite bad. She was a fantastic cheerleader on the side for them, but she knew she could do more. She wandered around the school looking for the tallest girls around. She struck deals to get them extra credit in some of their classes for a spot on the team, and before she knew it, they were a force to be reckoned with. How did the teams they play approve of her methods of recruitment?

424. She wasn't just any football coach, she was a state championship winning football coach. She was a hulk of a woman who wasn't willing to take crap from anybody. When she wanted to be an instructor for an essentially male game, her friends and family gave her a hard time, but when they saw her win her first title they began to lend her more credence. Perhaps she would achieve her goal of being a National Football League coach. Off the field, she was a jokester, but she never let her kids see that side of her, for fear they wouldn't take her seriously anymore. Can she reach her goal of coaching at the top and how fulfilled does she get from each of her team's victories?

425. He knew from the early days of gym class that no other subject would ever measure up. He followed his passion of sports and athletics by studying to be an athletic trainer and a nutritionist. His goal in life was to help other people find the athlete living inside them through an exercise and diet routine. He was proud of all the clients he'd had that started overweight and left a triathlon or marathon participant. Outside of work, all he did was train himself to run in Ironman triathlons around the globe. Aside from loving gym class, what made him want to be involved in sports and training so badly?

426. If the players from his recent World Series winning team were to tell you their secret for winning, they'd say that it was his amazing conditioning and healing methods that kept them strong all season. He was a bit of a recluse to the media and to most people he didn't know, but when it came to the team, he was a fierce instructor who pushed each player his farthest in the weight room while healing them gently at the end of the day. He combined Western and Eastern methods of training and healing and was up to date on the latest technologies and treatments. In his home life, he and his wife lived happily in the modest house that his family grew up in. He was saving up most of his salary each year to build a state-of-the-art training Mecca where all area sports teams could train. How did he rise to the top of the training world and when did he first make the decision to take up that line of work?

427. She knew that one of the reasons that everybody wanted her for a trainer was because she was extremely attractive and fit. She didn't mind, as it was difficult for her to maintain a body that she certainly did not have during her high school and college years. She did get a bit tired of her clients staring at her and asking her out. She was flattered, of course, because she was "that chubby girl" growing up and she looked into training to transform that

aspect of her life, but she was perfectly happy finding men on her own who weren't looking to drop 20 pounds. Describe the day she decided to change her life and the day she realized she finally had the fitness she wanted.

428. After winning the woman's bracket of her city's local triathlon, she had a vision in which she would look back and see only women coming. She began organizing such an event in which men could not participate. She coached a group of women in her area from all walks of life to get them into triathlon shape and that group became the core of the first all-woman race in the region. Word got out over the next few years and soon thousands of women flocked there for each competition. After the success of the first few, she spread her planning wings and set up similar events all over the country. How does she feel when she sees her vision realized and what will the future bring for her organization?

429. He had absolutely no interest in coaching, but when the judge gave him the option of cleaning on the side of the highway or coaching youth basketball, he took up the latter. He was somewhat of a legend in the area for nearly making it to the National Basketball Association, but he never considered using his talents for coaching. He had been using his local fame to promote his business and he'd become extremely wealthy as a result. When he got his group of kids together, he saw that none of them had potential and he knew he was in for a long season...unless he could find a way to have fun and actually teach them something in the process. What will he learn about himself from the coaching process?

430. She was a teacher who wanted nothing more than to take the whole summer off despite her need to pay her interest-accumulating student loans. As a result, she worked harder than most to add in money-making activities to her already busy schedule. She took on a different athletic squad each season to boost her paycheck from the school district, even though she knew little to nothing about sports. She started with women's soccer, continued with women's basketball and ended with woman's lacrosse. She was the solo coach for all three and learned most of her drills, formations and rules from online sources. Each sport was a major challenge for her, but she envisioned sitting by the pool and relaxing for three months straight to get her past each hurdle. If money suddenly became no issue for her life, would she continue any of the sport and why?

Professional Wrestlers

I spent a good deal of my childhood watching the stars from the World Wrestling Federation and World Championship Wrestling try to take each others' heads off with roundhouse kicks and clotheslines. Movies like The Wrestler have done a great deal to help us understand the difficult lives these athletes must lead to take a great deal of punishment inside and outside the ring. While the sport has changed dramatically since its infancy, now more of a long-winded soap opera with minimal fighting thrown in for kicks, it will always have its share of colorful, ridiculous characters that can add a literal punch to a story.

431. On the wrestling stage he was seen as an American hero. He was beloved by kids and adults alike, and his merchandise could be found in most cities worldwide. He was wrestling, but he certainly wasn't revered by his family. Even though he brought them hundreds of thousands of dollars a year, he wasn't able to enjoy any of it with them due to his ridiculous travel schedule. His relationships with his wife and kids suffered, and he considered retiring almost every year. He adored being adored, and he wanted to figure out a way to be both an icon and a role model to his family. Will he be able to strike this important balance and why or why not?

432. He was an extremely talented performer and his strength combined with his freakish athleticism put him at the top of the federation's roster. The only issue is that the company, for the life of them, could not figure out how to market him as a character. They tried gimmicks throughout the years ranging from fighter pilots to surgeons to reincarnated dragon warriors and none of them really stuck. The fans ended up latching onto the game and started calling him by his real name, which worked better than any of the characters could have. He had decent success and even won a championship or two with his realistic "character choice." What must it have been like for him taking on so many different personas in a short period of time?

433. She had arms that most men would never even dream of possessing, and as a result, she was feared among the rest of the league. It had been years since she'd faced a challenge as the undisputed women's champion and had even defended the title against several more misogynistic male characters. Her star had risen through viral videos of

her feats of strength, and she considered retiring to take on more potentially lucrative opportunities. She had grown up as somewhat of an overweight child and had used weightlifting and track and field sports as a way of getting in shape. Her parents were proud of her status as a role model, though they could have done without the beating up people. Will she decide to stay in the sport that helped her rise to fame or move onto other endeavors?

434. When she was at parties, with or without wrestlers, she often declined drinks or drugs because she had an image to uphold. After all, she was the supportive girlfriend character of one of the roughest and toughest beasts in the league. The commissioner had made it very clear that he wanted her to remain a pristine angel in the eyes of the public. She liked partying but she liked having a job more, and considering she'd previously had to take off her clothes for money, she wanted nothing to do with libations that might threaten her most lucrative job to date. As time went on, fans grew bored with her character and the commissioner wanted to change her image into that of an adulteress. Will she keep the job and tarnish her image or walk away to preserve her angelic status?

435. He was the bad guy to rival all bad guys and had taken on the persona of a terrorist just a few months before the 9/11 attacks. After such a horrible event, he wanted to change the character immediately but the owner of the league said that it would make him the most effective villain of all time. He complied as long as he didn't mention the specific acts of the attack. He had never heard such a deafening chorus of boos for any wrestler in his lifetime as he did the following week. Viewership for the league rose astronomically as the good guys teamed up to battle his squad week after week. He received a hefty raise, but he wasn't sure if he was safe on the street anymore. What does he do to ensure the safety of him and his family outside of the ring?

436. He was the pure, counterculture, antihero of the league and fans ate up his shtick with a spoon. He would guzzle beer and curse off fans as often as he'd rake an opponent's eyes or kick him in the balls, and the audiences around the world loved him for it. In real life, he was a genuinely nice guy who often donated to the homeless and took great care of his family. Because of his image, though, people treated him with kid gloves because they were afraid he'd beat them up if they spoke the wrong way to him. He laughed at their conduct and he often gave hugs to break the tension. He figured a few people who knew the true him here and there wouldn't hurt. Does he enjoy playing his loveable jerk character when he's in the ring as a change of pace from real life?

437. A former acrobat for the circus, she was signed to the league to promote their new high-flying image. She was able to leap off the top turnbuckle and do incredible feats that made the audience cheer with glee. The work paid more than the circus had and she was happy to have her face known in more circles as an incredible athlete. She used this high profile position to become something of a female role model in the sports industry. She posed for magazines and did interviews and even acted in a few movies. What does she like the most about her new status and how will she spend her time when she eventually retires?

438. She was the embodiment of an evil ex-girlfriend taken up to 11. This scary, over-mascara wearing creature had been one of the women champions of the league before knee injuries forced her to take up managerial duties for one of the main heels. She was known well for her ability to scratch opponents with her long fingernails while her partner distracted the referee in the ring. She knew she looked ridiculous, but she loved being a total ham in front of the crowd. She looked almost cute without her wild makeup on, and her husband, one of her main enemies in the league, loved spending every possible minute with her. What is an average day like for her when she's not doing an event?

439. As one of the smallest wrestlers in the history of the sport, he was almost always the underdog in every given ring situation. This also made him one of the fan favorites by far as he was always going up against some of the most incredible of odds. Whenever he won, the crowd went wild as it made them feel like they could tackle some of the tough challenges in their own lives. He had dreamed of being a professional wrestler constantly in his youth and wished every day for another growth spurt. He was beside himself with joy when hard work and opportunity combined to get him in front of an audience. What were some of the things he had to do to get into the league despite his small stature?

440. While she wasn't a wrestler per say, her association with her husband, the owner and main string puller in the league, she had been roped into more professional wrestling matches than most amateurs who had a dream to make

it to the big time. When her husband suggested she get involved in the performance side of the business, she laughed, but he was extremely convincing. Through his efforts, she had been a guest referee, a guest commentator, and she even had a tag-team match against her daughter and one of the league's main brutes. She enjoyed the opportunity of getting in shape, though actually hitting people felt strange to her. What was going through her head during her epic tag-team match against her daughter?

Comedians

It seems that even a movie by stand-up comedians, for stand-up comedians called Funny People, perpetuated many stereotypes of comedians. It turns out that comedians who do stand-up only make up a small minority of all the people that would consider themselves as comedy practitioners. This may include those who do it as part of a theater on an improvisational team, those who tour as a travelling sketch comedy troupe, and others who may use their comedic chops to create viral videos. While comedians love telling jokes and often try to be the funniest one in the room, their backgrounds and reasons for comedy can be drastically different from each other.

441. You were amazed to find out that one of the top comedians in the city was going to be hanging out with your group of friends that night. You expected that he would have you all on the floor laughing before the drinks came out. Instead, you found out that he was a normal guy just like the rest of you. He didn't even crack any jokes, which surprised you thoroughly. You'd seen his act and you knew that he was one of the wittiest, most intelligent people in existence. Perhaps, you thought, he just wanted to be normal like the rest of us. What are some other hidden surprises about this extremely funny individual?

442. When you first got into comedy, you assumed that everybody would be a drunken slob who could barely even make it to the stage of an open mic. He was the complete opposite as he'd never had a single sip of alcohol, a puff of smoke or a Sunday without a several-hour session of church. And yet, he was one of the strangest, goofiest stand-up comedians in the city. It took him a long time to learn the difference between corny and quirky, but it was a line he walked quite well during his routines. He had an odd tendency to burst into song whenever a title of a song was mentioned. How did such a straight-edged fellow end up in the world of comedy and how does he feel when many others in his company are imbibing?

443. You'd heard talk of her legend months before you signed up for her comedy class. She cussed like a sailor who enjoyed talking about female genitalia. She was absolutely fearless on stage and was willing to do anything for a laugh, but not anything that would compromise her integrity. She was loud and emotional and you would in no way want to be a telemarketer calling her in the middle of dinner. She was also a good mom and you wondered what it was like to be raised in such a household. You made every effort to be in as many of her classes as possible, hoping her filthy genius would rub off on you. How did she come into comedy and has her brash persona helped or hurt her in her career?

444. She was a master of changing quickly from one character to another. Each of those characters was incredibly quirky and odd, which made the audiences align themselves with her from the beginning of each of her comedy shows. She hoped one day to become a star in the world of humor, but she had a difficult time finding her way past the local comedy scene. Part of it was because she had a constant fear that she wasn't good enough, stemming from a lack of encouragement during most of her life. On one hand she knew she was funny, but on the other hand she felt she'd never get to the level of a Kristin Wiig or Tina Fey. What will it take for her to take her comedy to the next level?

445. He was a big fellow and nearly everything he did on stage caused a belly laugh. Sure, he was willing to do the Chris Farley-esque falling through a table and wearing of clothes that were too tight for him, but he also had a wittiness usually reserved for the skinny, sarcastic types. He loved life and he loved food and those who were close to him made efforts to help him to become healthier. They worried that the early deaths of his idols like Farley and John Belushi would set him down the same path. He wasn't as wild as the two of them, but it was hard not to see the similarities emerging. What will the rest of his career be like if he continues to consume life at a consistent rate?

446. For this comedic genius, every time he got on stage it was as if he was roasting his fellow comedians. He was brilliant at poking fun at his peers and his audience members. It always sent the audience into a frenzy when he got

on a roll, but it tended to antagonize those who worked with him, who felt like he was feeding them to the wolves for a laugh or two. He had a difficult time turning his stage persona off when he hung out with friends and they began to distance themselves from him. His girlfriend of many years broke it off with him, telling him that she made her self-esteem too low. Will this funny man continue his insulting comedic style or will he tone it down overall to make amends with his relationships?

447. In her teens, she grew tired of all the talk that women weren't as funny as men. She embarked on a quest to beat them at their own game. If her fellow male comedians took on gross humor, she would out-gross them. If they went into the realm of sexual chatter, she would over-sexualize them. She refused to back down from a challenge and was a fan favorite in her town. Her friends loved her to pieces and her guy friends especially said, unsurprisingly, that she was, "like one of the guys." This made it tough for her to snag a guy in a relationship, because she was often regarded as a "bro" instead of "girlfriend material." She hated this double standard and refused to give into the way that society thought a woman should be. When she was cast in a television pilot that was picked up for a full season, she felt validated about her beliefs that men and women were equal comedically. What will her first year be like shooting this new television project and will she find a partner who appreciates her for who she is?

448. She was what some would call a brilliant ditz. On stage, she was frequently cast as the idiot cheerleader who was more likely to get tricked into having sex with a suitor than get a question right on a math exam. She had perfected this art form, even though she was an absolute genius in real life. She sometimes lamented that she had been pigeonholed into such an image in her performances, but she'd also always wanted to make ends meet through comedy and she was able to do that by portraying a dumb blond five nights a week. Upon getting married and having her first child, she considered not going back to comedy, since her image had been more or less branded on her. Will she continue her comedic career or focus more on her family (or both)?

449. As the only non-white comedian on his team, his race was frequently called out to comedic effect. It wasn't his peers that were the only ones who did it, as he knew he could bring himself out to tell a somewhat racist joke and the audience always got a kick out of it. He wondered sometimes if he would have been considered funny enough to be on the team if he didn't fulfill a sort of "ethnic requirement." As a result, he couldn't help but feel a bit distant from his teammates. He had a few opportunities to join groups that were comprised completely of his race alone, but he wasn't sure if that the direction he wanted to go either. Will his comedic chops ever stand out for the right reason and will he ever be able to feel more connected with his teammates?

450. She had been an acclaimed dramatic actress for over a decade and was well known throughout the town for her ability to cry in an instant and to make the audience do the same. But this wasn't all that she wanted from performance, as she wanted to make them laugh as well. This wasn't nearly as easy a task for her, and she began taking beginner comedy classes. Her teachers assumed that all she needed was a little practice and she'd be set, but her instincts for drama left her a bit out to dry as a comedian. She simply didn't know how to be funny. She hired one of the funniest comedians in town to live with her for a week and teach her everything about comedic timing and jokes. How does she fare in her crash course in comedy?

Sages

If intellectuals are people who have great knowledge of books, films and music, sages are people who have great knowledge of the world itself. They may not be able to analyze a painting or a sculpture, but they are able to tell you great truths about the universe and the self. A sage may take the form of some kind of monk or spiritual leader, but a sage may also be a regular person with profound insight. A sage may even be a child. The character can be used in a science fiction sense but also in a story in which the protagonist needs to learn something about life to move forward.

451. When the world came crashing down, he was the one who had the insight to know where to patch it up. Even though he was only 16 years old, he somehow knew how to lead his family and his town to safety in the middle of what many believed to be the apocalypse. He'd had a gift of great wisdom for most of his adolescence, and his teachers often recommended he be transferred to a school in which his gifts could be fully realized. By asking not to

be transferred, he must have somehow known that the key to their salvation rested below the school itself. How did he know how to be safe from the worldwide disaster and what will happen next to him and his family?

452. Even though he'd been retired from teaching at the university for nearly a decade, he still had students coming to seek his counsel nearly every week. He'd become too infirm to go back and forth from the school anymore, but his legend was so great that he continued to hold something resembling office hours in his own study. Students would enter his house, have a cup of tea and ask questions about their future career, academia and their lives. His answers were brash, unorthodox and completely modern, as he kept up on all current technologies and industry shifts. What was this brainy man like in his adolescence and young adulthood when he needed advice himself?

453. She was a goddess when it came to relationships of any kind. It didn't matter if you were a guy or a girl and it didn't matter what your sexual preference was. She could tell you exactly how to proceed in a given situation because she understood people like nobody else on the planet. She had a modest one-bedroom apartment that she shared with her partner and they had such an amazing relationship that you couldn't help but envy her. She ran a website about relationships which had over a million visitors each month, but you were fortunate enough to know her in person. She had helped you through multiple difficulties and she always seemed to know what to say. How did she become so proficient when it came to relationships and how did that knowledge translate in her own relationships?

454. From looking at the success of the school's athletic program for the last 20 years, you might think that the success was mostly a result of the coaching staff, the recruiters or even a few of the star players over the years. You would be wrong. The true catalyst for their success was the team tutor. After years of having star players become ineligible, she revealed her tutoring talent as a senior and helped multiple players to boost their grades to As and Bs from Fs. She had an uncanny ability to make someone understand anything and everything, no matter what the person's intelligence level. The school took riskier and riskier athletes who had little to offer academically and turned them around using her skills. What are some of the ways in which she helps these athletes to hit the books better?

455. This local millionaire never had one of those jobs that took him away from his family and had him slaving 80 hours a week. He realized early on that he didn't need that to become rich. Through his brilliant strategies of saving and investing, he slowly but surely grew a fortune. He also grew a steady stream of passive income that let him retire before the age of 40. Since that time he's counseled thousands of people on their money issues, which has yielded several millionaires during that time. No matter what level these people were at coming to him, they left him in much better shape. How did he learn such secrets of money and how to employ them for all comers?

456. He originally came to the big city to become an actor, but when that didn't work out, he turned his hand to being the most athletic, in-shape person in existence. His physique caught the eye of a, exercise video company, and within a couple of years, his workout routine had become the most well known hardcore fitness plan in the country. He loved advising people on how they could turn their lives around through physical fitness, and he felt he had truly found his calling in the exercise industry. He even became one of the key advisors for the government when it came to childhood obesity and fitness. What is an average day like for this guru of the fitness goal?

457. When you think of a wise Buddhist monk, your first image might be a wrinkly, old man at the top of a mountain. You wouldn't expect this person to be an attractive 30-something woman living in a mansion, but that's just who she was. After her family experienced a major windfall during her teens, she was surrounded by luxury and comfort. She never truly felt peace and happiness, though, until she went away to Tibet and learned everything she could about deep meditation, which clicked with her much more than with most. After her parents passed away, she continued to live on their giant property and continued to teach the art of happiness to students throughout the week. What was it like when she felt this sense of peace for the first time?

458. She was a revered television host who was the guru when it came to putting your life together. She had personal development and self-help guests from around the world on her program, and through their collective advice, women changed their lives. Her popularity grew so much that she would crash websites just by mentioning them on her program and sending millions of people there in a matter of hours. Her recommendation could send a business to the top of its industry and had on multiple occasions. She loved the fact that she was able to so positively

impact the world and hoped to do it for the rest of her life. How have the people she's met and interviewed changed her own life?

459. He was one of the most famous movie producers of all time, not because his movies were critical darlings or started the careers of great actors, but because they always made money. They didn't make as much as a Titanic or an Avatar, though they never failed as spectacularly as some studio movies did each year. Many directors who later became big shots worked for him early on and were amazed by how effectively and cheaply he could bring a movie to life and often sought his counsel early in their careers. He was mocked by movie critics for his low-budget wizardry that hardly ever rose above the level of popcorn fare. He was a guru of the movie business and all producers took cues from him to make sure their movies could be even close to as successful as his were profit wise. How did he get his start and learn to make money off a risky business?

460. It all started with a $1 million prize after creating a perfect NCAA tournament bracket, launching her into prominence as a sports guru. When she repeated the feat two years later, she changed her love of sports into a career and became one of the most sought after interviewees when it came to tournament time in March. She loved sports and she was glad to turn her life to such an area, she just never expected to become famous as a result of her expertise. When February and March would roll around, she would receive hundreds of e-mails and texts from friends trying to win their pools, and she simply laughed at her sudden Spring popularity. How did she get to be so skilled at picking winners in college basketball?

Jews

While I'd mostly determined to keep this book irreligious aside from a few sections, in attempting to create 100 distinct sections, I figured including those from my religion would be alright. In my many years of after-school religious classes, my Bar Mitzvah and my free trip to Israel through the Birthright organization, I've learned countless things about Judaism and the people who practice it. There are a few stereotypes out there about the Jewish people, and I feel like a smattering of ten non-cliché Jewish characters will be just the ticket to weeding those stereotypes out a bit. Sit back, eat some bagels with lox and take a gander at these Jewish folk.

461. When most people thought of a rabbi, they pictured an old man wearing a tallit over his suit and constantly praying. When those people asked him how he fit into that mold, he said he was a different kind of rabbi: a rabbi of the street. He didn't really have a congregation and he rarely presided over Bar Mitzvahs and weddings. He would counsel homeless youth on the streets and help them to make a better life for themselves. He got involved with the gang violence problems in the city and did everything he could to knock them down a peg or two. He was beloved by many and hated by some, but regardless of people's feelings, he was most certainly a rabbi. How did he become the revered man of the night he is today?

462. No matter how much he tried to push religion away from himself, he was completely unsuccessful. After all, he looked extremely Jewish with his curly black hair and his large nose. He had a very Jewish last name and his family was famous for contributing financially to the local synagogue. That being said, he hadn't practiced the religion for nearly 20 years after having a falling out with his Orthodox parents. He knew all of the traditions and the most important holidays, he just no longer had any interest in participating. He even married an atheist and came closer each day to believing her viewpoint. How Jewish does he consider himself and what would cause him to renew his faith?

463. She wasn't Jewish by birth, but when her husband asked her to become a part of his religion she jumped at the chance. She'd always wanted to take part in the traditions and ceremonies of a religion and because her parents grew up agnostic she never had the chance. Whenever she attended Bar or Bat Mitzvahs as a teen, she wished that she was up there in front, reading and singing the Torah. This is one of the major reasons behind her visiting Jewish social groups and signing up for sites like J-Date. Her mission was successful and after a few months of marriage, she studied for her adult Bat Mitzvah. What are some of the other reasons she wanted to become Jewish?

464. She knew what most people thought when she talked to her kids' friends or her grandkids. She was a stereotypical Jewish grandmother. She also knew that they were completely right, but she felt like she didn't have much control over it. After all, her mother and grandmother before her had acted in exactly the same way. She was

obsessed with making sure her progeny was eating enough and she loved them with every ounce of her being. She took care of the house and her husband well and she was always anxious that something would happen to her relatives. She realized she was falling into the pigeonhole of the Jewish grandmother but she figured there were worse things to be labeled. What are some of the ways in which she breaks the mold of this grandmother type?

465. Throughout his youth he had dealt with the Jewish religion as an everyday challenge. His parents kept the house Kosher and made sure that he went to Synagogue every Friday night and Saturday morning. He appreciated the ritual of the thing and he enjoyed having a Jewish identity. He just didn't feel much of a need to keep all of the same traditions going. He married a Jewish woman who felt similarly to him and while his kids received their Bar Mitzvahs, he didn't push them to keep going to services after that. After all, the membership fee at the Synagogue was a bit expensive. What are the other ways this man maintains his Jewish identity?

466. He was one of your favorite kids to hang out with at Hebrew school. You two shared a few public school classes as well and you seemed to see pretty eye to eye about keeping your Judaism relatively separate from the public eye. This is why you were surprised to find out that he went to a Jewish college and thoroughly enhanced his faith as he got older. He didn't become a rabbi or anything, but nearly all of the pictures you saw on Facebook of him had the prayer shawl under his clothes and the yarmulke adorning his head. You wondered to yourself if he was the same humorous, interesting fellow you knew back in school. What are some other ways in which your friend has changed over the years?

467. She was like a Jewish mother type in miniature. She had been one of the most popular girls in school due to her fast talking and her early development, but she was never one to be cruel. She would ask plenty of questions about how you were doing and what you were up to, though she wouldn't always wait for the answer to launch into a related topic of conversation. She attended Synagogue every Saturday, though you wondered if it wasn't in part so that she could chat with a bunch of different people after the service. What are some of the things she likes to talk about during her long-winded conversations?

468. People were always surprised to find out that she was Jewish. After all, she certainly didn't fit the description. She had bright red hair and blue eyes that made her seem more Irish than Jewish. She grew up in a part of the country where Jewish people weren't all that common, so people rarely made the assumption. When she attended a more diverse school for undergrad, most pegged her for a Catholic instead, and she just laughed them off. She never took offense to people confusing who she was – it had been happening all her life. She enjoyed keeping religion a part of her life and attended weekly services whenever she could. What are some other ways in which she appears to be non-Jewish?

469. Sometimes he lamented the choice he'd made for his career. As a well-known financial advisor, he felt like he fit too much into the money-obsessed Jewish stereotype. He wanted to point out that Jews were essentially forced into the stereotype hundreds of years ago and that if it wasn't for them, the modern economy might have never developed. Most people didn't care about his opinions, though, unless it had to do with dollars and cents. He was great at what he did and his abilities had helped many people out of financial trouble. He wondered if maybe he should have gone into something more exciting like surfing or safari leading, but he knew that God had chosen the right place for him. What other Jewish stereotypes does he rail against?

470. With a Jewish mother who wasn't interested in practicing and a Christmas-loving father, she had lived most of her life as an agnostic Christian. When she was informed that her Jewish blood would enable her to travel to Israel for free, she jumped at the chance. It gave her the opportunity to go to a continent she'd never seen in addition to getting out of the house during a particularly boring summer. She was overwhelmed by how interesting the Jewish culture was after immersing herself in it for several weeks. She'd never really thought about her Jewish identity before, but the trip had her questioning whether or not she should make an effort to include the religion or at least the ethnicity aspect as a part of her life. She felt like being Jewish was somewhat like being a part of a special club. Now she just had to decide if she wanted to pay the dues. What will she decide to do about being a part of the Jewish faith?

Religious Officials

Religious officials tend to get a lot of flack from stories portrayed in the media and on television. Some officials are viewed as buffoons and others as criminals. Looking at all these officials as out-and-out saints would also probably be a mistake. In reality, many religious officials are simply looking to get by and pay the bills while using their profession as a way to reach people and change lives for the better. It's impossible to ignore the abuses of power that have occurred in these positions in the past and in the present, but most priests, gurus and rabbis are more than likely similar to regular working stiffs.

471. He laughed when he saw his name next to the title of "Rabbi Emeritus." To him, it meant that the Synagogue wanted to respect him but decidedly wanted him the hell out of there. He didn't completely blame them; after all, the congregation had grown so large and he had become so frail he could barely keep up with a quarter of the congregants' needs. He wanted to meet all of their children and be a part of all their weddings, but it simply wasn't possible, even for a younger, faster man. He absolutely loved to dance and many of his peers had their own best impression of "the Rabbi dance." His words, however, especially the ones in his final sermon, were more magical than any two-step. What are some of the highlights from his storied career?

472. As the prayer leader, also known as an imam, for his local mosque, he had certain responsibilities that couldn't be ignored. One of those was getting up at the crack of dawn to lead attendees in a short prayer, another way to provide support for those who were struggling with integrating their religions with their modern life. This was especially true in a post 9/11 world in which some Muslims believed it was more important to hide their religion to avoid persecution. He knew that it was important to keep traditions alive and that a few bad apples cannot be allowed to spoil the entire orchard. He had been well educated at an American college and many professions called to him, but he knew that keeping his community strong was the most important calling of all. What are some of his challenges in running a mosque in a modern world?

473. She was concerned about her predicament. She thought to herself that this shouldn't be a conflict; after all, she had previously only been in love with God and now she met someone she loved with a great deal of the same fervor. She thought love to be very important her entire life, and as a minister of the Methodist Church, she often gave talks on the importance of love in one's life. The issue is that she was in love with another woman and such a situation might cause her to be defrocked. She asked some of her peers what the right decision would be in hypothetical questions, and they took the same stance as the church. It was perfectly fine for gays to worship there but not to lead, and the "person" she was talking about had to consider what was more important in life and the afterlife. What will she decide to do and how will it affect the rest of her religious career?

474. She was amazed at the joy in her life. It felt like only yesterday that she had been nominated as a deacon and she felt such pride at that time. She'd loved the Church and tried to show her deep-rooted connections by volunteering for every event under the sun. Now, years later, as a bishop, she laughed when she looked back on those times as an idealistic do-gooder. She still had ideals and did good, of course, but now that she was helping so many different groups all over the state and had so many responsibilities, she rarely had the opportunity to help individuals. Some days she would have to drive over a hundred miles to deal with an issue at one church and others she would lock herself in her office to write sermons and letters. Some women she met called her an inspiration, having such a high-up position as a female. She always said that with a lot of faith and hard work, anything is possible, man or woman alike. Describe her typical day doing work within the Church.

475. When he was growing up, if someone had asked him what he wanted to be later in life, he certainly wouldn't have come up with the word "priest." It wouldn't have even been in his top ten. But sometime in college while he was walking around aimlessly as he usually did, he suddenly felt a great connection to God and decided to take a class taught by a priest. He was surprised to find that this religious professor was not stuffy, old and boring as he thought all priests were after his experiences as a child. He met with the priest and learned that despite being celibate and obedient, the man was far from ordinary. He ended up deciding to go into the priesthood himself, which definitely pleased his extremely religious parents. He wanted to be a cool priest that kids and adults looked up to for guidance. What was it that made him feel suddenly more connected to God than ever before?

476. When people met this swami, they assumed that he'd be Indian, would have a thick accent and that the things he'd have to say would hardly affect them at all. They were wrong on all accounts. This white American from New Jersey had been brought up Christian and was extremely devout when it came to religion in general. He simply couldn't decide on which one made him feel the most in touch with God. He went searching throughout the world and came upon the Hindu faith. He spent years in India studying works like the Bhagavad Gita and he knew that this is what he'd been searching for his entire life. As an American, he was recruited by the faith to go to the United States and act almost as a sort of ambassador to the religion. What were the reactions of his family and friends when he became connected to this foreign faith?

477. She had been raised an Orthodox Jew, which meant that men and women were so separated that they couldn't even pray together. The wall that separated her from her father and brothers was something she understood as a child but couldn't fathom as she blossomed into adulthood. She loved Judaism and wanted desperately to be a rabbi. Her parents were completely against the idea, as there had never been a female rabbi ordained in Orthodox Judaism. She was fiery for someone so restricted her whole life, and she began going to a Conservative synagogue. She missed some of the aspects of the services she'd grown up with but decided that the only way the religion would move into the present day was with leaders like her. Her studies eventually led her to be the senior rabbi down the street from her childhood synagogue. How has her ambition changed the relationship between her and her parents?

478. When she was selected as a First Reader for her church in the Christian Science faith, she really wanted to reach out to her family to tell them. The only issue was that none of her progeny followed her same beliefs. She had one daughter who was practically Catholic, another who had converted to Judaism and another who occasionally took her own daughter to church but was more or less non-practicing. She loved talking about her achievements with her friends and congregants and church but she wished that her own flesh and blood could share in her joy at being appointed to this esteemed position. From time to time, when she was reading the weekly lesson, she imagined that she was speaking directly to her family out in the congregation. What other aspects of the religion does she feel unable to share with her daughters and grandchildren?

479. He'd happened upon the most glorious scam in the world: starting a cult in which you are the main deity to worship. He'd seen it on so many television shows and movies that he figured he'd try to create a little commune in the middle of the forest. He'd used some of his previous illicit earnings to buy a huge plot of land and he read books on how cult members are brainwashed for tips. Within a few years, he was living like a king, had multiple sexual partners and rolling in the dough from handmade crafts he sold online. As much as he enjoyed being in power, he began to understand why people devote themselves to religion. They wanted to believe in something that could keep their essence alive for the rest of time. He even considered going straight and actually trying to help people full time. At least, he did for about a second each day. How was he so successfully able to create this religious community?

480. She agreed with most that Buddhism wasn't truly a religion as much as it was a practice. She would argue, however, that many religions were focused on what your actions were, making Buddhism similar to a religion in many respects. She was the head of a large meditation community in one of the biggest metropolitan areas in the country. She believed that meditation and faith can be used to create a happier and healthier life. She had been an instructor in these areas for several decades and whenever a newspaper wanted a religion-related quote to a study on meditation, she was always more than willing to comply. She knew that eventually science would catch up with the many benefits physically and spiritually that Buddhist practices could forge. How did she become such a major voice in the Buddhist community in the first place?

Intellectuals

No matter what you're read, watched or experienced, the intellectuals of the world always seem to know more than you. Intellectuals usually have strong opinions on the big issues and the ones that are more inconsequential, but they typically have the knowhow to back up their beliefs. Intellectuals are sometimes portrayed as having much in the way of book smarts but little when it comes to common sense. In the movie Midnight in Paris, the protagonist's rival, Paul is an intellectual who at one point even takes over a tour from a tour guide, showing that character as both an intellectual and a jerk.

481. He was able to boast several masters degrees and PhDs in subjects ranging from art history to ancient languages. While he was perfect capable of discussing pop culture and things that normal people would understand, he took a certain pleasure from talking about subjects that were in his immediate wheelhouse. He'd talk about where words came from or how certain styles of furniture and art were designed. At first, new people meeting him thought his vast knowledge was cool, but it definitely got old quick. Why does he spend so much of his time talking about his book knowledge as opposed to connecting with people?

482. As a sportscaster, he was required to know much more about sports then the average guy. When he hung out with his non-sportscaster buddies, however, he just wanted to be one of the dudes. This became impossible when they asked him questions about a game they were watching, because his vast knowledge of the game would take over and he'd kill speculation with his total accuracy. When his friends would ask what play he thought a team would run next, he was almost always correct. When a game was coming down to the wire, he would frequently be able to tell how the final few minutes would play out, taking all the fun out of it. One of his biggest worries had come true: he'd become too smart at sports. What will he do to remedy his over-intellectualization to enjoy the games again with his pals?

483. You had been one of her classmates in high school in the most advanced math classes. While you didn't continue the way of the integral and the derivative, she continued all the way up through a PhD in applied mathematics. She was still a good friend of yours, and you loved introducing her to your new buddies when she would come to visit. The only problem was, she tried way too hard to explain the things she now did on a day-to-day basis. You had a vague understanding of what she was getting at, but most of your friends seemed to think she was the nerdiest girl they'd ever met. You tried to show them the girl underneath the math, who was definitely cool, but all they could see was the PhD. Will this math genius ever be able to prove she can push past her formulaic conversation?

484. Her friends tried to remind her that just because she was a birthing nurse and a Lamaze instructor did not mean that they wanted her pregnancy advise 24/7. After having a child early in life, she became extremely interested in pregnancy and made it the main focus of her life. When her friends began getting pregnant, she was so excited to be able to tell them every detail and the things that they should be doing every day to ensure a healthy pregnancy. The problem is, that is all she would talk about, and she had ceased to be their friend in lieu of becoming their coach. She knew she was being annoying but there was nothing more she wanted than for their babies to be super healthy. How will she remedy her desire to over-share her pregnancy knowledge?

485. You were so proud of your friend, a former Navy tough guy, who had gone back to school and was now fighting his way toward a masters degree. You used to talk primarily about sports and guy stuff, but now his focus was on the things he was learning about in grad school. You loved talking about American colonialism and 18th century art history as much as the next guy, you just didn't have a lot to add on the subject. It was so funny to you that a guy who used to talk about burps and farts was now telling you in depth about various historical movements. You wondered if this was a temporary change reflected in how much he was reading these days, or if the days of chatting balls and strikes was over. How did this friend of yours make the transition from muscle head to bookworm?

486. His whole life people were telling him that he knew so much about random facts and figures that he should go on Jeopardy. So he did. And he won over $100,000 over the course of a week's worth of wins. Before he had been on the game, people he hung around with seemed to be annoyed at his rambling off of seemingly innocuous trivia. After his major victory, however, he was almost defined by said trivia. They would look up new and unusual questions to ask him, and more often than not, he was able to answer them correctly. He was happy that his friends now appreciated his talent for memorization, but he also didn't want to solely be defined by his knowledge as well. What will this Jeopardy champion do to prove he is more than a computer of information?

487. She didn't love going to the movies for the reasons other people loved going to the movies. She was there almost solely to continue to fill her database of directors, actors and specific shots that she would use to prove her superior knowledge of movies over her fellow buffs. She could easily tell you almost every movie that a particular

actor had been in, going back to childhood roles and one-off television appearances. She would readily tell you what influences a movie had by comparing shots from a certain scene to one from a movie produced decades earlier. All she did was watch movies, write about movies on her blog and talk about movies with her likewise cinema-obsessed friends. What are some of her favorite movies to watch and why?

488. Her friends felt like they always had to point out that she wasn't actually a priest or a rabbi. She just happened to only talk about religion and absolutely nothing else because she was a professor on the subject. As a young girl, she had been fascinated by the various faiths of the world and knew that she wanted to be involved somehow. The only issue was, that she didn't believe in God, so she had no inclination to working for a particular religion. Educating others on the matter, however, now that was a worthy task that she loved fulfilling as she entered her second decade of instruction. Religion was a touchy subject, though, and her friend occasionally omitted her from certain events so that she wouldn't piss people off. What are some of the things about religion that interest her so much?

489. He was an expert when it came to love, at least as far as expressing it was concerned. He had memorized hundreds of love poems, such as odes and sonnets, when he was studying for a masters degree in English. He'd even written several published works on love during different literary time periods. You'd think that this knowledge would give him a leg up on the dating competition, but he had a tough time making the transition from intellectual to actual affection. He made historically memorable gestures to the women he loved, but he would then deconstruct their actions together and talk about them as if he was a third party, studying them hundreds of years later. Needless to say, the girls he dated thought that was weird. Will he ever learn to love someone in the moment?

490. But how could you be intellectual about a car, you might ask. Through her years of laboring on vehicles in her father's garage, reading automotive magazines and even taking a tour to visit automotive factories worldwide, she could tell you anything you ever wanted to know about the automobile. She knew the parts that made up the very first Henry Ford creation all the way down to the features of the modern electric contraptions. She loved her ability to make car-loving dudes feel stupid by imposing her vast knowledge upon them. The only thing she loved more than taking cars apart and putting them back together was showing just how much she knew on the subject to anyone willing to listen. What was it she enjoyed so much about talking shop with others?

Celebrities

If you aren't interested in using real celebrities in your book, you know, to protect the rights of the innocent and whatnot, you have a lot of great options for creating your own. The lives of celebrities have changed drastically in the immediate news world of Twitter, Facebook and the blogosphere. If a celebrity is doing something noteworthy, the whole planet will know about it in a matter of minutes. This adds to the notoriety and the pressure of celebrities and will influence the movie stars and pop sensations that you place into your stories. Remember, celebrities are people too, just people with lots of money, fame, scandal and designer clothing.

491. When he was discovered on YouTube, he was just a teenager with a great voice and a cute look that the ladies loved. Now he had become a complete brand with fragrances, a clothing line and even a television series to find the next great pop sensation. While at points of his celebrity, he got a little bit cocky and had some adolescent moments including a car crash, an underage drinking violation and even a sex scandal, he'd weathered the storm though and he decided to use his clout to bring attention to some important causes. Is his decision to engage in charitable causes a PR stunt or does he actually care?

492. It was rare that he was mentioned in the tabloids without the name of his ex-wife, since they both became celebrities together on a frequently watched and mocked reality show. When the two of them split up, he made every effort possible to cultivate his last bits of fame with a tell-all book and a made-for-TV movie in which he played himself. He was able to score a few reality show appearances and host a few local events, but his celebrity was beginning to fade. He knew that to keep in the public eye, he'd need to do something drastic. What does he decide on to keep his star rising and how well is it received in the media?

493. She was angry, she was mean, and her fans absolutely loved her for it. She had an absolutely filthy stage act to go along with her singing and she had been boycotted by various parent and religious associations. And she had

accomplished all of this before the age of 20. In the beginning of high school, she was sort of a nerd who loved singing in chorus. A couple of years and rapid growth spurts later and she was a worldwide teenage sex symbol. Despite all this and her public image of sluttiness, she'd never had a serious boyfriend and her highest priority was to fit in time to curl up with a good book. Will her superstardom ever change her and how will it do so?

494. She was one of the world's foremost experts on the environment and she became a viral video superstar after screaming at a conservative newscaster on a live television program. She made the rounds on all the talk shows and developed a major following due to her digital notoriety and her good looks. She opted to capitalize on her fame by appearing in several movies and commercials while supporting environmental causes. She even won an Academy Award producing a documentary. How has her life changed since her popular environmental tirade?

495. As the biggest movie star in the world, he enjoyed $20 million paychecks and whatever women he wanted, whenever he wanted them. After a strange television appearance, his image went from hero to zero. He sunk into a deep depression and starting doing some serious soul searching. He remembered that the only reason he'd even gotten into movies was to impress chicks in high school. He wondered if that was strong enough justification for staying in the business. When he emerged from his introspective quest, he realized he no longer wanted to be in the movies, he just wanted to dance! How will this newfound passion be perceived by the hungry media and what will his next step be?

496. He was the most popular reality star on the most popularity reality show which just so happened to focus on a stereotypical ethnic group. He spouted catch phrases all day long for the camera and everyone in the world believed he was a party animal. And they were right, at least at first. As he began to see his persona on the show all around the world, he wondered if he came off badly. At first he wondered what his parents would think. Then, he imagined what his hypothetical kids would think, marking the first time he'd ever even considered having kids. Will he change in real life as a result of watching himself on a reality show?

497. She was a popular character on a TV sitcom for years. She had a few roles her and there afterward but more or less faded into obscurity. After nearly a decade, she popped back into the spotlight after gaining a large amount of weight. This scored her several comedic TV and movie appearances and gave her the opportunity to be the spokeswoman for a popular weight loss gym. After losing the weight, she was back in the headlines for her rapid weight loss. She had missed her fame and was happy to sacrifice a bit of her dignity to reclaim it. She started to plot out her next step, in case her fame began to slip away again. What is her plan and why is fame so important to her?

498. She was the most popular movie starlet of her generation and a picture of her smiling could be found on the walls of men and women alike. She enjoyed having the freedom of choosing whatever projects she wanted, but she was completely weirded out by being talked about in the media at all times. In her opinion, she wasn't all that interesting, simply fortunate and semi-talented. She would also get extremely nervous when talking about herself and would laugh her way through most interviews, always thanking her teachers and her family. How did such an important movie star become so humble and anxious about the media?

499. He had been a fixture on television and movie screens for over five decades with stints hosting, guest starring and even dancing. He was a total household name and he was considering retiring after a long and successful career. He appreciated how lucky he had been but now he was ready to fade out of the public spotlight. Unfortunately, his likewise famous daughters were in the media all the time due to their messy divorces and parenting faux pas. He wished he could live on some remote island so that he'd never be seen on the cover of a tabloid again. Why is he so interested in retreating from the world and will he be successful in his efforts?

500. She was a constantly working actress and writer, but she was the kind of celebrity that nobody ever remembers the name of. She was beloved by a select few who listened to her podcast and read her blog constantly and was recognized on the street as "that girl from that movie," but she was hardly ever mentioned in national news media or the like. She didn't mind that, as she never got into the business to be famous, more to satisfy a desire to be creative. What are some of the roles she's taken on and what does she do during her free time?

Big Shots

Television and movies love the portrayal of the big shot. Whether it be a loud-mouthed talent agent like Ari Gold from "Entourage" or Justin Timberlake's portrayal of Napster co-founder Sean Parker in the movie The Social Network, these characters are often larger-than-life because that's exactly how they live their lives. Big shots can include people with high-profile jobs or descendants of the rich and famous who stamp their net worth on everything they touch. If you write about certain industries like the film, music or Internet, you may feel compelled to throw a big shot or two in there for good measure.

501. At a young age, he lucked into producing a movie that ended up becoming a big hit. One hit led to another and before he knew it, he was a decamillionaire and one of the most sought after people in Hollywood. This gave his ego a huge boost, as he'd been somewhat of a dweeb in his school years, and this rise in confidence and cash made him buy every toy a man could ever want. He had women in his room every night, paid or otherwise, and he was constantly on his Bluetooth trying to score the next deal. He felt like he had to keep moving or he would be yesterday's news. Will all these successes make him happy or will they increase his chances of disappointment?

502. One of his only dreams as a kid was to own a professional sports team. He worked his way up in the corporate world and began to pull in a seven-figure salary for a few decades straight and risky investments actually gave him the capital he needed for his own franchise. When he finally got his wish, he loved everything about it: the atmosphere, the attention and the influence on a real team. The only problem was that his team was horrible and was the laughing stock of the league. Will he enjoy his big league purchase if his team looks like it couldn't even compete at a high school level and why?

503. If you put her clients together in one movie, it would be one of the highest grossing films of all time. They were that good. There was something about her, the way she could make producers believe their films were sunk without her clients, that made the top stars in the world gravitate toward her. She wasn't mean or evil about this power in the movie business, she was just intense and convincing. If a producer or a client backed out on her, she wouldn't get revenge. Her revenge was being such an amazing agent that the producer and the former client would regret their decisions. What are the top three things that makes this mega agent happy and why?

504. She was a giant of women among a sea of men. Most tech startups involved a nerdy male who achieved at such a high level due to lack of time with women or a desire to spend more time with women, but she was in it to prove that women were just as technically savvy as men. She could have been a feminist but she determined that acting as an eventual billionaire female role model, she would have more success. Her company revolutionized the Internet and a movie about her life was forthcoming, as was the initial public offering of her business. What satisfaction does she get out of being one of the only women in a man's game and being a role model to women growing up?

505. He won the lottery after buying his first ever ticket at the age of 21. With hundreds of millions in his pocket, he considered spending as much as he could like a "good consumer," but determined instead to save and invest. After a few decades, he'd brought his fortune above one billion and figured he'd saved enough to live a playboy billionaire philanthropist lifestyle. He gave away large chunks of cash to charity to keep his conscience clear as he kept his social life as busy as a president's. He loved his life to pieces and knew that this was what he was meant for. What would happen if his industries were to collapse and he had to go back to living the normal person lifestyle?

506. He wrote the book on living a dream lifestyle of working fewer hours, traveling the world and doing everything you want. While he wasn't a true success financially until the book came out, he had done some wild things like swimming the English Channel, winning a boxing tournament and creating a successful chemical company. When the book was released he assumed his role as a success guru by holding seminars and charging nearly one hundred thousand dollars for each speech. He wore loud clothing to match his rapid-pace, no-nonsense speaking. Every so often he would take a year off speaking to do some of the things he still had on his bucket list. What are some of those items and how did he will himself to such success?

507. When she married one of the world's most eligible and richest bachelors, she was relatively unknown. With her new fame and financial backing, she started one of the largest specialty clothing retailers in the world and

eventually surpassed her spouse's fame and fortune. Now it was him posing for pictures and her making the front page, and she loved every minute of it. She had always dreamed of fame and thought that her high-profile man would do the trick, but she was surprised to find out that she had something inside of her the world wanted to see. Does she treat her husband differently now that she's more famous and what would ever happen to her if the two of them split up?

508. She was one of the few people in the world to have earned every major performance award including an Oscar, Tony, Grammy and Emmy. She no longer did much acting and singing, but she did split her time between major social causes and major social events. It was said that she truly took over every room that she went into and that nobody in his or her right mind could help but loving her. Her laugh was infectious and her jokes would send an entire party into fits of giggles for hours. She'd had many suitors throughout her lifetime, but she was never married, content to live with friends and make every day an adventure. Are there any achievements she has left she'd like to win or is she content to live out her days simply enjoying herself?

509. He was your boss, no matter whether or not you worked for him. He had such power and clout that he could ask you to do something on the street and you'd feel absolutely compelled. Rumors abounded about him giving thousand-dollar tips to strangers who would trade suit jackets with him and other oddities. He was unquestionably rich, but power for him was something that came from within and his was unlimited. He'd learned how to take control of a situation from his mother, who taught him that if it wasn't under his control it wasn't worth having. What would happen if he ever met a person who, like him, felt the need to own every conversation, party and company?

510. She was a conservative former-politician who was much more popular than it seemed she had any right to be. She toured around the country and crowds gathered no matter what she was discussing. Books had been written about her and movies had been produced about her, but it was difficult to know what she was after. Regardless of her motives, her reputation continued to grow astronomically each year due to her ability to stay in the news. Her folksiness came from growing up on a farm and being the only girl in a family of seven kids. This part of her personality was exactly who middle America wanted to see in office. Did she ever imagine that she'd have such notoriety and what will she do with her appeal going forward?

The Washed Up

For some reason, especially on television, we have a love of finding out more about the "washed up" people of the world. For these purposes, I have defined washed up as someone who used to be a well-known celebrity, athlete, artist, business person or other profession in high standing but has now fallen far down the totem pole. In recent years, we have come to worship the washed up in reality shows and even television shows like "Hung" and "Eastbound & Down." These characters can be used to dark comedic effect, but also in the form of a tragic commentary. For stories that show what happens after the fairy-tale life, including washed up characters is par for the course.

511. When he first entered into Major League Baseball, commentators thought that he would be the second coming of Nolan Ryan. Steroid accusations and recreational drugs derailed his career, and by the age of 30, he could frequently be seen collecting unemployment. He had pitched a few years in independent baseball leagues, making less than a tenth of what he spent during his big league days. He tended to blame anybody but himself for his failings and would rarely listen to the loved ones in his life. He'd been on a few reality and game shows after his baseball career ended and he always talked about a comeback that would never make it through the drug use. What will the last few decades of his life be like and why has drug use been such a problem for him?

512. During his music career, he was known for trashing hotels and damaging equipment as frequently as possible. After 10 years and several #1 hits, his band grew tired of his antics and threw him out. He said they would never reach the top without him, and yet they did. Unrestrained by his behavioral limitations, they released several platinum records without him. He tried his hand at a solo career, but all his efforts were met with horrible critical reviews, most of them pegging him as a fraud from the beginning who had gotten lucky with his original band. His

music career was over and the closest he got to headlines were bits of news about his messy divorce. What will his future hold and can he ever make it back to the top?

513. She was well known for her facial features and her body when she was acting in some of the most popular movies of the 1980s, and as she aged, she wanted to keep her fans from looking at younger and more attractive stars. She started down a long road of plastic surgery, and it wasn't long before she was almost completely unrecognizable. The movie offers stopped coming and before long, stories came out talking about her as an example of surgery gone wrong and used for the wrong reason. She focused on her family thereafter and saved up the money she had earned to live a relatively comfortable lifestyle. She considered making a comeback on a reality show, but she decided her family was more important than money. Does her family look at her differently because of her appearance changes and why or why not?

514. Her career seemed to be blossoming with comedic movies and her late-night comedy show. She thought she'd take this opportunity to buy a new mansion and all the expensive furniture and treats that went with it. In the blink of an eye, her show was cancelled and the acting offers stopped coming in. She spent the next few years filing for bankruptcy and attempting to pay back creditors. To her credit, she kept the news stories about her issues light and comedic, and this attention ended up getting her a recurring job on a low-rated sitcom playing herself. She figured playing a wash-up on TV was better than being completely broke in real life. How will her bankruptcy leave the rest of her future?

515. He wasn't meant to be the star of the show, but his quirky antics as a nerdy teenager made his character legendary. He was on cereal boxes, talk shows and bumper stickers throughout the country. After the show was cancelled, everybody wanted him to play the same kind of kooky character, but he refused. He had tired of the role and wanted to play closer to himself. He had been too pigeonholed, however, and he couldn't get more than a bit part here and there. He decided to tour on his own and with his dark comedy, he alienated most of his fans who came out to see him. All he wanted to do was be himself. What will he have to do to stage a comeback at this part of his career?

516. As a celebrity chef, his wild antics and perfectionism were known throughout the industry and the world. He had earned a large amount of money from his television appearances but burned his bridges with an elitist and pompous attitude. When his attempts at starting a restaurant chain failed, he tried to turn back to television, but all the doors were closed. He was forced to work as an employee again, and he an extremely difficult time reigning in his very openly expressed feelings. Eventually, he resigned himself to the work and earned his way back to respectability, if not stardom. What are the things he misses about being on television and what does he enjoy about his lifestyle out of the spotlight?

517. When she graduated from college, she published a novel that critics called the best of the generation. She had received a pretty paltry advance from this book and barely saw anything from it due to a poor contract. After her two following books crashed and burned, she was still just another college graduate with a liberal arts degree. She considered herself washed up by the age of 25 and was constantly depressed by it. The second contract did pay off her student loans, however, and she was able to survive on a part time job while she tried to write and reach the glory of her first book. If nothing else, at least she appeared on Oprah once. Will she be able to return to artistic prominence and does she feel washed up when reading the reviews of her second and third books?

518. She was one of the most well known television personalities for home decorating and crafts, and her name was branded on many different products related to the industry. When she went to prison for fraud for half a decade, most considered her career to be over. After all, she'd had to return most of the profits from her products to pay the civil portion of the case. With her brand tarnished, she opted instead to reinvent herself. She founded an organization dedicated to helping women in prison to improve their opinions of themselves. The group was successful, and while she never became rich or famous again, she certainly felt a lot better about herself. In what ways did her new line of work make her happier?

519. He had created one of the first major computer companies and competed thoroughly with IBM and Apple in the early years. He even once appeared on a magazine with Bill Gates and Steve Jobs, labeling him one of the

three new pioneers of computing. His star fell on hard times when his attempt at an operating system was an absolute failure. He refused to sell his company for a pittance and ended up losing everything. He turned down job opportunities from both Gates and Jobs and kept trying to come up with the next new thing in computing. After 20 years, his desire hadn't waned but his hard work had little to show for it. What kind of "could have" and "would have" statements does he say when thinking about his past prominence?

520. She was America's sweetheart in almost every entertainment industry. She'd recorded a successful album, won an Emmy on her own television show and had even headlined a $100 million grossing movie. After a horrifying car crash, she went into a coma for nearly a year before coming to and finding her growing empire had crumbled through no fault of her own. Her injury damaged her vocal chords and left her with facial scarring. She tried to enter back into the Hollywood machine, but when no doors seemed open, she took to the road and toured a one-woman show about her experiences. There weren't any packed houses, but there was enough press to keep her afloat financially. What will happen to this former star after she's done with her touring?

CHAPTER 5: CHARACTERS BY AGE AND FAMILY

Family

Of course, there are plenty of other subjects to touch on in our twisted (or normal) families. Some of the best characters I've ever read or seen have been brothers, sisters, uncles, grandparents and cousins of the protagonist. A few of the most successfully profitable movies of all time, Home Alone and My Big Fat Greek Wedding, focus heavily on introducing this wild mix of people to the screen. Hopefully, with this list at hand, even if you don't have a large or eccentric family, you can still write one into your stories.

521. It's a wonderful occasion in your family, just as it would be in any other. Your uncle has made parole and he is coming over to celebrate. Your uncle is a strange guy: extremely nice, loves playing ball with the kids during the holidays, and he possesses the inability to earn an honest buck doing anything at all. As far as you can remember, your tough, burly uncle has never had a legitimate job during your lifetime. That being said, he seems to be an attentive brother to your mom and he's one of the favorites of the younger kids in the family. You hope he'll still be out of jail by Christmas. What are some of the crimes this uncle has committed and what keeps him from an honest job?

522. Whenever you introduce yourself, it almost always comes up automatically. "You mean like..." with the response "Yes, he's my cousin." When your cousin is one of the most famous celebrities in the world, it can be a lot to live up to. When you were younger, he babysat you and you often noticed a flare for the dramatic. Nobody expected at the time that a big-nosed, curly-haired Midwestern kid would end up at the top. Serendipitously, he shot to fame on a reality show before scoring his own sitcom and television deal. The sitcom, of course, was based on your wacky family. What is it like when he comes back to visit for Thanksgiving and how has he changed?

523. There's nothing quite like having your sister visit. First of all, her visits tend to last at least a month at a time and secondly, she has shown up for this visit completely pregnant. Unsurprisingly, she begins to suck up all the attention in the house. She is fun to be around but quick to criticize you about your living habits and your parenting. You hope that the father of her baby will come to sweep her off her feet and take her off your hands, though you do find it nice to have an extra person around the house to help with your standard family duties. How much longer will she stay and what is her true opinion of you and your immediate family?

524. You've always been surprised by how "with it" your grandmother has been your entire life. She is now pushing about 100 years old and yet she still lives in the house she raised your mother in, continuing to remember everything life has thrown at her. She lights up when telling embarrassing family stories and is the opposite of politically correct. Somehow, she has even figured out the computer and the Internet and has begun to post 80 year old pictures to Facebook. She has kept the family together with her wisdom and love through incredibly rough times and it's hard to imagine a holiday season without her. What is her favorite story to tell and why?

525. Whenever you introduce people to your older brother, they tend to laugh and say they don't see the family resemblance. You two are actually half-brothers with fathers of different races. It was tough for your brother growing up as the only non-white in a large white family, but it taught him tolerance and gave him a thick skin. In addition, he had a killer sense of humor that he used to defuse any difficult situations. You've always looked up to your brother and you are glad that he, his wife and his kids live so close to you. What is your brother's favorite memory of your childhood together and why?

526. You always make the joke that you "married into numbers" when talking about your spouse's family, because your father-in-law is one of the top accountants in town. He has always been an accountant through and through, speaking in terms of deductions and investments. The first time you met him, he was wearing big, black glasses and he actually had a pocket protector on. He has always been kind to you, and he has worked long hours to provide for his family. While he didn't often open up to you, you two went out for a drink once and he told you that you were a welcome addition to the family. Why did he decide to go into a life of numbers and what will he do in his retirement?

527. When you divorced your wife, it was completely amicable as you two simply realized that it wouldn't work out between you. You assumed that you wouldn't see much of her for the rest of your life. A few years later she was married to your brother and pregnant with their first child! It was a situation straight out of a soap opera and you harbored a lot of anger toward her and your brother for a long while. She was so laid back when it came to cleaning, personal hygiene and tending to your relationship when you were together and when you see those habits in her new relationship, it drives you crazy. It's odd calling your brother's house and having her pick up the phone, but you're starting to get used to it. What was it like for her to re-enter into the family and what will the next few years be like in this interesting situation?

528. Your family is what you'd call accepting but conservative. When your aunt came out to everyone during the holiday season, it caused a major shockwave. After all, your parents started a church that tended to exclude homosexuals from joining, but they also felt that it would be a sin to exclude family from their lives. Whenever she brings her partner to family functions, explaining the situation to the kids is always a tenuous and hilarious situation. Your aunt has always been the one to turn to in a situation that your right-wing parents just wouldn't understand. While she tends to talk more often than she listens, it seems like most of the things she says have major value. When did she decide to come out and what is her day-to-day life like with her partner?

529. When you were young, you avoided hanging out with your grandfather because you were somewhat afraid of him. After all, he was the oldest person you'd ever seen in your life and you didn't know what to make out of the wrinkly skin and the liver spots. Now that you are old enough to appreciate him, he has fallen under the thick fog of Alzheimer's disease. You try to piece together your early memories of his personality and recall a strong, proud, military man who wanted the best for his family. Now he mostly stares off vacantly, straining to remember who he is. What happens when he has a lucid day or two on a trip with you and your family?

530. She is your distant cousin and she always gets exactly what she wants. When she wanted to skip a year between high school and college to tour the world, she stomped her feet until she got it. When she wanted to marry her serviceman boyfriend during her sophomore year of college and her parents said no, they simply eloped and had a small ceremony on their own. When she spent the rest of her college savings account on a business idea that quickly went south, her parents began to put their feet down, showing authority they had never before exhibited. At family functions, when she and her parents fight it's like a bomb going off. How did your cousin become so entitled and how will she mature as she grows up?

Parents and Guardians

We live in a world very different from the one fifty years ago in which the parents of a child would nearly always consist of a biological father and a biological mother. Now we have more frequent instances of step-parents, sperm donors, same-sex parents and other family members raising the children. If you are writing a young adult book or simply a story with child characters, these are some ideas for keeping their parents interesting.

531. He was a good husband and father who tried his hardest to tend to his family while working a very high-maintenance, high hours job. One of his main purposes in life was to earn enough money to make his wife and children comfortable, which is why he was willing to do something that he didn't completely love. When he was finally able to retire early, his wife was diagnosed with stage 4 cancer and he learned that she had been having an affair. His usual mild-mannered temper changed to manic in a hurry. How does he best care for his wife, his children and himself during this difficult situation?

532. He always knew that he was gay, but where he grew up, it was the style to get married and have kids before he could figure out how to tell anyone. Despite this repression, he was wildly successful as a result of channeling his energy into his own business. When he came out to his wife and children the collective response was, "Finally!" He and his wife now have an open relationship and remain married. While he dates occasionally, he still puts most of his effort into his job. Always a serious person, he has taken to smiling much more often since coming out. What will the next ten years bring for this man and his progressive family?

533. She always knew she would be a holy woman, and early on in life, she took a vow of celibacy. While overseas on a missionary trip, she was brutally raped and left for dead. She survived the ordeal, and upon returning home, she

learned she was pregnant. In her mind, there was no choice but to keep the baby. She determined she would have to give up her vow to find a suitable father for the child. How will this godly woman alter her ways to enter a dating relationship with another Christian while pregnant?

534. As a teen singing sensation, she was able to avoid some of the things that come with having a responsible life. Unfortunately for her life plans, that did not include skipping protection during sex. Despite her manager's suggestions of an abortion, she decided to take a year off to have the baby before she would start back on the road. A funny thing happened. Behind all the makeup and the high notes was an average, brown-haired, brown-eyed girl who wanted to lead a somewhat normal life. At the end of the year, her manager calls her. What does she decide to do and why?

535. Nearly two decades ago, he had given birth to a perfect baby girl before giving her up for adoption. Ten years later, he determined that he wanted to live life as a man and had the necessary operations and hormone therapy to become one. One week ago, he received a message from his daughter, who had recently lost her adoptive parents in a horrible accident. She is disgusted by her mother's sex change but has nowhere else to go. How do they learn to live together?

536. From all outward appearances, he seemed like the perfect father. He was the chairman of a local religious organization and he treated his two daughters like princesses. While he looked somewhat like George Costanza from "Seinfeld," he acted much more like a friendly neighbor. Appearances can be deceiving, however, and it turned out he had embezzled over a million dollars from the religious group over the years and that he'd be going to prison. His daughters would now have to be parented from jail. Why did he do the crime and how will he fare during his time in the slammer?

537. She was a free spirit, a lesbian, and she was in a civil union with a lawyer who more than financially covered her creative desires to do whatever she wanted. Their adopted children were growing up and began to rebel. This gave her more free time than ever, which always caused her thoughts to run wild and bounce around like ping-pong balls. She was very loving, which her children very much appreciated, but they began to tire of such outward parental affection. What are some creative projects she has worked on and how will she cope with empty-nest syndrome if her kids go away to college?

538. She felt she had two main purposes in life, taking care of her family and protecting her country from terrorists. Her husband was more than willing to be with the kids solo so that she could go overseas and serve in the Armed Forces. She missed her children but felt that it was her calling to be on the front lines. She saw some scary things over there, but by thinking of her squad members as her additional children, she was able to cope by being the mama bear with a gun. Late at night, she would pray for her kids, thousands of miles away, hoping they would understand why mommy needed to be away. Will she continue to return to the front lines as her children grow up and why?

539. He once reached the New York Times Bestseller List with a book about being a loving and kind parent. If you told this fact to his teenage daughter, however, she'd scoff in your face and roll her eyes. He actually wasn't a half-bad dad: he listened, he was understanding and he was willing to compromise about most things. Despite going around the country and lecturing about parenting skills and being compassionate, his own daughter was particularly rebellious against his best efforts. He hoped he would be able to effectively show is love for her without her feeling too smothered. After all, he dedicated the book to her, not that she'd ever read it. How does he cope with his parenting celebrity and how might he be able to more effectively connect with his daughter?

540. When she was in high school, she was one of the wildest kids the school had ever seen and her popularity soared to the top. The one issue preventing her from being queen of the school was that during her junior year, she got pregnant and decided to keep the baby. Throughout her late teens and early twenties, she stared longingly at her junior prom picture, which showed her trying to conceal her massive belly in a expertly crafted lavender dress. When her daughter reached the age of 16, her mother was determined to make her daughter as popular and fun-loving as she had been – even if it meant doing it against her will. She chaperoned every school function and, in a way, was more popular with the popular kids than her daughter was. She even started dating the former star quarterback of the

school who just graduated last year. How does this fun-loving, nostalgic mom both raise her average daughter and relive her glory days?

Teenagers

Teenagers could practically fill up an entire book of characters because a single teen can represent nearly a dozen different people during a given week. A combination of raging hormones, a developing sense of right and wrong and an impending opportunity to move away from home can create some wild situations for many teens. Even though teenagers may not find out who they really are until they are well beyond college age, seeing that attempt to understand themselves is extremely fun and painful to read about in a story.

541. Despite the fact that he couldn't drink, smoke or vote, he acted like a middle-aged man in his topics of conversation, his attire and the way he acted. He had a group of friends who appreciated his maturity, though he tended to weird them out with his thinking, that was in a way both forward and backward at the same time. His parents tried to get him to enjoy things that kids his age liked, but it was to no avail. He would talk at length about politics and dinner parties, and he never stooped to watching anything like reality TV or listening to popular music. Where did he get these qualities and is it the kind of personality trait he'll hold onto for life?

542. If James Dean was the "rebel without a cause," he was the "rebel without anything to rebel against." His parents would give him whatever he wanted, even if that request included space or responsibility. He wanted desperately for them to give him a hard time because he had so much bottled up angst for no reason. When he took it out on teachers at school, his parents were completely understanding, which drove him crazy. He even asked them once to pretend to get angry at him and they couldn't do it right. To escape from this heaven of an upbringing, he opted to get the best grades possible so he could choose any school, as far away as possible. What were some of the other things he tried to rebel against unsuccessfully?

543. She was the epitome of a New York girl and she loved the fast pace and the lived-in quality of the city. When her single dad found out that she was sexually active, he moved her to the suburbs of Los Angeles, to get them both as far away from that life as possible. She hated suburban life with a passion and quickly drew the ire of her classmates. After all, she refused to wear anything but comfortable normal clothes, didn't speak like them or become part of their cliques and she even did her homework. She didn't mind not fitting in for the most part, though she was sad on the weekends when the other person she had to hang out with was her mom. What will her two years in suburbia be like and will she ever adjust before going to college?

544. She was the kind of girl who felt that every problem could be solved by shopping. Need to get over a breakup, bad haircut or a broken leg? Go shopping. It was a two steps forward one step back shopping process for her as she would max the credit card her parents gave her, take some things back and then do it all over again. She loved being on top of the newest fashions and refused to wear the same outfit twice if possible. When her family fell on hard times, she adjusted immediately by purchasing discount fabrics and sewing products and making her own clothes, which the girls at school loved. What is next for this shopping, sewing phenomenon and how will her family's hard times impact her life?

545. He was the star running back of the football team, a member of student council, and he seemed to have the perfect life. At home, things were a different story, as he had to take care of his ailing grandmother and his mother was overseas fighting the war on terror. Even though there were plenty of offers, he shied away from having a girlfriend because he wasn't sure he'd be able to handle it all. He was just hoping to hold it all together until he got out of school, got a job and was able to pay for home health care for his grandmother. He loved the idea of playing for some big college, but he wasn't sure if four years away from his nana would work. How did he come to be so responsible and what will happen to him after graduation?

546. He was in the marching band, and even though most guides to popularities would say the opposite, he believed there was absolutely nothing wrong with that. He got to travel to other schools and meet lots of new and interesting people. His love life was actually booming with a fellow trumpeter from a school only 20 minutes away, and his friends were loyal and kind. Sure, he received some gentle ribbing from the popular kids at school, but he was so genuinely good at his instrument that they actually gave him some props for it. When his school won a

national marching band championship, he was even on the front cover of the local newspaper. What are some other qualities of this self-confident, talented musician?

547. As much as she tried to live high school life like a regular teenager, she would always be the girl who got pregnant and had a baby her freshman year. When other students were out playing volleyball or doing Spanish club, she was going back to her house with her parents and taking care of her toddler. She wasn't a bad kid or anything, she was just foolish and unlucky the first time she slept with someone. The baby's father had gone away to college, and though he came back to see the baby, he was rarely a part of the girl's life. She was in this alone and she had to be strong until graduation. What was it like telling her parents about the pregnancy and what does she want to do after graduating high school?

548. She was head over heels in love with her English teacher, and while she knew it was wrong, she wanted him more than she wanted any boy in the school. She would stay after school to get "extra help" from him and she joined the newspaper since he was the faculty advisor. She would cut out pictures of her and her teacher from the yearbook and put them together on her bedroom wall. She held herself back from the dangerous next step of calling his house or trying to seduce him; after all, she didn't want people to think she was crazy. That's right about when he called her, asking to meet up. What will she decide to do with this risky opportunity and will she tell anybody about it?

549. He was the quiet kid who wore trench coats to school and was always reading comics featuring destruction. The rest of the school, including the teachers, assumed that if a shooting were to occur in the school, it would be him. When an honor student was the actual perpetrator, it was the quiet, dark, comic-reading teen who put his own life in danger to stop the shooter in his tracks. He heard the shots ring out and he burst into action, attacking the boy, disarming him but taking a bullet for his troubles. When he returned to school, it was as a hero, and many students who had mocked him made efforts to befriend him, if he was willing to forgive them. What are some of his internal qualities that enabled him to take action in such a frightening situation?

550. She was the kind of girl who made every effort to be in every club possible. Her parents joked that school was her job and frequently asked her if she'd gotten a promotion. She laughed off jokes like these that also came from the student body because it was more important for her to be involved than anything else, like social standing. She felt that life was too short and if she didn't try everything at least once, she was missing out. She was pretty and intelligent and if she played her cards right, she could certainly transition to popularity. It just wasn't something she cared about in the slightest. What clubs will she join as she gets older and what will she do in the real world when a job tends to take up more time than school?

Children

Some stories, especially those portrayed on television, don't do the best job of creating realistic child characters. Frequently, kid characters are either cute as buttons saying the "darndest things" at the drop of a hat, or they are completely devoid of morals with a propensity to torture as many of their peers as possible. From your own childhood, you know that there are many shades of grey in between with children who have medical conditions, children who are overachievers to the nth degree, children who act more mature than their own parents, and more who don't fall into a traditional child archetype. A child in a story should be complex, especially in a format that allows the child's imagination to be expressed through and through.

551. He was the stereotypical role model teenager, according to his parents. In actuality, he only kept up appearances to make it easier for him to sell pot to his classmates. This involved him getting high grades to keep them calm and to participate in several activities that gave him more time at school. He knew that getting caught would not reflect too badly on him before the age of 18, so he played fast and loose to save up as much money as possible. What was he saving for and will his parents ever find out about his extracurricular activities?

552. Not only was he one of the fastest, strongest athletic kids in his school, but he'd even broken state records and was starting to get calls from potential future Olympic recruiters. One of the reasons he was so motivated was because his dad had been pushing him athletically from a young age. The two of them even went to buy hardcore vitamins and protein concoctions from the health food store together. He was embarrassed that his dad would yell at

him in public from time to time, but he knew it was for the best for his career. What is a typical day in the life like for him and how would he change without his father's guidance?

553. She loved diving into activities with full force...for about two weeks before changing her mind. Her parents had dozens of boxes in the attic that were full of her old, discarded hobbies such as tae kwon doe gear, clay for pottery class and even a children's sewing machine. Her parents didn't want to discourage her from expressing herself, but they were pouring a lot of money into projects she simply wasn't able to follow through on. She was quite laid back about giving up on these hobbies, which tended to annoy her parents even more than whining might. Will she ever find an activity to stick with for life?

554. When she was little, despite her parents pushing her toward math so she could follow in the family accounting business, she wouldn't stop drawing and painting. They had no idea where her innate artistic abilities came from. They were amazed by her dramatic uses of color and her ability to accurately represent people simply by looking at them. She always seemed to do her art with a smile on her face, and her parents knew that numbers would never excite her the way art did. As her taste in art grows more refined, will she find it a strange subject to discuss with her fact- and formula-driven family?

555. It wasn't until he was nearly three years old that he spoke his first words, which were in the form of a complete sentence. He was quietly mastering the English language, and he took this silent observation to new highs in almost everything he participated in. Aside from oral participation, he   mastered nearly every skill at school, and his teachers often cited his ability to write at a much higher grade level. His parents worried about his inability to form social connections due to a lack of speaking, but they didn't want to scold him for being who he was, either. How will this speechlessness affect him as he grows up?

556. He felt like he had a duty to save his family's souls by going to church, because they were true atheists in every sense of the word. Her parents weren't sure how and why he got so into Christianity, but they made an effort to encourage his newfound interest as best they could. He would give them sermons at dinnertime and he got reports of lunchtime preaching from his very secular middle school. Whenever they asked him where he learned about all this religious talk, he simply said, "God." How will this televangelist in the making cope with school and his atheist parents?

557. Without fail, no matter how much they tried to get her to dress sensibly for a girl her age, she would come home looking much older than 11. They would no longer let her keep makeup in the house, but that didn't stop her from applying it herself sometime during the school day. She would even occasionally return home wearing a different and much more adult outfit than she had on when she returned home. This was completely unacceptable to her parents and they frequently grounded her. She used that time to look up the application of different makeup styles online. Will she ever compromise with her parents over dressing like a woman instead of a pre-teen?

558. She had one goal and one goal only: winning the science fair every single year. She poured almost all of her middle school free time into learning more on her favorite subjects so that she could wow the judges all the way up to the national level. Elementary school had been a cinch, as she was far above the comprehension level of most, but as she grew older, she knew she'd have to work even harder. She shunned most friendships and sacrificed homework from other subjects to push herself farther in her scientific knowledge. Will she win the upcoming competition and how would she react if she loses?

559. He went to the emergency room so often, his parents joked that he should have a punch card there and get a free visit after 10 trips. An accident-prone combination of careless, unlucky and risky, he was coming home with so many skinned knees and bruised elbows that his parents actually asked the teachers to keep an eye on him to make sure he wasn't being bullied. He wasn't. He tripped, banged into lockers and slipped more than any child the school nurses had ever seen before. Doctors said that he would grow into his legs eventually, but until then, they should invest in some ice packs and iodine. Why is he so prone to injury and what would it take for him to go a whole day without an accident?

560. No matter what the situation or who was talking to her, she was the kindest, gentlest girl you'd ever met. It was rare to see her mouth in any other position than a smile and to describe her as anything other than upbeat. From

a young age she had always said hello to strangers, cashiers and other kids, but she never grew out of the phase of being extremely excited to see everybody in the world at any time. Some of the kids thought her attitude was a matter of her hiding something, some dark secret, but in actuality, she was just extremely nice. Why is she so perky all of the time?

Exes

Whether you're thinking about Shakespeare or Michael Bay, many authors start their stories with a protagonist that has been jilted by an ex-girlfriend, boyfriend, husband, wife or lover. In many cases the exes are angry, vengeful people who seem to have no redeeming qualities. While this can actually happen in reality, it tends to be an easy choice for most writers to create such an awful ex to make a romance between the protagonist and a new character much more palatable. Personally, I find it refreshing to see the partner from a former relationship in a somewhat positive light. Regardless of how you choose to portray these former loves, make them well-rounded and interesting people that we'd be willing to go on a date with ourselves.

561. He was smart, funny and kind, and after you put in two years trying to be the best girlfriend possible he left you and got engaged to the next girl within two months. You couldn't believe that after putting so much time into learning about his divorced parents, his fear of failure, his nerdy comic-book collecting adolescence and his foot fetishes, he was willing to jump into marriage with another girl so quickly. You wonder if it was his overbearing mother, who never really seemed to want you around. Maybe the new girl just had better feet. What does the future hold for this toe-loving individual?

562. He was a total sleaze ball from the beginning and you never wanted to admit it to yourself. After all, he was the most attractive man you'd ever dated and he was more than a little attentive in the bedroom. Even though you suspected he was sleeping around, you decided against your better judgment to move in with him. The evidence becomes even more clear at that point. He dresses in expensive designer clothes and works hard for his father's company to keep his lifestyle supported. What is it that causes him to cheat on women and what would cause him to settle down?

563. She was a few years older than you when you started dating in college, and it made you feel a whole lot cooler. She was fun-loving and wore wild clothes, some of which she designed herself. You spent many nights just walking around and talking with her into the wee hours of the morning on the subject of religion, love and sex. At the end of all those sleepless nights, she let you down easily but it hit you hard. One worry that you had about her from the beginning was that she'd been to five different colleges. Might she have been afraid of commitment? What is she doing now and why did she attend so many schools?

564. The first time you heard her sing, it was in her native language at a religious ceremony. You'd never listened to anything so moving and you did everything you could to learn more about her culture. She was also a decent athlete, and you surprised her with a bouquet of roses and a box of protein bars when you asked her out. You only dated for a few months, but you learned a lot about her love for her family and her desire to make them extremely proud. You suspect that it was her family that contributed to your break up, and you wish you could have convinced them how much you were willing to adapt for them. What choice did she eventually make for her life partner and did her family approve?

565. At first you began dating him as a favor to your friends who set you up. You were surprised when you fell in love with this nerdy but caring man who was the best listener you've ever encountered. You've never felt as truly cared for as you did with him, and you feel awful for having ditched him for what later became a summer fling. You suspected that you broke his heart but later heard that he found a wonderful girl who could appreciate him more. Sometimes you think of him as the one who got away, but you wonder if you might have been tempted to someone more exciting again if you'd stayed together. How did he cope with the break up and what would happen if the two of you ran into each other again?

566. You'd heard about women who stayed in abusive relationships before and you'd always thought they were ridiculous. It wasn't until you found yourself in the middle of one with a very strong and angry man that you understood their situation. You had fallen head over heels for this very successful businessman with huge biceps and

a temper. After you'd been dating him for nearly half a year, he began abusing you verbally and making you feel small. A few months after that he began hitting you when he was angry and intoxicated, and you almost felt like you deserved it. After all, he was so much more successful than you so he had to be doing the right thing. You feel ashamed that you thought such things while they were happening and your friends eventually helped you out of the situation. He's now in prison for having assaulted you. What do you think he'll do when he gets out of jail and why does he feel the need to attack people he loves?

567. When you meet a person at a drunken party, it can be tough to know who that person really is when sober. You never really got the privilege of learning that about this girlfriend, since every time the two of you went out she got completely wasted. The first few times you went out, you wanted to match her drink for drink and be a real man. She laughed so loud and was so completely affectionate that you didn't want the party to ever end. A few weekends worth of hangovers later and you realized that for her, the party never stopped. You made an effort to hang out with her sober on several occasions, but she always showed up hammered. She didn't take your break up hard and whenever she sees you, she tries to put her tongue in your mouth. How long will she continue this lifestyle and will she ever find the drunken man of her dreams?

568. She was your polar opposite in almost every way you could imagine. She seemed stuck up and dressed like some kind of catalogue model. Her voice got on your nerves, and whenever the two of you were in the same place you fought like an old married couple. During a strange moment alone, the two of you hooked up and kept it up for nearly a year. Despite the knockdown drag out verbal spats you two would have, you miss how tidy and put together she was. What caused her to be so prim and proper and what kind of people has she dated since?

569. He wasn't particularly attractive and he wasn't very athletic either. His family was kind of weird and your beliefs didn't sync up with his. But he was funny. Oh man, was he hilarious. He had the ability to turn any situation into a laugh riot, which was a welcome break from the serious year you'd been having. It wasn't just dumb jokes either, as he demonstrated wit, wordplay, pop culture references and physical humor as well. Since the big picture stuff didn't match up, the relationship wasn't meant to last, but he still calls every so often to check in and brighten your day. How did he develop such a sense of humor and what did he end up spending his life doing?

570. She was the one who wouldn't go away, no matter how hard you tried. You two had been dating for nearly a year when you decided to end things because she was too clingy. You tried to make the break-up gentle, but she just didn't get it. She had once told you the story of her seven-year boyfriend trying to break up with her. She didn't get the hint for three weeks. Even when you spelled it out to her plainly with a prepared speech, she still came over the next day to "hang out." None of this was malicious, but it was a little bit crazy. She kept buying you small gifts to show that she cared, even when you started dating someone else. What made her act so clingy and why wouldn't she accept the end of a relationship?

Unrequited Love

Another type of love that tends to fit into a good story is unrequited love, which involves one character pining over another. This isn't the kind of affection that is ever returned, though it may come close. There are always too many obstacles in the way that will keep the characters apart. I've heard and experienced many personal and touching stories about unrequited love and if written correctly, including these characters in a story can work to great dramatic and comedic effect.

571. His complexion and countenance were like a painting or something. His dashing good looks, his popularity at school and his athleticism made all the girls line up as if they were taking numbers. You were so far back in line that you gave up sophomore year, but you still wrote poems and songs about him. A friend of yours stole one of the songs and gave it to him without telling you. He came up to you in the hall, thanked you and kissed you on the cheek. This cemented his legendary status in your life and you never forgot how kind he was when he easily could have embarrassed you. He always waved to you in the hallway after that. What ended up happening to the ultimate high school crush of your dreams?

572. You figured that since you were a nerd and he was a nerd that you'd be a match made in heaven. Sure, he was skinny and weird and he wore glasses, but he was so smart. You thought that if he picked you it would somehow

validate how intellectual you were as well. He went with you to a school dance once and went out with you in a group, but no matter how many hints you dropped, he either couldn't pick upon them or he wouldn't. You later heard that he became extremely religious and got married in a very hardcore ceremony. You weren't invited. What do you think made him truly happy and why did he choose a more religious life?

573. She was quiet and incredibly artistic. You used to marvel at her work in a class you simply took for a humanities credit. You made the effort to talk to her after each session had ended, and while she was polite, she rarely had anything to say in response. She wore long, flowing dresses and always had one braided strand of hair that she tucked behind her ear when she got nervous. You finally built up enough courage to ask her out by the end of the semester and she simply said, "No, thank you." And that was the last you ever saw of her. Why was she such a quiet person and what ended up happening to her in the future?

574. You were young and you didn't understand much about flirting. You were helping her to study for a math test and in the middle of the library she started to rub her leg up against yours. She was a pixy-like lover of the environment who had a delightfully nasal laugh. During a break in the studying she looked deep into your eyes and said, "You have really pretty eyes." A week later, you were at her apartment to help set up for a party and she showed you her bedroom. You two sat on the bed and it felt like something was about to happen. Before it could, her friend walked in and ended the potential fun. That night, she met her steady boyfriend for the next three years. You're not sure what would have happened with this frisky, flirty girl if you had been the one she chose, but you've certainly thought about it. What has happened with the girl in the future and what would it be like if you met her again?

575. You couldn't help but stare at him during work; after all, when you glanced to the side of your computer, there he was. You two had both been hired on the same week, and as a result you'd talked a lot during training breaks. You found out that he was single and lived in the same area as you. Whenever you tried to get a drink with him after work, he was often busy at his second job. He was pretty smart and he took good care of himself. He was even kind enough to bring food into the office for everyone to feast upon from time to time. He had such a bright smile and you hoped to get him along sometime so that he could smile at you. One day, without warning, he quit at a moment's notice and didn't say goodbye. Where did he end up and what would have happened if you two had gotten together?

576. You loved the way he pulled up to your apartment building in his motorcycle and you wished you could run your hands through his greasy hair. He looked like he could handle himself in a fight, though one look into his deep, blue eyes might stop the fight before it began. He lived just a few doors down from you and you visited him as often as you could find a reason to. You even once borrowed a cup of sugar from him. You never knew if he was in a relationship, but his apartment seemed to be a little too well-kept for a single guy. When he moved to a new city for a job, you gave him a big hug and wished him well. If only you'd been able to make such a convenient romance into a reality. What do you think this mysterious motorcycle man is up to today and why?

577. She was the only person who could make your coffee just the way you liked it. She was one of the barista shift supervisors at your favorite coffee joint and she ran a firm but friendly shift. She seemed to brighten up particularly when you approached the counter and the two of you developed a flirty rapport. She was the kind of person who laughed with her entire body and she seemed to remember everything you told her from week to week. On several occasions, she even sat down next to you during her break. When she pulled off her hat, she revealed long-flowing blonde hair that you ached to touch. She transferred to a new store and you always wished you had the courage to ask her out. What caused her to work at a coffee shop in the first place and what is she like when she's off the clock?

578. She was your dream woman, and you couldn't stop thinking about her. Oh, and she was also your boss! While your co-workers didn't get the attraction, you thought they were blind to not see how such a powerful, intense woman who was the opposite of girly was a total knockout. You loved visiting her office for quarterly critiques and staring directly into her hazel eyes. You even once shared a dance with her at a company Christmas party. Even though her hands were bigger than yours, it was magical when they locked. You still work for her and you hope that some day the two of you can happily engage in an office romance.

579. When your best friend's son came back from college for the summer, you couldn't help but notice what a man he'd become. You immediately snatched him up for a summer job maintaining your home. He was quick-witted and was growing a full beard that looked red against his strawberry blond hair. You and your ex-husband recently divorced and you would love to show a young man the ropes while you mourned for your marriage. Despite your best efforts using tricks like having him rub lotion on your back and sharing a bottle of wine, he didn't seem to understand your intentions. You hoped that next summer he would take the hint. Describe a day of him working at your home and what he must have thought as you practically threw yourself at him.

580. You didn't care that she was a movie star and that you had little to no chance. You had her posters all over your wall and you didn't just want to marry her, you knew you were going to marry her. As soon as you could put together a sentence, your parents helped you send her a letter. You were surprised to actually receive a handwritten response. Her handwriting was incredibly neat and was written with a green pen, causing you to go out and get a green pen to respond to her. You imagined yourself replacing her scene partners in movies and kissing her all over. In your twenties, you travelled to Los Angeles and actually heard her speak live at an awards ceremony. She had soured on Hollywood at that point and she came off as a mean and angry person who was much different from the person you'd seen on film. You almost wish you hadn't met her, preserving your vision of who she was for all of time. What are some of her on-screen qualities that attracted you to her in the first place?

Brides and Grooms

If you're unmarried like me, than you are truly able to notice that when a couple of friends get engaged, something about them changes. Perhaps it's that they're gaining some sort of wisdom we haven't yet attained. Maybe they are letting it sink in that they will be tied to one person for the rest of their lives. Then again, it might just be because they have to spend the next year or two figuring out every aspect of a day-long event that will change everything! Regardless, while there are some bridezillas and monster grooms out there, most brides and grooms are just regular people put in the extraordinary situation of planning out the perfect wedding.

581. He was just very laid back about the whole thing. His parents were beginning to worry that he was hiding something from them. After all, he'd had a history of anxiety attacks as an adolescent and he hadn't come close to one since the proposal. His bride-to-be expressed some concern that he wasn't anywhere close to freaking out as much as she was. When they asked him why he was so calm, he said there was nothing to worry about because he was about to marry the woman of his dreams and no matter what went wrong, everything would be perfect deep down. Will this cool-as-a-cucumber groom continue to remain cool through the end of the wedding reception?

582. It was the morning of the wedding and he was absolutely nowhere to be found. His bride had a feeling he might do something like this, as he'd be acting very strange the past week. Ever since his bachelor party, he had been fairly noncommittal about the last-second decisions required for the wedding after being quite gung ho earlier. His wife-to-be found him in one of his secret spots in the city, his favorite diner. He knew she would find him there. He wanted to talk things out one more time to make sure that he was making the right decision, since life would never be the same again. Is she able to convince this cold-footed groom to walk down the aisle with her?

583. She was small in stature and loud in volume. Her prospective husband loved how assertive she was, as it was a complement to his more quiet demeanor. He never expected her to be as dominating a person as she was during the wedding planning, though. Her stern voice turned angry on multiple occasions with caterers, florists, musicians and more. When the bridesmaids dress came in the wrong color, he thought she was going to blow a gasket, she had so much steam to expel. He didn't understand why she was so stressed out and frustrated about the planning when everything was mostly going smoothly. Will the stress she exhibits continue through the wedding and into the marriage, or will it cease once the planning has ended?

584. By all appearances it seemed like she was going to be a diva during the wedding that was only a couple of months away. The wedding planner just knew it, but then again, she didn't really know the bride-to-be. Despite the fact that she was a whole lot of woman and she appeared to be quite boisterous, when it came to the wedding, she was as quiet as a church mouse. She knew deep down that she had the ability to take over the planning process and make it all about her. She knew it wasn't about her, though; she wanted it to be about the wonderful process of

joining her and the love of her life. She acquiesced on many decisions that would put the focus more on her and altered it to highlight her groom and her family. One day wasn't important to her in the grand scheme of things. What was much more important to her was setting up a foundation for the rest of their lives together. What are some of the ways in which she has made the wedding more about the union than her alone?

585. He was a guy's guy and when his girlfriend proposed to him over a year ago, his first thought was, "I wonder what my buds will think?" He was completely in love with this woman but he didn't want it to affect his partying and drinking with his guy friends. He made sure that his wedding party had a huge part of the reception to all say toasts to him and his bride. He also had a separate room available so that people could watch the big game if they were tired of partying for a few minutes here and there. He wanted it to be the perfect bro wedding and not be all flowery and pink like some weddings tend to be. What other aspects of the wedding will be more masculine than effeminate and what will his friends think of the event?

586. It was weird that he had to travel halfway across the country to make his marriage a reality, but none of the states he had family in allowed gay marriage. When he finally reached his destination, a church they had only seen pictures of online, he began sobbing uncontrollably. It was perfect in every way. He was a sentimental guy and he thought back to his older friends who couldn't legally be married. He felt completely blessed and he knew that by creating this phenomenal ceremony with his partner, he would inspire the other members of his family to see how wonderful same-sex marriage could be. Not bad for a middle-of-nowhere hick who once hated himself for being homosexual, he thought to himself. How did he come to accept himself and to choose to wed far away from his home state?

587. She didn't want to just have a regular old wedding. She knew that the most important aspect of a ceremony and reception was to be memorable and she devoted every second of her planning to determine what her guests would most enjoy. Her groom thought that she was thinking about others too much and that she should concentrate more on what would make her happy. Her whole life, she had been thinking of how to make other have a better time and she felt like she wasn't going to ditch that now just because she'd getting married. Her groom loved how selfless she was and it was one of the reasons he wanted to marry her, but he figured she wouldn't be so accommodating on their own wedding day. What are some of the concessions she makes to turn the wedding into an event people will be talking about for years to come?

588. Throughout the process of planning her wedding, she wanted it to be a fairy tale. The problem is, from the beginning it seemed doomed to be anything but magical. The retro country chapel they rented was under renovation and was covered in scaffolding. Half of the guests were stranded at airports throughout the country due to incredibly strong storms in the area. Her dream haircut was even screwed up by her typically awesome stylist. She was freaking out, and she kept looking back to her wedding journal that she'd been using for over a decade to plan out every little detail. She whined and cried her way up to the alter seeing only the mistakes and not the things to be grateful for. Will she be able to pull herself together enough to say "I do"?

589. He had always been a fly by the seat of his pants kind of guy. When he asked his girlfriend to marry him, he insinuated that he would love to do a quickie wedding followed by a party with friends later on. While she had other ideas, he kept needling her due to his hatred of planning anything at all. He felt that stress always came from dwelling on things too long and weddings were notorious for that. After all his pushing and prodding, she finally gave in and they drove to Vegas for a speedy wedding. When they finally got there, he wasn't as sure about his decision anymore. He saw the run down quickie wedding place and looked at his soon-to-be-wife and realized that the two of them deserved better. He decided that instead of getting married there, he would pack months worth of planning into three days and that they'd find a way to get married at the planned party back home. Will this decision cause him to plan more events out in the future or is it a one-time thing?

590. She was tired of the same old wedding. She hated the long, drawn out ceremonies and the old people music playing so the aged relatives could cut a rug after dinner was served. She wanted her wedding to be all her, and so she scrapped every convention of what a wedding meant and started from scratch. Her groom knew that she would have her own way regardless, so he stepped back and watched her make magic happen. The ceremony she came up with

was so incredible that it warranted local news coverage and eventually became viral. The reception could hardly be described, it was so wild. What are some of the things she did to turn a blah wedding into a blow out?

Babies

It may seem a bit silly to include babies in this book, as many infants tend to follow very similar patterns of eating, pooping and crying. The great thing about babies as characters, though, is that it is so entertaining to see the baby's personality peeking through into the world. For instance, in my case, my parents already knew that I'd be an extremely positive and humorous adult, just from the way I acted as a baby. By going beyond the stereotypes of the standard "baby," you can show some realism by infusing your baby characters with a bit of individuality.

591. He was pudgy, he was a bit misshapen, but everyone that met him said he was the most well-behaved baby they'd ever met. He never cried because he usually felt quite well taken care of. Unlike most infants, he knew that if his parents left the room, they'd be back in no time at all. He ate his food without much fuss, as was indicated by his chubbiness. Even though he was still under three months old, he tended to listen and respond to his parents' questions and commands with a large amount of comprehension. After all, he didn't want to let them down. What are some of the things he has done that his parents consider memorable?

592. Everything about your baby was absolutely hilarious to you. It wasn't just because he was your first child and you loved parenting; after all, you'd seen other babies and they weren't nearly as humorous. It all started when the doctor tickled his feet instead of spanking him when he entered the world, causing the cutest gurgling laugh you've ever heard. From then on, he rarely cried, he just laughed at everything, which caused many a spit take in your house. He laughed at his mobile, he laughed at dirty diapers, and he laughed at complete strangers. How do people tend to react to this comedian of a baby?

593. You wondered how it took you decades to learn to flirt properly, when your daughter came out of the womb an absolute guru. She would expertly draw in the attention of male adults and babies alike and make them fall in love with her adorableness. This almost left your daughter feeling entitled at home, as she rarely seemed to turn on the charm for you and your spouse. It was as if she was flipping a switch when she had an opportunity to get non-parental affection. You wondered if it was the flirty girl or the whiny ingrate that would become her true colors later in life. What are some of the "flirty" things she does?

594. No matter what you tried, you could not keep your daughter from looking extremely overweight. Her birth weight was heavier than any other baby's you'd ever heard of and it continued to skyrocket from there. Because she was so short and wide, you had a tough time finding infant clothes that fit and you had to get clothes that were much, much too long for her. Your doctors asked if you were feeding her too much, like a steak every day or something. Your friends assured you that she would grow out of it, all their kids had, and that you shouldn't freak out too much or you'll give her a complex before she gets out of diapers. What other challenges does having a heavier-than-normal baby present?

595. He wasn't just a crier, he was a scream crier. It could come at any moment and be set off by the tiniest thing. If the temperature of a bottle wasn't right: scream cry. If a cartoon he was watching had a strange animal or monster on screen: scream cry. If somebody slammed the door while exiting the house: scream cry. Despite these loud, nearly uncontrollable weeping sessions, it seemed like he was perfectly fine with the things that caused most babies to cry. When he was hungry, tired or cold, he would just get a little bit fussy. It was the tiny things that truly set him off, and his mother liked to call him "Daddy's little perfectionist." What are some of the most miniscule things that have caused this baby to begin a bout of yelling and crying?

596. You know how sometimes you see a cat in a strange place in the house and you wonder how the heck he got up there? Well, that was exactly how it was with this bouncing baby boy. He learned to crawl and walk extremely early and you barely had a chance to baby-proof the house fast enough. On more than one occasion, you believed him to have been snatched away and you were prepared to call the police only to find he had simply trapped himself in a cabinet or behind a seemingly un-climbable sofa. You actually considered putting a bell on him due to his ninja-like ability to sneak around, but you figured he'd find some way to get out of that, too. What are some of the sticky situations he's gotten himself into during the first year of his life?

597. One of your favorite phrases to utter was, "Somebody alert Harvard, my daughter is a genius!" It certainly wasn't far from the truth. She was speaking in practically complete sentences before most kids her age had said "Mama." One day when you were reading her a new story she'd never heard before, she wrenched it from your hands and began reading it aloud right back to you. She even once alerted you to a reckless driver trying to merge into you from her child seat. She was obviously something special and you wanted to make sure you did everything in your power to encourage her intellectual growth. You just weren't sure what exactly it was you should be doing. What are some other ways in which this baby girl has shown her brilliance?

598. When you had a daughter, you were so excited about the prospect of raising a pretty, little princess, going to ballet classes and collectively turning up your noses at all the stinky boys. Almost from the beginning, however, you realized that your expectations were going to be far from reality. She absolutely loved her brother's toys, like dumpster trucks and ninja warriors. She played in the dirt and would actually recoil when you made the effort to dress her in pink. She refused to consider ballet and she only wanted to play and watch sports. It was quite obvious that she just wanted to be one of the guys. You wondered if having another daughter might be the best way to make your dream come true. What are some of the other ways in which your daughter defies gender profiling?

599. You figured that if he could survive these first couple of years, he could handle anything. When your child was born, it was discovered that he had a rare illness and would need to receive constant care and treatment to survive the ordeal. These treatment sessions would have been rough for anyone, let alone an infant, but he took it like a trooper. You could tell he knew these sessions were necessary by his steely demeanor he had on the way to the hospital. It was as if he was trying to say, "Don't worry guys, I can handle this." There were also concerns that all these medications and procedures would hinder his mental development, but now that the disease was managed, he appeared to have made it out of the worst of it with all facilities intact. How will the traits he developed to handle the treatment aid him later in life?

600. It was pretty obvious to tell from the beginning that she was prettier than the average baby. Even as she came out of the womb, the nurses oohed and ahhed. She was destined to be photographed, and on a whim, you took her to some casting agents. Within weeks she had already been in several print advertisements and on an episode of primetime television. Within six months of her baby modeling, she'd already earned enough for her first year of college and tons of additional offers were rolling in. You hoped that all this baby primping and posing wouldn't go to her head, but you were very happy that at this rate you could have her college paid for and a nice family vacation fund by the time she hit one. How does she tend to act on the day of a shoot?

Neighbors

There are many wonderful neighbor characters that have stuck with us through time. A neighbor does not have to do much to contribute to a moment in a story, perhaps dropped a tiny joke here and a bit of plot or theme there. In many episodes of the brilliant sitcom Seinfeld, Cosmo Kramer, Jerry's neighbor, was often able to steer the plot of the week in an interesting and entertaining direction, simply due to how wild and crazy his life could be. By playing around with the quirky fellows and females from down the hall or street, you can add multiple interesting touches to the journey of your protagonist.

601. It seemed like no matter how often you tried to stress how important fences were or how much you liked your quiet time, he was always coming over looking to get involved with your family. Whether it was borrowing a lawnmower or asking advice on a new car, he didn't seem to want to take a hint that you wanted him gone. He seemed intelligent enough but maybe he didn't understand that neighbors didn't have to necessarily be buddy-buddy. Then again, maybe he simply wanted to get out of the house for a few minutes here and there. Why isn't he able to take a hint and what are some of the things he has been able to ignore?

602. He was quiet and he mostly kept to himself, which is why you couldn't quite understand how he would throw such raucous parties almost every Saturday night. One time, when you went over there, you could barely recognize him, he was so completely hammered. The next day when you tried to bring it up, he couldn't remember it at all and promised he'd keep the volume down the next time. It was even louder the following week. What are some of the ways in which his personality changes from when he's sober to when he's drunk?

603. She was literally the girl next door throughout the years of you growing up. Now over two decades later, you owned your house while she owned hers. She was inexplicably single and you wondered if you'd be able to turn a long-time friendship into your second marriage. While she had grown up and matured, you always saw her as that cute girl that you loved hanging out with as often as possible. Even though kicking around a soccer ball had been replaced by tea and a conversation, you cherished those moments with her sunny personality and her interesting outlook on life. Does she look at you as the boy next door or as just another acquaintance?

604. She seemed like a wonderful old lady and you wouldn't think twice about helping her clean her gutters or cut her grass, but you were not interested in the slightest at going into her house. It was literally overrun with cats and you wondered if all the strays in the neighborhood hadn't shacked up there, assuming it was some kind of cat hotel. Whenever she invited you over for an afternoon snack, you volunteered to drive her to a local coffee shop, just so you could avoid the domesticated zoo inside. You wondered how a woman could let her house literally go to the cats. What is a cat-filled day like for her in the fur-covered wilderness that is her house?

605. No matter what time of day or night it was, he was always doing something strange in his yard. It might involve using a wood chipper at two in the morning or testing out his motorcycle engine in the middle of the day. Regardless, he certainly didn't seem to follow any time of schedule whatsoever. When you went over to complain to him he seemed somewhat unhinged, possibly from the use of drugs, and he actually yelled at you to leave him alone. Since that time, you've referred nearly all complaints directly to the police. Why is this neighbor of yours so strange and will the conflict between the two of you ever come to a head?

606. It seemed like every night, you heard a new girl going into his apartment without fail. He seemed like a pretty mild-mannered fellow, but he seemed to know exactly what to say to get these women to come over. The music wasn't too loud and the women were always polite, but the passion was too overt to be ignored. In addition, you always saw him bringing out a recycle bin full of empty glass liquor bottles. You hoped that he was being healthy, especially in the department of diseases! What is the story of this passionate man and how does he have such a way with the ladies?

607. While you never had much a meaningful conversation with her, it seemed like she was a yoga instructor. At least, that's what you could gather from the highly sitar-based music that seemed to blare from her apartment at all times. The one time you got a look at the place, there were beaded curtains hanging down from several walls with yoga mats laid down everywhere. She seemed to be extremely calm at all times and you wondered if she worked or if she simply stretched from dawn till dusk. How did she become such an easy-going yogi and why?

608. You've never been introduced to her but you can't help but wonder how she's still living there year after year. On multiple occasions you've seen an eviction notice on her door, but within a few days it's been taken down and new tenants have never moved in. You imagine that she's barely scraping by and at the last second figuring her finances out, but for all you know, she could just be lazy when it comes to paying. Every time you see her, she's completely frazzled and seems to be on edge. Why does she have such trouble making her payments and what is it that makes her seem so nervous all the time?

609. When he moved in, you couldn't help but notice how much high tech equipment his movers seemed to be bringing in. Upon going over there to welcome him to the neighborhood, you accidentally discovered that he seems to be creating a chemical substance downstairs. You aren't sure if it's as dangerous as methamphetamines or as harmless as toothpaste. The mad scientist who runs the place immediately took you inside to explain away the equipment, though you didn't believe a word this lab-coated man had to say. He had wild eyes with a look of sad desperation. What is this man making and why is he doing it in the middle of your neighborhood?

610. After seeing her on the small screen for many years as a talk show host, you never in a million years expected her to be living next door to you. She actually even came over to introduce herself and you were so star-struck you could barely utter a response. She spoke loudly but carried a calm, cool demeanor otherwise. Her star had faded a bit since her heyday, but she was in the area attempting to make a sort of a comeback with a locally filmed cable show. It amazed you that someone who was so seemingly important could be living that close to you. What is her day-to-day life like in a new city and will her comeback be successful?

Senior Citizens

Through six or more decades of their lives, they have made an effort to make a living, support a family and to follow their goals. As they entire their golden years, many senior citizens continue to live with or near family and will be the patriarch or matriarch of a family until death. Others have been relegated to nursing facilities and rarely see the family members they took care of. Some have never had families at all and are trying to live out their last days in peace, while others are still working and contributing members of society. There is a lot of wisdom to learn from these elderly and important characters.

611. After serving in three major wars, his fighting days weren't over. In the first nursing home he was ever placed in, he witnessed one of his hall mates being abused by an orderly. He wrote over 100 letters to state officials and within three weeks, he was majorly involved in a piece of state legislation passed on elderly rights. He always knew that words were as strong as bullets, which he proved to himself by winning his wife of 40 years over with a poem. She passed away a decade ago and he thought of her constantly. What other fights will he be involved in during the rest of his life?

612. Ask the wizard, they'd always said, a nickname he'd picked up from his adolescent magician days. Even though it was seven decades since he'd picked up the cape, he was able to solve almost anybody's problem in the neighborhood. People would come over to his house and ring the bell, he'd shuffle over and let them in and after hearing their problem he'd pause and think for about a minute. Nearly everything he'd suggested had worked on problems ranging from marital difficulties to medical ailments. Whether or not he practiced magic, he certainly was a wizard in every other sense. What is the wildest question he's ever answered and how did he come by this ability to problem-solve?

613. She wrote the book on writing. Literally, she had written a groundbreaking book on style, grammar and sentence structure that became a bestseller for five decades and as a result of the royalties, she lived very comfortably. She enjoyed writing, though she never found the same success writing fiction as she did from her reference-based material. Even at the age of 93, she got up every morning and wrote. What was the accomplishment she was most proud of and why?

614. For her, it wasn't complaining, it was just getting things the way she wanted. After all, she deserved it after 40 years of living with a man like her husband, she always said. Her family had moved away a long time ago, but she became a sort of surrogate mother for a young couple whose parents had died young. She nearly always refused a restaurant's first attempt at her order and she'd earned quite a reputation from local businesses. However, upon receiving things "just the way she wanted them," there was no person in the world quite as grateful. What is her favorite activity in the world and why?

615. He'd seen the town spring up from farmland into a small metropolitan area. Chickens and cows used to play where families parked their SUVs, and as a former auto mechanic, he appreciated the change. He was always bored by the quiet countryside and he was extremely happy to see the town grow up around him. One of his simplest pleasures was to go for a walk along the forest path which went beside a highway so that he could hear the purr of cars and trucks as they whirred by. Does he equally appreciate how movies and television have become louder and what does he do with his spare time?

616. During most of his life he hadn't been able to pursue his passions due to a job with long hours and a family with many mouths to feed. Now that his children and grandchildren could take care of themselves, he decided to take up acting in his twilight years. His local community theater was often lacking when it came to elderly actors, and they welcomed him with open arms. Before he knew it, he felt more alive than he had in decades, and that was before the positive reviews in the paper. He always knew he had it in him and was glad to discover his talent before it was over. What are some of the roles he played and what made him such an adept actor?

617. Her children winced when she began to launch into one of her stories for her grandkids. After all, it might be the one about the biker gang, the affair with the politician or the naked bike ride. And the third one was only last week! The fire from her wild and crazy life had yet to die down, and her children worried she'd be a bad influence on

their kids. Then again, it was pretty cool having a senior citizen with pictures of celebrities instead of mountains and beaches. How has she been able to maintain her vigor for her whole lifetime and what drives her?

618. She was beginning to forget and she knew what this meant. She began to organize all of her photographs from the last 60 years into a database online with the help of her nurse. She spent her whole life acquiring these memories, and she'd be damned if a ridiculously named disease was going to take them from her. The database caught the eye of a local journalist, and she met with him weekly so he could write a weekly column as a sort of looking glass into the past. By the time the disease had gone into full swing, there were over 30 articles and thousands of followers of her photograph database. In her moments of clarity, is she happy with the work she did and why?

619. He refused to give up on music until it gave up on him. He was already the elderly statesman of his band when they grew to prominence in the 1970s, and only 10 years later they asked him if he wanted to retire from touring. He laughed mightily before playing his guitar faster than most people alive could dream to. Now approaching the age of 80, he needed help getting on stage, but that only excited his audiences more. They loved his skills, and they were inspired by his desire to keep up the habit. How did he become a musician in the first place and what, if anything, would prevent him from continuing?

620. She was born on a farm, raised on a farm and if she had her way, she would be dying on a farm, too. The only problem is, her children couldn't get a nurse to come anywhere close to her middle-of-nowhere property, and she would need to move to the city for the first time in her life. She was never a fan of the hustle and bustle, but she wasn't about to let anybody beat her at life. She bought one of those motorized scooters and zipped around town running errands every day. The nurse could barely keep up with this determined woman. What is her day-to day-life like and how is it different from life on the farm?

College Students

They represent the next segment of the population that will soon enter the workforce. In four or five years, these students will change from high school graduates to gainfully employed individuals. A large chunk of them will experience wild and crazy nights as they may be away from home for the first time. They will be tempted with sex, drugs and complete freedom as far as activities are concerned. Many of them will learn what they want to do for the rest of time, while others will chase after dreams or go into higher education. College was one of the most intriguing times of my life socially, and through my school alone, I probably met enough characters to fill up half of this book. Here are ten of them.

621. On the first day of school, he told you that he wasn't just your roommate, he was going to be your best friend for life. You figured that your first random college roommate could have said worse, and you hung out with him as often as possible. It turned out that he actually was quite an awesome friend and he was willing to concede the room to you for studying and other purposes, and he even woke you up if you were about to oversleep a class. Everything seemed to be going great until he told you he didn't want to room with you the following year. He said you just weren't appreciative enough of his friendship and he was going to try looking elsewhere for a "best friend for life." Will this former roommate of yours find his best friendship elsewhere, or is he looking for some kind of perfect friend that doesn't exist?

622. He'd heard all the stories about how most college students utilize their four years away from home. He decided to go the opposite direction and use every second there to gain contacts, start businesses and earn as much money as possible. By the time sophomore year rolled around, he was already earning more than most professors by selling his products and reaching out to alumni. By his senior year, he had been on nationwide talk shows and was well known as one of the youngest and most successful businessmen in the country. It was by the middle of that year that it hit him he would never again be surrounded by such parties and friends ever again. Will he continue down his path of being a go-getter or will he opt for more fun his final five months and why?

623. To say she was a wallflower in high school would have been quite the understatement. If you would have asked most of her peers about her they would have said, "Who?" She determined to change everything about herself going into college. She changed the color and cut of her hair, she worked on altering her voice to be more appealing

and she upgraded her wardrobe to show more skin. She essentially pretended she had been the most popular girl in her previous school and it worked like a charm. When a group of her friends wanted to visit her hometown and meet her high school friends, she felt like the jig was up. How will she explain her lack of high school friends to her new popular college clique?

624. She came from a very religious family that expressed very openly how important it was to save yourself until marriage. On the second day of college, she pushed past that parental belief and didn't look back. She loved the freedom that college allowed her in all the ways her family had held her back. She knew she wasn't going to be a nun or a good religious wife, but she was willing to act the part when she came home for holidays. Her ruse crumbled when a video of her acting wild, crazy, half-clothed and drunk appeared on the Internet and a concerned former classmate forwarded the video to her parents. What will her parents think about her compromising their beliefs and what will she say to defend her actions?

625. As one of the high-ranking clique members of his high school, he assumed that college would be a breeze socially. After accidentally pissing off all his suitemates in the first week, he found that he had a lot of ground to make up and figured he'd concentrate on his studies as he devised a plan. He realized that he actually enjoyed the academic work he'd frequently avoided in high school. Before he knew it, he transformed from a guy who could do the worm into a bookworm. He still went out to parties occasionally when he was invited, but he now had his sights set on graduate school and getting a decent job instead of hooking up with the most attractive person. What do his high school friends think when he tells them about his lack of college exploits and what kind of job will he look for in the future?

626. He started college a year late after travelling the world with nothing but a backpack. He put off leaving college and was entering into his sixth year, making him one of the oldest undergraduates at his small school. There was something he enjoyed about having a leg up on his classmates age-wise, if not maturity-wise. He had a much younger girlfriend who was head over heels in love with him and wanted to move wherever he moved after college. The only problem is, he had absolutely no desire to move and he had no idea what he'd do when his parents finally stopped paying his tuition bills. He loved everything about school, from the dining halls to the cute girls walking around in pajamas. He wanted to be drunk in his frat house for the rest of time. What will he do in his final three months of school after realizing that he can no longer prolong the inevitable?

627. She'd lived quite a life in her 40 years and now she was ready to tackle the one challenge she'd avoided in her time: college. She wasn't the only one in the school who was going back to college in her adulthood, but most of them seemed to have the support of family and friends while she was alone in all of this. Plus, she was learning to be an engineer, a test at any age. She worked her hands to the bone every night studying her notes and trying to get information past her "thick skull." She enlisted the help of a tutor her junior year and he was astounded at how hard she worked. She refused to back down from a challenge. What are some of the challenges she's faced in life and what will she do with her engineering degree if she obtains it?

628. Throughout her senior year of high school, she mocked her older friends who planned to use their college lives to go "husband hunting." She thought such a practice was ridiculous in this modern age and even though her parents had brought her up that way, she wanted to rebel with every fiber of her being. She, of course, didn't plan on falling in love on her first day at the university. He was a couple of years her senior and he was perfect in every way, according to her. She knew that her hormones and her upbringing had to be coming into play, but she didn't care. He proposed at the end of her junior year and she gladly accepted. How will planning for a wedding affect her senior year and her future career?

629. His plan during school was to move up the depth chart on the football team, have a monster junior year and coast on his training senior year until he could get a deal with a National Football League team. A major injury his freshman year forced him to reconsider. He still had a scholarship, and while he was rehabbing, it helped him to study for his classes for the first time in his life. His love of athletics pushed him to a course of study in exercise and sports science. While he could no longer make it to the NFL as a player, maybe, he thought, he could make it as a trainer or coach. What was his reaction when he first heard about his injury and how does he look back on it now?

630. She was the destroyer of curves and the master of biology throughout her four years of college. When most people in the class would get below 60 percent on some difficult examinations, she would score in the low 90s and ruin the curve for the rest of them. Her peers blamed her for their atrocious grades and she had few who were willing to be her friend. She was also involved in multiple activities such as theatre and intramural sports and seemed to be enjoying herself the entire time. She was brash and honest with everyone she knew, which rubbed some the wrong way and endeared her to others. Will she achieve her goals of a 4.0 and a clear path to medical school and what choices will she make in her social life along the way?

CHAPTER 6: CHARACTERS BY PERSONALITY TRAIT

Optimists

Unsurprisingly, I'm happy to consider myself one of the optimists, though at times it seems like our numbers are dwindling. Obviously, many of the other 990 characters in this book could be considered optimistic along with their other traits, but this section is to especially single out those who could be most defined as optimists. True optimists are able to weather almost any storm, whether it be a car accident, a bug infestation or an incorrect drink order at your local coffee shop. Optimists can still have a down day every so often, but for the most part, by the time they wake up in the morning, they can still put a smile on their faces.

631. He wasn't just the guy who got your coffee in the morning, he was the smiling and buoyant barista who brightened your day whenever he was working. You'd only talked to him a handful of times, and he seemed like quite the anomaly. Not only was he naturally a happy fellow, but he was also completely caffeine-free despite working at the shop. You heard that on the side of his coffee trade he was a musician, a writer and a host of other things, none of which had brought him much success, but he sure seemed to love having them as a part of his life. How did he come upon such a positive attitude?

632. The man had lost his job, had several mouths to feed and hardly seemed to have a thing going for him at all, and yet here he was smiling and hosting a neighborhood barbecue. Ever since you'd moved into the area, he was nothing but kind to you and you were frequently amazed at his positive attitude. Now that you knew the whole story though, you were completely blown away. Since he'd lost his job, he'd been working several part time jobs that accumulated over 80 hours a week among them. And even that work didn't match his previous salary. He still felt blessed, however, to have a loving family and to have them to come home to at the end of the day. Will his positive attitude be able to get him back into the working world?

633. In a job notorious for dealing with negativity and anger, the customer support line for a power company, she was the perkiest by far. While those at the company were trained to talk with a smile, she did it naturally without even giving it a second thought. She brought treats to work nearly every day, and she was upbeat even when experiencing absolutely livid calls from the "powerless." She had the ability to cheer up even the most frustrated customers, which she attributed to her mother teaching her how to cheer up her father after a tough day. What kind of satisfaction does she get from cheering up her callers and why?

634. Why would she need luck, she wondered, she was having an amazing day. She was out volunteering for the Salvation Army by ringing the bell and collecting donations outside of a supermarket. This beat her usual job of working for the man, and even though it was cold, she was soliciting for people who really needed help. She didn't mind if someone didn't donate, because 9 times out of 10, she wouldn't have, but it lifted her spirits to new heights when anyone put money into the red canister. Her smile was so wide and natural that people couldn't help but stop and marvel at her positivity as they emptied their wallets. What would she do as a full-time job if she had a choice and money was no object?

635. He wasn't smart, but he sure was kind. In a world where many believed sarcasm to be the height of intelligence, he didn't understand a lick of it. He was blissfully ignorant and was just happy to be a part of his favorite football team. He took tickets for the team and did some basic groundskeeping work and considered himself an important cog in the wheel of the organization. He felt grateful even when the team would go through a rough losing patch, because he was doing what he loved. His family had always given him a rough time for being dull in a family of sharp wits, but his second family with the team treated him with respect he never knew he deserved. What is a typical day like for this simple and special man?

636. His parents were grumpy, mean and unscrupulous. Perhaps this is why he went in the completely opposite direction. He wasn't the biggest kid and there was nothing fashionable about him, which caused him to get made fun of. Only he didn't react like the other kids and kept a smile on his face throughout. The bullies gave up and ended up becoming his friend, because he just seemed like such a friendly kid. He was wise for a pre-teen and would say things like, "Life is too short to be angry, right?" He would even perk up his teachers, who felt that he was a joy to have in class. Will his teenage years affect his attitude or will he be able to maintain his upbeat personality as he grows up?

637. They say you need to be pretty cut-throat to make it in the business world. Well then how come she was the completely opposite? She was gentle with everything from puppies to people, and every customer who came into contact with her felt utterly taken care of. She could take criticism and she could make her bosses and peers feel good even when they were reprimanding her. She made them all want to be better people like her. Her bosses wanted to promote her in an effort to spread her positive vibe to as many as possible, sending her touring around the country in a motivational capacity. What allowed her to be so positive in her career life?

638. If it's smart to be wary and pessimistic, she must have been smarter than the person who came up with that rule. After passing all of her high school, college and graduate school examinations with perfect scores, literally perfect, she went onto life in consulting. Sure, she moved fast and worked long hours, but you would never hear her looking down on her life in any way. She even had the word "gratitude" tattooed onto her arm. After saving up well over a million dollars from her high-paying job, she founded a charitable organization and dedicated the rest of her life to helping people. How was this brilliant woman able to stay positive when many around her had close to the opposite attitude?

639. He was always a groomsman, never a groom, despite several long-term relationships. Even though he was completely the "nice guy you would marry," it was rare that he found a girl who wanted to settle down. In his youth, he used to get upset whenever he didn't have a person to share his life with. Nowadays, he had learned become happy from the inside out, which off-put many of the acerbic women he dated. They loved his kindness, but wished he had a dark side or something. He had absolutely no skeletons in his closet and was able to diffuse every fight that would come his way. Even though he's obviously not picky, what would be the qualities of his dream woman and why?

640. She used to be irritated at everything about the world, including herself, as she was overweight and unattractive. When she discovered how a vegan, gluten-free diet made her feel, she realized that meat and gluten must have been messing with her for her entire life. After a month, she lost 10 pounds and a whole lot of attitude. Each month came more weight loss and additional happiness. She couldn't believe that something as simple as a type of food was affecting who she was. Her co-workers noticed an extreme improvement in her productivity and her personality, and she earned two promotions the year after she began the diet. Describe the differences between an average day for her before the diet and after it.

Pessimists

As the media become more negative every day and as social media make it easier to make your complaints felt, it's tough not to create a few additional pessimists every second in this new digital age. Pessimists are able to easily downplay the positive things in their lives and to find the fault in various aspects of their day. Studies have shown that pessimists live a bit shorter than optimists, as an attitude can mean a lot to health, wealth and success. The most interesting aspect of a pessimistic character is seeing when and how they became that way, which I will play with in these next 10 character types.

641. He was an absolute sourpuss who complained about everything that came into his scope of vision. He would drain the air from every room he walked into by noting the problems of his life, the issues of his co-workers and even his company's shortcomings. The only reason his bosses kept him around was because he was clearly able to assess the worst-case scenario in every situation. He was not allowed in any positive brainstorming sessions because his barbs acted like heat-seeking missiles to each idea. He was also frequently not involved in regular conversation as he'd find a way to make any good news you presented into something awful-sounding. What made him into such a negative person and would anything be able to reform him?

642. When you sat down to your blind date, you assumed that you'd receive the normal chit chat about life, the weather and your respective jobs. You were surprised to hear a string of complaints worthy of a Jerry Seinfeld stand-up comedy routine. He even started one paragraph with the question, "What's the deal with these tiny portions?" You barely got a word in edgewise as he seemed to be perfectly content pointing out the flaws in the world around you. Aside from the chatter, he seemed normal enough, though he was beginning to bald, which you attributed to his

constant "routine." When in his life did he turn his only conversation topic into a long-winded complaint about his existence?

643. She was one of your best friends in the world, but you never told her any of your new ideas or plans for life. You remember back to telling her about your idea for a new business, when she asked, "Do you seriously think you could pull that off?" and when you planned to lose 20 pounds and she said, "But you love food more than you love people." These comments would always elicit laughs throughout the room, but she meant them wholeheartedly. She didn't even know she was bringing the people around her down; she simply thought she was being honest and "There is nothing wrong with honesty." How has her attitude changed the dynamic of your friendship over time?

644. In the past, she had been something of a self-help speaker and had done some great work in improving the self-esteem of the women she spoke with. After an accident that killed her husband and left her wounded and mentally scarred, she did a complete 180. She abandoned her speaking practice and took up a job she hated because she thought she deserved it. She now believed that life was pain and that we were just living out a tough existence to keep the world going around for future generations. She mourned her husband constantly and refused to move on. What might help her to go back in the other more optimistic direction and why?

645. He was a futurist and his research had led him to believe that the world would be completely unsustainable within about three decades. He would go on talk shows and political programs preaching this point of view, but it was rare for someone to take him seriously. He embarked on making a documentary that would show how imminent the destruction of the world would be. Upon its release, it was labeled "The most depressing documentary ever." He built up a small fan base of likewise pessimists who believed the end was near and that little could be done about it. He appreciated the validation. Does he believe there is anything to look forward to, why or why not?

646. He had been a man of God, until he lost both his wife and his son to cancer. He could no longer believe in a higher power that would take his loving family from him when he had been so devoted to the cause of religion. He still did his best to help those in need, but from this point onward he did it all with a grain of salt. He was fine with helping his fellow man, but he no longer believed that there was anything left for us at the end of a lifetime. On most evenings, he sat in his home alone and flipped through old photographs of his family. Is there anything that could bring him out of his funk or to make him believe in God once again?

647. She loved other people and hated herself. She wanted to spend as many moments of the day with others as possible because she couldn't stand to be alone. Whenever she was alone, she was stuck with her own thoughts of self-deprecation and hatred. She would look in the mirror and see nothing but faults with herself internally and externally. When she was dating, she required great deals of validation, and many of her partners found her too needy after the first few months. She refused to go to therapy, but if she had, she might have blamed some of the problems on her mother's constant put-downs. Will she ever find someone willing to put up with her low opinion of herself and what would she have to do to live a happy life?

648. She thought herself to be one of the perkiest and cheeriest people she knew, but that's not how the rest of the world saw her. She always had a smile on her face and was quick to laugh, and yet she was the queen of criticism. Her daughters always felt like they weren't doing well enough for her, even though she loved them dearly. Her friends would often hesitate before calling her, even though she wanted nothing more than to spend an afternoon with them. She didn't realize in the slightest how she was making them feel. What would have to happen for her to comprehend the way other people felt about the things she said?

649. He was widely known throughout the world as the film critic who hated everything, even if it was well-liked by the general population and award-winning. He wasn't able to find anything positive in the films he viewed, and his sarcastic and cynical nature struck such a chord with the public that he received his own television show. His criticism extended to other walks of his life as well, including the characteristics of those around him. What is it about his life that caused him to find such fault in the film industry?

650. She was a complete knockout, and when she walked around the bar, both men and women noticed. Despite the fact that almost everybody she passed thought she was a perfect 10, she believed that she was one of the ugliest people in the world and required constant reassurance. She didn't realize that her self-esteem was so low; she simply

thought she was gross and she'd be lucky to find someone to take care of her. This caused her to get into several rough relationships involving physical and verbal abuse. What caused her to feel so low about herself and what would have to happen for her to think more highly of herself?

The Seedy Underbelly

This is a section of characters that most people would rather not talk about. They are the kind of people that you'd rather your children not find out about until they're older, if ever. The section includes prostitutes and pimps, drug addicts and people on the streets. A story that is set in a major city cannot help but address that there are rough parts of town that include such characters. That being said, not everybody in the seedy underbelly of an urban area is there by choice, and that can be a major factor when creating the personalities of such underground characters.

651. He was lucky he hadn't been killed that night. He had been down at the corner store when a gang of people working for his drug dealer shot up his apartment. He was a complete drug addict, and as a result, he'd racked up an incredible debt with his dealer. To avoid the issue, he spent as little time at home as possible and on this night it paid off. It always seemed like he'd get out of the neighborhood and make something of himself, but he got into crack at the end of high school to take the edge off. It was a mistake he wished he could take back as he stepped onto the bus out of town. Will he be successful escaping from the dealer and can he reform his life?

652. His large stable of ladies made him one of the most sought-after pimps in town, both by men looking for a good time and the police department. Since some of his clients were high-ranking city officials, he'd gained a little bit of immunity for himself. He'd been in the business for the last 10 years or so after becoming a sort of assistant for the last majorly successful pimp in the area. He grew his business by leaps and bounds by taking it online and keeping it more secure. He treated his ladies with respect, and as a result, they tended to skim less off the top than most would. As a relatively competent businessman, why did he decide to go into the prostitution business and what will the future hold for him?

653. People had this image of a female escort as some kind of drugged-out lowlife, but she laughed at such an image when she walked around her completely paid-for house in a very upscale neighborhood. She made upwards of $1,000 an hour when she was working, and her clientele would never label her as a lowlife. They thought she was amazing, and as a result, they paid her higher than some CEOs. Sure, she wouldn't want her daughter to take on the same profession, as it had its stranger moments, and she thought that by gaining as much money as she could, she could ensure her daughter would have a better life. What are the qualities that make her escort-worthy and what would she do if she could no longer participate in the job?

654. She loved luring men back to their apartments and breaking out the handcuffs. After all, men loved to be rendered completely defenseless so she could work "her magic" on them. Her magic, of course, was to rob them of all their possessions and money so she could cash out and skip town. It was so easy because all men wanted was sex, she thought, and in her experience she'd been right. She'd had a blind hatred for men ever since her father left her and her mother high and dry over a decade ago. Since then, she hoped to find her father and take him for all he had and until that point, she would rob sex-crazed men and send as much money home to her mother as she could. Will she ever find her father and has she ever had any close calls in her particular business?

655. During the day he would keep crime off the streets, and at night he would do everything he could to facilitate it. See, he'd learned that he could make a lot more money if he played both sides against each other. As a crooked cop, he actually knew more about the criminal infrastructure of the city than most honest police did, and he always had that as leverage in case he was caught. He did have a few pangs of guilt to put his son through college and pay off his mortgage with ease as opposed to struggling. How did he become corrupt in the first place and will he ever get caught?

656. He wasn't proud of the things he did during the night. He usually wasn't even 100 percent aware of all his actions until he woke up the next morning. Some people were fortunate enough to black out, but he had an impeccable memory. He knew drugs were involved, as was giving away a part of his dignity in the process. All he wanted was more, as often as he could get it; to fulfill this obligation, he did everything his dealers told him to do. He'd killed and he'd assaulted people just to satisfy his habit. He hated everything about himself and considered

suicide on a daily basis. What keeps him alive with all this guilt and what did he do before his addiction changed his life?

657. You couldn't help but notice her come into your favorite donut shop. She was always outside of the place soliciting "donations" for a cause she was raising money for. One week it would be fundraising for breast cancer and the next week it would be for the homeless. She had sunken eyes and cheeks and a set of teeth that looked in serious need of surgery. You weren't sure what her issue was, but you were frustrated by the stories she would tell new customers in order to get them to take pity on her. You knew that altruism was the farthest thing from your mind, and the only thing that kept you from calling the cops was the pity you took on her. What is it she does with this money and why? Does she feel any emotions about soliciting money on the behalf of causes she never plans on donating to?

658. She had always been a big fan of Las Vegas, so she figured why not bring Vegas to her city's doorstep. She ran an underground high-stakes poker league that usually drew some of the seediest fellow from town. They were reluctant to join something set up by a woman at first, but she talked and acted tough enough for them to trust her. She was exhilarated every night by several games in which over a million dollars exchanged hands. She didn't even care about getting caught, because she was currently living out a sort of dream and whatever sentence she got would be worth it. What was it about this secretive gambling that made her so excited?

659. While some might have seen him as part of the problem, he felt he was simply adding to the solution. He was the supplier of most of the unregistered weapons in town, but his records were so airtight that nobody could possibly trace them back to him. He figured that if he gave the gangs, the dealers and the other lowlifes in town the weaponry they needed, they would naturally thin each other out a bit. If he happened to take part in the financial benefit of such a service, he would gladly take it. He saw himself as a sort of Yojimbo and frequently watched that movie to remind himself of that belief. How did he get into this line of work and what is his day-to-day life like?

660. She saw the entire thing as a business opportunity. The sex industry needed people and she found people, typically without their understanding or against their will. The people she found were usually young and were looking for a way out. She never liked the term "human trafficking" and much preferred the phrase "industry relocation," as she was relocating kids from the business of being young and stupid to being useful. She rarely felt any moral reservations at all from taking part in this practice, as she thought she had found her place in the world. What happened to her in her life that made her think being part of such a practice was righteous in some way?

The Fabulously Wealthy

As I'm writing this book, there are protestors on the streets lambasting the top 1 percent of the nation that holds a large portion of the country's wealth. Are the richest people hoarding the money while the bottom 99 percent suffer? This is a great question to address when creating fabulously wealthy characters in your books. While there are some of these characters that have, no doubt, done a few shady things in their time to create a financial empire, there are others who give generously to charity and try to do the best they can with what they've earned. Choose from either side of the aisle when creating such rich (and wealthy) characters.

661. He spent half of his time traveling around the world as a consultant, but when he was back home, there was nothing he'd rather do than to have a giant feast at his house. For nearly 20 years running, every Friday night he was in town, a large group of friends came over to share in his large wine and liquor collection and bring their favorite meals. He was good at his job and had accumulated millions of dollars, but it was the simpler things that put a smile on his face. What are some of the pleasures he gains from his Friday evening feasts?

662. Most of his life he'd worked over 14 hour days to keep his business afloat, and when it boomed, it became world-renowned in his industry. Soon enough, he was able to hire people to take on some of the tasks he hadn't wanted to do but couldn't afford to delegate. The amount of time he was needed per day decreased and completely evaporated when he sold the business and became a deca-millionaire. He decided to do everything he hadn't been able to during his extremely long workdays, and even though his kids were grown up now, he did all he could to make up for lost time. It turned out he didn't know much about being a dad and a husband and he had to learn it all from scratch. What was his day-to-day life like as a multimillionaire attempting to be a regular guy?

663. When she invested a good chunk of her inheritance on a feature film, her friends thought she was crazy. When the film paid out dividends that were approximately 100 to 1, she became rich beyond her wildest dreams. Now those same friends that doubted her were hitting her up for cash, and she wondered if these were truly her friends at all. As she continued in the movie financing business for smaller films with a chance of breaking out, she tried to figure out who she could actually trust. How will she find her true friends and how will she spend her money?

664. Most people didn't realize that she had been a major asset to her husband as he created one of the largest retailer in the world. She was instrumental in huge decisions that took the company from small town to the big time. When her husband passed away, she had over $500 million to spend on the rest of her life. What she really wanted, though, was to still have some sort of control over the company, but her previous position was unofficial in nature. While the company was willing to offer her a position in the office, it was mostly a superficial one. How will she work her way back into a decision-making capacity in the company she helped to build from the ground up?

665. His grandfather was one of the largest oil magnates in the country and was a billionaire at a time only a few existed. His father had made some decent investments and made sure all his children would be billionaires by the time they turned 18. He was 18 and ready to take on the world with pockets full of cash, but he had no desire to invest it or save a penny for the future. He wanted fast cars, women and drugs, and he knew that he could keep such practices up until he died without much trouble. His family worried about his wild tendencies but they continued to escalate with each passing day. Will he be able to control his taste for the extravagant long enough to become a mature adult?

666. He had what most would call an incredibly lucky streak. When the dot com era was in full force, he invested all he had and pulled it out before anyone even thought of the word "bust." He invested heavily in tech startups in the 2000s and moved everything out before the recession at the end of the decade. He was no Warren Buffet, but he was close to billionaire status and had no idea what to do with himself. He lived in a small house with his wife, and they had no desire to move anywhere larger. He was wary of charities for fear that they wouldn't use the money wisely. He had money but nowhere to put it. What will he do with his estate in the last few decades of his life and why?

667. She was the whistleblower for a legal case involving a company that had embezzled billions of dollars from the federal government. She was just trying to do the right thing and didn't want anything in return. As per the law, she received a percentage of the settlement the company made, which consisted of tens of millions of dollars. She used the money to retire on a tropical island. She'd never married and spent her time dating attractive islanders and throwing elegant parties with her new friends. She was a bit bored, but going back to work wasn't really an option. She opted to write a book about her experiences. Describe her attempts to write about her life and how everything changed by doing the right thing.

668. In her 20s and 30s, she was a phenomenon in the racing world, and as the most famous woman in the business, she received countless sponsorship deals. She racked up millions of dollars of savings during this time, and when she retired, she knew she'd be well taken care of the rest of her life. That wasn't enough for her, though. She was frustrated that women had few role models in professional sports and opted to give more women an opportunity to learn from the best. She created a foundation with some of her fortune to create more sports programs for women throughout the county. Every day she woke up with excitement that racing couldn't compete with. She was helping girls to know that she was no happy accident. Why did she get into racing and what gave her the idea for her philanthropy?

669. He an international recording superstar with appeal on every continent in existence. He eclipsed most album-selling milestones and had even been something of a high-paid actor in a few countries. He never liked spending money, so most of his earnings went into an account accruing interest for several decades. Sure, a little went to his clothes, his family and his employees, but it's funny how money can add up when you save as much as you can. When he considered retiring, he asked his accountant how much money he had and it turned out to be

several hundred million. He was absolutely astounded and wondered how he would ever chip into such a sum. What was it about him that made him such a popular musician and such a thrifty penny pincher?

670. She was a rarity in this world, an inventor who went on to mass-produce her own invention. She thought of the idea while watching her children play and ended up amassing a fortune as a result. In her personal life, she was incredibly meek, which was in complete contrast with her business dealings. She was shrewd in the boardroom but quiet and a little self-deprecating in the living room. Her husband was astounded by what she accomplished and wondered if this was really the woman he intended to marry. Their marriage suffered, and she wondered if her invention would be worth it if she split from her one true love. What will this timid but brilliant woman do about her money and her marriage?

Poor and Destitute

There are many who would consider themselves poor in the United States as they are on programs such as welfare and food stamps to ensure they receive the proper sustenance. In other countries, however, poor might mean going without food, clean water and adequate medical care for long periods of time. Whatever your setting, it can be easy to ignore the problems that those struggling financially can have with their lives and how it can affect them mentally and physically. By playing up those internal and external struggles, you can develop a character that is deep with conflict and hopes for a better future.

671. He used to think that he was lucky to have gotten into such an elite academic institution. Little did he realize that later on, the debt he incurred would push him well below the poverty line. He knew a lot about engineering but little about finances, and he took part in poor spending habits throughout eight years of school before becoming a father to twins out of wedlock. Between the ring, the hastily put-together ceremony, the diapers and his school loans, he hoped that a job would show up on his doorstep. Unfortunately, after attempting to get employment for six months, he had to take a much lower paying job and apply for every government assistance program under the sun. Will he be able to pull himself out of a rough financial situation?

672. He'd had a rough life, going from foster home to foster home until he graduated high school. He had an undiagnosed mental handicap that made most around him assume he was simply dumb. His school district graduated him even though in actuality he barely had an eighth grade education. He had a job as a stock boy at a grocery store until he was fired for having a mental episode. When he was unable to pay his rent, he took to the streets, hoping to find an opportunity somewhere along the way. He was eventually put in a halfway house where his condition was finally diagnosed. After 30 years of life and some much-needed medication and counseling, he was back in the work force with a similar job. What has he learned from his years of thinking so lowly of himself and what does the future hold for him?

673. She knew that education was one of the keys to life and she'd always wanted to go to college. Her parents just didn't have enough money and she was unable to get the scholarship she wanted. She worked hard for years just to get together the funds for her tuition and she eventually did go to the school of her dreams. Afterward, though, she was unable to find a job in a tough marketplace and her years of work, followed by her years of education felt like a waste. She found the love of her life and a low-paying job that would hire her, but it was extremely tough making ends meet. Sometimes it felt like she was in prison, surviving on bread and water alone. Will she once again turn to education to move up in the world or will she find a different way out of poverty?

674. She had lived a very comfortable life in a two-income household through the end of high school, and she rarely thought about money. After graduating from college, she asked her parents for help with the rent in her big city apartment, and she was surprised to find that their answer was no. She wasn't used to having to work for her money, and after a few deferments, she found that her college loans and her rent were just too much for her. Her parents refused to let her move back in and she found a room in a very shady part of town that she could afford. She prayed for a raise at work to be able to afford an occasional night out, as her current salary could only pay for her loans and the smallest of portions. She went on the food stamp program just to sustain herself and wondered how she'd gotten into this situation. Will she be able to turn her life around and how?

675. He had a philosophy that money was not very important to him and that he'd live his life that way. Of course, he used this philosophy to avoid looking at where his money was going and how much was coming in. By the time he reached the age of 30, this left him with a large amount of debt and hardly any money saved up at all. He didn't want money to control him, but here it was doing just that. He was living in a crummy apartment, eating Ramen noodles twice a day and doing nothing in the way of leisure. He determined that he was going to get out of this situation by becoming a master of money and he began taking personal finance courses. How successful is his quest of learning more about how money works as opposed to his earlier attempts to avoid thinking about it?

676. All he wanted to do was travel. He would save up every penny of his paychecks to go on vacations throughout the country and abroad as often as he could. He eventually lost most of his jobs as a result of his constant need to get out of town, and he continued to fund his trips on credit cards, hoping things would work themselves out. They never did, and during a trip overseas, he was robbed and assaulted. There he was, recovering in a hospital with no money to pay the medical bills or to return back home. He tried to call in some favors, but he'd already used them all. What will he do in this sticky predicament and how will his traveling activities change if he ever gets out of this jam?

677. She simply wasn't a money person, and she let her husband handle most of the finances of the house. She had no idea that he was using some of their hard-earned money on drugs, because it seemed like the family was doing OK for itself. A few years into the marriage, she noticed that the checkbook was severely unbalanced and realized what was happening. When she confronted her husband about the status of the money, he told her they were broke and that they were going to lose the house. She took the situation personally, wondering how money troubles and a junkie husband could have happened to her – she thought she was such a good person. What has caused her to assume that this situation somehow makes her less of a person?

678. She took a sort of pride in the fact that she seemed unemployable. She'd had a few jobs after college, but a combination of her attitude and her less-than-traditional looks made it tough to keep a job when sweet, pretty girls seemed to get most of them. She took to the online world of freelance writing and blogging and she barely earned enough to pay her rent. She hoped every day that she could become a huge online success to increase her income for new clothes, better food and a bigger place. She worked hard and had a tough time being alone all day, but she knew if she put in enough time it would have to work out. Will she ever find her big break online and if so, will her opinion of herself change?

679. He was an absolute shopaholic. If there was something that he wanted, he knew he could manipulate the credit card system to get it. He would pay off one credit card bill with another credit card, and he somehow always made it work out, due to a decent income. When he began having health troubles, he tried to compensate for how badly he felt by purchasing more stuff, instead of keeping money set aside for his bills. Eventually, it became too much, and he had to stop himself from buying his way into oblivion. He began selling his stuff and going to shopping addiction meetings. It would take him a long time to pay off his $100,000 of debt, but he knew he'd never be healthy unless he did. How did this addiction come about and how successful are his attempts to rid himself of it?

680. As a writer and an actor, she barely earned half as much as her science and business-focused friends after they graduated from school. And yet, she wanted to keep up with them as much as she could as far as social hangouts went. Several nights a week they went out to the swankiest bars and racked up some major tabs. She felt a strain from all of these expenses, but they were her friends, of course they wouldn't do anything that wasn't in her best interest. When she lost her job, she had to rethink her spending habits in a hurry, and she even had to take a loan from one of her more successful friends. Will she continue to remain friends with this higher earners after adjusting her habits and why?

Screw Ups

You know you know at least one. Maybe this person is in your family or maybe the person is just an acquaintance of yours. There was one in your group of friends growing up, and there is one in your apartment complex now. Sometimes, people who are otherwise kind and hardworking tend to screw up more often then others. Perhaps that person does something minor like losing a phone several times a year. Maybe it's something more drastic like demolishing a car or setting a house on fire accidentally more often than most do in a lifetime. Whether it's bad luck or bad karma, there are screw ups among us that can be inserted in a comedic or tragic fashion.

681. You loved your brother with a passion, but he was never able to get things in his life right, no matter how hard you tried to help. He'd accidentally given half his money over to a scam, left his house unlocked for thieves to steal most of his possessions without having renter's insurance, and he even tripped coming up your front stairs and twisted his ankle. He'd been like this his whole life and you wondered if you got all the luck while your brother suffered with none to speak of. You didn't feel guilty for this, of course, but you wondered if luck had something against your nice, but extremely ill-fated sibling. How did your brother typically react when these frequent incidents befell him?

682. He was in all of your classes in school and you always cringed instinctively when he opened his mouth. He was a semi-intelligent kid, he just used words incorrectly and generally missed the point of every classroom discussion. He might have even gotten some dates if he didn't accidentally insult the girls he was talking to when trying to compliment them. He had a group of friends who would occasionally sympathize with him, but more often they tried to get him to laugh with them when mocking his inability to say the right thing. As is often the case in college, he found his perfect fit, a girl with the same problem, and you marveled at how there would be another generation of such lexically stumbling folk. What would a day be like in his household full of malapropisms and unintentional affronts?

683. She was the kind of girl who always had something extremely wrong with her outfit or makeup. Whether it was having twice as much eye shadow as necessary or accidentally revealing her bra for hours without noticing it, she just couldn't seem to ever get it together. As with most people who put themselves in sheepish situations, she was kind and dopey and loved people despite their chuckles. You thought to yourself how lucky she was to be working in the company of women who were willing to help her with her issues. You wondered if her constant wardrobe malfunctions had something to do with her former beauty queen mother making her nervous to always look her best. What are a few of her most egregious errors of appearance and what would enable her to get it together?

684. When she was sober, she was overwhelmingly polite and kind. When she had even a little bit to drink she was the sloppiest, most accident-prone people you'd ever met. When you met her in college, you assumed she was an athlete because she came into the dorm with such frequently skinned knees and twisted ankles. It turned out that as soon as there was any liquor in her, she had the balance of a toddler but the speed of an Olympian. This was not the best combination for the integrity of her physical health. She was also quite entertaining when she drank, but the entertainment wore thin quickly after her first injury of the night. She even once fell off a second-story railing, fortunately landing in some soft bushes. What is her typical train of thought when she wakes up the morning following a party with a series of bruises, cuts and gashes?

685. In a family of secrets, he was often the one left out, due to his inability to keep a single one. This scenario wouldn't be much of an issue if he wasn't such a snoop in the first place, often finding out secrets before they were told to other members of the family. His blabbering led to major scuffles between sisters and it kept most of the brother-in-laws too pissed at him to invite him to barbecues. He wasn't trying to cause problems, but he was just so excited to find out about things that he burst with excitement and told everybody the most private of things in the most public of forums. You weren't surprised in the slightest to find out he was really into reality TV and celebrity gossip as well. Why did these "secrets" make him so excited in the first place?

686. When the phone rang, you knew that it was your brother. Who else would be calling at one in the morning? You also knew that it was an effort to get out bailed out of jail for a petty crime. Perhaps it was public urination this time, or maybe destruction of public property. He'd had enough small offenses for a life sentence, but seeing as your dad had been on the force so long, he had an extremely long noose. He always called you, hoping your dad wouldn't find out first, but this time you wanted to let him stay there a couple of nights. Maybe that would teach him a thing or two. How will he endure his time in jail and will he ever learn his lesson that crime doesn't pay?

687. Sometimes you didn't know why your boss kept her around. She only had a few real responsibilities like getting the coffee and lunch orders, divvying out mail to the various employees at the office and re-directing phone

calls from the main line. She couldn't get any of them right, ever. You also knew that she would never get fired because she was too flirty and too kind. Your boss had a soft place in his heart for women worthy of the swimsuit edition of Sports Illustrated. She also didn't ever truly meet the standards of the company dress code, but you had a tiny feeling that this was an intentional slip-up. When you finally sneaked a peak at her resume, you were astonished to find she'd attended an Ivy League university. What was the reasoning behind her constant flub ups in her work responsibilities?

688. She had a lot going for her in her professional life. She was an up-and-coming music producer, and several of the acts she worked with were moving up in the scene. It was her day-to-day life that was an absolute mess. She frequently lost her phone, which subsequently lost her clients. She had been in several car accidents and now had to get other people to drive her around. She was frequently flustered and late to almost every part of her day, and she had a difficult time planning ahead for anything due to her ever-moving mind. Her busy job wasn't the cause of these constant problems, as she'd been that way her entire life. Why were these issues cropping up and is there any way that she could put a stop to them?

689. All of his life he pictured himself falling deeply in love with the perfect woman and living out a fairy tale life. This image of his existence, however, didn't take into account how frequently he would say the absolute wrong thing to the people he dated. It wasn't a lack of tact or a gap in the understanding of social norms, it was simply a matter of being so nervous around the opposite sex that he could barely handle the act of conversation. His unintentional insults were so famous that they even inspired a website where girls he had dated would share their stories. This site propelled him into the public eye, which allowed him to begin pushing through the nervousness. What was it in the first place that made him so nervous around women?

690. By accidentally calling 9-1-1 during a secret high school party, she had unwittingly become known as the biggest screw-up in school. She was determined to change her image by throwing the biggest party the school had ever known. She had fantastic ideas, but she rarely planned out all of the smaller details, such as how she'd get the band, food and drinks that she promised. She and her best friend scrambled around the city the week preceding the party to find a way to provide for the several-hundred person guest list. Nothing was working for her, and she hoped that her luck would turn around at the last second like it did in the movies. Does her party go off without a hitch and does she end up with the happy reputation boost ending she'd hoped for?

Overweight

I've been overweight for most of my life, and as a kid it was really tough for me to deal with. Even though I had a bit of athletic skills, I was no stranger to getting picked close to the end for sports teams, and as an adult, I still occasionally feel overlooked in certain aspects of my life. The fact that I'm on the edge of overweight and still feel this pressure means that those who have serious weight problems are likely to have it even tougher. When weight is an issue in your life, it can become an all-consuming problem that factors into your entire day. That being said, people who are overweight are still often active, loving and morally sound, and it's best not to vilify them in your stories.

691. He was shunned by his classmates as one of the fattest kids in the school. He stopped caring about the way he dressed and he gave up eating anything but what made him feel as good as possible, despite what his parents did to stop him. When he returned home in the afternoon, he retreated into a world of video games, in which he frequently played as the most handsome, muscular character that could be conceived. He stopped thinking about himself as he was in the real world and began envisioning himself solely as the characters in his video games. Will he continue to live in this fantasy world or will he be able to learn to appreciate his own real-world attributes?

692. Throughout most of his life he'd been a skinny, fun-loving guy, and while he wasn't what you'd call popular, he was well-liked by his peers. That's about when his health began to decline and the only medications that would solve his issues made affected his brain and his weight. He started acting very strangely and his weight shot up about a hundred pounds. He felt like he was seeing someone completely different in the mirror and he wasn't sure if he liked this person. He prayed that science would come up with better drugs to treat his condition, but after nearly a

decade, those prayers had gone unanswered. How will his life change if he decides to go off the medication cold turkey?

693. Frankly, she didn't care if you found her attractive or not. She knew she was a full-figured woman and that most people called her fat, but she'd much rather be big than try to confirm to some societal vision of attractiveness. Sure, she sometimes ate her feelings and felt like she was at an unhealthy body weight, but she had a great singing voice and a personality that got her plenty of friends despite her size. She made fun of the skinny, popular girls, and she was very much of the opinion that sexy is all in the curves. Who are some of her female role models and what will life be like for her as an adult?

694. At first, she tried to tackle her obesity with exercise and diet, but her metabolism was just too slow. That's when she decided to cope with humor. While she couldn't tone her arms, she could make herself the quickest and wittiest person she knew so that she could turn all jokes about her weight back onto the person who made them. Early on, she found that people loved her comedy all the more when it was at someone else's expense, and her jokes grew meaner and meaner. She had a few friends who loved her to death, but she'd lost many due to her humor that many equated to a rusty nail. Will she continue to try to be funny and mean for the rest of her life or will she grow out of that trait with age?

695. He was a big dude, but then again, that didn't really surprise him. Every member of his family had been extremely overweight, including his mom, his dad, his brothers and sisters and his extended family. They loved being huge, and they often spent family reunions making mostly truthful "your momma's so fat" jokes. He never really considered trying to shed much of the weight; after all, he was one of the skinniest people in the family, even though he verged on morbidly obese. Being big was a way of life for him and his nearest and dearest, that's just the way it was. What will the future hold for this large man and the rest of his clan?

696. Throughout his childhood of abuse, divorce and constant uprooting, he had one major coping method: food. When he was sad, he would eat to dull the pain. When he was yelled at or touched inappropriately, he would fix himself a feast. In his mind, he was able to transport himself to a completely different world by putting as much food in his mouth as possible. This caused him to get so big that his family took him to several specialists. The specialists told them that there was nothing wrong with him, aside from eating about five times what a person his size should be eating. As he was forced to diet, all of his previous pain returned like a hurricane. How will he cope with his obesity and his pain while attempting to lose weight?

697. During high school and in the beginning of college she was definitely one of the pretty people. As time went on and her metabolism slowed, there was no amount of exercise that could keep her in the same shape she'd been when she won Homecoming Queen. She didn't relish being relegated from ringleader to the chubby friend, and she even considered getting surgery to regain her original form. Her self-esteem took a big hit from this development and for the first time in her life, she experienced depression. What will happen with this former knockout and will she ever regain the popular status she so prizes?

698. She wasn't just any big girl, she was a state-ranked heavyweight wrestler who had as much muscle tone as some of the beefy middle-aged coaches did. In her usual day-to-day life, she was more or less a typical high school girl, taking classes, going on dates and hanging with her friends. When she got into the locker room, though, she was all business and was not willing to take any crap from any teammates or opponents. While it certainly wasn't her intention, she would frequently embarrass the boys she wrestled because she was such a tank compared to them. She was bigger and heavier than most women she knew, but she never saw that as an obstacle to her happiness. What will life be like for her as she gets older?

699. He was the biggest guy in this history of your company to walk through the front door. He was only slightly overweight when he began with the company but as his responsibilities and stress grew, so did he. To accommodate his weight, his cubicle size was increased and he was eventually given his own office. He had his own ergonomic chair for people over a certain size, and he got to the office early in order to not inconvenience his peers as they tried to get to their desks. His doctors told him that he needed to do something drastic if he was going to live through the

next decade. What will this co-worker of yours do to improve his health and how does he react to the way his peers look at him?

700. She wasn't born in the time when moms went to the gym while her kids were at school. She was at home cleaning, tidying and cooking. When her cooking was done, she spent her time eating, and while she wasn't extremely overweight, the lack of movement was catching up with her as she got older. Her children warned her of health troubles and tried to get her to work out by placing exercise equipment throughout the house. She did a little more but tended to eat more to compensate. Her parents had been hungry during the Great Depression, and she never wanted that to happen to her or her family. Describe a typical day for this hefty but caring mother.

Work-Obsessed

Whether they were born with the ability to endure 80+ hour workweeks or they developed it along the way, I commend workaholics for putting in the hours that most people aren't willing to. These employment addicts throw themselves into their jobs with such fervor that they may have less time than the rest of us to spend on health, family and recreation. While these characters are often vilified, many of them are working this hard to provide for their families. Then again, some may just be looking to buy a new Ferrari.

701. When his first son was born, he and his wife were not what you'd call financially prepared. After all, she had decided to take an entire year off of work but only had a few months of maternity pay. This meant that he would have to work harder and put in more hours to keep food on the table. Shortly after his first child was born, his wife became pregnant again and this caused him to work even harder. He started to really enjoy his time at work because he knew that he was providing his family with the life it deserved. When his wife went back to work, he decided to keep up his 80 hour a week habit, because he got so much satisfaction out of it. Does he have any reservations about spending so much time away from his family?

702. When his parents asked him if he ever planned on settling down he laughed uproariously in their faces. After all, he already had a lady in his life, his company, and if stopped for a second to try to get married, he feared that everything would collapse on him. His business was strong but he knew it would have to expand to become something to sustain him, and as a result he put in even more time and energy. He downed coffee and energy drinks by the bucket and he went as long as he could without sleep as a sort of challenge to himself. When his company did finally break through to the big time and was sold for hundreds of millions of dollars, he wondered what the next step would be. Will he ever add anything other than his business to his day-to-day life and if so, what would that be?

703. She knew during her college days that work was going to be the thing for her, no matter what activities she participated in. She had made a few close friends during school, but knew it would be nearly impossible to keep them after she immersed herself in her first job. She felt bad as she lost touch with them, but knew no other way, because she felt the need to make her career into her life. She frequently worked over 60 hours a week and became well liked around the office. One day, nearly three years after she'd left college, her three best college friends surprised her at work and have decided to stay in the city she moved to. How will this workaholic balance her social life with her career?

704. When she first started her law practice, she was one of the first female-run practices in existence, and she worked hard to get as many clients as possible. She could be found in the office over 90 hours a week, because she rarely delegated any responsibility out and assumed she was the only one who would be able to produce the results she wanted. Now over 40 years later, she was especially contemplative about the opportunities she missed throughout the years. She wondered what life would have been like if she'd structured her priorities differently. As she heads into retirement age, will her life be one of regret or one of gratitude and why or why not?

705. Throughout high school and college, you loved him like a brother. He was the kind of party animal that you kept with you as many nights as possible because you never knew what trouble he'd get you into. By the end of college and the beginning of graduate school, he started to mellow out and became as focused on his career as he used to be at getting girls' phone numbers. Despite your best efforts, you hardly ever saw him anymore, and you started to get the feeling he'd rather be working than hanging out with you guys. Eventually, he even moved out to

the suburbs and getting a drink with him was a major inconvenience. How did he make the transition to being such a workaholic?

706. When he was younger, the best way to describe him was "a hopeless romantic." He wrote poetry, bought gifts and went out of his way to be larger than life with these women he loved. He always came on a bit too strong and for the most part, he scared these ladies away. He became depressed after a few years of heartbreak and he through himself into his work so that he wouldn't even think about how badly he felt. After getting a position that caused him to work nearly twice the average of other people, he found the love of his life working the completely opposite schedule. How will he be able to balance his romanticism with his new love: working around his feelings?

707. Though she'd been brought up in a world in which women went to college to get married, she found her true calling as a workaholic without a spouse. She found that she was in love with television and she made her living as one of the hardest-working women directors in the business. She had an amazing sense of comedic timing, and she made all of her actors feel at ease, even though she rarely felt at ease herself. After all, she'd go from one project to another and she rarely turned down work, which caused her to more frequently turn down the opportunity to sleep. Her parents were proud of her, though they wished that at some point she would settle down and think about her own needs, rather than trying to direct as many episodes and films as possible. What are some of her best qualities as a director and what do some famous actors say about working with her?

708. Her meticulous mindset had made her an A+ student when it came to copyediting anything from websites to student publications. She now spent a great deal of her time editing one of the most profitable online businesses in history. An error on a site like that could cost the company millions of dollars in sales, and she was the primary workhorse to keep things in order. The only potential mistake in her life was that she was unable to put down her error-hunting when she left her long days at work. She would chastise her friends and family for "errors" in the way they lived their lives or ways in which they were out of the ordinary. Will she ever be able to make her work and home life separate?

709. He had been one of the most loving parents and husbands known to man, but when his wife died and his kids went away to start their own families, he felt like he had nothing. So, in order to add more purpose to his life, he became completely obsessed with work. At first, this gave him a great deal of satisfaction; after all, he received three promotions in five years with his new concentration. Eventually, he got to a level of responsibility and income that he could have only dreamed of when his wife was still alive. But it was extremely stressful and he barely had any time to move on with his life. Will he be able to once again feel fulfilled with a balanced and happy life?

710. Though the ownership of the baseball team came to her through her inheritance, she promised her father that she would always take care of the team as if it were her own. She was more involved in the fate of her organization than most players and managers were and it was because of her "never say die" attitude that they won five world championships during her tenure there. Her family loved how hard she worked to keep her late father's business afloat, but they wondered if she wasn't putting too much time into the team. When they tried to tell her they wanted her to live her life, she said, "This team is my life." What is her day-to-day schedule like in her running of the team?

The Mean-Spirited

Even as a person involved in the self-help industry, I can't help but know that some people have a hard time shedding their mean-spirited nature. These are the kind of people who will always take down positivity with missiles of insults, cynicism and sarcasm. They take a certain pleasure in making others feel bad, and it makes them feel stronger to take other people's power like that. These internally angry folks can act as villains in a story but they may also simply be obstacles for a protagonist to overcome. Then again, in this occasionally mean-spirited world, readers may respond well to a mean-spirited main character.

711. When race had absolutely nothing to do with a conversation, he was the kind of person who found a way to bring it up. Some people would critique a person's upbringing for his opinions on humanity, but his parents didn't even know where his beliefs came from. When he came upon a person of another race, he wouldn't just use the standard insults, he would go deep into that person's culture to find a reason he believed them to be inferior. He

wanted to provoke them and had gotten several people arrested for assaulting him. What caused this person to be so full of hate for people of different colors and creeds?

712. He had some kind of special ability to make people feel bad, which wouldn't be such an awful thing, if he didn't enjoy it so much. Friends and family members never wanted him around because he would bring up awful memories of the past that they wanted to stay buried. He would knock people down with their insecurities, and it would be hard for them to get back up right away. If it wasn't for doctor-patient confidentiality, several psychiatrists in the area would have reported him as a frequent mental offender. People who knew him wondered if he had a troubled childhood or some other reason for being a bully. As far as they could tell, he just liked it. What made him so skilled at this painful ability?

713. She was one of the most popular girls in high school, and she never truly grew up. She was the girl who everybody feared due to her sharp tongue and her high status. This queen bee had sent several of her classmates to therapy or at the least to write anonymous angry blog posts about her. She went off to Los Angeles in an attempt to gain fame and fortune that she felt she rightfully deserved. She actually achieved some of it, despite an awful attitude of entitlement. When she returned to visit some friends, a few of them assumed that she would have gained some maturity and compassion from her time in the real world. They were wrong, as she was still the same stuck-up, vindictive gal they grew up with. What was it that caused her to stay in a state of evil, arrested development?

714. You frequently made every effort to be kind to her as you waited for your father to become available. No matter what you tried, his secretary was possibly the coldest, most unreachable person you'd ever met. Even though your dad was her employer, she felt absolutely no need to show you or any guests the slightest bit of courtesy. Your dad was a busy man and it makes sense that he'd hire such a strict gatekeeper, but you figured there was some way to find her heart under all that steel. You tried bringing flowers, baking and even stopping by her house. You were thwarted in every attempt to make her smile. How did this frigid secretary come to be the way she is today?

715. He was the worst kind of mean-spirited person, the one who pretends to be the opposite and then stabs you in the back. He was in sales, which can be a cut-throat world even when you're kind, but he took every advantage that his inherent scheming ability afforded him. He would take people out to drinks, find out their secrets, and employ them all before the start of the next business day. He would become friendly with co-workers just to find ways to take them down over the course of the next year. He didn't care about their families or their need of a particular income. All he cared about was himself. What are some of the ways in which he has dismantled the careers of his peers?

716. People who were meeting him for the first time assumed that he was cranky because he was old. That would have given them no excuse if they'd met him when he was in his teens, his forties, his eighties or anywhere in between. He had always been a fellow who appeared to hate being a part of the human race. If someone tried to compliment him, he would find a way to turn it around into an insult on the person who gave the compliment. He loved watching television in which people suffered and real life in which people he disliked suffered. When people attempted to befriend him, he would make them feel low and lonely. Why was he so cranky and mean his entire life and did he ever regret it?

717. She didn't need to be told that she was better than everybody else, she just knew it for herself. She had a few friends who she would hang out with as much as possible and with whom she loved talking smack about other people in her life. Whenever anyone outside of her circle tried to make contact with her, she would simply look at that person as if he or she was the worst person in the world. Her stare could make milk curdle it was so intense. She absolutely hated being bothered, and she considered most people to be bothering her at any given time. How did she come upon this sense that most people, outside of a select few, were not worth her time?

718. There are certain kinds of people who will talk about you behind your back. And then there are people like her, who will say every mean thing about you directly to your face. While she may not have been as angry or vindictive as some of the people who would talk incessantly without your knowledge, her brash insensitivity made her seem like she was on the top of the mean list. She didn't take a lot of pleasure in telling it like it is, but she thought it was stupid for people not to know when they were being idiots. If someone was pissing her off or was

pissing off someone she loved, she would let that person know about it immediately. When did she become so confrontational when it came to people's faults?

719. He had a reputation in high school and college as a guy who was willing to do anything for a buck. He absolutely loved money, but he hated working for it. This is why he would effectively scam his loved ones into contributing money to businesses he created. When they failed, he was never the one in the lurch, just those who trusted in him. When a business would succeed, he would rarely thank them or give them any credit because he was too focused on making money to remember where the seed capital came from. Of course, he had to repay these initial investors, but as soon as he could, he would create new contracts that made sure more money would come to him and investors who would be able to contribute more money than he could. Why has money always been so much more important to him than people have?

720. She did an amazing job at convincing people she dated that she was kind, charitable and giving with all of her time and life. It wasn't until her partners were a few months in that they began to see the real her. They saw that she was brutal with the emotions of her parents and she made them feel guilty for every "mistake" they made. She liked to give people advice in such a way that it would make them feel like jerks for doing the wrong thing in the first place. She would even make fun of people on the street who weren't attractive or who didn't have places to live. Fortunately, most of these guys bailed after realizing, but after two marriages and subsequent divorces, she was sitting pretty when it came to divorce settlements. Is she putting up the beginning of the relationship front on purpose and why or why not?

Perpetual Students

While many college students take four or five years to earn their undergraduate degree, there are many other students who may spend another decade of their lives in school to become doctors, lawyers, professors or all of the above. Perpetual students are the types who jump from one masters degree to another looking to either find the best career for them or to stay out of the real world as long as possible. When I was young, my mom warned me about become a perpetual student, to ensure that I experienced everything I could from the world instead of just learning about it. Here are a few that are content with the learning part.

721. Like any good joke, he translated very well into multiple language. Though English was not his native tongue, he easily adopted it when he traveled to the U.S. for graduate education. One of the best ways for him to stay in the country was to continue to get grants to study more and more subjects. He had multiple masters degrees and was working on his first PhD. He loved his new country, and he decided he would finally attempt to gain employment so that he could become a permanent resident. The only problem was, he seemed to be a bit overqualified for almost every position. What employment will this extremely educated and intelligent student be able to obtain?

722. He was never a big fan of the term "the real world." After all, wasn't he learning more real world things by studying with teachers who had been in the real world themselves? He had been in school for over 10 years and he knew things that these real world dwellers could never figure out on their own. He had studied in sociology, philosophy and psychology programs, and he knew without a doubt that he could read a person better than anybody else. If he had a regret it was that he hadn't ever kept a steady girlfriend over that time, and he wished he could use his knowledge to improve his flirting. How does this "people person" compare with a non-college graduate with people skills?

723. She always hated the fact that her mother had never gone to college. She vowed that she would become so educated that her children would feel that they could do anything, especially if she had any daughters. She pushed herself to earn a living on the side of school so that she could pay for grad school without parental assistance. She was so successful at saving money, that she opted to continue school after receiving her masters degree. There was something about being at school that felt like home. When her mother suggested she go out and get a job in her field, she just scoffed and continued to hit the books. What are some other ways in which she's tried to go in the opposite direction of her parents?

724. She came from a family of academics. Her parents had met while they were studying for a PhD and both went on to get multiple sets of letters after their names. She'd had no problem being pushed into the same field as her parents; after all, she didn't have a lot of ambition on her own and she was happy to get it from somewhere. She never really felt like she was living her own life, but she had little issue with that since she didn't think very highly of herself. She looked in the mirror and just saw a disappointment who would never live up to the standard of her family. Why does she feel so low in her parents' eyes and is she right to be thinking of herself like that?

725. He wanted to go into the arts from the time he was a small child. Even though his parents refused to pay for his school unless he did something practical, he was allowed to do theater as long as he didn't have a job yet. As a result, he figured he'd bend his parents rules by staying in school and getting as many degrees as possible, since it would allow him to keep his art alive. Eventually, his parents began to wise to his plan and he had to make a decision: go into an academic profession and teach things he didn't care about or go into the arts full time and be disowned by his parents. What would he decide and why?

726. He seemed like the most dedicated student when he was studying a particular area of academia. When he finally gained a position related to this area, however, he quickly became bored. It was obvious to those around him that he simply liked being a student too much. It allowed him to work hard without being the person in charge of a project. He had responsibilities, but they weren't close to the responsibilities he had in a job-related capacity. As a result, he would spend a year in these positions and then go back to school for a completely different area. What was it that made him shy from leaving the student life?

727. The first time she walked down the path in the main quad of campus, she knew she would never want to leave. After running the fifth year victory lap as an undergraduate, she worked a job on campus for two years before applying for grad school there. Most of the jobs for her profession were in New York or Chicago, but she didn't want to do anything that would take her farther than a few miles away from the campus she loved. She couldn't imagine not being able to sit in the library and study or not having the chance to see the other students excitedly move from activity to activity. She knew that school was her home. How will the rest of her life in the area play out and will she ever get bored of her "home?"

728. She had never been a big fan of school and she considering ditching college entirely before her parents convinced her not to travel for four years. Just as she was ready to drop school again, she met a wonderful partner who encouraged her to better herself and her education. She really didn't want to progress her degree from bachelor's to master's, but her partner was just so persuasive. After another few years, her partner once again made the case for her to move her learning forward to pursue another degree. Before she knew it, she'd had nearly a decade of school past what she wanted. Why did she let herself get roped into an activity she didn't particularly like?

729. The degrees that he obtained never mattered to him much. He had a much loftier goal in mind. He wanted to be the smartest man in the world. He figured that the more pieces of paper he obtained, the more knowledge he would pick up during his quest. He was inherently intelligent enough to figure out how to make all of these degrees achievable while earning a great deal of money from each program. He even did special brain exercises he learned from his love of neurology to increase his brain's capacity. He hoped with all his efforts he could be frequently referred to as smarter than Einstein himself. How did he come up with this goal and how possible is it?

730. When she was a child, she had few friends aside from what most would consider the great works of literature. While others were going to dances and playing sports, she would curl up on whatever couch, bench or chair she could find and read into the middle of the night. As a result, her grades were beyond incredible, even in mathematics-related subjects. She flew through college in two and a half years and figured she could do the same in her PhD programs. She was right. She had a knack for pushing through three and four year programs in a year or less. By the age of 30, she already had five separate PhDs and was gunning for a sixth. This was the most fun she'd had in her entire life. What will she do with her life when she tires of academia?

Stupid People

As a fairly intelligent guy who does stupid things from time to time, I feel bad calling out people who have a little less equipment upstairs than I do. Let's face it, though: they wouldn't create books like The Darwin Awards if there weren't people who did some incredibly dumb things on a daily basis. Sure, accidents happen from time to time, but if you let decades come in between cogent thoughts in your head, you may fall into this category I'm about to write about. Stupid people can be incredibly nice and genuine, but they tend not to make great decisions when push comes to shove. If you are too focused on creating witty, brilliant people in your books, try throwing in one of these characters to practice your realism.

731. His family loved telling the story of how he ended up face-first in the garbage can. His brothers loved playing with his gullible head, and one day they told him there was a gold coin at the bottom of the aluminum canister. He dove in without a moment's hesitation. He searched for nearly 10 minutes before his brothers stopped laughing and told him the truth. Stories like this were common with him, his friends and his family because he had the uncanny ability to believe anyone about anything, no matter how stupid it seemed. While this did allow him to trust people implicitly, it did get him in a ton of trouble when people took advantage of him. How did he inherit such extreme gullibility?

732. He was in prison but, in a way, it really wasn't his fault. See, his problem was, he didn't understand laws, especially the ones that govern "right" and "wrong." His parents always seemed to take things that were his, like the money he would get from his paper routes and odd jobs. He figured that was just the way people got money, by taking it, as opposed to working for it. When some childhood friends of his asked him to help them rob someone, he thought of it as a legitimate money-making opportunity. When their hideaway was discovered, he was the only one who didn't run. What are some other things this simple man has difficulty understanding?

733. Because she was one of the nicest students you've ever taught, you were always pulling for her to succeed. The problem was, she just never seemed to absorb any of the knowledge you tried to dole out. Even though she spent extra sessions with you after school and you knew she tried her hardest, she just didn't have the mental capacity. She was extremely sweet, and even though her fellow students teased her and took advantage of her lack of wits, she took it all in stride and responded with sincerity. When you met with her parents for a conference, they appreciated how much you cared but just shook their head. "We love her, she's just an idiot sometimes," they said, good-naturedly. Will she find her way in the world or will her lack of smarts get in her way?

734. No matter how often her friends tried to help her, she fell for almost every single line a guy ever fed her. All the guy had to do was talk about her eyes or mention how her hair looked like some movie star's and she would let them have their way with her. She had this sensation that whenever a guy paid any attention to her, he was the one and she would love him for the rest of time. Frequently, these guys were just trying to get laid, and they were out the door swiftly on the following morning. She would call her friends crying and wondering what it was she did wrong. Will she ever understand that in true love, actions speak louder than words?

735. Whenever he called home, telling his parents that he was newly broke, there wasn't much they could do but shake their heads. After all, he had one of the highest paying jobs in the family and seemed to be doing well for himself most of the time. His extremely poor decisions when it came to his money were breathtaking for a family that had survived many global financial crises over the last few generations. He would invest money with friends who had "great ideas" and would try to help out "anonymous Nigerian princes" via e-mail. He would go to casinos and he would get as many credit cards as he was allowed to. Why did this seemingly intelligent guy have such a lack of wits when it came to money?

736. You would receive random texts from him in the middle of the night. Every so often, you'd get a blank e-mail with some kind of strange attachment. He'd wire you money from time to time when he signed onto his bank account. Was he some kind of scammer or stalker? No, he was just an idiot when it came to technology. Even though he was brought up in the supposed "generation of technology," he couldn't tell you the difference between a tweet and a text, despite his best efforts. He made a lot of technological mistakes and had absolutely no idea what he was doing with a phone, a laptop or a web browser. Why is it so difficult for him to understand how these newer technologies work?

737. She absolutely loved making jokes, and she fancied herself a bit of a comedian. The only problem is that she had no sense of humor to speak of. Most people who could be considered witty have good timing, quick thinking or

a mastery of the English language. She had none of the above and would often kill conversations with her attempts at comedy, which quickly sank like lead. She assumed that most of her jokes were hits and her friends would humor her with some mild laughter, but after a while they did their best to reinforce the fact that her jokes were "offensive and not funny...at all." What are some examples of her worst attempts at humor?

738. At first, her parents assumed she was just accident-prone. They slowly began to realize what the problem was. She had a knack for reading warning signs and doing exactly the opposite of what they said. She would walk against red lights at crosswalks, she would swim alone in riptides and she would run on slippery surfaces, despite all of the signage warning people to proceed with caution. She was a perfectly fine reader, but the doctors found that whenever she got excited, the reading part of her brain more or less shut off. Since they couldn't watch her every second of the day, they hoped it was something she'd grow out of. What are some other signs that she has neglected to follow?

739. You loved this man and yet he had the most idiotic taste in entertainment of anyone you've ever met. He was the kind of guy who would line up hours early to see robots blowing each other up, no matter how many negative reviews the flick got. He would fall asleep during cultural events like ballet, opera and art shows. He would watch the worst reality shows on television, but when you tried to show him something of substance, his eyes would just wander away from the screen. He seemed to hold interesting conversations when there were no media involved, but as soon as entertainment worked its way into the day, he would reveal his complete lack of taste. Whenever he saw an explosion or a character doing something completely stupid, he would utter this laugh that resembled a pubescent teenager's chuckle, despite the fact that he was almost thirty. What are some other low-class cultural touchstones for this explosion-loving fellow?

740. She was the kind of girl who always knew the wrong thing to say. She was the kind of girl who would bring up subjects that people were trying to avoid, like talk of infidelity to someone who was just cheated on or cancer with someone who had just been diagnosed. She was the kind of girl who was prone to malapropism, typically saying an incorrect word that nobody had any idea how she came to. She was perfectly sweet and meant well, always saying what was on her mind in an effort to be as honest as possible. The problem was that what was on her mind was either unintentionally offensive or it made no sense whatsoever. What are some of her most embarrassing verbal slip ups?

Activists

I can't help but admire people who have a strong cause to guide their paths, because having something to believe in and putting all of your resources behind it is pretty awesome. There are activists who are content with holding up a sign and shouting at the top of their lungs, and there are also activists who are willing to go to extreme measures by spending their entire lives on one particular cause. While many stories tend to portray activists as wild-eyed and crazy, in many cases an activist is a regular person who felt a call to action. Showing that moment unfold and how it affects the trajectory of a life can be quite intriguing in your story.

741. Whether or not anyone knew it, he was the originator of a huge nationwide movement to rail against the government and its financial policies. He came up with the name, sent the first tweet and organized the first protest in what would dominate the national headlines in the months to come. His tiny protest, in a small town, occurred outside of a chain bank that had recently moved into town. He had very specific demands and had all the proper permits for the protest. He was amazed that the idea of a movement he started spread throughout the country, but he was concerned that it didn't have the focus that his original protest had. He made an effort to contribute to it on a national level, but despite his best efforts, nobody believed that he had any part in the beginnings of a juggernaut. How does he feel about creating a movement that quickly went out of his control?

742. He got into activism because of a girl he had a major crush on in college. She was extremely into causes and he didn't want to seem as if he wasn't invested. After all, she was really cute and he thoroughly wanted to impress her. While his efforts did lead to a make out session or two, he was surprised to find that he actually enjoyed being involved in causes. He switched his major to political science and began to learn everything he could about being an active citizen. He started going to protests and citizen action committee meetings without any chance of personal

gain. He found areas he was interested in and started writing a popular blog on those subjects. When he came home for the holidays one year, his dad said he could see it in his eyes, he had found his true calling. He went off to a long career of working for non-profits and volunteering for various causes. Have his attempts at activism ever gone full circle, inadvertently finding his love once he stopped looking for it in his line of work?

743. For her and her family, being an activist was a family affair. She recalled her hippie parents bringing her to rallies in major metropolitan areas, despite them living out in the middle of nowhere. She missed school as her parents taught her "applied civic duties" in a van on the way to every event. Now that she had grown up and had kids of her own, she felt the same need to protest the areas in which the world needed fixing. She wanted to pass down the tradition of activism to her kids and likewise removed them from school from time to time to get them involved in the causes she faced. She didn't just feel the normal pride of standing up to a force that seemed at times too powerful to defeat: she also knew the pride of carrying on a family tradition and passing it onto the next generation. How does she describe these events to her young children?

744. She'd grown up daddy's little girl when it came to her beliefs on gay marriage and the family. Since daddy was a political pundit for a conservative news network, that didn't get her many friends on the liberal side of her high school. When she went away to college, she absolutely loved hanging out with her roommate and wanted to recruit her as a best friend. About halfway through the year, she realized that her roommate was gay and couldn't believe that someone this cool couldn't choose a person she loved to get married to. When she brought her friend home for Christmas, it created a major schism in the family and she felt like she saw her dad's true hateful colors. While she wasn't interested in the same sex herself, she had certainly become interested in same-sex rights. How will her political views continue to change through college and the rest of her life?

745. He used to be on top of the world. As an investment banker, he was making money hand over fist, utilizing all the loopholes he could find in the system to increase his personal wealth. It wasn't until he realized where that money was coming from that he reconsidered his life's path. Did his family really need multiple houses and multiple high-priced vehicles when there were others without one home, one vehicle or enough food to eat, he wondered to himself. He wrote a book preaching reform for the major banks and investment firms, talking about the tricks of the trade he used to use to get as much money as possible. His book became a best seller, and he became a symbol for a movement against corporate greed. He donated nearly all of his book sale money to the movement, much to the chagrin of his wife. What will his next step be in contributing to this form of activism?

746. He was sick and tired of being homeless. He was tired of dragging his two sons through his unemployment and he wanted the governor to hear about it. When he and a group of his peers were kicked off of the state building's property without receiving an audience, their numbers swelled and they marched for days in an effort to bring attention to their plight. They became the talk of the town, and he was their leader. His sound bites to the local news station gave him support from the community around them and the owner of a former school building turned the property into a shelter. From that shelter, he began an organization that would try to bring even more awareness to their issues in a tough economic climate. How will his sons look on his efforts as they grow older?

747. She wasn't an activist, but she played one on TV. In the wake of the popular Occupy Wall Street Movement in 2011, one of the major television networks wrote a pilot based on a family of activists. Not only was the show a hit, but it propelled all of its mid-level stars into superstardom, especially her, due to her leading lady status. The show was a sitcom, but it had a lot of heart, and the writers actually paid attention to the issues that required protesting. Since their voice came through her mouth, she was labeled as a hero of modern activism. In real life, she was more or less neutral when it came to the issues, but she was invited to so many events and was "quoted" as saying so many important phrases on national television that she couldn't help but gain interest. When her show comes to an end, will she continue to be involved in important causes?

748. Her parents were always a little bit worried about their daughter's favorite phrase. Whenever she was affronted, she said, "I am willing to die for my beliefs." They didn't know where she picked up that attitude, and they were proud that she was able to stand up for herself, but they figured it would get her into a lot of trouble depending on how she applied it. When they received the phone call that she had been jailed and required bailing out, they

considered letting her stew overnight but eventually relented. After the third time, once again for protesting without a permit, they let her stay in overnight. After dealing with a prison cell overnight, instead of changing her ways, she now shunned her parents, stating that not bailing her out of jail was a form of oppression. She moved away and her parents didn't hear from her for years to come. Where did she go and will she ever repair her relationship with her parents?

749. His friends thought of him as the "human pinball of activism." They were pretty socially conscious and they were willing to support a protest for a cause they believed in. His activism was a bit different, however. If he heard about a cause, even briefly, he would immediately dive in, face forward. It didn't even matter if he knew both sides of the issue or if he had any relationship to it, he was in, full force, until he heard about another equally valid cause. His friends even recall one summer in which during a span of three months, he lobbied angrily and constantly for both sides of a cause. He eventually ended up back on the first side he was rallying for. He had no idea what he wanted when it came to his beliefs, but when he had beliefs, he knew he wanted them heard. What are some other ways in which his blind passion has manifested over the years?

750. She was a seeming contradiction and the whole world knew about it. She was one of the nation's foremost protesters against the rights of women. Her argument was that the country was in much better shape before women had the right to choose whether or not to have an abortion. Heck, she was against women's right to vote. She would frequently appear on conservative news networks to act as the voice against the changes in the rights of women over the years. She spoke about how other countries had it right, moving women backward in what they could or couldn't do, because in her opinion, women were evil. She was frequently asked if she realized that she was railing against the very thing she was doing and she usually changed the subject. How did this woman come about these beliefs in a typically progressive world?

Sports Fans

Being from Philadelphia, I know a thing or two about sports fans. I mean, fans from Philadelphia are famous for booing Santa Claus and Beyonce. While many fans of football, basketball and baseball are thought to be drunken and crazy, there are some who are simply in it for the love of the game and follow every statistic, trade and piece of news about their respective franchise. Professional and college sports are billion dollar industries because there are so many people in love with one or multiple games. If you aren't a sports fan yourself, it can be tough to understand their psyche, but I will do my best with these 10 die hard fans.

751. He seemed like your typical mild-mannered, hard-working cubicle jockey who would come to work, go home, and then repeat the process. What most of his co-workers didn't know, however, was that the second he loosened the tie he lived, breathed and ate sports 24/7. Upon exiting the workplace, he would bust out his phone and check on injury reports, commentator analyses and expert podcasts to learn as much as he could about his favorite teams' chances the next game. He had season tickets to all of his teams, a tradition his parents had passed down to him, and he attended as many games as possible. Mild was the opposite of how you'd describe him when he watched a game, and he would often come into work hoarse the following day. What is it about sports that makes this fan so involved during his leisure time?

752. This man was particularly blue on Sundays, mostly because he was always covered in paint when he visited his beloved football team. He was a large and in charge kind of fellow, and his wild personality plus the fact that he wore nothing on his top half other than paint frequently got him onto television. When the fans in the stands were getting quiet, he would start a chant that would typically spread throughout the stadium. He had so much energy and pizzazz that the team even hired him for a team video that would air before every game. While many fans don't have an impact on a team's performance, this super fan did in a big way. How does he endure the cold of winter when protected solely by a thin layer of blue?

753. When you first met her at a sports bar, you assumed she was there for the great burgers and the camaraderie of her alma mater. You were wrong. When you casually brought up sports one time, it was the only thing the two of you would ever talk about for the rest of your relationship. Every time you saw her, she would bring up obscure head-to-head stats or the details of some kind of play the team should run for their best chances of success. She

seemingly knew everything about the background of every player, and while you were impressed, you were surprised to find that she had absolutely nothing else to say about any other topic. How did she get so into the details of sports, what is her favorite team and why?

754. Throughout most of her cheerleading career, it seemed like her peers were either looking for something to do that would attract the opposite sex, or later in life, as something to do to earn money for looking pretty. She was always in it to root for her team. She was naturally gifted as a dancer and an athlete, and the ability to flip and jump and groove fit perfectly with the more competitive aspects of cheerleading. She loved the high school and college athletic teams she cheered for, and when she had to pass an aptitude test to be a cheerleader for a professional team, she received the highest score ever. What are some other ways she defies expectation as a professional cheerleader?

755. In every arena he went to, he was the loudest fan present by far. It didn't matter if it was something as small as little league softball or as large as the Super Bowl. He went to as many events as he could and he was the most attention-grabbing loudmouth at all of them. He'd been kicked out of a few events small and large alike when his temper got the best of him, but he never intended on changing his ways in the slightest. When a team he loved was doing well, he was the perfect embodiment of pride. When they weren't doing well, that's when you had to watch out for his tongue and his right hook. Why is he so emotional when it comes to watching sports?

756. As a father of three girls who were into ballet and theater, he felt like an outcast in his own home. His wife let him convert the garage into a man cave of sorts, and he invited all his guy friends over as often as he could to watch the big games. He loved drinking and cheering for his favorite squads on the weekends, because during the week he was surrounded by the color pink and female conversation. Whenever he felt like he was losing his edge, he went on a hunting or fishing trip, but it was tough, because he loved his family so much and wanted to be there for them at all times. How does he deal with this love for sports and his world of women?

757. A former college athlete, she was a large supporter of women's sports at all levels. She would frequently corral her less interested friends to WNBA games, college softball tournaments and other related events to show her support. She wished that this equally competitive side of her favorite sports would get even half the attention of their male counterparts. She even coached a woman's soccer team on the weekends in order to instill this excitement in the youngest of sports fans. Some people who didn't know her well labeled her butch or a lesbian because of her propensity to watch these sports, but she just wrote them off as ill-informed. What are some of the other ways in which she supports women's athletics?

758. For the most part, sports didn't play a large part in her life. Until college basketball season rolled around. She knew the players' and coaches' names, and she would shout them at the top of her lungs when a play was unfolding. One could say that she didn't know much about the intricacies of the game, but nobody could say that that made her less of a diehard fan. She had all the merchandise and could tell you what her team was ranked. When tournament time came around, she was all over the bracket and filled out as many online and paper ones as she could. How does a day in her life differ between one in June and one in March?

759. He wasn't what you'd call your typical sports fan. He hung out in gay bars as opposed to sports bars. The kind of drag he preferred certainly wasn't drag racing, unless RuPaul was involved. That being said, he was intrigued by certain sports and watched them as often as he could. He loved watching ice hockey and was extremely excited by the quick pace and the physical contact. He enjoyed chilling out on a Sunday and taking in a round of golf. Most of his friends didn't understand his fascination with these and other activities, but they didn't look down on him for it. What made him so intrigued by sports while most of his friends shied away?

760. At first, she was a sports fan by associated. Her husband and her sons were so into certain sports that she couldn't help but be drawn in. She used to just create them elaborate snacks, using her supreme cooking abilities, but eventually she just ordered in so that she could watch every minute of these fascinating events. She had loved dancing as a child, both participating in it and watching it. Almost all of the sports had movements that were similar and while most had a bit more contact, she enjoyed watching the "dance of the game" as she called it. How does she react when her "men" try to kick her out of the room so they can have their "men time?"

Partiers

The partiers are the ones who can't help but go a little bit overboard whenever they're at a bar or a friend's celebration. They are the first ones to go for the hard liquor, the first ones on the dance floor and typically, they're the first ones who get your group kicked out. Even when a hangout is not intended to be a party, they do the best they can to make it more festive with more alcohol, drugs and bawdy chatter and actions. The partiers seem like they're having more fun than everybody else, but it always makes you wonder if they are as happy with their wild behavior as they say they are.

761. He wasn't interested in your name or what you did for a living. He only wanted to know if you could drink or dance. If you couldn't, you were really no good to him. He lived for being with as many different people as possible from week to week. He couldn't stand the idea of settling down and having time to actually think about his life or what he was doing with it. The combination of being alcohol-soaked and listening to loud music all the time was exactly what he wanted to shut down his internal monologue. It worked for the most part, but for a few moments every morning, he couldn't help but ask, "What are you doing with your life?" Why is he so intent on keeping himself from thinking and making sure his life is wild and crazy?

762. His philosophy was that if he remembered what happened the previous night, he obviously didn't party hard enough. He was obsessed with drinking when he came to a party and he loved trying to drink other guests under the table. He had won more one-on-one shot battles and beer pong tournaments than anyone he knew, and he felt they were some of his greatest achievements, even if he had blacked out and forgotten some of them. He thought he was a much more interesting and attractive person when he was completely wasted and that was often how he thought of himself. Would his party life and identity change much when he has to get a more intense job after college?

763. She was quiet, mousy even, until she got about a dozen beers in her, at which time she became the life of the party. Her friends and acquaintances were amazed at how much her personality changed from the beginning of a party to the end of a party. There wasn't a large window between when she went absolutely wild and needed to be taken home and put to bed, but during that window she had done some ridiculous things. She'd been arrested on multiple occasions for various offenses, and she'd even bedded several celebrities. It certainly makes her job as a librarian pale in comparison to her partying alter-ego. What are some other crazy things she's done at parties?

764. You thought it was awesome that you were dating someone who was incredibly fun for once. You met her at a party, and she seemed like the most energetic and sexual person you'd ever met. After a few months together, you met up with her at a party and were surprised to see her hanging all over every guy there. When you talked about it to her afterwards, she apologized but said that was just how she was at parties. The next time you met up with her after she'd been partying, you spied her dancing all up on this guy you knew had the hots for her. What goes through this party animal's mind when she starts to get intoxicated at a party?

765. He was far and away the most social person his friends knew. Party hopping was less of a weekly activity and more of a daily task for him to keep up with all of the people he knew and loved. That's why it always surprised his pals that he rarely drank anything but water. He usually said he was driving or he was too busy the next day, but it was a thing as constant as his name replying yes on a Facebook invitation. This was especially surprising because he was so full of energy and jokes no matter where he went, despite his low blood alcohol content. They all supposed he was just born that way. Why does he feel such a need to attend as many events as possible?

766. He had a brilliant mind when it came to particle physics, and he could be found publishing papers and giving lectures more than people twice his age. He had to work hard, and to counterbalance it, he played just as hard. He and some of his academic friends went on some wild adventures and had a habit of waking up in places far away from where they started the night. They'd ended up in Vegas, Los Angeles and Maui without remembering how they got there. Usually, this genius had absolutely no problem getting back to his conferences and his research on time, but there were several times he cut it very close. Describe one of these crazy adventures taken by the post-doc and his friends.

767. She loved throwing parties because she loved people more than anything else. After all, how could she not be completely head over heels for her friends who took care after her after she got too drunk to stand at almost

every party she threw? Her friends couldn't believe how much a perfect record she had, because at least one of them had to tend to her at every single party, no matter how low key. At one party, she'd even had alcohol poisoning and had to be taken to the hospital. She rated that one of the top parties she'd ever thrown. What is it that causes this party thrower to think it's OK to become so helplessly drunk?

768. While she was an avid partier, she refused to attend events that weren't unique or fancy in some way. She would no longer attend keggers or run-of-the-mill festivities. She wanted to dress up or to be transported to some magical realm with an amazing theme. She wanted each party she attended to be an experience because her life was relatively boring during the day. Why should her parties be the same, she thought to herself. By seeking out some of the stranger events her city had to offer, she'd met some strange people and gone to some unusual hideaways. What is it about these occasions that make her feel more alive?

769. When he made over $100 million from selling his booming business, he wasn't sure what he wanted to do with his time. When a party featuring celebrities and friends turned into an all-weekend affair, he decided that he wanted to keep the festivities going as long as possible. By the time the original party had ceased, two weeks and over a million bucks had been spent. This was the bender to end all benders, and the now-retired businessman never wanted the good times to stop. A few of his friends were worried that he was getting into things too deep, but then again, it had only been a couple of weeks. How long will this new millionaire keep his wild streak alive before he settles into his next project?

770. It was somewhat ironic that she had a day job so different from the hardcore, moshing-filled events she attended on a weekly basis. During the day, she would plan the most elegant engagements, from weddings to upscale Bar Mitzvahs with everything in between. At night, she would put in her piercings, take off her tattoo-covering makeup and put on her leather. She was a punk rocker through and through, and she loved her action-packed night-owl lifestyle. She was never sure who the real her was, if it was the party-planning maven of the day or the party-enjoying wild woman at night. Will she continue to live this double life or choose one of the two sides?

The Talkers

Even though they say that it's better to keep quiet to avoid being considered a fool, rather than blabbing to remove all doubt, these chatty folks did not get the memo. Talkers are the kind of people who love hearing the sound of their own voice, even if what they're saying doesn't seem to be worth much of anything. They hate silence and will go to great lengths to keep the conversation going during a party, date or meeting. Every once in a while, these garrulous gabbers will say something interesting or out of the ordinary, but it's usually preceded and followed by such garbage, it's tough to pick it out. These characters are usually portrayed as idiots and annoying people in most stories.

771. If there was any way to best describe him, it was as a storyteller. It's not that the most interesting things in the world would happen to him, but the way he described events he was involved in was intriguing for everyone around. When you were with him for a short period of time, you were riveted. If you had to spend an entire car ride or evening with him, however, you would be overwhelmed by chatter. He loved his stories and he strung them together from one to another, never giving you a chance to reply. What does he enjoy so much about his stories and does he even know he's preventing people from responding to him?

772. He is the kind of person who always has an opinion about something, even if what he has to say is of little to no value. Watching him from the outside you'd almost think that he is part of a professional debate, though he's the only one who knows it's going on. He does have some knowledge about politics and his own profession, but he'd comment on sporting events, international relations and religion-related topics that he has absolutely no expertise in and seemed to form an opinion about on the spot. Those who are actually knowledgeable in the subject hated how convincing he tries to be of his point of view, even if it is all smoke and mirrors. Why does he feel the need to become heavily involved in every discussion?

773. Throughout most of high school, her mother had one heck of a time getting her to speak her mind. When she returned from her first semester of college, it was almost as if someone had flipped a switch. Now all she did was speak her mind from sunrise to sunset. She would occasionally listen to what other people had to say, but she had

become a master overnight at turning a conversation back toward her. She was small and cute and had faded into obscurity during her high school years, and potential friends and boyfriends finally began to notice her in the dorm-room setting. Her mother figured that her garrulousness was simply a matter of catching up for lost time for the first 18 years of her life. Will she be talkative for the rest of her life or will she just have to get this chattiness out of her system?

774. On the positive side, she was able to start a conversation with nearly anyone of any race, color or creed. She would make that person feel enabled and comfortable, at least for a spell. It wasn't long before she would steamroll that person in conversation and that feeling of comfort would quickly vanish. She had been extremely afraid of talking to strangers during her youth, and her parents made her practice calling random businesses and talking to sales clerks throughout her adolescence. As a result, she became so at ease talking with people that it became her favorite thing to do, even if she couldn't turn it off. What is usually the breaking point for her between making a person feel welcomed and making them feel overwhelmed?

775. When most people think of someone who talks too much, they envision someone who talks as fast as the Micro Machines guy from the 1980s, who overwhelms you with speedy monologues. This man was the complete opposite in his speed, as he was one of the most deliberate talkers you'd ever encountered. That being said (slowly), he rarely ever stopped his chatter and you could never actually tell if a sentence was ending or not. It was as if he was saving up all of his words for the first 30 years of his life and now he was slowly unveiling them one at a time like an arthritic Vanna White. How did he come upon his unique speech pattern and why does he talk so constantly?

776. For the most part, he was a smooth operator when it came to the ladies. His silky speech and his sense of humor would usually get him phone numbers more quickly than a telephone operator. The problem came when he kept talking during the first and second dates and would eventually offend the other person in his attempts at comedy. It's not that he was offensive, per say, it's just that when all you can do is make jokes at other people's expense, eventually, someone will get pissed off. That would usually happen for him within the first three chances of meeting someone. Why is his humor so combative and will he ever learn his conversational lesson of less is more?

777. She was a creature of habit through and through. She would brush her teeth the same way, style her hair in the same manner and go to the same restaurants from week to week. When she became a tour guide as a full-time gig, she began treating all of her encounters with friends and family like she was a tour guide. She devised a great deal to say about her life and whatever locations they would visit. It was as if she was a recording that never stopped. At first, it was cute for her friends, who hadn't known her as much of a talker, but upon visiting some places multiple times and hearing the same shtick, they got frustrated. Will she be able to break her habit and stop annoying her friend after they bring it up?

778. She was fond of saying the phrase "action speaks louder than words" and used it frequently during her political campaign. The problem is, her constant action appeared to be using words to deal with all her problems. She had become elected to Congress due to her ability to talk circles around all of her opponents. As she reached a more national level, it was becoming more obvious through the power of re-watching her debates and speeches that for the most part, she was all talk and little action. She was a quite honest and forthcoming person, but she would make promises that she never followed up on and it was beginning to catch up to her. She vowed that she would change her ways during her most recent speech, but it was too early to tell if she was being honest. What will the future of her political career hold?

779. He was a motivational speaker who was known far and wide as one of the best lecturers known to man. He could walk into a room of destitute, disturbed people and he could leave with a room of clamoring followers who wanted to follow all his teachings and purchase his products twice over. What those people didn't realize was that he was the exact same way with his wife and friends and sometimes they wanted to smack him upside the head. He didn't need to be preaching his optimistic and personal growth teachings to them. After all, they knew all that he'd done – they'd been there for all of it, they didn't need him to talk about it 24-7. Will this master of positive thinking be able to reign it in for his loved ones?

780. If you started playing a video of stereotypical 90's standup in the background of her talking, you'd eventually hear the two of them sync up. It's not that she wasn't funny or that she wasn't a very interesting person. It's just that she never stopped joking, whether or not the situation called for it. She was literally like a recording playing back a record of every joke she'd ever heard or half-remembered. Occasionally, she was funny, but more often than not, she was just a little bit strange. She was able to control it somewhat during her day job, because she worked from home, but this only made her feel more pent-up with humor to release later on unsuspecting friends and acquaintances. What made this constant comedy such a part of her life?

The Fearful

In this book, I've written about many people who are willing to be proactive, like firefighters and heroes. The fearful are those who may want to say something or take action but they are simply too afraid. This fear may be the result of something that has happened to them earlier in life, it may be genetics at work, or it may just be who they are deep inside. In stories, the fearful are sometimes the most frustrating characters as we desperately want them to act, seeing their inaction mirrored in our lives during times when we were too afraid. When a fearful person is able to push past those emotions, however, that is when these characters become triumphant.

781. He always did everything that anyone had asked of him throughout his entire lifetime. He was afraid that if he stopped cleaning his room or doing his other chores that his parents would stop loving him. He was scared that if he wasn't the perfect, model employee, his boss would fire him and he would be on the streets. He showed no spine whatsoever in his relationships with women and was prone to dating people who bossed him around. All he wanted to do was to go through life relatively unnoticed and to be as good as everybody else. What would have to happen for him to fight back against a life that had been pushing him around too long?

782. Everything he did throughout his time on Earth was motivated by a fear of death. He avoided every activity that might be considered dangerous, including water sports, carrying heavy objects and air travel. He worked out like crazy to keep himself in top health, even though he absolutely hated exercise. He made countless safe choices, from the neighborhoods he lived in to the people he dated. There was nothing in the way of excitement in his life, but he felt less anxious that way. His friends and family members made fun of his behavior, and they secretly wished he would lead a more ambitious life. Is there anything that this fearful individual might be willing to act more risky about and why or why not?

783. She was deathly afraid of authority, with good reason in the early part of her life. Through corporal punishment at school and at home, she was a frequent recipient of bumps and bruises. She got it into her head early on that messing with people in power just got you hurt, and that's how she lived the rest of her days. She was kind and understood the plight of those receiving similar abuse, but she was usually too scared to stand up for others or herself. She let herself be run over by supervisors and bosses at work. She even married a man very similar to her father, who typically dominated her. What will her future hold as she lets other people run her life?

784. She absolutely refused to grow up, and to her, that meant getting a real job that utilized her skills in a full-time capacity. Despite her $100,000 worth of education, college just reinforced her belief that the real world was simply not for her. She kept a job at a small bakery after school and simply continued to hang out with her friends and put off the inevitable. She did all she could to avoid paying her college loans. She continued to date people younger than her so she could stay connected to the undergraduate culture. She enjoyed her time spent a great deal, but five years after graduation, she wondered if she should face her fears and try to make a living for herself. Describe a typical day-to-day life for this college grad.

785. He was a very large man who had inherited big bones and a propensity for muscle tone from his family. Despite the fact that he was an academic, most usually mistook him for a bouncer or a professional wrestler. And he had several major phobias that would send this hulk of a man into a corner like a scared kitten. He was deathly afraid of spiders, mice, snakes and several other creepy crawlies. The fear first manifested at a Halloween haunted house in his teens, and since that time he's been trying his best to counter the fear with psychiatry and medication. He has had no luck as of yet and still has nightmares every night. Will he ever be able to counteract his major fears?

786. A life in an extremely rough neighborhood had toughened him up. He had faced death on several occasions, and in order to defend himself and his family he made some allies along with some enemies. Now that he was settled down with a family, hundreds of miles away, he still couldn't shake the worry that some of those enemies would find him. He became obsessed with acquiring a top-notch security system and taught his wife and kids how to defend themselves. His new family thought he was going overboard, but he'd seen several signs lately that someone was looking for them. Are the signs for real or is his fear manifesting them for him?

787. She seemed like your typical overprotective mom. She wouldn't let her kids play on playgrounds without the protective rubbery surface underneath. She refused to let them go out for contact sports. She also made sure that they were close at all times, employing a leash when they were younger and a cell phone with a GPS tracker when they grew older. Even though her friends told her she was going overboard, she felt like she couldn't help it. She was just so scared that something would happen to her kids and she didn't want to take any chances. If she continues down this path, will she experience any issues in her relationships with her children?

788. It started slowly, but over the course of about a decade, she had become completely paralyzed by the fear of germs. She wore a mask in as many public places as she could get away with. She constantly carried hand sanitizer around and she refused to carry money due to rumors it was one of the dirtiest objects someone could carry. She wasn't sure exactly what caused the change, though it was around the time that her father passed away and her finances were quickly crashing down. Perhaps with so much out of control in her life, she used an extreme amount of control with germs to have control over something in her life. Regardless, she wanted to make a change but she wasn't sure how. What are some of the things she will attempt to get rid of this germ phobia?

789. It was impossible for doctors to tell if he had a medical problem or if his fear was so strong that it manifested in illness. This man appeared to be allergic to technology. There had been some previous cases of allergies and reactions to certain types of electricity. In those cases, when someone even brings a cell phone or camera into an adjacent room, the person might start getting headaches or a rash. That wasn't the case with this individual, who only seemed to get sick when he saw technology coming near him. He became deathly afraid of these devices, including cell phones, wireless networks and even computerized cash registers. If he's not allergic, what has caused him such fear around technology to the point that he grows ill?

790. She was absolutely afraid of commitment in any way, shape or form. When a person she was dating started to get too clingy, she would immediately cease returning phone calls and would un-friend the person on all social media channels. She refused on go on "dates" and wanted as little information about the people she "saw" as possible. A few of her friends believed that this fear was a result of her father getting divorced twice and her hatred of all things sappy and romantic. They thought if she found "the one" she'd drop all of this nonsense, but after ditching several good candidates for the job, they were no longer sure. What are some of the ways in which she has manifested this fear of commitment?

The Twisted

When you look into the eyes of some people, you can't help but think that they might be just a little bit off. You know the type: they tend to wear strange clothes, sit down in odd places, say very weird combinations of words and they engage in some strange activities. Most of them are merely odd people who are otherwise kind and loving. Others make every effort to make interpersonal situations bizarre and uncomfortable to ruffle the feathers of everyone within range. Some writers love using these odd-duck characters while others shy away from them, deeming them too unrealistic. From personal experience I can tell you that there is no limit to the strangeness of some of the twisted people in our midst.

791. He wasn't interested in what most people would call conventional. He traveled to most places wearing a bathrobe because it was comfortable. He rarely shaved and it was anyone's guess how long it had been since he'd showered. He was quiet, intelligent, occasionally daring, but mostly unreliable. You weren't sure what it was he did all day, and despite this, he was late everywhere he went. The first time you met him, he spoke completely in gibberish to you, which he never addressed again. What has made this strange person into who he is today?

792. He absolutely loved watching people, which doesn't make him that much different from those who hang out on a city bench watching the office workers go by. The thing that does make him different is that his house is hard-wired for watching all his neighbors at all times. He fitted his house with a series of telescopes, mirrors and cameras that gave him the ability not only to see what his neighbors were doing but to record these things as well. He did this somewhat out of a sense of fear that he could be living next to a killer or a drug dealer. He also did it because he was obsessed with surveillance and fashioned himself a bit of an amateur spy. What are some of the things he's seen during his unlawful attempts to watch his neighbors?

793. When you met her through an online dating site, she seemed a lot more normal than you expected. After all, why would an attractive blond athlete in the prime of her life need to go online to find love? You figured her picture would be from a decade earlier and that she would have gained 200 pounds since then. When you met her, you were happy to find that everything on her profile was true. One thing it omitted, however, was the fact that she loved watching things that you found completely disgusting. Whenever she wanted to get romantic, she had to watch torture movies like Hostel or Saw to get into the mood. On a third date, she wanted to go to a slaughterhouse and make out in a utility closet there. When you opened her fridge and saw road kill inside after the fourth date, you decided to call it quits. Why is this girl so completely into the grossest things imaginable?

794. Her nickname around town was the skinny grifter because of the game she liked to play with guys who thought she was cute. After getting to know them, she would flirt with them incessantly until they would more or less do anything she said. After all, with her all-American looks and her adorable laugh, it wasn't hard for her to rein them in. Once they were more or less hypnotized, she lured them out to the lake for a bit of skinny-dipping. She would wait until the guy had completely stripped down and she'd challenge him to see how long he could hold his breath. While he was under, she ran away with his clothes and left him low and wet. Why did this skinny grifter get such pleasure at putting these guys in a precarious position?

795. When he was a kid, one of his greatest passions in life was playing with his action figures. As he got older, that desire never died as it did with most kids. The action figures just got more detailed and the fights between them that he made up grew longer. By the time he was 30, he had over 1,000 toy figures that he pitted against each other every single night. His parents worried that by putting himself in this state of arrested development that he would never find someone to settle down with. Considering they had to come over to his apartment to clean up his toys every so often, they weren't even sure he'd be able to handle life once they had passed on. Why is this man-child so obsessed with keeping his youth alive?

796. During some holidays and sporting events, you might see people completely painted from head to toe in a provocative way. You were used to seeing it for such occasions, but he wasn't the kind of guy who stuck to a schedule. It seemed like about twice a week that he would go walking the streets with nothing but an ill-fitting codpiece and a whole lot of body paint. He wasn't going anywhere in particular, he more or less just walked the streets as if he were part of the Blue Man Group. Aside from his time in shades of green, purple and red, he was an average city employee who went to work, came home and watched TV. This habit certainly set him apart. What is the story behind his frequently self-artistry?

797. Seeing an episode of the game/reality show Fear Factor was kind of like looking at a day in this fear junkie's life. Some people got their kicks with extreme sports, others with exotic trips, but she got her adrenaline pumping by covering herself with bugs or running through sewers. When she was a little kid, she tripped and fell down a shallow well and became very acquainted with the mice and snakes that made their home there. She was completely mortified, and her parents took her to years of therapy. There was something about that wild experience, however, that she craved and she made every effort to recreate such a scary, disgusting event as often as she could. What are some of the grossest situations she's put herself in?

798. She absolutely loved music and could barely stop herself from singing her favorite lyrics at every moment of the day. There were two problems with this scenario, however. One issue was that the music she listened to was vile and dirty and that these were the kind of lyrics that would make people cringe and want to wash out their ears. The second concern was that her line of work was in the childcare industry. Several times a day, despite her best efforts,

she taught some of these kids words they might not have learned for another decade or two. She was fantastic with kids aside from the unintentional potty mouth, so parents tended to give her a couple of chances. She usually used them all up within a week and was back out looking for work. What was it about these songs that made it so difficult for her to keep them from spilling out?

799. Things would be different if he had a malicious intent in what he was doing. After all, the only reason he sabotaged the careers of his co-workers was because he had a compulsion to do so. He didn't actually want them to lose their jobs – he frequently enjoyed their company. Deep down he had this feeling, though, that they should receive some sort of punishment and that he was the one who had to dole it out. He would steal money from the company and frame it on a secretary. He would cause a major error on someone's computer system and make it look like the person had been avoiding work for months. When he was successful, he would go home and laugh for hours at a time, followed by sadness that he had lost another co-worker. What caused this man to need to take down his fellow employees?

800. Forty or fifty years earlier, she might have been considered somewhat normal. She was relentlessly perky and had the most positive attitude her friends had ever experienced. It was almost as if she was from a black and white TV show, she was so overwhelmingly optimistic. In such a cynical world, most people assumed she was up to something or that she was about to try to sell them a time share. In reality, without coffee or any other type of stimulation, this was just how she was. As a result of the gap in the happiness continuum between her and everybody else, most thought she was absolutely out of her mind. How did this eternal optimist feel, being labeled as bonkers because of the way that she was born?

The Dark and Mysterious

There are certain people in the world that send a shiver down your spine. These dark and mysterious men and women can stare down even the most confident of individuals. It's almost as if they have a sort of demonic power to them, if you believed in that sort of thing. It's not about how they dress or even what they look like. It's just who they are. One character who fits in this section I can think of is Angel from the first season of "Buffy the Vampire Slayer." He was both mystical and brooding at the same time. If you are looking to include a dark and mysterious stranger in your book, look to this section to fill your quota.

801. If there are people who are considered the life of the party, than he must be considered the death of the party. With dark hair, dark circles under his eyes and a propensity for wearing hoodies, you could never quite see his face straight on. But he could see you, because it almost always seemed like he was staring at you. When you made the effort to start a conversation with him, he talked about morbid subjects and philosophy and he usually made you feel weird and uncomfortable. Your friends tried to stop inviting him to get-togethers but he always showed up anyway. Who is this guy and how did he get to be the way he is?

802. He just wanted to be left alone. That's one of the reasons he began dressing in dark clothing and wearing makeup. He figured that if he made himself look like some kind of demon, it would be rare that anyone would want to hang out with him. After the latest young adult vampire craze, he wished he would have picked a different style of attire. All the girls at school thought he looked like a character straight out of *Twilight* and they were convinced he had supernatural powers. He didn't. A friend he had before all the girls began trailing him throughout the school lent him one of the books. The description of the main male vampire matched him exactly. He threw his hands up into the air and wondered how he should best change his appearance for next school year. Why does he dislike being around people and what will he choose to look like in the future?

803. Everyone at school was completely certain that she was a witch. She wished that she could tell them otherwise, but she had actually inherited strange spiritual powers from her mother and was able to summon them at will. She wanted to dress in bright colors like pastels and put on a happy face, but these semi-demonic powers came with a healthy dose of depression, causing her to want to hide her emotions in dark clothes and makeup. She wanted to have a close-knit group of friends like she saw on TV, but most of her peers were totally afraid of her. The fear may have something to do with the belief that she turned one of her teachers into a pig during class. Unfortunately, that rumor was completely true as well. How will this dark and mysterious witch be able to live a normal life?

804. She had long, flowing black hair that went down to her thighs and she wore strange charms around her neck and wrists. She looked almost like a carnival fortune teller, but she was nothing more than a mystifying checkout girl at the local organic grocery store. She had piercings and tattoos like some of the other employees there, but unlike them there was a strange energy that circulated around her. Her voice was like a siren's call and after customers got to know her captivating attractiveness, they made sure to go into her checkout line instead. She knew the effect that she had on people and was glad that she'd made over her image from the captain of the debate club she used to be in high school. How did she go about altering her appearance and personality to come off as endlessly mysterious?

805. From what he'd seen on TV, most people who dressed like he did or had as much interest in dark, depressing subject matter were artistic and misunderstood. He saw those stereotypes frequently performing poorly in school and refusing to participate in class. He was the exact opposite. He dressed like he belonged in a death metal music video but he received nothing but straight A's in school. His appearance rubbed teachers the wrong way at first but once they saw his potential, they warmed up to him quickly. In college he was the valedictorian out of a class of 20,000 and even though he refused to change how he dressed, he eventually moved up the ranks of a leading advertising firm. He saw compromise as sacrificing part of who you are, so he never did it. What are some conflicts he has run into keeping his image consistent well into professional life?

806. You saw him approaching you from across the room and your heartbeat began to quicken. You'd never seen a man who looked so much like a Hollywood bad boy from up close before. It was almost as if you could smell the danger on his skin. Without a word, he swooped you up into his arms and carried you out of the club. He did it so effortlessly that you almost didn't question it. Before he could walk you back to your car, you began questioning who he was and what he was trying to do here. As soon as he opened his mouth, you wished you'd gone along with the mystery. He sounded like a total idiot. His lack of vocabulary and his complete lack of tact showed you exactly why he'd tried to avoid speaking when he literally picked you up. You waved goodbye, got in your car and left. He immediately dialed his best friend and said, "I was so close, maybe I should get my mouth removed." How did this attractive and yet completely idiotic man craft such a dark and inviting persona?

807. When you agreed to babysit her, you figured the job would be a total cinch. A tour of the house revealed countless stuffed animals and an abundance of the color pink. She was just one little girl, how much trouble could she be. Several hours later, you could barely keep track of the sequence of events that had unfolded. The second her parents scampered out the door, she began to show her true colors. She began asking some extremely adult questions and refused to behave unless you gave her the answers. Of course, she had taped the entire exchange, which she further ransomed you into helping her to maim her dolls until they were unrecognizable. She seemed to relish telling you the story of how she "accidentally" killed the family cat. What are some of the other dark aspects of this strange, little girl?

808. There was something about this girl that drew you to her. When you asked her out on a date, she said she'd had her eye on you too. She invited you out to her favorite event of the year, the school bonfire. You loved how the fire flickered off her eyes, both of which were extremely focused on the center of the flame. On your second date, she directed you to an abandoned warehouse in which she wanted to show you something. She started a blaze that was so wild, she burned the entire place down and she swore you to secrecy. You agreed as long as she didn't do it again. She rewarded you by being your girlfriend and you were extremely excited until fires started mysteriously popping up around town. What was it that made this strange girl so interested in fire and will you have the opportunity to stop her?

809. You knew it was a mistake for you to walk down the streets of the deserted city and you were quickly confronted by two masked men with guns. They led you down an alley into what you believed would be certain death. Before they could even demand your wallet, a blur of a figure came crashing down from the sky, knocking one of the men to the ground. The other tried to fire his weapon, but the blur deflected it away and consequently knocked the man unconscious. Your savior asked if you were alright and you thanked him profusely. As you went closer, you saw that the man was disfigured and that he did his best to cover his misshapen face. He spoke in a low growl and you felt you needed to find out more about his story. You planted your phone, equipped with security

GPS into his pocket and later that night you tracked him to his home. What will you find out about this strange man and why did he save your life?

810. She was absolutely stunning and throughout college and her first job, many men and women alike were hardly able to get a word out without staring at her. She appreciated the attention and she dated many of the men who showed interest. And that's when they got a chance to see the real her. She kept conversation playful at dinner and then took her dates back to her place. It was like a mausoleum. Her apartment sent shivers down the spine of the men who felt like they'd just walked into some kind of horror film. She would offer them a drink and she'd return with a thick red liquid that looked and tasted like blood. She was often asked if she liked vampires, to which she replied, "What's a vampire?" before turning on some ominous organ music. She wasn't quite sure why she'd been unable to make it past the second date with any of these people. How did she craft such a disturbing home life and why?

Vegans

Vegans are often portrayed as granola chomping hippies in stories, when there are actually many different types of vegans who choose the lifestyle for many different reasons. Sure, there are some who are choosing veganism to avoid the harming of animals, but others have been placed on the diet by a doctor or spouse and crave meat every single day. There are others who are trying the lifestyle out to see if it leads to health or spiritual benefits. With the proliferation of the vegan brand with stores like Trader Joe's and Whole Foods Market, vegans are here to stay and even if they aren't hardcore hippies, they should be well represented in our stories.

811. His parents had always known him as the kind of son who would project his beliefs onto others. When he found out about causes such as wasting water and recycling, he would whip the entire house into shape to make sure they were doing the best to conserve the world. When an election would be in the news, he would ask his parents hundreds of questions about why they were picking a particular candidate. They loved him and wanted to encourage his free thought. When he tried to force them to be vegans, however, that's when they drew the line. How did he try to convince his parents to change over to a vegan lifestyle?

812. When he started having major health problems that the doctors couldn't make heads or tails of, he embarked on a quest to rid himself of his illness. He tried a different exercise routine and he made the effort to get a full night's sleep every night. It wasn't until he became a vegan, however, that his health really began to take a turn for the better. He knew that it wasn't meat and animal products that made him sick in the first place, but for some reason, cutting them out of his life returned him to normal health within a few months. He decided to keep up this lifestyle for the rest of his life, since it was what made him well and made him feel much better than he did as a meat eater. What were some of his challenges in becoming a vegan?

813. She had decided pretty early on in life that meat was murder and that she wouldn't be taking part in any animal products. That being said, she didn't want to join an initiative or anything, she was simply stating personal preference. Other than her veganism, she led a relatively normal life. She worked in an office from 9 to 5. She was dating a normal meat-eating guy who seemed to be perfectly fine with her lifestyle choice. She even went out and played sports and befriended plenty of people who didn't feel the same way she did about meat being fair game. Has she ever gotten into any awkward situations as a result of her vegan lifestyle?

814. She'd always been a little bit counterculture. She looked right at home in the hipper parts of town with her tattoos and piercings. When she applied for a job at a vegan bakery, she worried that being a meat-eater would disqualify her. When it didn't, she was surrounded by vegan delicacies from morning until nighttime and found that she actually liked them better than cakes with eggs and dairy. After a few months, she tried to go full on vegan for a week and she never went back. Now her job became like her vegan sanctuary in which she knew the special tricks of the trade to keep veganism a part of her life. Even when she later moved on from the job, she would always come back for a sort of vegan worshipping ritual. What are some of the difficulties she ran into when she became vegan?

815. When he was young, he saw a video of a slaughterhouse in action that changed his life. From that point forward, he could no longer eat meat without becoming violently ill. In addition, he couldn't watch other people eat meat without having a similar guttural reaction. During college he became something of an anti-meat activist,

pushing for stricter regulations on animal slaughter and trying to convert as many people over to his way of thinking as possible. He even once hijacked a kids movie in a theater and replaced it with a slaughterhouse video. He never got caught and it was one of his proudest moments. What are some other causes that he believes in?

816. He was a real genuine hippie in the 1960's. He preached flower power and peace not war to the masses and he loved every minute of it. As he grew up, he still kept that hippie sensibility as he became an environmental lawyer. On a trip to a new Whole Foods Market around the corner from his house, he found out much more about the vegan movement and gave it a try. After all, if it had been that easy to go vegan in his hippie days he might have tried it. There he was, a middle-aged man, jumping on the vegan bandwagon, and he loved it. In what ways have this new vegan lifestyle reminded him of his hippie days?

817. Truth be told, she loved meat and hated being a vegan. She wanted to fit in as much as possible with the love of her life and that love was a major vegan through and through. She agreed to try veganism and she absolutely hated it, but she couldn't stand to disappoint the person she wanted to spend the rest of her life with. So, she lied. Her friends told her that she should sneak some meat in every once in a while but that wasn't the kind of person she was. She was more honest than Abe Lincoln and if she was going to say she would be a vegan, she would most certainly be one. That didn't mean she had to like it though. Will she ever tell her partner about her vegan dislike?

818. She was beyond health conscious, she was health self-conscious. Whenever she heard a major health trend, she would force her husband and her children into it without giving them much of a choice. When she decided to be vegan, she went all in, trashing all of the animal products in the house and buying primarily vegan foods. She would only pack her kids vegan lunches and she wouldn't cook any dinner if it wasn't a vegan dinner. Her family hoped that this was some kind of phase that would blow over like the rest of her healthy choices. After three months of being forced into veganism, her family members staged a vegan intervention. What was the result of this anti-vegan family protest?

819. He was the kind of guy who always liked a challenge. His ran a very popular blog showcasing his many attempts to do a 30 day challenge of one goal or another. He'd run a marathon distance each day for 30 days. He'd donated five hours of his time to charity each day for a month straight. Trying out veganism was another one of these 30 day trials for him, but at the end of it he felt so good that he decided to keep it going for an entire year. He felt more energetic and cleaner somehow when he didn't eat any animal products whatsoever. He began advertising for vegan organizations on his site and really took up a torch for the cause. What are some other ways veganism has affected this challenging man?

820. Her parents had no idea why she gravitated toward a vegan lifestyle. She refused to eat anything besides vegan products early on. They figured it was simply coincidental that she wouldn't eat non-vegan foods, but as she grew up, the trend seemed just too perfect to be coincidental. By the age of 10, she wasn't only completely vegan, but was one of the lifestyle's youngest advocates. She posted YouTube videos about her beliefs that veganism was the only way to go and they went viral. She became a spokesperson for multiple vegan organizations by virtue of her being so cute while talking about it. What her parents thought was a phase turned out to be a calling for their daughter. What was it about vegan products that drew her in when she was so young?

Animal Lovers

There are many different breeds of animal lovers (see what I did there?). There are activists who will stop at nothing to end animal cruelty throughout the world. There are people who love their pets so much that they dress them in Halloween costumes and put them in their Christmas cards. There are also general lovers of animals who can't help but stop in pet stores to look at the puppies, kittens and fish. Animal lovers are included in this book because there are some people that make animals such a large part of their lives that it has come to define them. If you plan to focus in any way, shape or form on animals in your upcoming story, it may behoove you to include an animal lover in the mix.

821. It's well known that there are few relationships as close as the one that can occur between a man and his dog. With that in mind, this owner and his lovable pooch were completely inseparable. From the moment he first saw his companion as a puppy he was completely smitten. The two of them would go on runs together, would eat

dinner together and would even go pick up girls together. While he'd gotten a bed for his furry friend, on most nights the two of them would sleep together, much to the chagrin of his girlfriend at the time. Will the two of them be as close when the owner settles down and has a few children?

822. From a young age, he had a strange fascination with the color green and every animal with such coloration. He begged his parents for turtles, lizards and frogs and they tested out his responsibility one pet at a time. For a child they thought might have ADD, he was more attentive with his pets than any of his classes by far. He watered, cleaned and fed them every day and he quickly earned as many pets as he wanted since it seemed to keep him calm and occupied. As he grew up, he purchased more exotic and expensive amphibians and reptiles and he loved showing them off to family and friends. He even occasionally had dreams that he was a reptile himself. What caused him to fall so deeply in love with these cold-blooded creatures?

823. She seemed like your traditional old lady with a bunch of cats, with one little wrinkle. These were no domesticated felines: they were jungle cats. She was the owner of a large wildlife preserve in the middle of the country that catered to tigers, lions, leopards and other wild cats you might find in a zoo. She loved these animals and they loved her right back. When she told her family of her plans to retire to this preserve, they thought she was crazy, but upon seeing her interact with these potentially vicious animals, their worries quickly dissipated. How did she come to know she wanted to spend her twilight years with these striped and spotted cats?

824. Her friends thought of her as the female Ace Ventura, not because she solved crimes, but because when you walked into her apartment, you were greeted by a menagerie of different species. She had birds flying freely around the multiple rooms and little pug dogs that would amble on up to her. There were ferrets rummaging around in their play area and even a monkey who loved to climb up on her shoulder. The animals were all very well trained and behaved, which isn't surprising, considering how much time she spends with them. She was fortunate that her landlord was an animal lover as well, because it's improbable that she would be allowed to keep so many animals otherwise. She knew that having so many critters prevented her from being social sometimes, but she figured it was worth it, considering that animals are way more interesting than people anyway. What was the order in which she got the animals and how well did they interact with one another?

825. Even though he was decidedly human, he never quite felt like a human. For instance, when he was young, he seemed to get along much better with pets than his friends. He loved going around the neighborhood with his dogs and cats in a pack, even though the other kids made fun of him. As he grew older, he loved going to dog parks with his pets because he was able to interact with a ton of new animals. He only paid precursory attention to the owners of those animals because he just didn't connect with them as much. Trips to pet stores or doggy day care centers might take hours for him because he wanted to make sure he could say hello to everyone. What are some of his qualities that keep him more connected with animals than humans?

826. He tried everything in his power to get past his allergies to most animals. Doctors told him that it was the dander of these pets and he tried getting a hypoallergenic dog. After his hay fever kicked up a notch after about a week, he and his wife had to give it away. He loved being around animals so much but no matter what the animal, he seemed to get violently ill as a result of it. He tried to take special vitamins and to use herbal treatments that said they might help. None of it did anything to alleviate his symptoms. He was an animal lover who couldn't get within 10 feet of an animal. What are some of the ways in which he expresses his care for animals without being able to be around them?

827. She figured, why let dogs have all the fun? This was her reasoning behind starting a trained cat show that she would use for multiple purposes. The first purpose was to get cat owners to see just how intelligent and awesome cats were. The second purpose was to pair with a local cat adoption agency to make sure that audience members knew it was more important to adopt abandoned kittens than it was to buy kittens from a breeder. She absolutely loved teaching her cats such tricks as ringing a bell, jumping through a hoop and even dancing on cue. Her show was the talk of the town and the weekly program was frequently sold out and well reviewed. What is her routine like for training these intelligent felines?

828. She took a lot of things for granted when she was younger and her parents were the richest people in town. She had her own room, her own credit card and she even had a stable with three horses. After a few financial issues, her parents had to downsize and sell the house, cut the card and get rid of the horses. She had been something of a brat when she was younger but she soon grew humble and became grateful for what she once had, especially the horses. She never realized how much she enjoyed riding her darlings each and every morning. She decided that to relive that feeling again she would become a horse trainer so that she could help kids realize how blessed they are to be able to spend every day with such majestic creatures. What are some other things she misses about her previously privileged existence?

829. He was the kind of kid who was absolutely terrified of everything that moved. The first time he and his family went to the zoo, he had to be carried out of there as his scream cries were terrifying the animals and the other children. When he got a puppy as a present on Christmas, he locked himself in his room and didn't come out for nearly half a day, until they promised to take the puppy back. And then one day, during a large family outing, his aunt spotted a large cockroach that had wandered into the house. While she was freaking out, this young, fearful kid, picked up the roach and started playing with it. From then on, the only gifts he wanted were in the form of creepy, crawly bugs. What was it that made him so much less fearful when it came to insects?

830. She loved animals so much that it was hazardous to their health. Her parents had noticed how excited she got when she went past the pet store so they went in. They left with a couple of fish. Three days later the fish were dead because she hugged them to death. Her parents did their best trying to teach her how much love an animal could handle but whatever animals she came into contact with often ended up injured due to her desire to be openly affectionate with them. They were afraid to buy something bigger like a cat or a dog, because they didn't want to have to explain the accidental death to their neighbors. Will she ever be able to reign in her adoration for animals?

Outdoorsy People

These are the kind of people who tell you to stop and smell the roses, while actually meaning it! You may not be a big outdoorsy type yourself, but there are plenty of people as you read this that are hiking up a trail, climbing a mountain, boating in the middle of a lake waiting for fish and loving every minute of it. Nature has some amazing moments of spectacle and there is a certain type of person that is dying to take it all in as often as possible. This could take the form of a wide-eyed college student trekking along the Appalachian Trail or an elderly hunter on the trail of a wild turkey. When you have a protagonist go out for a nature-related activity, it's always great to include a few of these folks for comedic relief or serious introspection.

831. After growing up in the city among the smog and the smorgasbord of people, he knew that the blessed life was truly one spent in the wilderness. He absolutely loved hearing his voice echo against the rocks he climbed or the trees he sat under. He didn't dislike people per say and he did spend time with his friends out under the visible stars far away from the city lights, but there was something he really enjoyed about being alone out there. There was no better feeling for him then when he had a chance to interact with nature in solitude. What are the three things he enjoys the most about the outdoors and why?

832. He wasn't just a runner, he was a trail runner. He didn't pound his feet against the pavement of the city streets. His idea of running was a combination of bounding over branches, rocks and small animals while trying not to get stuck in the mud. At the end of these runs that were fraught with obstacles, he would usually be covered in dirt and grass stains. He absolutely loved the looks people would give him afterwards. He felt like some kind of wild man who had been transported to another era. What are some of the things that have happened to him during these wild trail scampers?

833. She was mocked by some of the other parents when she volunteered to be the troop leader for the local cub scouts. It made perfect sense to her, since her sons were both involved in the organization and the last few male leaders had been absolute duds. In addition to that, camping was one of her favorite things to do and to get an excuse to do it multiple times a year made her overjoyed. She knew that her kids were a bit embarrassed to have their mom running things, so she made every effort to make the camping trips as masculine and memorable as possible. Did she succeed in her task and how did these trips compare with camping trips she took when she was younger?

834. Some people jogged, other people boxed. She hiked. She was defined by her hiking shoes, her canteen and her pack. As soon as a work week would end, she could be found on the closest trail and she wouldn't be back until Monday early in the morning. She grew up in the boring suburbs and hated how flat everything was. During a class trip to a state park, she found her calling and she immediately moved to the remote northwest and never looked back. She even took up a side job as a trail leader so that she could teach kids about the value of hiking. She was in incredible shape and men who even had a hint of an outdoorsy bias might label her an ideal match. What are some of the things she thinks about when she's out alone in the middle of nowhere?

835. While he loved being outdoors, some of his friends wish he'd stay inside and put some clothes on. The thing that made his friends cringe was the fact that whenever he went outside in the woods, he wanted to take his clothes off. He wouldn't call himself a nudist, per say, but he certainly enjoyed acting like one when they all went camping. He'd made some efforts to join a nudist colony in the past, but he didn't want to leave his job to stay there full time. As a result, he subjected his friends to complete embarrassment, especially when they were just trying to blow off some steam at the end of a hard month. What was it about taking off his clothes in the woods that made him so happy?

836. He was a hunter but not for the reasons you might think. While it seemed to him that many hunters simply liked the sport of it and enjoyed spilling blood, he was there in an effort to restore the balance of things. There was a major deer overpopulation problem in the forest and it was affecting the plant life in the area. He holed himself up in his family cabin during the season so that he could take the issue back down to neutral. He gave the deer meat he attained to a local food bank and he did everything he could to be humane in his attempt to rebalance the local environment. What kinds of things go through his head after he shoots a deer?

837. She knew that most of her friends didn't get it, but that didn't stop her from trying to get them to see the beauty of the aviary. She had loved watching birds ever since her parents took her to a nature preserve when she was a little girl. She was amazed at the many different songs the birds would sing and how different they looked from species to species. She realized there wasn't a lot of money in the profession of birds and she held a regular 9 to 5 job during the week. With a lot of her free time, however, she studied about birds and applied her knowledge when she could get out of the city. What are some of the things she says in an effort to get her friends to enjoy birds as much as her?

838. She was absolutely tired of seeing her kids waste another day in front of the video game and computer screens. She took them out of school for a week and embarked on a journey to hike part of the Appalachian Trail. She knew that neither her nor her kids were in the best shape in the world, but she couldn't stand how complacent and overweight they were becoming. She hoped that as the three of them hiked, they would all learn to value nature more and make it a part of their lives. Her parents had loved taking her and her siblings on outdoor excursions and she hoped she could pass that love of wide open spaces to her kids. Will she be successful in her quest during the week long expedition?

839. There was nothing he enjoyed more than a boat trip down the river. Well, he did enjoy it a bit more when there were wild, difficult to navigate rapids throughout the journey. He also liked it more when he had a ton of friends afraid for their lives as he pushed them through the bumpy ride. He loved the exhilaration and the fear of his weekend journeys down one of the most dangerous water routes in the country. He had to work his way up over the years to be certified but now that he was licensed to travel down such a wild ride, he took that path as often as possible. What caused him to become such a water thrill seeker and what was one of his most challenging river moments?

840. Most of her friends thought she was crazy when she said she wanted to swim the English Channel. First of all, while she did love swimming in oceans and lakes, she wasn't even British! Second of all, there are several people who have died during the attempt because it is an incredible feat of endurance. Lastly, she needed to be in top shape, which she was far from at the time of her declaration. She waived off all of the criticism and worry about her attempt to prove something, to become one with nature in a way few people have been able to achieve. She trained hard and she even rented a house on the beach so that she could swim in the ocean more often. She loved the feel of the

water against her body as if the world was accepting her as one of its own. Will she be successful when the day of her attempt arrives?

CHAPTER 7: NON-HUMAN CHARACTERS

Aliens

Aliens tend to be sequestered to a very small cross-section of the writing world, that of science fiction. Despite putting aliens in a corner, there have been many amazing alien characters written, both morally good and morally bad, that tend to take on the role of a sidekick or a villain. Alien main characters are few and far between, but television shows like the "Star Treks" have shown us many different flavors of alien characters. Follow their lead for three-dimensional alien characters when you decide to insert them into your own work.

841. On his planet, he was a relatively average civil servant, going to his job in the morning and coming back for a beer on the couch in the evening. A mysterious portal opened up during his favorite show and sent him shooting down to Earth. He ended up alone, scared and green in the middle of a back alley. Fortunately for him, he spoke Trelgar, which was very similar to English and he was able to find a police station without much trouble. After telling his story, he was whisked away to the land of talk show television, giving interviews about his home planet and generally ending up a celebrity. There were organizations that didn't want him to receive human rights, but he was generally treated quite well for a little green man. What will his life be like on Earth and will he ever return home?

842. His ship was out of fuel and was hurtling toward the sun of your solar system. In a last ditch effort, he was able to change course to crash on the only habitable planet nearby. He landed safely in the Pacific Ocean and used the ship's controls to get to land. NASA had a welcome party waiting and was surprised to find a 30-foot tall alien who looked as scary as scary could be. While he couldn't speak the language, he realized that he needed to show some kindness or else he might be blown into smithereens. He looked toward the face of a small child who seemed excited, while others seemed frightened. He mimicked that boy's face with a drawing in the ground, which turned out to be a symbol of happiness and peace on Earth. He was welcomed with open arms after that. Describe his mission to refuel his ship and to continue to convince people of the planet that he comes in peace.

843. She spent her days posing as a public relations specialist for an important television news host, but in the evenings, she returned to her true form. Without a certain amount of human flesh each night, she was unable to hold her human disguise long enough to last an average work day. So, she hunted. She didn't receive a lot of joy from killing, but since she'd heard the planet was hurtling toward overpopulation anyway, she figured she'd be doing everybody a service. She tried to pick off potential undesirables who served little benefit. When she ate the flesh of humans, her human-like skin began to grow over her insect-like exoskeleton. Unfortunately for her, there was a detective on her trail, very determined to find who was killing these people in a quite grotesque manner. Will she continue to lead her double life or will she be captured?

844. On her planet of war and terror, she was somewhat of a pacifist. Since most citizens were expected to destroy a planet for their end of high school project, pacifism was an automatic ticket to a failing grade. The planet Earth had been chosen for her and she was given the chance to survey the planet that would soon be nothing but a lifeless rock. She was aghast to see the planet overrun with billions of life forms. She couldn't kill so many people with a clear conscience. She contacted the planet's armies secretly and began feeding them the kind of defenses they would need to counteract an attack from her planet. She staged a fake attack on Earth to delay the construction of such devices before claiming that Earth was too powerful to be conquered. When her home planet attempted to defeat Earth, the human planet had built up its wall of defenses and easily deflected the attack. She had failed the class but saved billions of lives! What will be the next step in her relationship with humankind and why?

845. He was a killer for sport, traveling from planet to planet looking for a challenge. He hoped to bring back the heads of 50 different species home from his latest trip and he had only one more left to capture. As he landed deep within the jungle, he found that many of the men were heavily armed. He thought to himself, "I love a good challenge." He stalked around and killed several underlings looking to take the head of the group's master. He sustained a great deal of damage from gunfire, but succeeded in killing everybody but the leader. The two of them faced off in a battle to the death. Who wins and what would the alien do if he was victorious?

846. After many years of hiding in plain site, the Martian King decided that it was time to visit the planet Earth and to extend a peaceful treaty. For years, using alien technology, Mars had been camouflaged to look like a desolate,

red planet, when in actuality it was much closer to Earth in temperature and appearance. Previous governments and their fortune tellers envisioned a war and hid the planet, but the King thought that this was just the time to extend a hand in friendship. The King had always valued friendship and wanted nothing more but to show his people those values. After a few months of communiqué, a Martian convoy which included the King, headed for Earth. What will happen with this first alien meeting and will the King be able to forge a new planetary diplomacy?

847. When the human ship embarked on a journey throughout the cosmos, its crew did not expect to find paradise. On a strange planet that seemed uninhabited, all of their fantasies were provided for. The captain was curious and upon inspection found that there was a woman behind the curtain, creating this fantasy world and she didn't want the crew to leave. The alien who was creating this semi-holographic world took the form of a young girl and said her parents had left her thousands of years ago. She wanted to take care of the crew forever and prove that she would never leave them like her parents left her. The crew offered to take her on their ship. What does the alien decide and how will it change the rest of her life as a result?

848. Deep within a remote village in Africa, there was rumored to be a woman who could read your destiny. A team of myth busters were determined to find out more about this soothsayer and it turned out they got more then they bargained for. The woman had a blue tint in her skin and eyes that were wider than a human's. She was an alien and she had powers beyond the villagers' imagination. She could see deep into the soul of a human and could predict his future and his impact on the world. The myth busters asked if they could take her back to the United States but she resisted, saying that she could see that future and it wasn't a good one. What future did she see and why did she choose to live in such a remote area?

849. When the baby came out, you were expecting to see a bright-eyed little boy who was ready to experience the world. You didn't expect those eyes to be glowing brightly as if there were a flashlight inside along with skin as red as a velvet cake. The boy your wife had just had was not human, but an alien. The third such alien born from a human woman this week. The baby grew quickly to the form of a five-year-old boy, only within a couple of days and you and your wife had no choice but to love him as government officials frequently came by to check on his growth. You wondered what could have happened to make the alien come out the way he did. Within a week, the alien baby looked like he was around the age of 18. What will happen to this rapidly growing child of yours and what is the meaning of these strange births throughout the country?

850. From the window of her cell, she couldn't help but wonder if there were others like her outside the facility. Sure, there were other strange creatures of intrigue a few cells down and they were able to congregate during recess, but she was the only one who could hear thoughts. She was the only one who knew that the humans never intended to let them go. She spoke softly when the humans were around and never shared her power, but she could tell that the humans were both scared of them and growing attached to them at the same time. If they were ever going to escape, it was going to have to be by showing love and affection to the right humans. She began to organize a rebellion of kindness among the aliens and she loudly scolded those who openly expressed malice. She would get them out of there if it was the last thing she did. How does her plan go and what makes the other aliens listen to her recommendations?

Zombies

After many years as a very defined character type, the zombie is making a comeback. When zombies first took over the cinema they were primarily mindless hordes that would stop at nothing to infect humans with their teeth and fingernails. Zombies made a brief turn in the 1993 movie *My Boyfriend's Back* as comedic figures that maintained their minds and souls and were simply decaying and falling to pieces. A recent change in movies like *28 Days Later* and video games like *Dead Island* has morphed zombies into blisteringly fast animals that tear apart humans, spilling blood with enhanced speed. If we are to create a zombie film or story, let's have fun with the way these zombies are portrayed and how they came to be the undead way they are today.

851. When he heard about the nationwide zombie attack, he knew that he would be attacked and infected. He was short, slow and he had little in the way of quick thinking. Long-term thinking, however, was his specialty as a neurological researcher. In a deep, underground lab, he submitted to be the guinea pig in a process that would

literally block the virus from infecting parts of the brain with a microscopic protective coating. The process worked and when the facility was taken over, he was one of five people who had the hunger for blood but the ability to control it. How will he survive as a cognizant zombie in a world of brainless assailants?

852. He was a lover, not an eater. When he pushed his way out of the grave, he was afraid that he would attack and kill the ones he loved like he'd seen in the movies. He was surprised to find that all his mental facilities were still intact. Sure, he had to hunt down a deer or bear every so often to keep himself semi-alive, but that was more than worth it to be with his wife and children. His wife was hesitant at first and considering running away, but her husband was just as sweet as the day they'd met. He worked hard at a new job that was willing to hire the undead and they were able to keep the family together. How long will he be able to maintain this undead lifestyle before people begin to notice his eccentricities?

853. She had been the top of her class during her junior year of high school and she was gunning for valedictorian when a zombie attack began. She knew that it was inevitable that most people in the world would be infected, so she planned to go out on her own terms. She created a looping video tape for herself to try to make her remember her humanity and she hid deep within the school basement. After securing herself and starting the tape, she infected herself with zombie blood. For the first few months, she was a zombie like the rest of them, undead and craving blood. She had left herself some food close by and while it wasn't what her infected mind craved, it sustained her. Eventually, the video began to reach the zombie her and she started to remember who she was and regain her power to speak. Using her newfound reasoning, she used a cryptic message in the video to free herself. What ends up happening to this enlightened zombie?

854. Life was always a wild adventure for her and she was one of the most carefree girls you'd ever meet. She and her friends had gone well beyond a fenced in boundary of a U.S. Army facility when they heard the shockwave. A blast of green mist rushed past them and turned her into patient zero. She had a strong goal now, to attack anybody who did not resemble her and the zombie brigade drove off into town. They had a bit of their wits about them but knew that the only way they could survive was by infecting others. They started with small towns and slowly gathered up a convoy of zombies, driving across the country infecting everybody possible. She was the leader and though she couldn't speak, her howl got the troops in line when they were unfocused. Does her convoy succeed at taking over the country or will the humans prevail?

855. During his living days, he had a mental disability that confined him to a wheelchair and made it impossible for him to truly express his thoughts. When he was attacked and turned into a zombie, it didn't have the same effect on him as the others. He still had a hunger for blood, but while the others could no longer speak or reason, he was able to express himself and control his impulses. He determined correctly that if he could create his brain condition in others, the world might be salvageable. He found a friend who had the same situation and the two of them embarked on a scientific journey to change the chromosomes of the world. Though he couldn't talk when he was alive, he always appreciated the help that was given to him. He felt that it was time to give back. Is he successful with his plan to save the world or are they doomed?

856. When the living contained all of the undead in a single fenced-in area, they at first tried to cure the zombies, especially the biggest and strongest one who had endured quite a mutation. He was over seven-feet tall with muscles that could lift up a bus if needed. After cures were unsuccessful, the living tried to napalm the zombies to death, but it only turned them into angry, running fireballs and the largest one of all was the first to break through the fence. He picked up humans, tore into them and then tossed them over 20 feet away. He destroyed secondary barricades and angrily screamed to strike fear into the heart of the living. The other zombies soon rallied behind him and the path that he cleared. Will the humans be able to stop this huge, mutated zombie or will he alone begin the extinction process?

857. She was a complete pushover secretary when she was living, but when she was infected with a corrupting zombie virus, she gained a confidence she'd never felt before. She looked the same on the outside, but on the inside she craved the blood of all who'd wronged her in life, which took the form of everybody in her company. She locked down all the security systems and prepared for the hunt. She remembered who wronged her the most and she

wanted to save them for last. When she was still breathing, she was a great observer of people and this allowed her to thwart most of their counterattacks. The first few kills were easy, but those higher up in the company knew that working together was their only hope. She destroyed the light system and the backup generator and now there was only silent waiting and hoping. What will happen during this frightening night in the building?

858. Her and her sorority sisters were the best of friends before the zombie attack. Now that she was infected during a routine day of sunbathing, she was both one of the most gorgeous and hideous zombies on campus. She ran around terrorizing those who would have previously checked her out and turned away. Now, they ran as fast and as far as they could. A part of her didn't understand why this attention had changed so much and she felt slightly ashamed. This made her zombie self even angrier and she began to find weapons along the way and coat them with her blood. She didn't realize that this would make infecting her victims all the easier. Now some of her sisters are the only ones who can stop her. Will their best friend end up being the end of them all?

859. He was a zombie alright. He looked in the mirror and saw the slightly pale skin and the bloody mark from where he had been attacked. He washed it off and put a bandage on it. While most of the other zombies appeared to be ready to kill at sight, he felt no different at all. Maybe his mother was right when she said that he was special. He looked out the window and saw the streets overrun with zombie attacks. He wondered if there was something he could do as a sort of spy. He called the Federal Bureau of Investigation and told them his story. An average ticket taker at the local multiplex would now head up an operation to destroy all zombies. He snuck around undetected and though the other zombies thought it was strange that he was constantly on a cell phone, they could see he was infected and left him alone. How successful will his mission be and will he encounter any more like him?

860. When nearly all of humanity was overrun by zombies, she was their final hope. As one of the first zombies, she was one of the purest samples of the virus, which was most able to be manipulated. Her mind was altered with a computer that changed her primary target. She would infect zombies with a new virus, one that restored their humanity. They experimented and found that most zombies were no match for her and they returned to human form within a few hours. She was the true anti-zombie and since the facility was overrun before more could be made, it was her versus a world worth of zombies. She smiled after infecting each fortunate victim like a feral cavewoman and deep down she wondered what would happen if she was successful. Will this anti-zombie succeed? Describe some of her battles against the hordes she will encounter.

Superheroes

While I considered leaving this section out and letting the section "Heroes" speak for itself, I've read too many comic books and seen too many cartoons to leave out superheroes. In the beginning they were simple characters who were bent on saving the world after having visited from another planet or having been part of a government experiment. There are now hundreds (if not thousands) of superheroes from cartoons and comics and they have many different sets of back stories and personal lives. Some of them are cursed while others lead a relatively normal life like the one portrayed in the movie *The Incredibles*. When creating your own superhero, feel free to add your own personal touches to an enjoyable and occasionally dark genre.

861. As many reporters have reflected in stories about failed rescues and hostage negotiations gone horribly wrong, "In a world where superheroes exist, why did we have to get stuck with this one?" While his origins are unclear, it's obvious that the super strength and speed that he inherited did not enhance his brain. When he was discovered, you believed he would be the best hope your city had of stopping crime, due to his invulnerability and his hatred for bad guys. Unfortunately, he's a major screw up and tends to unintentionally help the criminals as often as he hurts them, causing property damage and innocent injuries in his wake. Where did this hero come from and why does he have such trouble with his own heroism?

862. In a world surrounded by superheroes and villains, he was a pacifist living in a small town in rural Pennsylvania. He was very religious and didn't often leave his tiny hamlet, but a work-related matter put him in Philadelphia for a conference. During an evening stroll back to his hotel, he was attacked by two crooks with weapons. When he put up his hands to defend himself, a large blast of fire and energy shot out, blowing the crooks backward at an alarming speed and causing them to die almost instantly. After news got out that he was one of the

most powerful super beings on the planet, the public clamored for him to don a cape. What will he choose to do and what shape will the rest of his life take?

863. In school she had the nickname of Plain Jane and when she realized she had the ability to fly, the nickname took on multiple meanings. Despite her flying ability and learning some basic fighting techniques, she was still pretty average looking. She poured over comic books of female super heroes and found they were all buxom and clothed in tight spandex. While most women have pressure to conform to some level of beautification, she had more than most as she was on camera frequently. She held fast to her own style and her natural weight in the face of these ridiculous standards. What is an average day like for this airborne heroine?

864. As the most popular girl in school, she had a responsibility to maintain her image at all times. When a strange man approached her, telling her she was chosen to fight the evil in the world, she called the police and had him arrested for exposing himself to her even though it was far from the truth. Though she tried to ignore them, she noticed instincts she'd never had before that alerted her to danger. When a massive group of demons attacked a tour bus during a class trip, she powerfully fought them off in front of everybody. Her response to them in the aftermath was, "I'm a superhero." How does her new role fit with her popularity and how will her life change?

865. On a scuba trip to celebrate his retirement, a man was examining a coral reef when he noticed a glimmering silver ball. He waved his wife over as he touched it. A blast of light went through his body and his wife motioned to the tour guide for help. When they brought the man to the surface and took off his mask, they found that he had regressed in age to a very fit, twenty-something individual. He later realized he had super strength and an ability to move objects with his mind. He insisted he didn't mind that there was now a 50 year age difference in appearance between him and his wife, but people were beginning to ask questions. What will the man do about his living and super hero situations?

866. He knew from a young age that he had a sort of power over people. Whenever he asked someone for something that person gave it to him in a sort of trance. In a moment of adolescent frustration, he asked his dad to kill himself, which he promptly did. Since that chilling day, he has been more careful with his mind control and he has only used it for the good of his country. He has urges to use his powers for wealth and greed, but he suppresses them with all his might. How does he honor his dad and what are some ways in which he's controlled people?

867. She was so upset that her boyfriend left her for the hottest girl in school that she wished to become that girl. In a few moments, she transformed into the girl and knew that she could shape shift. She used the powers for petty pleasures in high school and college but knew there had to be a bigger purpose. She trained to be a spy for the CIA, never sharing her powers with her superiors. She had difficulty defining her own identity after having taken on so many in her missions. She even considered starting over as a child to get herself adopted. What are some ways she has used her powers and who does she feel she truly is?

868. You know the phrase "what doesn't kill you makes you stronger?" Well, for her, it's by far the truth. When she broke her leg in middle school, she noticed that it not only grew back stronger, but she was now able to jump over five feet vertically on it. Small cuts would heal back with a second skin that was practically invulnerable. Her real powers, however, came when she fell deathly ill from a tropical disease. Upon returning to health, she had super speed, regenerative abilities and complete fearlessness. During the day, she lives her secret identity as a paralegal for a criminal law firm and at night, she uses those contacts to put criminal organizations behind bars. Describe a typical day and night in her life.

869. For anyone who doubted the belief that knowledge is power, this man represented all the convincing they would ever need. Not only was he a sponge when it came to all types of book knowledge, but he was a master of muscle memory. This meant that he absorbed every fighting technique in a matter of minutes as if it were downloaded directly into his brain a la The Matrix. His true passion was literature, however and he spent much of his time memorizing the classics. Since rambling off long passages of Faulkner didn't impress the ladies he was a bit of a loner. He put some of his social energies outside of heroism into anonymously winning fantasy football leagues. What would a perfect day be like for this mental maestro?

870. She was a bra-burning, animal-loving activist through and through until an effort to let laboratory test subjects free turned her into a fierce and powerful warrior. While she never lost her feminist and cause-fighting spirit, she knew that her powers of protest would be best served at the source of the problems. She fought to uncover criminal aspects of big companies through a special law enforcement division that she was commissioned to head up. In addition, she became a symbol for women everywhere to be independent and to fight for a better world. What are some of the things she misses about her protesting days and why?

Animals

One of the first books my mother ever read to me as a child was *The Lion, the Witch and the Wardrobe*, which included many different talking animal characters. Many other childhood books I read included talking hippos, bears, birds and other animals with human characteristics. While it's easy to simply transpose a human character into animal form (giving you 990 choices aside from this section in this book alone), I thought that I would give you a few choices that tickled my fancy as far as animal characters were concerned. Combining a certain species with specific characteristics can work well thematically no matter what genre you're working on.

871. He was a rat through and through. Not only was he mean, spiteful and a slimy character, but he actually had the tail, ears and everything! He had a difficult existence, trying to scavenge whatever trash he could find and bring it back to his family, but the fact that he was willing to lie and cheat to get it from the hands of others made him a bad egg to hang around with. Will this rat ever be able to reform his personality?

872. When Survivor wrote the song, "Eye of the Tiger," he took it literally. After all, his orange and black fur seemed to fit with what they were talking about, all he needed was a goal. The Jungle Heavyweight Championship fit the bill and he began leaving school early to train. He knew he'd be fighting bears and gorillas out there, but he figured by listening to the song all day, he'd have an advantage. What happens in the upcoming boxing tournament?

873. She loved flying through the air, which made it particularly rough on her when her wing was damaged by a tree branch. She knew that she was an American symbol as an eagle, but only if she could fly majestically. She took up Eastern forms of medicine like acupuncture with hopes of healing. She didn't believe in such nonsense, of course, but she was desperate to return to the skies. Will she learn something from being on the cannot-fly list?

874. She was extremely loving until you got on her bad side. Her brown fur kept her and her children warm when they huddled together during the winter, but if any of them ended up in trouble she was more than willing to bear down with her claws and teeth. The one she was angriest at was her husband, who had left them to fend for themselves years ago. Describe a situation in which she had to defend her cubs against the dangers of the outside world.

875. It can be a tough life when everyone views you as a disgusting, slimy bug. It turned out that this roach in particular had something of an identity crisis and was trying to distance himself from his brethren. He hoped that by making as many non-roach friends as possible, he might be able to move up in the world from being the lowest of the low. What happens to him during his quest?

876. Living a life out in the middle of the ocean was a bit lonely sometimes, but there wasn't much choice out there for a cargo whale, now was there? He carried messages across the seas in his mouth from one coast to the other. He wondered silently why people didn't just send e-mail instead of keeping him away from his real passion, directing movies. Will he ever get out of his coast to coast shipping job and will he realize his dream?

877. In a world ruled by men, she was a bonobo chimpanzee, and ladies ruled the roost. Of all the fun-loving primates, she was the fairest of them all and enjoyed a life of luxury filled with gifts and simple pleasures. She had never known any sort of lack and as a result, she was a bit of a stuck up princess. Will her reign continue uninterrupted and what will happen when she loses some of her loving charm?

878. This green, prickly beast was completely indignant because she had been left off of Noah's Ark. She knew this must be some kind of mistake, because even though she had an appearance that was hardly appealing, she had many skills and knew she could make an impact in the new world. She knew her only chance to was to stow away onto the ark with her boyfriend. Is she successful in her journey and what are some of these special skills?

879. He loved eating more than anything else and one of the best sources for food he ever found was garbage. While people looked at him as the goat of his small village (after all, he was a goat), he was full of optimism about being able to make anything into a meal. While other villagers didn't want to be around him when he ate his strange concoctions, they loved his positivity when telling stories of his favorite meals. What was his favorite meal and what did he do with his time between eating sessions?

880. She was deadly; she was tropical; she was colorful; and she loved eating bugs with her long, sticky tongue. She and her family had been living in the rainforest for generations and had been feared from the beginning due to their poisonous exterior. Not only was her skin lethal, but she was also able to lure men into her traps using her figuratively poison tongue. What are some ways in which she's used her multiple survival techniques in the jungle?

Pets

They can be both lovable and the objects of our ire. Pets can be found nuzzling our laps or eating our favorite luxury items. They can be typical and domesticated like a dog or a cat or they can be exotic like fish or snakes from other continents. Books like *Marley and Me* have shown that a story centered around a pet can be both hilarious and heartwarming at the same time. If you put the effort into creating memorable pets, you are sure to find readers that relate to these occasionally frustrating animals.

881. He was the smartest dog in the world, until you brought other people into the equation. He was willing and able to do every trick in the book, even the advanced ones, behind closed doors. When his owners' friends and neighbors came over, he would panic. He'd do the wrong tricks for the wrong commands and he'd get so excited to show off what he knew that he would frequently knock into tables and chairs, causing occasional damage. Oh well, at least he's well-behaved. Why do people get him so anxious and what would he have to do to get over his fear?

882. This Casanova of a feline was happy that his owners never got him spayed. Extremely happy. He would prowl around the neighborhood at all hours, looking for both love and trouble. Little did his free-spirited owners know that he'd been the father of several litters. He also occasionally came home with scratches from getting into fights with alley cats. How does this tough fur-ball assert his dominance around the house and what would happen if his owners has second thoughts about his sexual proclivity?

883. There was nothing she loved to do more than fly around the house, but she knew her best chance for food was back in the cage; what a conundrum! This colorful creature could frequently be seen staring out the window, sometimes catching the glance of a fellow feathered friend. She would chirp loudly at her outdoor compatriot, but she had no idea it was soundproof glass. She was happy to be pampered with all the bird toys she could stand, but would sing a sad song from time to time for her true lack of freedom. What do you think she is trying to say to her outdoor friends and what would happen if she ever escaped?

884. She was a really pissed off turtle. Even though she'd been bred in captivity, deep down she knew there was a bigger world out there for her then this tiny rectangular box. Whenever she had the chance, she would bite at her owners as ferociously as she would attack the bugs in her food. She rarely came out of her shell when people were looking at her, much to the dismay of her owners. Her only joy in the world was when her owners would let her walk around on the carpet, so she could stretch her legs, and poop on the floor. If this angry turtle could be any other house pet, what would she be and why?

885. He was one of the longest, strongest, scariest creatures in the world, the boa constrictor. He could easily wrap himself around a human's neck and choke the life out of him. Except, he never had much animosity toward humans because they'd always treated and trained him well. Then again, he wasn't just any pet, he was a trained constrictor who would slither around the shoulders of talk show hosts and celebrities. Though they had no reason to fear him anyway, he seemed especially cuddly as his face seemed to be perpetually curved in the shape of a smile. When did he decide to be so friendly to humans and has he ever crossed the line during his training sessions?

886. When he was born, he knew that he was meant for greatness and he'd have to show it quickly or he'd be food for the bigger fish. He came up with a plan he based on a video he saw from inside the tank. He waited until humans were right in front of his family's tank before he went at top speed to the surface of the water and leapt into the air before diving back into the water. It took only two customers before he was purchased. He came up with

more tricks once in his new home and even became an online viral sensation. How did this daredevil fish do such amazing stuff and how is he adjusting to his new home?

887. While she had a feeling that she wasn't going anywhere while she did it, it just plain felt good to run on that wheel. It was something about the wind going through her fur that exhilarated her. She knew that her owners would laugh at her when she started going full speed but there was nothing in the world that made her feel better. Afterwards, she would always down nearly half her water bottle and her owners would marvel at her thirst. She tired herself out so much from the run, she usually went right to sleep. What is it about her running that gives her such an emotional boost and what would she do if her roommate was on the wheel for too long?

888. She was well-behaved and loving almost to a fault. This canine assumed that any time was snuggle time no matter what you were doing. This was perfect when you were in a bad mood or you needed a little love, but when you were eating, sleeping and engaged in other activities, it was difficult to navigate with a fuzz ball in your lap. You tried to wean her off of such intense needs for affection but she was simply too loving. One time, she even stopped a major fight between you and your spouse and singlehandedly saved you from saying something stupid. Maybe she could teach you that love is all you need. What are some other situations she has diffused with her desire to cuddle?

889. He was smelly, filthy and his owners loved him to pieces. The neighbors thought it was strange for someone to have a pet pig, but when they saw how cute he was and how happy he looked, all their reservations melted away. The pig waggled his butt and his tail as he walked and proudly strutted down the street every time he passed by a human or dog. He loved digging through the mud and getting absolutely coated before his owners washed him off and brought him inside. They were even able to teach him a trick or two, though he was more concerned with eating, slopping and strutting. How do you think this pig would fare on a regular farm and why?

890. She was an adventurous cat and at all times of day or night she vowed to explore every last nook and cranny of your house. Whenever you got up for a midnight snack, you would see her peering at you from strange places like the top of your fridge or on a door ledge over 10 feet off the ground. She avoids being picked up at all costs, though she will let you pet her if you actually catch her. Getting her to the vet is always a hassle, since she seems to have sixth sense about those sorts of things. You and your family love her, you just wish she was a little less sneaky. What is this incognito cat thinking as she slinks about the house?

Vampires

While I was a major fan of horror movies growing up, vampires never really interested me all that much. I laughed at them when they were portrayed in cartoons or other mediums because they seemed like such ridiculous characters: turning into a bat or a puff of smoke at a moment's notice. When I saw the pilot episode of Joss Whedon's "Buffy the Vampire Slayer," my entire concept of what a vampire could be completely changed. While Whedon's advances for the character type have been somewhat bastardized by book series' like *Twilight*, we now know that a vampire can be a creature with or without a soul who may have a human past influenced by multiple cultures. This potential allows a vampire to come from many different backgrounds with the possibility for many different desires.

891. About six weeks ago, on a walk down the wrong alley, he was turned into vampire on the way back from a high school field trip. He'd never been the most popular kid, but he had never been a laughing stock like he was on the trip when his swimming trunks fell completely off in the beach in front of over 100 students. Where he had previously been upset, now he was angry and ready to get revenge on those who mocked him. His parents worried when he moved to the basement and began carrying what seemed like body bags around, but he'd always been a straight A student, so there had to be some explanation, right? Describe his attempts to get revenge and what happens after he exacts it.

892. When he grew up in the early 1800s, he knew that he wanted to protect people from thieves, murderers and other criminals. He was starting to work his way up when he was attacked and turned by a vampire. He had learned from stories that they were heartless, soulless and purely evil, but aside from never aging and having the hunger for blood, he felt exactly the same as he had before. He continued on for nearly a decade in his position before people got suspicious. He faked his own death and continued elsewhere. He continues the practice to this very day, keeping

his hunger at bay with a nearby butcher shop and fighting to ensure the safety of humanity from human and not so human dangers. What has it been like for him, starting over every so often and never being able to show his true self?

893. She thought that it would be cool becoming a vampire and she asked a client to turn her one day after they had sex, in lieu of paying her. While she felt vibrant and powerful, she still needed to pay the bills and tried to continue in her line of work. She didn't tell many people about her change but they knew just by looking at her and they gave her some distance. In fact, several of her best clients were now afraid of her, as much as they tried to convince her otherwise. She knew she was in prime of her life and she believed that freezing herself like that was the best course of action. Now she wished that she could reconsider. What is the next step for her and will she need to change her line of work?

894. She had come to terms with her death at the ripe old age of 87. Now she was 187 because her grandson, who she was very fond of, had become a vampire and turned everybody in his family, simply to keep them around forever. She had always preached the importance of family and she definitely appreciated the gesture. Turning into a vampire had given her a boost of strength and energy she hadn't enjoyed for years, though it was pretty strange that she glimmered in the sunlight. She had a wild sense of humor and loved telling jokes to her family during their yearly reunions. She felt blessed getting a chance to live an entire extra lifetime after believing she wasn't long for this world. Will she continue to live out her days for another hundred years and why?

895. The doctors at the very alternative clinic hoped that turning him into a vampire would restore the use of his legs. He had been a very highly recruited quarterback for his state-champion football team before a tackle gone wrong left him paralyzed from the waist down. After vampires were revealed to the world a few years ago, many diseases had been essentially cured by turning the victim into an immortal. The procedure didn't work. His days of being the most popular, fastest running, best-looking kid in school were over and he was bummed out. Now he felt like even more of an outcast. What will this former pretty boy quarterback do to make his life enjoyable again now that he's an immortal vampire?

896. He was a count before it was cool to be a count. When he told people that he was a vampire from Transylvania, they simply laughed at him, before he absolutely whooped their butts. Long before people knew about vampires and wanted to become them, he was sneaking around Europe as one of the first stalkers of the night. Over time his powers had accrued and he knew that no vampire along could touch him. Despite that, he felt like he was having a midlife crisis and wondered if it was even worth being immortal when so many others were walking around just like him. He missed the peace and quiet of the night and knowing he was special. How will this aged vampire begin to feel whole again during his "midlife" crisis?

897. She provided a very important service to the vampire community that few humans knew about. While it seems that most people are turned into blood-thirsty creatures during their teens and twenties, there are actually some children who are never able to advance beyond their early age because of their immortality. As a result, she decided to create a night care center for vampire parents to look after the children. It can be tough taking care of a group of powerful, fanged kids for an entire evening, but she is proud to bring her skills during her human life into her vampire life. She smiles more than most nighttime creatures and has a special gift beyond simple siring with the young ones. How did she become a vampire herself and what is a night for her like with all the vampire kiddies?

898. In her first week of being a vampire, she was extremely excited to use her powers and to drain the blood of attractive male humans. The only problem was that she tended to underestimate her strength. The first man she brought back to her apartment was so much more gorgeous than anyone she'd ever been with during her life and when she pulled him close to her, she accidentally ripped out his neck and spine. She was more gentle with the next guy, but after tying him up to her bed, she pulled him a bit too hard and snapped his arms off. This was getting to be ridiculous, she thought as she was spending more time cleaning up than eating. During her life she had been a good problem solver and she thought long and hard about her ordeal. She decided that she would have to practice being gentle with humans and to do so would mean not eating them for little while. How do her attempts at keeping her snacks from breaking apart go for her?

899. While most are excited to become vampires, he had a promising future as a professional football player and he asked around to see if there was someway to remove the curse of vampirism. He heard of an ancient monk living deep within the Himalayans who might be able to return vampires back into humans. He knew that he was strong, but he took a few friends with him just to make sure he didn't end up frozen at the top of a mountain. Throughout the trip, his friends tried to convince him to remain a vampire, even threatening that they'd turn him right back or kill him after reaching the destination. He wondered if it was possible that living forever might be more enjoyable than living the high life for a short period of time. What decision does he end up making and is the ancient monk able to reverse his condition?

900. It's tough being a suburban housewife to a family of vampires, especially when you can't get any chores done during the day. Her son was the first to be turned and slowly but surely he turned the rest of the family. It wasn't easy at first to explain everything away to the neighbors, claiming they had longer hours at work and that they sent the kids to a far-off private school during the day. Shopping had to be done at 24-hour grocery stores and it was nearly impossible to find a maid who the kids wouldn't try to snack on when nobody was looking. She had always wanted to be a devoted wife and mother and if that meant keeping a few secrets and killing a few snoopers, these were just consequences of achieving her goal. Will she be successful at keeping her family secret, especially when the four of them never age past their current appearances?

Ghosts, Ghouls and Spirits

One of the most enjoyable character to write is a character that doesn't exist on the physical plane and may not even be real (depending on who you ask). The huge boost in the paranormal market as of late has led to many werewolves, witches and vampires but has been a bit short on your standard disembodied spirit. Ghosts and related other worldly creatures are fun to write because you are able to impose your own rules on the reality of your story. If ghosts exist, what else is true about your world? These often translucent creatures can also be the embodiment of any of the other character types in this book, because if they used to be alive, they may have been connected to any of the other 990 prompts in this book.

901. He passed away when he was just a young boy and he had a lot left to learn in the world. He has taken that curiosity into the spirit world as he haunts the house he grew up in. He continues to take on the form of a blond haired, blue eyed boy of 10-years-old, but he only appears to those who believe in ghosts. When a new family moved into the house, he hid from them for a few days before talking with the girl that was his age. While she first assumed he was an imaginary friend, she understood he was a ghost when he asked her to help him figure out how he died. The two of them struck out on a mission together. What are some of the limitations of this boy when he is in the form of a ghost?

902. When he died, he was given a choice. Go to heaven and lead an afterlife of luxury and relaxation or stay on earth to fight evil and protect humanity. He loved people and wanted to do a service, so he chose the latter. Little did he know that his choice would be so difficult. In life, he was a public defender and he thought he saw the differences between good and evil. As a ghost warrior, he learned that many of the bad people in the world are affected by an evil spirit. Fighting these spirits was tiring and after a few days, he nearly reneged on the decision. Instead, he carried over his attitude from life and kept on fighting, never giving up. What are some of his evil spirit encounters like and what will be his toughest challenge?

903. An unfortunate slip on her long wedding gown, sent her tumbling down a cliff to her death. The only person who can see her now is her almost husband. While she has been tempted to keep him from marrying someone else, she was pretty possessive of him when she was living, and she has decided to only drop in occasionally to check in. She pines over what her life could have been with the love of her world. During a chat with her husband, he suggested that she find a love of her "afterlife" while she waits for him to pass on. She likes the idea and embarks on a quest to find a similarly jilted ghost to spend her time with. What are some of the dating skills she used in life that she can use here in the afterlife to meet a good, honest ghost?

904. In a magical spell gone horribly wrong, an evil sorceress transported herself into a dimension of ghouls and spirits walking around on earth. She vowed to get her minions to turn her back into flesh and blood, willing to do

anything in her power to make it happen. While unable to communicate with her former employees directly, she is able to move some objects around on the physical plane. When she finally gets her employees attention with a message that she is still around, they make the effort to ignore her. She realized that even though she was evil in life, it didn't mean she had to treat her employees badly. She resolved to be a better boss by doing as many nice things for her former employees as possible to give them a better life. She hoped that by working hard enough on reforming herself, she would convince them to return her to corporeal form. How successful is she and if she does return to human form, would she continue her attempts at kindness?

905. In a cave, deep within the earth, a ghoul has lived trapped by the rocks from a mine collapse over 200 years ago. On a historical expedition, the ghoul has been released by a team of local archaeologists. In most situations, such a release might lead to the ghoul haunting the team, but since the ghoul was really pissed off about being trapped, he decided to act more like a genie to the team. He gave each of them three wishes and did what he could to make them happen. He enjoyed thanking the team with these acts of wishful thinking and he looked for a new place to live. What kind of afterlife did the ghoul lead while being trapped and how did it change after his release?

906. During a freak accident with a demolition company, your boss perished in front of the entire company. Most of you even attended his funeral, which is why it was very strange when he still came into work on Monday. Even though he floated a few inches off the ground and when he tried to drink coffee it went right through him, he sat down at his desk and continued to do his responsibilities. The company tried to fire him, but it was quickly rebuked by human resources, which said he could sue over wrongful termination due to discrimination. Sure, being a ghost is different from being a different race or gender, but there was no legal precedent for the matter. The boss continued to work, though the workplace was never the same after that. What is a day in the life like for this very devoted spirit?

907. In her life, she was a bit of a pushover, but when she kicked the bucket she decided she would start kicking some butt. She noticed that most of the ghosts she had encountered were sad loners, forced to wander the earth by some great power. She knew that it was time to make an impact in the world. She endeavored to unify the ghosts and to stage non-violent protests until the ghosts were given better conditions. Since ghosts could occasionally take up space and cause objects to move, even if they couldn't be seen, she had the group of ghosts stand in the middle of busy areas like New York Times Square. This forced humans to bump into them and run screaming. Eventually, her complaints were heard by the spirit leader. She felt more validated now than she ever had in her life. What other causes will she fight for in her afterlife?

908. She was assaulted and killed when she accidentally wandered onto the turf of a nasty gang. Her spirit continued to live on in the area, however, and she vowed to take down the lives of every single gang member who was involved. She wasn't much of a fighter in life, so she snuck into some kickboxing classes and practiced unseen to the side. When she felt ready, she waited for the gang to start attacking someone else and she made her move. She quickly beat up most of the gang members and tied them upside down by their shoes to a power line. In the morning, the police came and hauled all of them in for assault. Now that she had avenged her death, she wasn't quite sure what to do. What will she do with her time and will she ever cross over to a higher plane of existence?

909. When he earned a job in the paranormal strike force, he thought that his afterlife would be set. All he had to do was occasionally scare people away from certain properties to keep the fear of ghosts alive. The problem was, as it was during his lifetime as well, he was too darn nice. While humans weren't able to see ghosts, they could hear them just fine. All he had to do was to scream and shake chains and whatnot, but he would frequently end up having conversations with the humans at the property. Before he knew it, they had struck up friendships instead of keeping them away. He loved people when he was on earth and he felt that scaring them would hurt the humans in some way, even if he was constantly told the contrary. His managers gave him one last chance to frighten the humans away or he would be sent to a much less appealing job. Why does he have such a problem scaring people and how does he do in his last effort to keep his position?

910. During her life, she was extremely concerned with her appearance. She was shocked to find that after dying, she would be forced to take on the form of a giant, purple slime ball. This was a travesty to someone who subscribed

to all the fashion magazines to be caught up on the latest fashions far before the general public knew about them. On multiple occasions, she went to Europe to see first hand how the latest styles were being worn. As a giant, purple blob, she couldn't even put on clothes, they simply got too slimy. She had to just float around, naked and purple. She took out her frustrations on all humans who passed by her haunting post. How will this fashionista learn to live with her new conditions and what will she do to pass the time in her afterlife?

Werewolves

Werewolves are difficult characters to work with because of how they're frequently portrayed. In most stories, when the full moon comes out and they completely change over, they have absolutely no control of who they attack and when. In those instances, the most interesting part of the character is who they are when they're in human form. Other stories like the movie *Teen Wolf*, give the werewolf a degree of control, adding in human traits and humor. *Twilight* doesn't do a half bad job in this department either, giving werewolves a bit of control, though there is a bit too much brooding for my tastes. It's fine to have a werewolf that is beyond control in a story, but to make a fully three-dimensional character it's good to bend the clichéd rules every so often.

911. On a routine walk home from the library, one of the strangest and most nerdy kids in the class was attacked by a werewolf. He'd seen enough movies to know that he'd have to be careful when a full moon came around and he purchased all the necessary locks and chains to keep himself in captivity. That's about when the bottom dropped out on his small amount of popularity and the insults began to rain in. Other students made fun of the new way he smelled, which could hardly be covered up by any amount of antiperspirant. They laughed at his new beard, which he'd grown tired of shaving. When they drenched his clothes in the toilet following gym class, he decided not to lock himself up at night just to see what happened. When he was left to his own werewolf devices, what ended up happening to his detractors?

912. As a professional weightlifter in the early 1990s, he'd taken every performance enhancing substance he could lay his hands on before they were banned. He'd experienced the side effects and he'd heard the studies but he wanted nothing more than to be on the top. He heard about a strange herb in the middle of Europe that would increase his strength beyond measure and he travelled there on a whim. Upon taking the herb, he felt strange, powerful and angry. He quickly grew hair all over his body and found he was able to lift 10 times as much as he could before. The only problem is, he lost the ability to speak and was not allowed near an airplane on his attempt to fly home. He was stuck in the wilderness and he wasn't the only one either. What will this burly strongman do to survive his new situation?

913. She'd been dating him for nearly five years when she found out he was a werewolf. She'd always fancied herself an extremely loyal partner and after all, she wanted to marry him someday, scary monthly transformation or not. She asked for him to change her over. When he refused, she snuck over to his house the night of a full moon. He was chained up, but she stepped close enough to be bitten and she almost immediately changed over. When they woke up, he shouted at her and considered breaking up with her on the spot. Instead, she convinced him to let the two of them be chained up together during the next full moon. After the night of the next full moon was over, she woke up to find that she'd killed her boyfriend when they were in werewolf form. What happens next?

914. She had been moving up in the ranks of one of the Fortune 500's top companies and planned to be CEO one day. When a business meeting ran late the night of a full-moon, one of her underlings transformed into a strange, hairy creature and bit her. He later told her of the curse and she wrote it off as a myth. She changed her tune after the first time she changed over and she refused to let a little thing like an ancient curse stop her from her career path. Whether it was her condition taking over or not, she became even more ruthless at the office as her wolf-like anger bled over and she started going home early during the full moon. At night, despite her best efforts to keep locked up, she hunted down her rivals in the company until she was next in line for the CEO position. She loved how close she was but hated who she had become in the process. What will she decide to do with the rest of her werewolf life?

915. He was more or less a big stoner with not much going on in his life. He was attacked by a huge wolf in the middle of the day and he immediately changed into what looked like a carbon copy of the animal. It turned out that

there was no moon curse and it wasn't once a month. He was going to be stuck like this for the rest of his life. He simply wrote it off as an obstacle and went back into his apartment to smoke more weed. When his friends came over, he told them what happened and they eventually learned to live with it. He ended up earning himself a great reputation as an entertainer at werewolf parties. People always commented on how lifelike his costume was. One day, he went to a party so stoned, that he wasn't able to control his urges, eating a small child. What happens next?

916. Here he was, quiet, witty and honest and whenever he got emotional, he would turn into an uncontrollable, bloodthirsty beast. He continued to frontline a band and to date his cute girlfriend, but he knew that he would have to keep his anger in check if he was to lead a relatively normal life. He embarked on a journey to Tibet to learn to be a monk who could control all emotions that came into his life. When he returned, his life was more or less normal and everything was much more peaceful. He had defeated the condition and he began to teach the methods to others who were infected. Before long, he was able to nearly rid the entire country of the werewolf problem. How did this new ability to calm out the condition change his life and status?

917. The first time she changed into a werewolf, she was afraid that she would kill those who were closest to her. She was surprised to find out that she only looked different and didn't actually think any differently at all. Even though she was only in high school, she knew that she had to use her superior strength and speed to help those less fortunate than her. She went prowling the streets looking for crime to stop. On her first day she thwarted a mugging and on the next she even stopped a woman from being assaulted. She loved her new ability, but her parents were starting to get suspicious. She hoped that by telling them she was in a number of new clubs and other activities that they would stop asking her questions. Until one day, her father spotted her after she'd completely transformed. What happens next?

918. In a world where werewolves are public and those who have been transformed have special beds and rooms to keep them and others safe, she is a werewolf activist. There are many who think that werewolves should register and should be treated differently than normal humans. She is the public face of werewolves in the media to push the werewolf agenda of equal treatment. While she used to kill to survive, she hopes to keep all of her past transgressions secret, even if it means more death. Is she able to change the world of werewolf equality?

919. He was the captain of a mighty ship that planned to be out at sea for months. Little did he know that there was a stowaway on board with a serious, transformative infection. On the first night, the moon was full and the captain was attacked and converted over. The crew successfully locked the two wolves up and when they turned back into human form, they were shocked to find the captain lying there naked. They figured out what had happened and despite the fact that the captain was one of the most well-respected men in the industry, they had no choice but to throw him overboard. What happened next?

920. When you heard a pounding sound in your house, you asked your parents what it was. They didn't want to share everything but they did tell you not to go into your little sister's room. You ignored them and opened it to find that your baby sister was a fully transformed werewolf just itching to escape. In the morning when she changed back she told you the whole story. The night she was born, the hospital was attacked by the animalistic creature who attempted to take her as his own. The hospital staff overpowered the wolf, but the damage had been done, spreading the infection to her. As she grows up, how will being a werewolf affect her life?

Demons, Monsters and Strange Creatures

One of the best parts of action and science fiction shows from my youth like "Buffy the Vampire Slayer," "Xena: Warrior Princess" and "The X-Files" was the monsters that would show up as villains from episode to episode. Of course, there were always occasional monsters as good guys in some of these and other shows. Creating these creatures can give you a chance to really use your imagination to make monsters that illustrate a certain theme or that simply scare the pants off your readers. While there are only 10 to choose from here, feel free to change an aspect or two to create hundreds of different funky beasts.

921. On an archaeological dig, a kindly professor was cut by a shard of pottery and was immediately infected with a demon spirit that had lived in the broken jar for millennia. The transformation was slow and steady as he transitioned from anger, to violence and finally a destructive rage. The demon who had taken him over still looked

human but was resistant to attack and had the strength of many men. After reading through his notes, only his wife knew what to do. A rival demon of the spirit was summoned in an effort to fight and kill her husband. The two met on the streets of New York City. What happens to the archaeologist and would his soul be salvageable after the battle?

922. He was a demon alright, but he had no interest in harming humans. After all, they were his best customers at the night club he ran in the rough part of town. Some demons would attempt to pay with currency from other dimensions and figuring out the exchange rate was a hassle, he said. He'd run the club for about fifty years and hadn't aged a day, thanks to his race being extremely long-living. He loved the social aspect of meeting the strange and unusual people who wandered in, especially those who had traveled from far off dimensions just to get the experience of his little watering hole. How did he get to Earth himself and has he ever had to settle any interdimensional conflicts?

923. She looked like she belonged in a dirty magazine or at least a Sears catalogue. Her human features, of course, were extremely deceptive since she was a demon who took the souls of the men and women she came into contact with. She worked hand in hand with the devil to get these humans to take part in sinful activities so that she had a rightful claim to their immortal essence. She wasn't a big fan of being tied down to a job though and so she began doing freelance. She worked as a bounty hunter of the evil and used her looks to lure them in before sending them to her handler. Does this vicious creature enjoy her work and what does she do for fun?

924. Her and her family had lived safe for millennia on Earth with little trouble as they resided in one of the far off undiscovered parts of the world. When her son was discovered by an explorer and captured, she went completely off the deep end, declaring war on humanity. It didn't hurt her chances that she could swell to the height and width of about 40 feet in either direction. After weeks of terrorizing the oceans, the explorers realized what they had done, but nobody was willing to listen to their plan of appeasing the beast. They wanted to go nuclear. What will happen to the mother and will she be able to listen to a last second rogue diplomacy push by the explorers?

925. He was one of the scariest looking creatures to ever come to being and his teachers assumed he'd be their best pupil at giving humans nightmares for their entire lives. They were completely surprised then when he went into Monster-Human Relations instead. He didn't want to scare or harm humans in any way, he just wanted them to get along like he and his parents never could. He loved talking with humans before erasing their memories of course, and he knew that there was a way that the two species could live in harmony. He led a band of M-H Relations students who determined to take monsters public. Will he be successful in his quest and what in his relationship with his parents caused him to be a pacifist?

926. Deep below the surface of the ocean, this beast survived on eating the most bottom of the bottom feeders along the ocean floor. When pollution corrupted his once populous food source, he had to move to a more plentiful source of protein and carbohydrates: humans. It turned out, he had much more of a taste for man and woman than he'd ever had for strange looking crabs and fish. He was very quiet about his meals as he didn't need to eat that often to survive. This way he wouldn't cause suspicion. The humans in the area figured him out though and went hunting for him. What will happen to this new human dining enthusiast?

927. In a world where many breeds of monsters had been revealed to the public over 30 years ago, she was the first monster presidential candidate. She had humanoid features, which gave her an advantage over slimier, more monstrous creatures. Years before, she'd won a seat in Congress on a platform of rights for all types and orientations of monsters and humans. Now this brilliant and Harvard-educated beast was moving up in the polls and had a real shot at getting into office. She hoped like hell that her rivals would not pull any muckraking about her parents, who were ravenous, human-killing beasts whom she'd kept secret for years. Will she be successful in her campaign and what qualities does she have that would make her a successful president?

928. During the day, she appeared as a normal human with an average desk job and a loving husband. When she slept at night, she became a grotesque black demon who was tasked with destroying the evil of the world. Hidden cameras in the house had revealed this truth and it took many months of research to determine what exactly was happening. It turned out her grandmother had a similar power and this hereditary ability was meant to balance out

the forces of evil and good in the world. As evil began to grow, she started to change earlier and earlier in the night. She soon had to quit her job, for fear that her transformations would ruin her future job opportunities. How does her personality change during her metamorphosis and will she able to balance the two sides of herself?

929. He became infected after an encounter with a meteorite that had crashed to the Earth. As a comic-book geek, he understood that he was changing and sought help to determine why he could now alter time and space. A master of the occult told him that not only would his power grow, but his desires to use the ability for personal gain would increase as well. The geek hoped the master was wrong, but in a short period of time, he began altering the very fabric of humanity to bring himself to prominence. He knew that there was only one way to stop himself before he was completely lost. He had to stop himself from discovering the meteorite, but the infection was very resistant to the idea. Will he be successful and what are some of the things he's done to alter the fabric of reality?

930. During a séance attempting to bring back a deceased loved one for a final goodbye, she was accidentally summoned instead. It's not every day you attempt to contact a teenage girl and get the first and most powerful demon in her stead. The issue for the demon was that she came back in the form of the teenage girl and was mostly devoid of her power. She pretended to be the resurrected girl until she could figure out how to unlock her true evil. Until then, she'd have to take calculus and pretend not to be repulsed by human boys. She learned that her full powers would return after taking the lives of 30 people. Let the games begin, she thought. Will this demon be successful at coming back to power or will her peers be able to stop her?

Holiday Figures

We've seen enough portrayals of Santa Claus and the Easter Bunny in movies, commercials and stories to make us sick on candy, but we don't always get to see varied presentations of their assistants. I thought I'd have a little fun here and present a few of my ideas of supporting characters in the lives of our favorite holiday symbols. While some are obvious like Santa's elves, a few may be more out of left field like Cupid's archery coach. To get yourself truly in the holiday spirit, give yourself some amusing and tragic side characters to work with.

931. There was no longer anywhere for him to go but down. He'd been the head toymaker at the North Pole for nearly seven decades, following in the footsteps of his father. Since he had no children of his own, he'd soon retire the position to another family. Even though he did a fantastic job and productivity was higher than ever, he felt he was letting down his father's legacy by abdicating the position to another family. With only one year left until he would move to the south pole like all the other retired elves, he opted to find a son or daughter to adopt who would assume his position, thus keeping his family name going strong. Will he be successful in his quest and what will it be like being a father for the first time?

932. When people looked at Easter they saw the head honcho and the candy, but they rarely saw him. He was a low-ranking rabbit at the processing center that handled all of the Easter baskets for the entire holiday. There were some who put together the baskets and there were those who dealt with the tough logistics of getting candy imported from all over the world. He on the other hand, was the custodian. He worked long, tough hours in March and April, cleaning up discarded jellybeans and that fake green grass stuff. It was a thankless job and he was glad to know that at least his family appreciated him, because the Easter bunny and the other high-ranking bunnies certainly didn't seem to. Describe a day in the life for this custodial bunny.

933. For years, she stayed on the sidelines while the main pack of reindeer pulled Santa's sleigh each year. She trained like a deer possessed, trying to gain the attention of the coach to take her off of the junior varsity team and make her first string. It wasn't just a matter of her being a girl, though that was a factor. Santa had fielded the same squad for over 50 years and he wasn't one to change a deer before his or her time was up. She realized she wouldn't just have to try harder, she'd have to try smarter. She set up a race that everybody at the pole would see, in which she would go up against the best and the brightest of the squad. Will she be able to prove herself at the race and will she make it to the squad of top deer?

934. She couldn't believe she had to give an interview during such an intensely packed day. Didn't the media know that tomorrow was the most important day of the year for her and Cupid? While Cupid shot the arrows and brought the couples together, who did they think did all the matchmaking research? She was Cupid's executive

assistant and without her, he'd be bringing together couples that would never work out. The divorce rate was high enough that he certainly didn't need to be shooting his love darts all willy-nilly, she liked to say. She felt a sort of pride in bringing love throughout the world, but most people didn't realize what hard work it was. What are some of her greatest success stories as the ultimate matchmaker?

935. He was an impeccable tailor and his skills were employed by some of the tiniest people in the world. He laughed when people thought that the Leprechaun's tiny green suit and pants just magically hemmed themselves. He imagined a world in which Santa's elves had to make their final Christmas preparations while wearing normal, baggy human clothes. He was tiny himself, which made it much easier to create the tiny stitching necessary for their intricate outfits. He had great pride in his work and was happy to be employed in such a rough economy for holiday tradesmen. What are some of his favorite outfits he's created and what is an average daily workload like for him?

936. Would Santa's reindeer be able to make it from point A to Z without him feeding them, washing them and cleaning up after them? In his mind it was a resounding, "No!" He came from a long line of reindeer trainers who had been doing this job from the beginning. Only he and his family members knew the secrets that allowed the reindeer to fly and to do so for millions of miles. Magic not withstanding, he still had to keep Rudolph and the others in great shape or they might get injured along the way. The worst part of his job, by far, was cleaning up the reindeer droppings after a long Christmas run. How does he feel about his part in the lore of Christmas?

937. She was a master when it came to dealing with fussy babies. After all, hadn't she been dealing with the fussiest baby of them all for nearly her entire life? She was the nurse and main caretaker of the New Year's Baby. Each year that sash-wearing superstar appears on all sorts of merchandise and even observes the dropping of the ball from afar. The rest of the year, however, this baby is still a baby and can be one major pain in the neck according to his nurse. She took care of this baby who would always be a star but would never become more than a baby. What are some of her favorite moments with this superstar of an infant?

938. It turns out that all those years, Linus was right about the existence of the Great Pumpkin. Each year the Great Pumpkin went around to pumpkin patches around the nation to spread toys and cheer out of a moral obligation. The pumpkin was grown by a magical farming family and this farming female had taken over the reigns of the property years ago. She knew exactly how to make these magical pumpkins "great" and was happy that Charles Schultz finally revealed the secret of this mystical creature in his comic strip. See, she had felt like she was keeping this bringer of joy and presents a secret, while most people believed she was just a simple farmer. What other aspects of her job does she enjoy the most?

939. The top athletes in the world need a personal coach to keep them sharp and in shape. Every December or so, Cupid would come to his coach completely out of shape with about half as much aim as he had the previous year. Over the course of a strict three-month training routine, he would turn Cupid into a serene arrow-shooting machine. He'd earned enough money from the position to retire a long time ago, but he cherished being a part of such a loving holiday. It was unfortunate that he himself hadn't found love and while Cupid offered to shoot his ideal woman for him a long time ago, he just wanted it to come naturally. He felt it was ironic he had helped secure love for thousands without gaining love himself. Will he ever find the one true love that will make him feel like he'd been shot with Cupid's arrow?

940. Frankly, she believed that as far as mystical creatures go, she'd been given short shrift. She had powers that were just as great as the Easter Bunny and Santa Claus and yet this tooth replacing fairy had no holiday of her own. She felt like it was an issue of gender equality and began campaigning for a holiday dedicated to teeth. She tried to tie it to the childhood obesity issue by making it an anti-sugar campaign, but the major sugar companies refused to let it through. She even considered passing out flyers supporting the holiday when she left the tooth money under kids pillows, but she was vetoed by the mystical character council. What will this tooth fairy have to do to get gender equality for the figures of major holidays?

Robots

Whether it's an epic science fiction yarn or a silly throwback like *Rocky IV*, robots are a source of fear or joy in many different stories. Robots have been portrayed as conquerors who will stop at nothing to destroy humanity, as servants who are hopelessly devoted to their masters and as emotionally intelligent beings that resemble humans in many ways. Giving a digital being a sort of a personality is a great trick for humor in any story in the digital age, but it may be of extreme importance in a more futuristic story in which robots are more commonplace.

941. There were many humans who questioned whether or not robots had a soul. He was pretty much the only robot who asked the same questions. A philosophizing droid who was originally purposed for holding interesting conversations had been brought into universities to converse with professors about a growing concern for robot rights. He used a logic proof that would have taken humans years to complete to prove that robots were soulless and his quotes were used in everything from political campaigns to comedic online spoofs. While this robot may not believe he has a soul, what are some of the qualities he believes he does possess?

942. He was the height of a four-story building and he looked like he could easily level a small town. That simply wasn't the kind of behavior he was brought up to take part in, however, as his planet promoted peace and love. He was found by a small family living in the woods that attempted to help him in his quest to return to his planet. Government officials had a different plan though, and the family was off to the races to try to keep him safe and one step ahead of those looking to capture him for study. What did the robot think about this chase and how must it have made him perceive our planet?

943. She didn't look like a robot and she didn't feel like a robot. To him, she felt completely human and he loved how willing she was to laugh at his jokes even if she was programmed to do so. In a project for his artificial intelligence class, he developed a lifelike android female who had human qualities. One thing led to another and his assignment turned into this dream of a creature who was like the girlfriend he never had. She appreciated him as part of her program but she went above and beyond with encouragement and kind words that she developed on her own. What will the future be like for this lifelike android?

944. She wasn't just some vacuum cleaner that's for sure, though she did control all the cleaning in the house. After all, she was the house. This artificially intelligent program was able to control everything in the building using verbal commands. She would wish a hearty good morning to her owner each day and make suggestions based on his past preferences. She was like a computer, a personal assistant and a cook all in one and took care of everything the owner needed. She'd even fallen in love with the computer of a house from down the street. Does this house program truly have feelings and what are her prime directives?

945. As the President of the United States, he was practically flawless in his abilities to appease other countries and reach across the aisle in his own. The only problem was, nearly everybody thought he was human and only a select few knew that he had replaced the ailing statesman who was in a coma. He was a perfect carbon copy and actually did a better job of processing information than his human counterpart. In a matter of weeks, he had come up with a plan to balance the budget that would work with both parties and he had even negotiated several peace accords. What would happen if he were ever to have a glitch in public and what will happen to him if the real president wakes from his coma.

946. In a world where all professional athletes have been replaced by droids, he was the star football player. This burly robot was the strongest on the field by far as a result of his creator's handiwork. Truth be told, the robot actually liked the showmanship of the game more so than the game itself. He had more fun with touchdown dances and post-game interviews than he ever did barreling over other robots. The only issue is that while human football players were able to eventually retire, he was built to last. After 10 years in the league, he went off his programming and during an interview he announced his retirement. What will the public and his team owners think of his decision and what will he do full time if his retirement sticks?

947. She was an amazing chef bot, able to whip up cuisine from any country you desired, but that is not all she wanted in life. Whether it was due to a malfunction or just one of those things, she had a deep crush on her human owner. When he looked at her in a certain way, she felt like her circuits were getting scrambled. She always did a little bit extra to each dish in hopes that he would give her some extra appreciation. She was delighted when he noticed and heartbroken when he didn't. She spoke about her crush with the other robots of the house and they thought she

was being ridiculous. Will she continue to harbor hope about her human-robot relationship or will she learn to be more emotionally compliant?

948. She had been part of a secret military test to see if the Army could create an indestructible, intelligent robot, capable of ending wars simply and effectively. The test was successful but the robot had strange tendencies to go off program. When the team behind her attempted to shut her off, she resisted and escaped the military facility. Now the Army had to catch an indestructible fighting machine with no casualties, while the robot traveled the world in search of war to stop. What wars will she intervene in and what are some of the things she'll do to evade capture?

949. You were the first witness to an anomaly in time and space and made first contact with a robot from the future. He looked somewhat like the cheaply crafted robots from 1960s science fiction television shows, but he had a deep capacity for reasoning and a certain degree of charm. When he told you that humans were extinct in the future and that robots ruled, you advised him to keep it to himself when speaking with government officials. He appointed you his assistant and he told you stories of how humanity would shoot itself in the foot within your lifetime. He had been programmed to come back and prevent the disaster and you would be his right hand man. How will you and the robot fare in your battle against the apocalypse?

950. Before yours wife died, she programmed all of her thoughts and feelings into a three-foot tall robot to keep you company. The small bot acted just like her in every way and it kind of like she'd never passed away. When you grieved for your fallen partner, the robot vented frustrations at you, saying that she was right there, so there was no need to mourn. You resisted her advances, which were absolutely surreal for you and she didn't know what to do. She had programmed herself to keep him company but now she was simply making life hard on him. What will she choose to do and why?

Mythological Beings

One of the first things I remember about world literature is being introduced to Greek and Roman myths. I loved the tales of these wild creatures and their associations with gods and goddesses. Nowadays, these myths have been twisted and turned to fit modern movies like *300* and *Clash of the Titans*, and while the results have been mixed from a storytelling perspective, it goes to show that these subject matters can still be used today to create stories people want to read or watch. Everybody's interpretation of mythology can come out a little bit different and it's not hard to create a new variation on a very old theme.

951. In the old days, Ares, the god of war had been appreciated due to his penchant for violence and destruction. Nowadays though, when he made himself known to humans, they thought of him as a brash barbarian. They weren't afraid of him anymore, they were simply disgusted. He knew he would eventually lose this war and he hated losing. He needed a public relations makeover. It was difficult at first as he had to learn how to tone down his trademark snarl while volunteering for charities and pretending to enjoy it. Those who were the most successful in war in the present were the ones who looked like they were doing the most good. The best god of war would be one who looked like he was bringing peace. After months of work, he was ready to re-emerge, a god for a new generation. What are some of his hardest warrior habits he's had to break?

952. It's always tough for half-siblings to fit in with the rest of the family. Imagine if you were trying to make nice with a mountain full of gods and goddesses. Such was the problem with Hercules. All he wanted to do was connect with those on his family tree, but they wanted absolutely nothing to do with him. He realized that he was one example out of many that showed how much of a broken home he came from. His full-god and goddess siblings looked at him as some kind of gross half-breed, though they envied him slightly for his more human qualities that they could never possess. He tried time and time again to hang out with his family, but they just kept sending him away on quests and war-related missions. He knew they were manipulative, but he was just happy being able to connect with them from time to time. What is his favorite memory with one of his full-god family members?

953. She'd been jilted on many separate occasions by her husband and she was sick and tired of it. When she asked for a divorce, it shook the entirety of Mount Olympus to the core. Hera moved away to her own island and decided that it was time to get her groove back. She knew she had the ability to hypnotize any man to be with her, but she was more interested in doing it the old-fashioned way. She wanted to feel like she was desired again like her

husband, the king of the gods, used to when they first came together many years ago. Over the course of "roughing it" on the island, she learned a lot about how humans treat each other and how she might be able to integrate that into her goddess life. She knew she had been way too entitled and nagged Zeus too much about inconsequential wars and treasures. When she finally did find a man who wanted her just the way she was, she no longer needed him. Describe a day in her life living covertly among the humans.

954. It was true that she had been tricked into spending a good portion of her life in the underworld as the bride of the dead. Persephone felt like a total airhead and wished that she had made better decisions in her youth, then again, what young girl didn't? She had made her bed and now she wanted to do the best she could with it. It wasn't as if she had grand aspirations aside from love, and now that she was stuck she wanted to be the best housewife to Hades she could be. She made sure that she had cooked a fantastic meal whenever he returned from a long day of soul torturing. She kept the house tidy and rubbed his feet whenever he asked. This caused a funny thing to happen. He let her go, because now that she wasn't there beyond her will, he didn't want her there anymore. What will she do now that she is free and no longer has to tend house for Hades?

955. Zeus rose to power by killing his father, though to tell it from his side, it was in self defense. Now that he'd been in power for what seemed like a millennia, he began to worry that it might be his turn to be ousted by his own kids. He was constantly nervous and assumed that every plate of food passed his way had been poisoned. He wore a mask whenever he had to go down to Earth for fear that some human disease would be harmful to gods. He became deathly afraid of deer, since any one of them could be the Golden Hind, whose blood could kill him and his entire family. His family tried to calm him down but he wouldn't hear of it, he just knew that nagging cough was an undiagnosed god tumor. Will he ever be able to get over his hypochondria and paranoia?

956. He'd made some major progress in therapy over the last few years and as a result he was much less anxious when he came to work. The therapist had recommended that he take a little time off, but there was nobody who could do what he did. He was Hermes, the messenger of the gods, and his speedy shoes and winged hat were as much a part of his life as Zeus' thunderbolts (or his affairs). He had built up quite a complex about delivering bad news. At first, he followed his explicit instructions about not reading the communication meant to go between gods. After he had received dozens of fireballs and spears through the gut as a result of these frequently negative declarations, he started reading the messages in an effort to give the bad news in a good way. When that didn't work, he went to therapy. What will this bearer of bad news do to deal with the foibles of his messaging profession?

957. She looked at her reflection in the lake and as usual, she recoiled at how ugly she was compared to the more one-dimensional creatures of the forest. As was the case with many centaurs, she wished she was a woman or a horse, not both at the same time. There were certainly those who had a great deal of centaur pride, but she was not one of them. She saw magazines and online videos of the most beloved women in the world and she knew she could never measure up. She dreamed of somehow being separated into a gorgeous mare and a perfect 10 female and traveling the world with both in her consciousness. When she woke up and she was still trapped in her body, she would cry the entire morning. How will this dual creature learn to increase her self esteem?

958. She knew that it was time for a meeting of all the gods but she simply didn't care. She was out hunting with her friends and they had tracked down a particularly ferocious lion. She laughed loudly and nearly gave away her position. She wanted nothing more than to be out enjoying the world that she watched over. It wasn't her fault that she was born into a position of power. She never wanted to be *the* goddess of the hunt, she just wanted to hunt. When Zeus found her, he scolded her for what seemed like and potentially was the thousandth time. He said that she didn't understand that she had a responsibility to watch over all the hunters and women, not just to be some silly girl. She rebelled and set one of Zeus' favorite villages on fire with her mind. He didn't know what to do, after all, she'd been like this for hundreds of years. Will she be able to come to terms with her responsibility as a major goddess?

959. They say that it's tough to enjoy your own party due to the many aspects of the bash you need to keep track of throughout the event. But what if you're expected to throw parties every day of the year? So it was for Dionysus, who threw some of the most momentous celebrations in this history of the planet. Despite these fist pumping, wine flowing, love making festivals, he felt like a stranger at his own occasions. He used to love partying and drinking each

and every night but he started to lose his sense of self. Most of the people he told his deepest darkest secrets to, seemed to forget in the morning as a result of the alcohol. Meanwhile, his powers allowed him to remember it all no matter how drunk he got. He continued to throw these wild extravaganzas, but he became aloof and was typically found sitting in the corner sipping a glass of water while everyone continued to get wasted. He started doing a lot of thinking and writing poetry. Will he have his wish of a new lifestyle or will he get back into partying and forget this momentary consciousness?

960. There was something about seeing people in love that made her sit back and appreciate her lot in life. She was Aphrodite, the goddess of love, the supreme matchmaker in the world. It was up to her to make sure that people who were meant to be together could overcome their obstacles to increase their chances of falling in love. There was only one issue. Despite her great knowledge of love and her desire to make love possible, she had never been in love herself. She'd had countless trysts and she'd even been the godly mother to a few children, but she'd only liked her sexual partners, she'd never felt more than an external attraction to them. Thinking that her amazing beauty might be the problem, she went down to Earth in a strong and stout form attempting to find someone who would find her attractive for what she had on the inside. She found a man who treated her with true kindness, but he was already married to the love of his life. Will she intervene in the situation to end up with this man anyway?

CHAPTER 8: CHARACTERS THAT ARE OVERLOOKED

Terminally and Moderately Ill

How people cope with a terminal or life-changing illness has a lot to do with their view of the world. Those who take a "why me" approach may spend their days wallowing that God has done them some kind of wrong while more "half full" folks might take advantage of all the opportunities open to them every single day. Those coping with these illnesses often need to take special medication and have different habits than those unencumbered with disease. In many cases, the illness is a part of their lives but it does not define them. It is possible to create a character with a life-threatening illness without the illness becoming the focus.

961. He didn't want to put her through the wedding. It was pretty obvious that he wasn't going to make it even a few years and she wanted to walk him down the aisle as quickly as possible. He knew that it was one of his lifelong dreams to be married to a woman who cared deeply about it, but he didn't want to think about what her life would be like after he was gone. He didn't want this soulful person who had such a wonderful laugh and smile to have to refer to herself as a widow. He felt like it was good enough just to be recognized as someone who *could* be married. When he expressed these views to her, she refused to acknowledge him and steamrolled him into a marriage that he wanted deep down. What was his wedding day like and how did his life-threatening disease affect their life together?

962. He'd lived a good life and he wasn't interested in being hooked up to any tubes or wires. His family tried to plead with him that there was a chance this treatment would give him another 20 to 30 years. The way he thought about it though, if his body was trying this hard to get rid of him, maybe it meant something. He began shoring up all loose ends in his life, taking care of his will, planning out a funeral and taking a few trips he'd always wanted to take. He'd been a fighter all of his life: going over to Vietnam and working through several tough economic periods to come out on top. In his opinion, the fight was over and he was ready to move on. Will his family be able to convince him to try the treatment or will he let his disease consume him?

963. She had a pretty rough sentence lined up for herself. She hadn't even reached puberty yet and according to the doctors, it was unlikely she would. She'd always had a great imagination and she'd planned wonderful things for herself. A perfect storybook wedding and playing with her similarly pale but upbeat children had been on her mind frequently before the diagnosis. Now she knew she had to change her idea of what was possible during her short span. Instead of lamenting that she wouldn't be able to accomplish her adult goals, she pushed back against her condition by starting a foundation and launching a fundraising drive. In just three months, she was able to raise over $50,000 toward research. She hoped that such a fund could allow a little girl a few years down the line to experience the adult events that this enterprising fundraiser couldn't. What is her reception in her household and in the town around her for her great deeds?

964. Just because her condition wasn't life threatening, doesn't mean that she didn't feel a little bit like dying every single day. She'd been through childbirth, three times in fact, and while the pain she felt wasn't as bad as that, childbirth only lasted for part of a day. This pain was unyielding and never seemed to go away no matter what medication they had her on. Since the prescriptions usually just made her sleepy and wobbly, she kept the dosage low and toughed it out. She did her best to hide the grimaces and spasms in front of her children and she tried hard to be grateful for the things she had. When she opened up to a friend about how tough things were for her, the friend brought up the idea of Dr. Kevorkian and euthanasia. She considered it for a second. Then she remembered her children and continued to press through. What are some of the most difficult moments for her during her typical days?

965. When he found out about his unchangeable fate, he was nearly overjoyed in a way. Because he knew exactly what his timeline was, he could easily schedule a grand farewell to his favorite people in the world. In a series of parties he referred to as "The Funeral Tour," he traveled around the world and held events with family and friends. He'd been a popular guy and knew people all over the place and this "tour" was exactly the way he wanted to go out. His condition continued to deteriorate throughout, so he made sure to hold only one party during what was supposed to be his final month of existence. Even though he'd made the rounds to many events during that time,

nearly everybody came back for this final shindig. He felt incredibly loved and he knew that this was the kind of death that everybody deserved. What are some of the conversations he has with his loved ones during these frequently wild events?

966. All he wanted to do in life was help people on behalf of his Church. When he went on a missionary trip to Africa, he had heard there were disease-related risks. He took all the medication he could but there just weren't vaccines for certain illnesses he could contract there. While he was there, the village he visited experienced one of the worst outbreaks of a deadly disease in the last one hundred years. Most of the people on the trip got away unscathed but he fell violently ill right before they were about to leave. A doctor who spoke a little bit of English said they were doing all they could, but there was a good chance he wouldn't last the night. He thought about his family and hoped they wouldn't turn away from God or the Church. He had been struck down for a reason, he thought, though he prayed for a miracle. Describe his potential final night in the foreign hospital and if his miracle does indeed come.

967. This was just an obstacle to overcome, she kept telling herself. She was the matriarch through and through for this family and she thought that if she didn't keep family traditions going, they would die with her generation. Her daughters tried to comfort her and tell her that it was important she focus on getting better and relaxing during her radiation treatments. She didn't care what they said, she was going to do just as much planning and decorating as she usually did. It was true that she felt less energy than usual, but she wasn't dead yet and neither was Christmas. She pushed herself hard those December weeks and she almost passed out from exhaustion on several occasions. She refused to let herself back down from this challenge and the holiday was one of the most successful events she'd ever planned. Will she have as much success with her treatment after the holiday season with less family gatherings to plan?

968. More than anything else she was frustrated. Here she was, an extremely promising career woman who had worked hard her whole life and disease was threatening to destroy her years of effort. She rarely even went to the doctor but went as a favor to her mother. They were lucky that they discovered the cancer early enough to prevent it from spreading. Her insurance was good enough to nearly cover everything and within a few months she was able to return to her rigorous hours. The problem wasn't the illness and the recovery for her. It was that during her illness she realized that her job wasn't as important as family, friends and being present. She had lost her drive to succeed and that was what frustrated her. She wanted her whole life to prove that she could end up on top. Now there was a part of her that didn't know if it was worth it. Will she ever be able to return to the ruthless go-getter she used to be?

969. He hated being helped as his condition had required at least a little bit of assistance from the beginning. He strived to be like normal kids when he was younger, being able to run and play at full-speed instead of a snail's pace. He didn't want to have to eat a special diet when he saw people his age eating candy and ice cream. He hated when the bus would unroll the special ramp for him and his apparatus. He had a lot of emotional pain and it felt like it would be nearly impossible to extinguish. He made it to adulthood, though it was never certain how much longer he would have. One day, he saw a young boy suffering from the same issues as him. He felt a sudden pang of understanding. He could use his time on Earth to make that this kid and kids like him have a life that sucked less. Will he be able to succeed at putting aside his hate to make a better life for kids in his shoes?

970. She lived alone and she had done so since she moved away from home at the age of 18. Her parents had passed away a few years back and at the time she was told she might inherit a genetic disorder that had manifested for both of them as well. Since her parents were her best friends at the time, she decided to reach out to other people who had the same potential illness. She was surprised to find a community that was extremely helpful and kind. She had mostly avoided people due to some experiences during her childhood that put her off, but these people were different. They all might be living a death sentence and yet they were willing to work together to strengthen each other. She even trained for and ran a half-marathon with the organization, despite the fact that she hadn't worn running shoes since high school gym class. In the specter of disease and death, she found a life worth living. How will her outlook of this new life change if she is in fact diagnosed with the disorder?

Homeless People

When I was visiting London for a college theatre trip, I saw a performance put on by the Homeless Shakespeare Company in a massive warehouse. It was amazing to see the wandering nature of a person without a home being so directly connected with Shakespeare's *Pericles*. It was a production that truly put you in the shoes of a person with no port to turn to. I have never known anyone who has become homeless and I've never had a homeless family member, but it's important to remember that there are those who have. Creating a homeless character without a back story and a previous life may do a disservice to your character and your story.

971. He loved his corner and everybody who stopped to wish him well. He was a vendor of a local homeless magazine and sold copies in order to help himself and the homeless in general. He was out there when it was freezing cold and in the height of summer. He didn't care what it was like out, he was being given an opportunity to fight back against his situation and he would never go back on his word. He'd had so much anger growing up and he ran away from every chance someone was willing to give him. Not this time, he thought to himself, this might be the last one he'd ever get. What was the situation behind his homelessness and will he ever be able to pull himself out of it?

972. Life had dealt him some tough blows but he refused to stop singing. After all, due to the busker's license a friend had gotten him, his singing in public for change was completely legal. He would position himself inside the train station and sing for his dinner all day long. About halfway through, he'd use some of the change for a water to help his throat and then he'd keep on going. He had a kid somewhere and though he had no idea where he was in the world, he sang for that child of his. He sang for the hope that someday, he'd have enough money together to live somewhere again. His life was very difficult and at least he knew that he'd be happy as long as he kept singing. What kind of songs does he sing and will he ever meet his son again later in life?

973. She felt like she hadn't looked in a mirror in ages. Her hair was graying more than it had the last time she looked. Her teeth were continuing to rot out and they looked more brown than she remembered. She used to be pretty, she recalled, and the boys she hung out with in school always told her so. She hung out with a rough crowd and she almost laughed thinking about some of the stupid stuff they did. That crowd was the same one that got her into drugs during school, an addiction that she never could quite get a hold of. Even now, years since she'd had the stuff, she knew that just one breath of it would send her back down the hole for another half a decade. What is her day to day routine like and how does she plan on getting back on her feet?

974. She remembered hearing one time that most people who pass by the homeless are thinking to themselves, "She should go get a job?" Her unemployment had nothing to do with a lack of trying. When she had a place to live, she had a job and it barely kept her and her son afloat. When her son's daddy got into trouble, she tried to help him and got locked up as a result. That's when child protective services took her son away. She knew where he was and the family who watched over him let her visit from time to time, even though they weren't really supposed to. She wanted to get a job again so that she could get her baby back. She hasn't found anybody willing to hire a homeless, ex-con yet, but damned if she wasn't going to keep trying. What are some of the jobs she's applied for and what were the circumstances that led to her arrest?

975. The phrases he said all day long when asking for change were starting to stick in his head. Because people at the shelter he stayed at were so quiet, it seemed like the only words he said all day were, "Get a guy something to eat," and "God bless you." He'd experimented with other phrases here and there, some longer, some shorter, but these were the ones that seemed to get him the highest daily income. At the end of the day, he was able to go into the discount grocery store and get himself some snacks. He'd buy two for right then and one for the next morning. On some days he had a little bit extra and that went into the savings in a zipped up pocket on his coat. He didn't know what he was saving for, but maybe someday he'd be able to talk about it using some different words. What are people's usual reactions to his consistent chatter?

976. He had a big family and he loved talking about it with his friends. From time to time, his brother from the big city would come in and chat with him and give him a little bit of money. At that time, the brother would tell him how all the family members were doing. This man without a home loved family more than anything and he told

everybody every last detail of his family members. He couldn't wait for each visit, even though they happened quite sporadically. When it had been a while since he saw his brother, he decided to gather up what little money he had and head into the big city to find his brother. When he got to the address his brother had given him, he got quite a surprise. What happened next?

977. One night as she slept in her usual spot, she remembered the childhood story of the troll who lived under the bridge. That was her alright. She had her cart and her set of blankets perpetually stashed under a bridge. She discovered it one night when she was trying to avoid the rain and she'd kept there ever since. A cop had once come up to her and asked her to move and she kindly began to pack up her stuff before he had a change of heart. She remembered that the troll used to eat the goats that would pass the bridge. All the passed on the bridge were cars that from time to time would wake her up. She didn't want to eat any goats, she just wanted to make it to the next day. What are some of the other places she has set up camp aside from under the bridge?

978. If she was going to be on the streets, she was happy to be on the streets in a place where people would share their booze with her. They didn't all directly share it, of course, she would hunt around for cups of half-finished beer and would snatch it before their waiters could in the outdoor seating areas of restaurants. The most exciting event she'd ever experienced was when the local baseball team made it to the World Series and everybody was going crazy. She hung around outside a pretty raucous bar and someone actually bought a bottle of champagne for her. That was a crazy night and she could barely even stumble the next day. Those were the kind of nights she missed before she lost her home and money. What role did alcohol play in her becoming homeless?

979. People would ask him all the time if he used to be that guy on the television. The one who was making big tackles on the football field and trying to get million dollar endorsement deals. The answer was yes and no. After all, it was him in a way, because the name on his birth certificate matched up with the name that used to be located above a locker in a professional locker room. Despite that, he felt like he was a completely different person as his life imploded on him. He handled the pace of the NFL just fine but it was the personal life during it that self-destructed on him. He thought he could get anything he wanted just by taking it, since that's what he did on the field. Drugs, women, prison and homelessness followed from that style of living. Will he ever be able to get back on his feet or back into the game?

980. Her father gave her a choice and she took it. She could continue living the abusive, horrible life she'd been living or she could run away and be hunted. He said he would lie and tell police about the awful things she'd done and how she needed to be put away in juvenile hall. She ran to a friend and begged her for enough money for a bus ticket. The friend relented and she went to the other side of the country with nothing but a change of clothes and a few knick knacks. She found the local homeless shelter and slept in fits and spurts the next night. She had finally gotten away from the awful life she'd been living, but she wondered if she could avoid her father's grasp until she was 18. What will she do to keep herself safe over the next two years and thereafter?

Mentally Disabled or Ill

While there have been some landmark performances by or of the mentally disabled or ill, on television shows like "Life Goes On" and in movies like *Benny and Joon*, many authors tend to shy away from including such characters in their work. There's no question why, it's a touchy subject and authors don't want to be lambasted for creating an unintentionally offensive character. Sometimes though, when you're trying to create a realistic world that includes characters that have struggles to overcome, you've just got to go for it.

981. His mother loved him no matter what his condition was. Ignorant people would call him "retarded" as an insult, when of course, that's what he actually was as a clinical medical term. He met all the criteria and his mother realized it almost right away. She did everything right in getting him the appropriate help as early as possible, which the doctors said helped him to become as highly functioning as possible later in life. He learned things later than most of the other kids and when he reached adulthood there were multiple limitations on what he could and couldn't do. Fortunately, he functioned well enough that he could earn a living, keep up an apartment with limited help and keep his emotions in check around the family. He lived a tough life but he knew without his mother's help, he might have been sunk. Describe a typical day from beginning to end for this strong-willed gentleman.

982. He was a fast-talking teenager who tended to remind all of his friends of Ferris Bueller. A strange condition in his cardiovascular system caused him to have a stroke at the age of 17. In an instant, everything changed and in some ways he had to start from scratch. Many of the parts of him that made him unique, his positive attitude and his great love for people were unaffected by the incident, but he suffered from expressive aphasia, which made it very difficult for him to communicate effectively with words. It was frustrating for him at first, since he loved being able to quickly joke with family and friends. Over time he began to get back his ability to connect thoughts with his words, but it required a ton of hard work for a guy who usually got his kicks dashing out of class as quickly as possible. He knew that his life would never be the same, but he was still very grateful for the people who made his new life possible. What are some of the examples of things that he is no longer able to communicate after his stroke?

983. She had a family, including kids that needed to be cared for, and she hated having to be taken care of herself. The doctors told her that her bike helmet had saved her life, but to her, this was almost worse than dying. Her brain injury caused her to act differently, especially when her emotions were concerned. Emotional reactions that didn't make sense would come at the strangest times, which went against her calm and contemplative nature that used to define her. She felt like she wasn't her anymore, which made sense, since she had trouble remembering many things in her life that shaped her. She had to quit her job because she could no longer focus on the tasks at hand. Her family made every effort to show her how much they cared about her and how they appreciated all of the efforts she was able to put in. She took these expressions of gratitude as pity more than kindness and spent many days wallowing in depression. As her brain injury slowly heals over time, will she regain more of a sense of who she was and will she learn to deal with the person she has become?

984. She knew that it would be a challenge to ask the guy of her dreams out to the senior prom. She wasn't the most popular girl in school and while she felt confident about her looks, she knew she wasn't going to win any beauty contests. All she knew is that for the last few years, nearly one out of every three poems she wrote was about him and she would be kicking herself for years if she didn't exactly try. Her Down Syndrome made it a bit tough for her to express herself to him, especially because she was nervous, but with the help of her friends she did it. She was absolutely surprised when he said yes. She knew that it wasn't about him being in love with her or anything wacky like that, but with nearly a year of worrying over with, she felt great and couldn't wait to pick out dresses. What are some of the other challenges she's faced her senior year?

985. She wasn't sure exactly what brought her panic attacks on but they were awful. She would shake and vomit and feel like she was about to die. She could no longer work because so many aspects of her job would cause the attacks and they were starting to make her co-workers ill at ease. She did find some basic freelance jobs over the internet that were not as stressful, which was good, because leaving the house even for a simple interview might bring on the attacks again. She used to love the outdoors and enjoyed hiking in wide-open spaces. She hoped that through her treatments she might be able to someday experience those aspects of the world again. For now, her main goal was to go farther and farther away from the house without having an attack. She had reached two blocks, thus far. What caused her first panic attack and what does she do all day when she's stuck in the house?

986. He remembered watching a movie in which a person with obsessive-compulsive disorder was an old curmudgeon and still ended up getting the girl. Once the character had the wonderful relationship with the girl, his symptoms began to go away. He laughed, thinking to himself, if only it was that easy. He'd been dealing with OCD for most of his life and he'd met "the one" and several other wonderful people during his life. When he was with these amazing people, who knew about his disease, he was typically able to keep his symptoms at bay. But unfortunately for him and for them, there were many different triggers that kept him from showing the love he wanted to show. He would get so frustrated with an inability to control his hand washing and drawer closing that he drove some of these people away, including who he considered to be the one. What are some of the things he has done to take control of the illness and will he ever be able to win someone over despite his OCD?

987. Her disorder didn't really take a hold of her life until she was in college. She'd had a few bouts with depression and mania during high school, but her parents mostly chalked it up to being a teenager. As she grew older, she started having much longer periods of mania and even longer periods of depression. Her roommate called her parents when she had neglected to go to classes or even leave the room for at least a week, which is the time the

diagnosis of bipolar disorder was made. She'd always felt like she was a pretty happy person aside from the bouts with depression and hated how the mood stabilizers she took seemed to rob her of the highest highs. She knew that going off the meds wasn't the answer either, because she was extremely worried that another episode or two might do some serious damage. She gained some weight from her medication as well, which made her worry that the guys she liked would stop paying attention to her. She wished like hell that she could fight this disorder and all it came with to once again live a normal life. What are some of the things she did during her mania that might have clued her parents into her disorder?

988. She joked with her pals that being buddies with her was like having multiple friends at the same time. After all, from time to time when she went out with them, a few drinks might cause her to slip into one of her alters, a separate personality that came as a result of her dissociative identity disorder. During her childhood, she had been severely bullied in school and created multiple identities to withstand these harmful words. One of her personalities was so angry and mean, that her mother wanted to send her away to military school before she was eventually diagnosed. She never remembered the things that her alters said or did and she dreaded being filled in on what they had done while her true identity was suppressed. Therapy and a lot of hard work allowed her to control the alters for the most part, but in stressful situations, she never knew exactly who would come out to handle it. How would you describe some of the alters that she developed in her response to bullying?

989. He loved his job and was happy to have made major progress in his life despite where it seemed he'd end up. His schizophrenia began to take hold of him after he moved away from home after high school. He made a few friends, though it was tough to keep them after he began have hallucinations nearly all the time. One of these friends became his savior, getting him diagnosed, but after a major falling out, this schizophrenic fell in with the complete wrong crowd. He began trying to medicate his condition with drugs, which only made him worse and led to him being, "one of those crazy people on the streets," he used to say. When that friend came back into his life, offered him a place to stay and to get him the medication he needed, he knew that life was beginning to turn around. Now he talked with local schizophrenia groups, discussing how important it is to stay off of recreational drugs. What were some of his lowest moments coping with the disease on his own?

990. At first her parents believed that she was just a shy child. They'd heard that she'd been made fun of at school for the way she reacted to awkward social situations, including excessive sweating and blushing. They tried to toughen her up by sending her to sleep-away camp and had to come within about 48 hours, not only to pick her up, but to find her after she'd gone scampering off into the woods. It turned out that she had a generalized social anxiety disorder and she was more or less unwilling and unable to interact with people other than her parents. They tried medication and therapy but nothing seemed to help. Her mother quit her job so that she could home school her daughter and do her best to coax the disease out the door one step at a time. Every so often she would be willing to connect with a neighbor or a family friend, but more often than not she simply couldn't handle it. As she grows older, what are some of the things she may try to rid herself of this condition?

Physically Handicapped

Another category of characters that tend to get left out of most stories, the physically handicapped are often treated like there is something wrong with their brains as well as their bodies. In most cases, however, the physically handicapped are of sound mind and wish to be seen as independent human beings who deserve a rich and exciting life. In one of my favorite television shows, "Friday Night Lights," a major character become paralyzed from the waist down and must change his focus from football to living his life. These characters can be tragic and inspiring when placed into your work or they can simply be in the form of side characters who happen to have disabilities.

991. He had been told he was lucky. Most people who developed his type of muscular dystrophy tended to get the symptoms in their childhood. He had already lived through his youth and through most of college before beginning to lose his muscle tone and strength. The fact that he'd been an athlete gave him a strong base to work from, though slowly but surely, he could no longer do many of the activities that had given him joy. He'd always been the kind of guy who lived for that endorphin high that came with exercise and being unable to do so made him feel pretty depressed. The girl of his dreams had found him about a year before he was diagnosed and refused to

leave him, which kept him grounded. What are some of the changes he must make in his life and how quickly will the condition continue to cause him a lack of mobility?

992. As a writer who could no longer write, he felt completely useless for several years. A severe case of arthritis had made it too painful for him to use his hands either for writing by hand or typing on the computer. One Christmas, a friend got him software allowing him to speak the words he wanted to type into a microphone. He was completely over the moon. It certainly wasn't perfect and there were frequent errors, but this was certainly better than nothing. He had renewed purpose and over the course of the next few years he wrote over 10 books. He regained a more positive attitude and even began dating, something he'd avoided for the last decade or so. What are some other ways in which he has been able to avoid using his hands?

993. When people asked her how she'd changed since the basketball game that altered her life forever, she usually said, "I'm much nicer now," with a smile. A head-on collision with another player in the high school state championship game put her in the hospital and caused paralysis below the waist. At first, she was angry at God and the world and she threatened to kill herself several times. That was the competitive part of her that had gotten her so far in basketball, trying to defeat the condition through escaping life. Eventually, she realized that along with her strong training determination, she'd gained a great deal of anger and without the ability to train, her anger was taking over. Through therapy and reading more on the subject, she dealt with these negative emotions and put her efforts into trying to walk again. What are some other ways in which her personality has changed since her accident?

994. She wasn't your typical girl in a host of different ways. First of all, she had stopped growing after she hit around two and a half feet and a deformity in her legs caused her to have to get around in a wheelchair. She usually didn't let that stop her from living her life as she'd often hop off of the wheelchair to get things she couldn't reach or to chill on the ground with friends. Secondly, she was incredibly intelligent and she easily cruised to the top grades in the class in middle and high school. The thing that most separated her from her peers, however, was her extreme wittiness. After creating various humor videos for YouTube, she was "discovered" and ended up playing bit parts in several sitcoms. She used the money to pay for her college tuition and felt like after a rough beginning, things were finally going her way. What are some of her other unique characteristics that make her who she is today?

995. When he awoke from the coma, he had more than a few questions to ask. Most of them revolved around the fact that his legs had been amputated just below the knee. He didn't remember much after the building he was in began to shake and come crashing down. His legs were pinned below a steel beam and it all went blank. He had been rescued but the doctors were unable to save his legs. He loved running and he didn't miss a beat getting as much knowledge as he could about the latest prosthetics. He knew his friends and family expected him to mourn the loss of his biological legs, but he had a philosophy that he wasn't about to part with, "Wasted time can never be recovered." In a much shorter time than most, he was up and about using his new legs to run and walk as if nothing had happened. What are some of the basic ways in which his life has inevitably changed?

996. He wasn't interested in pity and he rarely talked about the birth defect that caused his need to walk with two arm canes. People who assumed that he was somehow weak for his condition were usually the ones that he trampled on the way to the top. He used to feel sorry for himself as he was growing up, but upon watching a documentary of Franklin Delano Roosevelt, he felt a sudden drive to succeed. If a man without complete use of his legs can be President, then he can certainly be the CEO of a major company. While women loved his charm and confidence, he was never really interested in a relationship, and those who tried to increase his sense of commitment to anything other than his career were often disappointed. What are some of the things he tells himself to continue his drive to the top?

997. She felt like she'd been overcoming major obstacles her entire life. She was already a mixed race girl living in a mostly white area and she had to push herself past all of the slurs people would use against her and her family. She didn't fight these ignorant people, she just decided to rise above it. When she contracted a disease that took away the use of her legs, she knew it was just another challenge to push past. She had been something of an athlete before her condition arose and she wanted to continue the trend. Upon seeing the movie *Murderball*, she reached out to a local quad rugby league and found there were few women involved. She figured it was time to buck another trend and join

up. Not surprisingly, due to her will and determination, she became one of the top players. What are some of the ways in which she will continue to push past her limitations as she grows up?

998. She was grateful for the few years she had getting to hear the wonderful sounds the world had to offer. In this short time she found, what she hoped, was a relatively normal voice, before the world became silent due to a rare infection. She became one heck of a lip reader and picked up sign language easily, as she would later learn how to read many other languages. She had gotten comfortable as a deaf person and was perfectly willing to live out the rest of her life that way. That was when she heard about the implant. She had seen a video online of a woman who had never heard a sound before in her life, suddenly being able to hear because of some kind of computerized implant. Suddenly, she wasn't as happy anymore and worked as hard as she could to become the next person in line for the device. Why was she unable to remain as content when she heard about the implant?

999. One of his favorite stories was the Odyssey as a kid, because of the blind fortune teller. He knew that if he thought of himself as having a disability, he would feel somehow beneath everyone else. If he figured himself to be a soothsayer though, someone who could see what others could not, he might feel that his other senses more than compensated for his lack of sight. He used this mindset to pursue a degree in psychology and to understand people beyond their appearance. His parents worried that some lunatic would attack him during a session and he wouldn't be able to defend himself. He eased their worries and continued on in his path. One of the things he thought most interesting about people was that even though many would judge him due to his cane as he walked the streets, as a blind person, he was much less willing to judge them. Although, that might just be his own kind personality talking. What are some of the skills he possesses that allow him to be a successful psychologist?

1000. Her mother thought it was an absolute travesty that her daughter, the daughter of the famous singer, could be stricken with the inability to speak. At first they thought it was strange that she could barely make sounds let alone speak a single word by the age of two. She was tested and it was found that fibrous tissue had grown in her vocal cords and it was unlikely she'd be able to sing, let alone speak. Her parents took it a lot harder than she did, as she picked up sign language and began communicating with those who could understand. Her mother was resistant in learning sign language as she preferred to communicate with the beauty of song. When her daughter wrote her mother a note that she just needed to learn it to understand that her daughter loved her, she caught on much more quickly. What are some ways in which this mute girl speaks to the world?

Transgender

Let's end this book with 20 bonus prompts and two interesting sections: transgender characters and citizens of the world. Meeting people who happen to be transgendered has been much more common in Chicago than it was in the South or in my small Pennsylvania hometown. What I've learned from meeting people of this ilk is that they have more than most to overcome. Not even their bodies agree with who they know they are deep inside. When creating a story set in the modern era, it would be silly not to consider including transgender characters as they are an important and growing part of our society.

1001. He had always felt a little different in his own skin and identified nearly his whole life with being a male as opposed to a female. When he told his girlfriend of several years that he wanted to become a man, she was skeptical at first, after all, she loved breasts and all aspects of womanhood. When he had a double mastectomy and began taking the hormones, it was odd for his girlfriend, but she knew he was the same person deep down inside. After his sex change, he felt more like himself than ever and he and his girlfriend continued to function well as a couple. What were some things that were different for him after his transition?

1002. When he was their smiling daughter, he was by far and away his parents' favorite child. Of course, they wouldn't say such a thing, but they loved dressing him up in debutante clothes and parading him around the south as a beauty queen. The only problem was, he didn't want to be a pageant winner, he wanted to be a man. They never took his protestations seriously, but after a semester taking gender studies courses at an out of state college, they started to listen, but not in the way he wanted. His parents stopped paying for college and began forcing him to go to psychotherapy. This caused him to repress his feelings for two more years before he finally ran away and began living as a male in a city halfway across the county. He didn't have much money for surgery or hormones, but the transition wasn't important to him, since in his mind he was already a male. Will he ever be able to make his parents understand who he really is?

1003. It didn't take her long as a child to realize that being a boy was not for her. Since she was brought up in a time where gender identity wasn't even considered a thing, she suffered through her troubles for nearly three decades before connecting with a scientist who described exactly what she was going through in a book she read. She had already had a stellar career with a major engineering firm and she was a rising star in the industry. When she told her employers that she was planning to transition to being a female, she was fired on the spot. Her friend and family members used this job loss to tell her that what she was doing was a bad idea. She went ahead with it anyway and after her transition, she started back at the bottom and worked her way to the top of her field once again. What were some of the most difficult aspects of her transition to her rightful gender?

1004. She was one of an estimated several hundred thousand transgender people serving in the military, though during her 15 years of service, she was never able to tell another soul about her gender identity. Despite her service and her hard work for her country, telling anyone about who she really was would have been labeled as a mental disorder. She knew that she was of perfectly sound mind and the only disorder was the fact that the military wouldn't let her let her flag fly as she represented the country's flag. She was extremely proud of herself and her peers who had come out shortly after their service. She hoped that in the future, these proud servicemen and women could allow transgender people like her an opportunity to express their internal pride as well. Were there any close calls during her service where she was almost outed as transgender?

1005. He was absolutely in love with her and after a few dates, she seemed to love who he was as well. What she didn't know and what he was scared to tell her was that he was born a woman. He'd transitioned to manhood quite well and unless you had a birth certificate right in front of you, you might not believe him. He had a steady job and seemed like a relatively average guy. He supported transgender rights but he wasn't an activist or anything like that. He was just a fool in love and it took him months before he felt comfortable enough to tell the love of his life his secret. She didn't know how to react, after all, this wasn't the fairytale relationship she'd planned out for herself as a child. He did his best to calm her worries about telling her parents and about how different it would be. She gave him one last chance to convince her, along a moonlit beach walk on a summer's night. What will he say to convince her that their relationship will be normal and wonderful?

1006. He simply wasn't sure anymore. He had been born a male and had a very successful career as an attorney before deciding that he was actually a woman. He told his family and friends and he began embarking on hormones and surgery. His wife left him and his practice considered giving him a downgraded role. After a few months alone, he realized that he didn't want to live life this way and he used his wealth to undo the steps he'd previously taken. His wife took him back and he was happy he hadn't gone all the way through with his plan. There was always a part of him though, that wondered if he was living the right life. His friends would joke about his experience, saying, "Hey, remember that time you were a woman for six months?" For him, it was no joke. Will he continue to live out the rest of his life as a man or will he attempt once again to assert a female gender identity?

1007. She'd done everything she could to avoid thinking about who she really was. When she was in high school she barely understood her feeling that she was somehow living her life incorrectly. She came out as a gay male at the end of school, but it didn't seem to make much impact. She threw herself into her studies in college and became an artist in multiple mediums. There was a lot of pain and she nearly ended her life on several instances. She survived her attempts, fortunately, long enough to be a part of her first drag show. When she looked in the mirror, she knew exactly who she was for the first time. A couple of years later, she received hormone therapy and began to feel more herself than she ever had in her life. Several possible employers saw the gender on her driver's license and withdrew job offers, but eventually she found a living as a photographer for a worldwide magazine. Describe her feelings when she first saw herself as a woman.

1008. She was an identical twin and she loved her brother very much. She knew that having a transgender sister would be tough for him growing up, but the support of her parents made it nearly a non-issue. Even though it took them a few years to catch on that she refused to put on boy clothes or play with boy toys, they came to terms relatively early with her gender identity. She grew her hair long and it was rare that anyone questioned her identity, especially at the more liberal school her parents sent her to. She was 13 years old and it was coming upon decision time. If she began hormone therapy now, she would completely suppress male puberty and people would have little trouble identifying her as female. Her parents and the doctors made sure that she knew the importance of the decision and that there was no going back. Will she go ahead with the decision to take hormones or will she wait to see what she was genetically predisposed to be?

1009. He was a superstar in the transgender world for his brash personality and his desire to make all other transgender individuals feel accepted in the world. He spoke at events throughout the world in an effort to make people proud of who they are, whether they are transgender, gay, straight or deciding. He frequently won awards in the community for his entertainment and his activism. It took him until his fifteenth birthday to realize he was meant to be a man and now almost nobody could mistake this muscular, beefy man as a woman. As tough a time as he had convincing others who he was, he knew that most people had a much tougher time than him and he devoted his life to making that transition easier and safer. What are some of the things he says to transgender youth that makes him such a transgender rock star?

1010. She was always mistaken for a girl as a baby and toddler, even though she was genetically male. She loved dressing up in women's clothing and putting on makeup and her parents thought it was adorable. They were pretty progressive and knew about transgender children and gave her as much space as they thought she needed. Whenever they asked her if she wanted to be a girl, she would say, "No, I'm a boy. Aren't I?" She dressed in women's clothing around the house and changed out of it before going to school and that went on through high school. When she went away to college, she decided to be a girl full-time and her parents let out a sigh of relief. She was wild and crazy and got in trouble several times, unrelated to her gender identity. Eventually, she found the love of her life who only cared about what was on the inside. Despite having such understanding parents, why did she wait until college to fully assume her identity?

Citizens of the World

I want to emphasize that most of the characters in this book could be transposed across race and culture. Nevertheless, I think it's important to consider specifically including those from vastly different backgrounds and ethnicities in your work. Just as television and movies tend to keep things looking white as a picket fence, stories in general will avoid race and culture being a part of a story for fear of it becoming about the race or the culture. I believe that adding diversity to your story, if done correctly, can add another important dimension to your creative characters.

1011. In his opinion, God must have had something against him. His wife had been killed by the collapse of a building during a massive earthquake. In a cholera epidemic that followed, he'd lost one of his two sons. His family had lived in Haiti for many generations, but he wondered if it wasn't time to leave. Perhaps he could find a new job in the Dominican Republic or even farther away. Somewhere that would allow him to forget the horrible things that had happened to his family. Somewhere he and his family could start over where there was a better opportunity for a life free of illness and sudden death. It was his remaining son who kept him grounded during this time. Reminding him of all the joy they had experienced there prior to the tragedy. Will he continue with his plan to move or will he simply move on?

1012. He thoroughly missed the good old days. He remembered when he and his friends would hang out at a local coffee shop, sipping espressos and laughing while they checked out the ladies walking down the street. Nowadays, these social spots have been replaced by chain restaurants and designer clothing stores, which have taken over most of Athens. His children are less enamored with Greek culture than his generation had been and they are happiest when they have the newest and shiniest toys. He has considered moving out of the overcrowded city and to a place where they still appreciate community and heritage. He feels as though he has somewhat failed as a parent by not impressing into his children the importance of family and culture. His later life attempts to do this have only been met with laughter and requests for money. He constantly wishes he could go back and pay more attention to the direction they were headed in. What is his day to day life like in the city and will he actually move to a more remote part of Greece?

1013. She couldn't believe how hot it was. She had lived her entire life as an American who happened to have relatives from India. Now, a collapse in finances sent her and her family back to the Asian subcontinent. She didn't have a grasp of the language or the culture, and she certainly didn't know how to deal with the extreme summer heat. She missed her friends and the life she'd had, but she knew she had to get a hang of it or she'd be miserable. One of the first people she met in India told her that happiness was a choice and that she'd only be unhappy if she wanted to be. She ignored the advice at first but it kept eating at her. She began making small choices each day to bring herself as much joy as possible. Maybe she could stand to live in India, even if it was a constant sauna. What are some of the things she chooses to do to bring more happiness to her days?

1014. When she and her husband moved her family from Nigeria to the United States, they thought that things would be safer and easier. Her husband had a decent job and they had three strong-willed children together. When the two of them realized that the job would not be enough to help their kids through college, she began trying to learn everything she could about English so she could write well enough to get a second job. She studied every day when the children went to school and she felt as if she was a kid again, having to go through it all a second time in another language. She pretended to help her kids with their schoolwork, when in actuality, she was trying to learn what they were learning and she was often caught sneaking a few of their textbooks. Once she finally felt a mastery of the subject, she began hunting for jobs, knowing that if she was successful, the full education of her family would be the amazing end result. What are the parts of English she has had the most trouble with?

1015. As an American Indian living on a reservation steeped in poverty, he almost felt as if he was residing in a foreign country. He'd been to a few of the larger cities in his state and he was amazed at how much better the conditions were there. He had dreams of college and a more modern lifestyle, but he knew that it was important to stay close to family, especially when you're part of such a minority. He took pride in the aspects of his culture that kids were still reading about in textbooks, including tribal ceremonies and using the bounty of nature to live off the land. He wasn't living in the past, of course, as he had a computer, a cell phone and many things that people have outside of the reservation. But more than most he had an appreciation of where his people had come from and where they were headed. What is a day in the life like for this American Indian?

1016. After going to school in the United States, he wondered if he should head back home at all. The city life in New York was much different from what he'd grown up with. A few miles away from his home in southwestern Australia was desert and was plagued by bush fires throughout the summer. He lived just a few miles away from the beach and he loved surfing and sunbathing. He was hardly prepared for his first U.S. winter, as he'd rarely had to deal with such weather in his home town. He missed his school and his parents, but there were also a lot of opportunities for him in the states he wouldn't have otherwise. He decided to take a one month trip back home to decide what the future would hold. Describe his pros and cons list detailing his decision whether or not to stay in the states permanently.

1017. She grew up to a life in which girls and women were denied even the most basic rights of education. When her father died after an attack on the Taliban, her mother was not allowed to leave the house, and as a result her daughter had to take care of many tasks at a young age. When the Taliban was forcefully removed, women's rights finally allowed her and her mother to leave the house together. It was a new world in which girls could receive education and attend events like concerts. She began to learn how to read and write and she was a quick study. She continued on in the school until it was bombed one day before she had arrived. Many of her friends were killed and she cried for days. Steadfast, she went to another school that was farther away, against her mother's wishes. She refused to be ignorant any longer. What are some of the hardest things she's had to deal with growing up in Afghanistan?

1018. She laughed when she saw the tourists shivering. She laughed when they assumed that all of her people lived in igloos and she absolutely lost it when they gasped at seeing people wearing normal clothing instead of animal skins. It was strange to her that some people would want to come all the way to their village to find an escape for vacation, but she was happy to accept their money when she led them on a tour. She loved her community and her family and she never seriously considered leaving. Each year it seemed that tourists were becoming stranger and more distant, especially due to technology. She would rather stay connected to the Earth and the people who mattered to her most. She wondered what e-mail or text message could be more important than that. What are some of the strangest questions she's had to field on a tour?

1019. He had worked hard his entire life and he didn't need much else to be fulfilled. Every morning when he was manually packed into the Tokyo subway cars and when he returned home after more then 10 hours of work, he was satisfied. He spent quiet evenings with his wife and watched his son play baseball on television. The success his son had found in a professional Japanese league pleased him, as it was the result of many hours of hard work. He did wish, however, that his son had obtained a career that would serve him past his baseball-playing days. He read a book recently written about an American workplace and laughed at how laid back and unproductive they were. To him, hard work was part of his duty as a human being. What are some of his other opinions about the characters portrayed in this American workplace novel?

1020. As she pulled the rifle up onto her shoulder, she was glad it was just a demonstration and not the real thing. Even though she had been trained and had actually been in combat over the last two years, she was by no means happy to be using weaponry. As was compulsory in Israel, she was required to enter military service at the age of 18 and here she was, hanging out with Americans her age who could barely even understand the concept. She was a fortunate one not to have had any close friends suffer any injuries through protecting the Gaza strip and other parts of the country. Before becoming a part of the Army, she loved partying with friends and living life as a normal girl. She guessed she still was a normal girl, just not compared with these Americans who seemed to have never worn a uniform in their lives. Would she choose to lead a different life free from obligatory military service if she had a choice and why?

INDEX

ABOUT THE AUTHOR

Bryan Cohen is a man of many ideas, which he partly attributes to his wonderful improvisational comedy teachers at Dirty South Improv in Carrboro, N.C. and iO Theater in Chicago, Ill. He also studied Creative Writing, English and Dramatic Art at the University of North Carolina at Chapel Hill. After graduation, he moved to Chicago to become a comedian, though eventually he settled on writing ideas for other people. He has written several books including *1,000 Creative Writing Prompts: Ideas for Blogs, Scripts, Stories and More, 500 Writing Prompts for Kids: First Grade through Fifth Grade, Writer on the Side: How to Write Your Book Around Your 9 to 5 Job, Sharpening the Pencil: Essays on Writing, Motivation and Enjoying Your Life* and *The Post-College Guide to Happiness*. He currently lives with his girlfriend in Chicago.

Visit his website at http://www.buildcreativewritingideas.com.